ALPHONSE MUCHA

IN QUEST OF BEAUTY

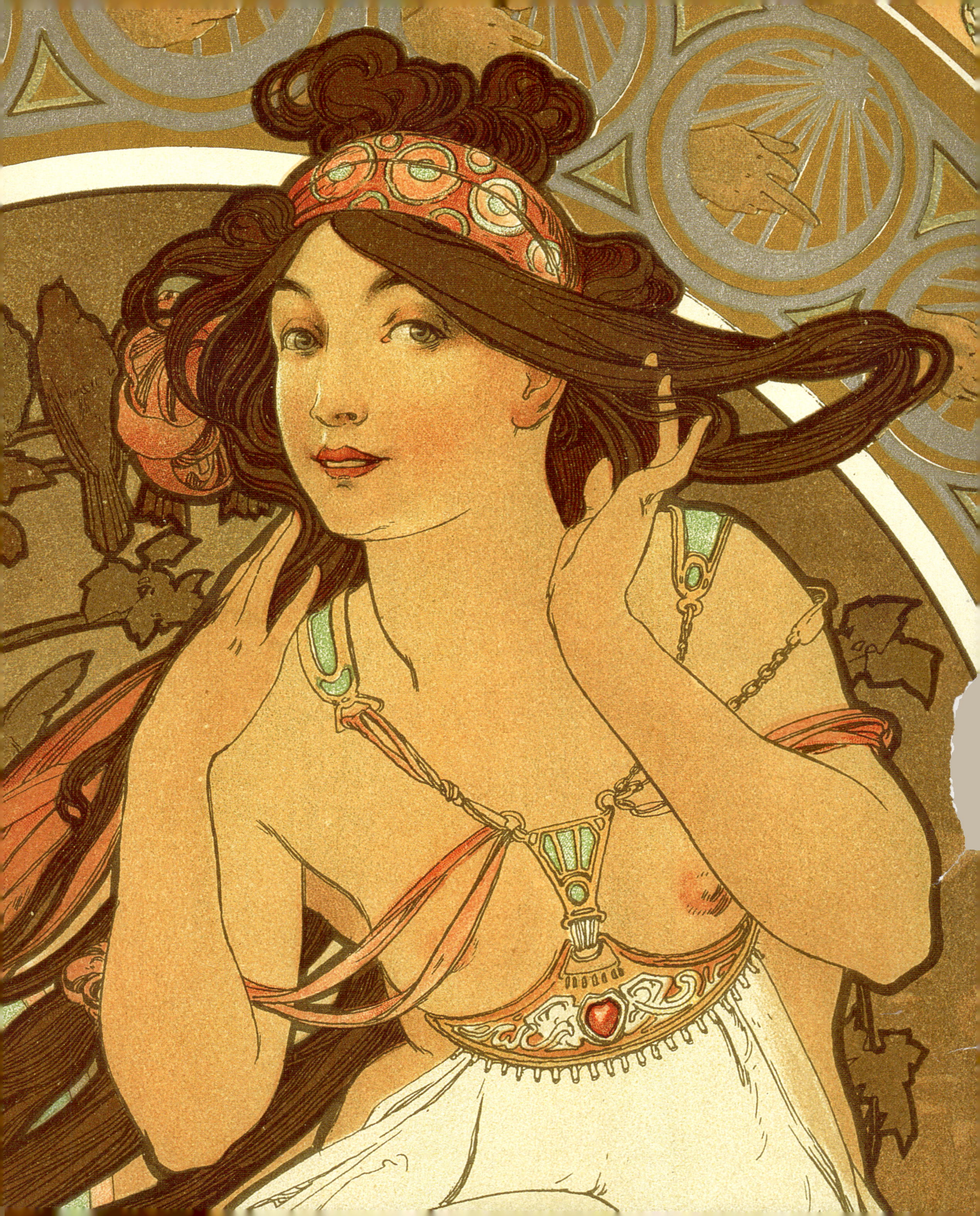

ALPHONSE MUCHA
IN QUEST OF BEAUTY

TOMOKO SATO

WITH ESSAYS BY

PAUL GREENHALGH & CLAIRE ALLERTON
ALISON BROWN
SANDRA PENKETH
JO MEACOCK

Mucha
FOUNDATION PUBLISHING

Published on the occasion of the exhibition:
Alphonse Mucha: In Quest of Beauty

Participating Museums:
Russell-Cotes Art Gallery & Museum, Bournemouth
Sainsbury Centre for Visual Arts, Norwich
Kelvingrove Art Gallery and Museum, Glasgow
Walker Art Gallery, Liverpool

First published in 2015 by Mucha Foundation Publishing

In association with Mucha Foundation, Prague
www.muchafoundation.org

ISBN 0 9536322 9 6

Editors: Sarah Mucha and Tomoko Sato
Designer: Roger Kohn

Made and printed in the Czech Republic by Graspo CZ a.s.

Front Cover: Study for the poster for *Lance Parfum "Rodo"* (detail)
Back Cover: *The Passing Wind Takes Youth Away*
Inside Cover: *Language of Flowers:* Plate 35 from
L'Album de la Décoration (vol. II)
Page 2: *Music* from *The Arts* (detail)

Measurements are given in centimetres. For two-dimensional works sizes are given height before width. For three-dimensional works height before width or diameter, followed by depth. Widest dimensions are given for the measurements of objects of irregular shapes.

CONTENTS

FOREWORD

The Mucha Foundation was founded in 1992 by the artist's family with the mission to preserve and conserve the Mucha family collection and to promote the work of Alphonse Mucha to as broad an audience as possible. Mucha believed passionately that art was an essential benefit to humanity and that it should be seen and enjoyed by as many people as possible, and the Mucha Foundation continues his legacy by actively promoting his work. Since its creation, the Foundation has worked with museums and art galleries around the world to introduce Mucha's work and has organised some fifty Mucha exhibitions, including the first British retrospective outside London *Alphonse Mucha: Master of art Nouveau,* which travelled to Edinburgh and Hull in 2000-2001.

We are delighted to return to the United Kingdom with a new exhibition *Alphonse Mucha: In Quest of Beauty* and this accompanying book. Focusing on Mucha's graphic works from his Paris period, which became synonymous with the Art Nouveau style, the exhibition looks at the development of his style and the ideas behind it, in particular, the idea of beauty - the core principle underlying his artistic theories and philosophy.

Reflecting the concept of the exhibition, the book highlights three key themes drawn from Mucha's art: 'Women – Icons & Muses' (Chapter 1); 'Le Style Mucha – A Visual Language' (Chapter 2); and 'Beauty – Power for Inspiration' (Chapter 3). Whilst the first two chapters explore Mucha's contribution to Art Nouveau in Paris, the final chapter throws light on his work after his return to the Czech lands. Each chapter makes links between Mucha's work and philosophy and key works from the four participating Museums – Russell-Cotes Art Gallery & Museum, Bournemouth; Sainsbury Centre for Visual Art, Norwich; Kelvingrove Art Gallery and Museum, Glasgow; Walker Art Gallery, Liverpool. By creating a parallel display of Mucha and his contemporaries' works, we are able to examine to what extent Mucha's aesthetic and spiritual concerns reflected the spirit of his times.

Many people have worked together to make this exhibition and book possible and we are deeply grateful for the enthusiastic support of all the participating museums and for their wonderful contributions to the creation of this beautiful book. We would especially like to thank Sue Hayward, Helen Ivaldi, Sarah Newman and Duncan Walker from Russell-Cotes Art Gallery & Museum; Professor Paul Greenhalgh and Claire Allerton from SCVA; Neil Ballantyne, Pippa Stephenson, Alison Brown and Dr Jo Meacock from Glasgow Museums; and Sandra Penketh, Xanthe Brooke and Myra Brown from National Museums Liverpool Above all, special thanks to Tomoko Sato, curator and author; her scholarly contribution towards the understanding of Mucha and his work and her innovative and creative approach to exhibition making are the inspiration behind this exhibition and book.

Finally we hope that, whether you are a seasoned Mucha enthusiast or are coming to his work for the first time, this exhibition will communicate anew the interests, passions and concerns of his artistic vision and you will find it not only appealing but also surprising, stimulating and challenging.

John Mucha
President, Mucha Foundation

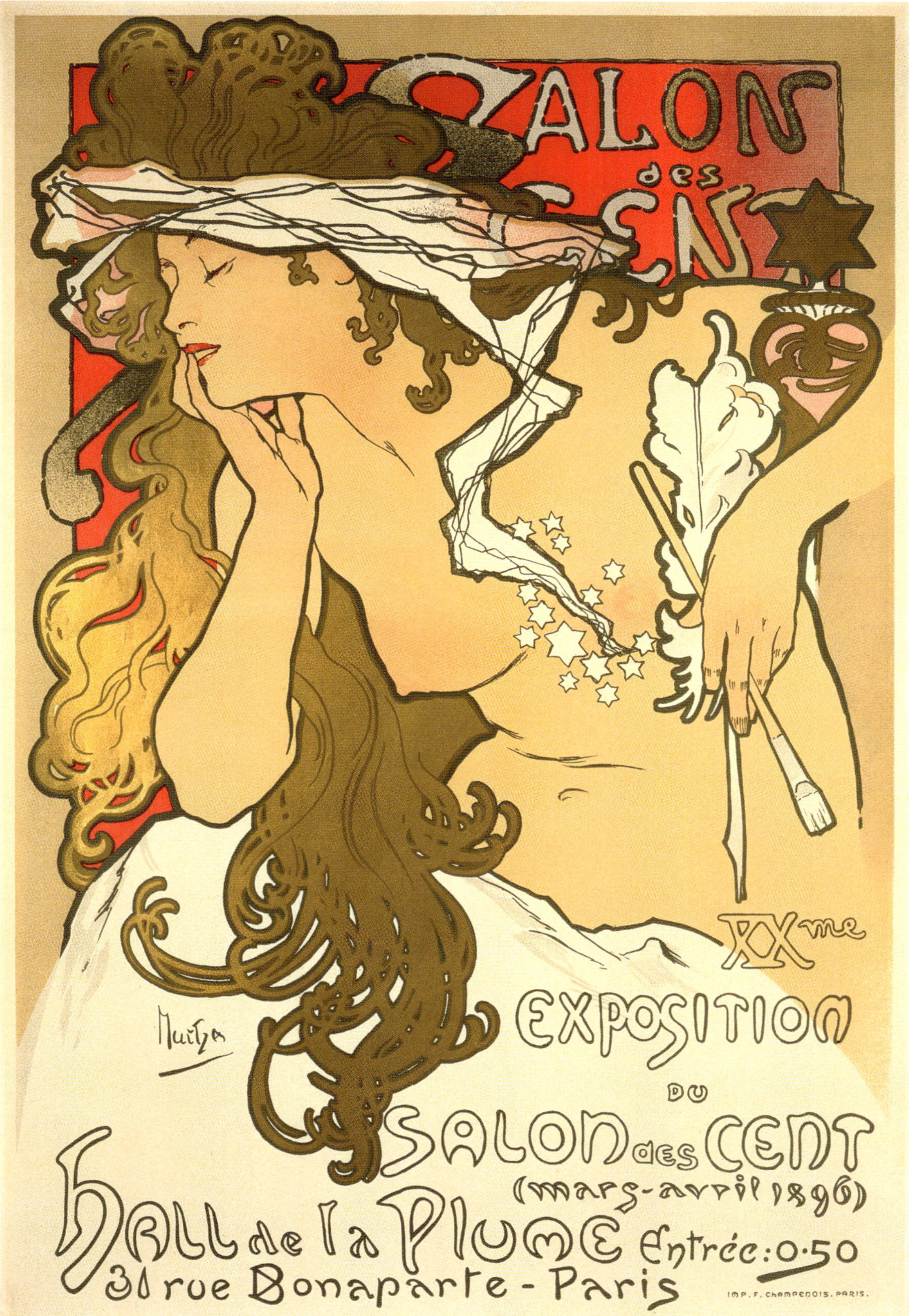

SALON DES CENT:
20th EXHIBITION
1896
Colour lithograph
63 x 43

ALPHONSE MUCHA: IN QUEST OF BEAUTY

TOMOKO SATO

'The mission of the artist is to encourage people to love beauty and harmony.'

'I prefer to be someone who makes pictures for people, rather than who creates art for art's sake.'

Alphonse Mucha

Czech painter and decorative artist Alphonse Mucha (1860–1939) is best known as a leading exponent of Art Nouveau, especially in the field of poster work. Beginning with his first Sarah Bernhardt poster *Gismonda* (see p.22), which made him famous overnight on its appearance in Paris in 1895, Mucha produced some 120 executed poster designs between 1895 and 1904[1]; many of these are regarded as icons of Art Nouveau today. Along with this large body of work, Mucha left an enduring legacy through his style, famously known as *'le style Mucha'*, which is characterised by the image of a beautiful woman in an elegant pose arranged in a harmonious composition with flowers and other decorative motifs taken from nature. These features became key elements of the Art Nouveau style, revived in the 1960s and continuing to inspire new generations of artists across the world – from the 'psychedelic' graphic designers of the Swinging Sixties to Japanese *manga* artists from the 1970s onwards.

Despite the lasting influence of Mucha's style, little attention has been drawn to the theoretical aspect of the development of his style, somewhat obscured by his huge success in the genre conventionally categorised as 'commercial art' as opposed to 'fine art'. Nevertheless, his surviving writings in the Mucha Archive[2] reveal hitherto unknown aspects of the artist both as a thinker and as an articulate writer on aesthetic theories. Above all Mucha's lecture notes, posthumously compiled and published as a book *Alphonse Mucha: Lectures on Art* in 1975[3], demonstrate his clear vision of the roles of art and the artist as well as well-formulated theories on the basis of which Mucha's style was developed (see pp.44,87). The following is the introductory passage of one of his lectures:

> *'The aim of art is to glorify beauty. And what is beauty? Beauty is the projection of moral harmonies on material and physical planes. On the moral plane, beauty addresses itself to the evolution of the spirit, and on the material plane, it addresses itself to the refinement of the senses through which medium it reaches the soul.*
>
> *The expression of beauty is by emotion. The person who can communicate his emotions to the souls of others is the artist.*
>
> *To communicate with the souls of man the artist must address himself to the senses of the body.*
>
> *To arouse the interest of the senses, to awaken them to his speech, the artist must know how to charm. This charm consists in the perfect harmony which should reign between the media of communication employed and the faculties of senses which he addresses.'* [4]

As asserted here and elsewhere in his writings, the idea of beauty occupied the central part of Mucha's artistic philosophy. For him beauty is the symbol of 'moral harmonies' (such as goodness and virtue) and possesses an inherent power to inspire; the artist is 'a priest at the altar of beauty'[5] to 'communicate' the message of beauty to the wider public. Thus Mucha logically explained his stance –

Fig. 1
FLOWER
1897
Colour lithograph
66.2 x 44.4

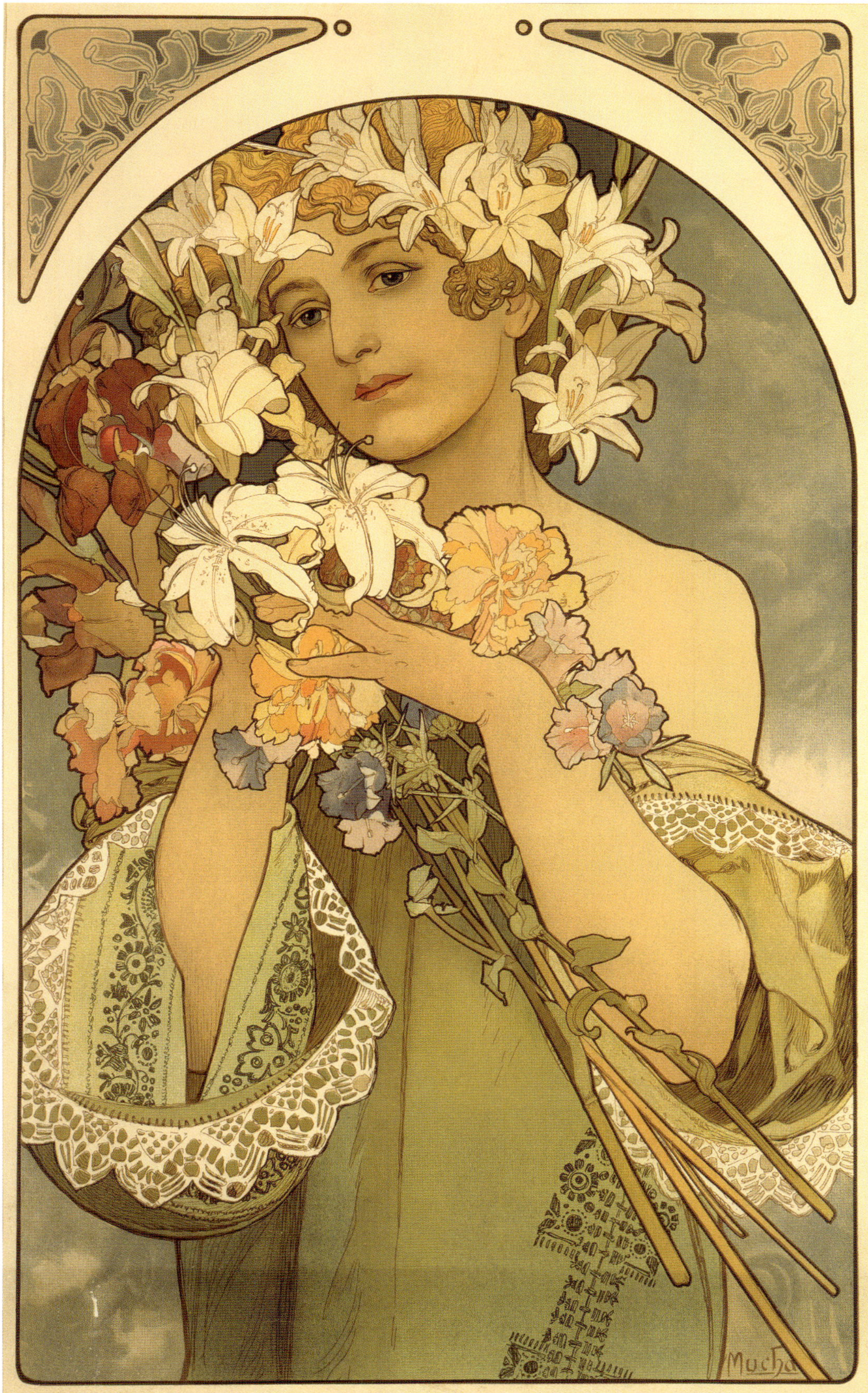

that the artist's methods and techniques should evolve from the need to communicate with the audience – which opposed the 'art for art's sake' doctrine, one of the most fashionable ideas in modern art, and in order to achieve this communication he advocated the use of modern scientific knowledge concerning the psychological conditions of visual perception in artistic expression.

Perhaps the most remarkable feature of Mucha's artistic philosophy is this unorthodox synthesis of moral and aesthetic principles with scientific rationalism, which demonstrates influences from diverse artistic and intellectual ideas prevalent in late 19th century Europe such as Symbolist and Neo-Platonic aesthetics, Morris-inspired 'Art for the People' ideals, Spiritualism, parapsychology, and, above all, Czech Nationalism.

Mucha was born in 1860 in Ivančice, a small town in the South Moravian Region of today's Czech Republic. By the time of Mucha's birth his homeland had been under Habsburg rule for 240 years[6] and his nationalist consciousness was formed early in his life. His childhood years coincided with the peak period of the Czech National Revival – the movement established in the late 18th century to restore the Czech language, culture and national identity, which had been all but eradicated through the Germanisation policy of the Habsburg monarchs. The 1860s saw the fruit of this effort with the emergence of the first regular Czech-language newspapers, *Čas (Time)* and *Národní listy (The National Paper)*, in 1861; this was followed by the foundation of important institutions in Prague to inspire Czech Nationalism. The Sokol gymnastic organisation was founded in 1862 to promote nationalist ideology through physical and moral training (see p.137 left). The forum of Czech artists, Umělecká beseda, was established in 1863 to foster national music, literature and visual arts.

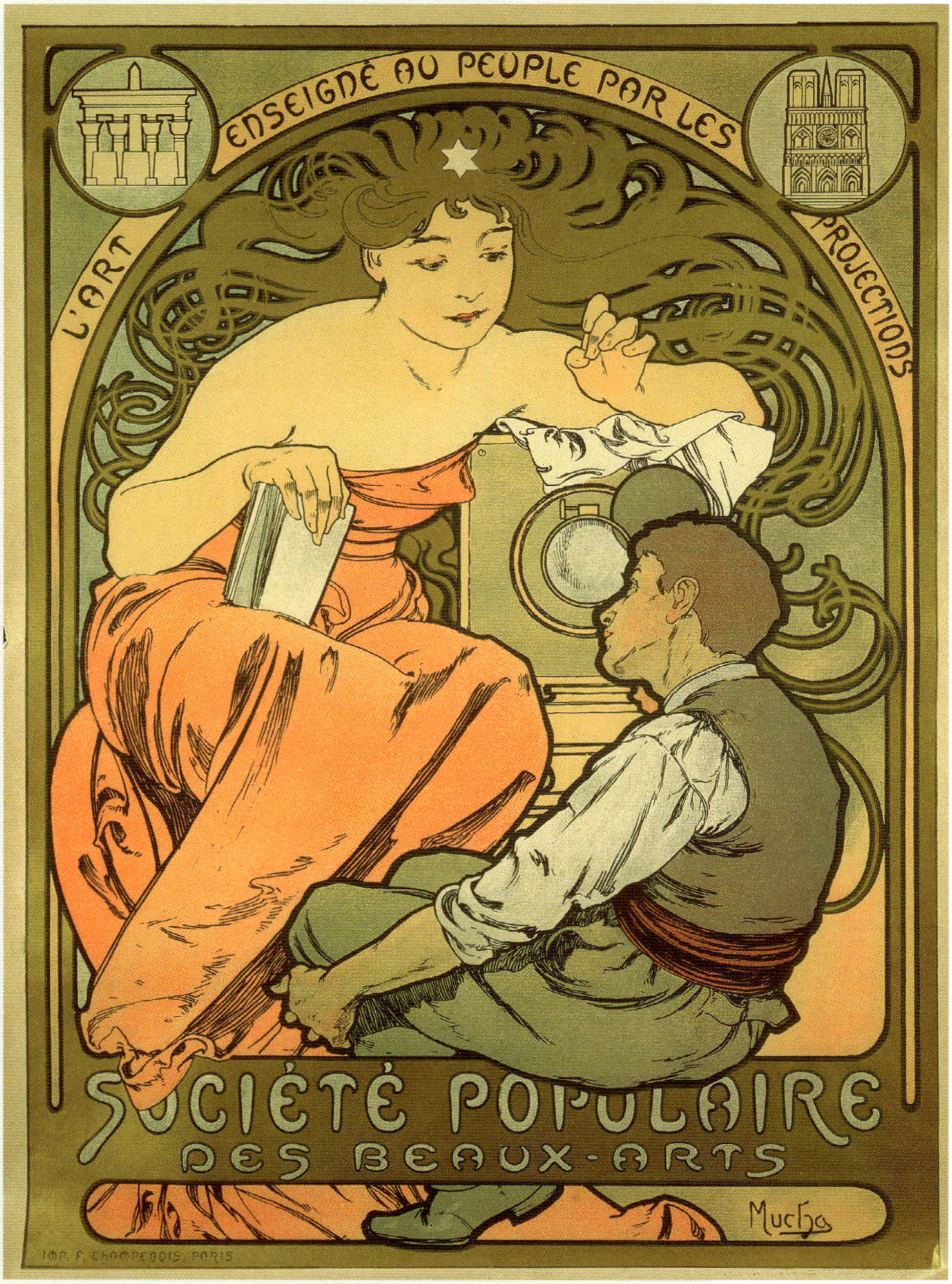

Fig. 2
SOCIÉTÉ POPULAIRE DES BEAUX-ARTS
1897
Colour lithograph
62.5 x 46

The foundation stones of the National Theatre – a symbol of the Czech national identity and political independence – were laid in 1868 with much pomp and circumstance.

As a student at the Slovanské Gymnasium in Brno, the capital of Moravia, Mucha spent his formative years in the intensely patriotic environment created by this new Czech renaissance, imbibing its ideology and influences. There was a revived interest in Moravian folk art and culture among the intellectuals and students in protest of influences from Vienna[7]. Its lasting impact was later manifested in Mucha's posters and paintings with his conscious and consistent use of Moravian decorative motifs such as the exquisite embroidery and lacework on folk costumes and the stylised flowers decorating folk crafts (Fig 1; also see pp.38, 81). Leoš Janáček (1854–1928), the future composer whom Mucha met during his time in Brno, was similarly inspired and later became a leading figure in modern Czech music with his distinctive style inspired by Moravian and other Slavic folk music. Furthermore, works by eminent artists and musicians such as Josef Mánes (1820–1871) and Bedřich Smetana (1824–1884) served as examples of how art could serve the nation through its power of inspiration. After leaving school Mucha was actively involved in patriotic activities in his hometown, joining Sokol and using his artistic skills to design flyers, decorate a meeting hall and contribute illustrations to local satirical magazines. In this cultural setting Mucha formulated the concept of art as a means to respond to the nation's needs. In 1879 Mucha left Ivančice to pursue his career as an artist with a sense of mission for the future of his homeland.

Mucha was initially trained in Vienna as a scene painter at the beginning of the 1880s, and he received his formal training at the Munich Academy of Fine Arts (1885–1887) and at the Académies Julian and Colarossi in Paris (1887–1889). Thereafter he worked abroad continuously – mostly in Paris and making several trips to America – until 1910 when he eventually returned to his homeland to fulfil his long-term goal through the creation of *The Slav Epic* (1912–1926), a cycle of twenty monumental paintings depicting the history of all Slavic peoples as a monument and inspiration for Slavic unity (see pp.138–139). Thus Mucha maintained his artistic ideals from his youth throughout his time abroad but during the 1890s the nationalist focus of his vision expanded to more universal concerns about society and the future of humanity as a whole under new influences such as *'l'art social'* and Spiritualism.

The late 19th century saw two strands of thought about art: 'art for art's sake' and 'art for the people'. While Mucha was particularly critical about the former, which he considered to be 'unsatisfactory'[8] because of its 'emphasis on mere techniques' rather than moral content[9], he was drawn to the latter, which naturally fit with the purpose of his art. Additionally, during Mucha's time in Paris there were vigorous discussions amongst thinkers and artists about the idea of advocating social reform through art by distributing culture to the wider public, as debated by contributors to political-art magazines circulating at the time such as *L'Art Social*, which was founded in 1891. William Morris (1834–1896) and the ideals of the English Arts and Crafts Movement were among the greatest inspirations to these debates.

Mucha was aware of Morris's work especially through Frederick Delius (1862–1934)[10], the English composer and an admirer of Morris's teachings, who was in Mucha's circle of friends at Madame Charlotte Caron's Crèmerie[11] in 1894–1895 together with Paul Gauguin (1848–1903) and the Swedish writer August Strindberg (1849–1912). Mucha also met Morris's French follower, Henri Cazalis (1840–1909) around 1897. A physician and social thinker, who was also known as a Symbolist poet and writer under the pseudonym of Jean Lahor, Cazalis published *W. Morris et le mouvement nouveau de l'art décoratifs* in 1897 and in 1903 he founded the Société Internationale de l'Art Populaire in order to promote 'beauty in life and the ennobling of the masses by culture and aesthetic education'[12]. Mucha became one of the inaugural members of this society along with René Lalique (1860–1945), Emile Gallé (1846–1904), Eugène Grasset (1845–1917) and Victor Horta (1861–1947).[13] During this period Mucha was also involved in the Société Populaire des Beaux-Arts, which was founded in 1894 by the lawyer and Masonic social reformer, Edmond Benoît-Lévy (1858–1927). The society supported poor young artists and developed an education programme to popularise fine arts using magic lantern shows – equivalent to today's slide presentations – for which Mucha produced a poster (Fig. 2) free of charge.

Influences from this 'social art' movement on Mucha were reflected in two areas of his work in Paris. The first was the innovation of decorative panels *(panneaux décoratifs)*: a new type of posters without advertising texts intended for aesthetic appreciation and decorative purposes, which was launched in 1896 with *The Seasons* (see pp. 82–83). Of his decorative panels Mucha later wrote:

> *'I was happy to be involved in an art for the people and not for private drawing rooms. It was inexpensive, accessible to the general public, and it found a home in poor families as well as in more affluent circles.'*[14]

The second was the creation of a ready-to-use 'design handbook' for craftsmen and manufacturers, *Documents décoratifs* (see p. 95), which was

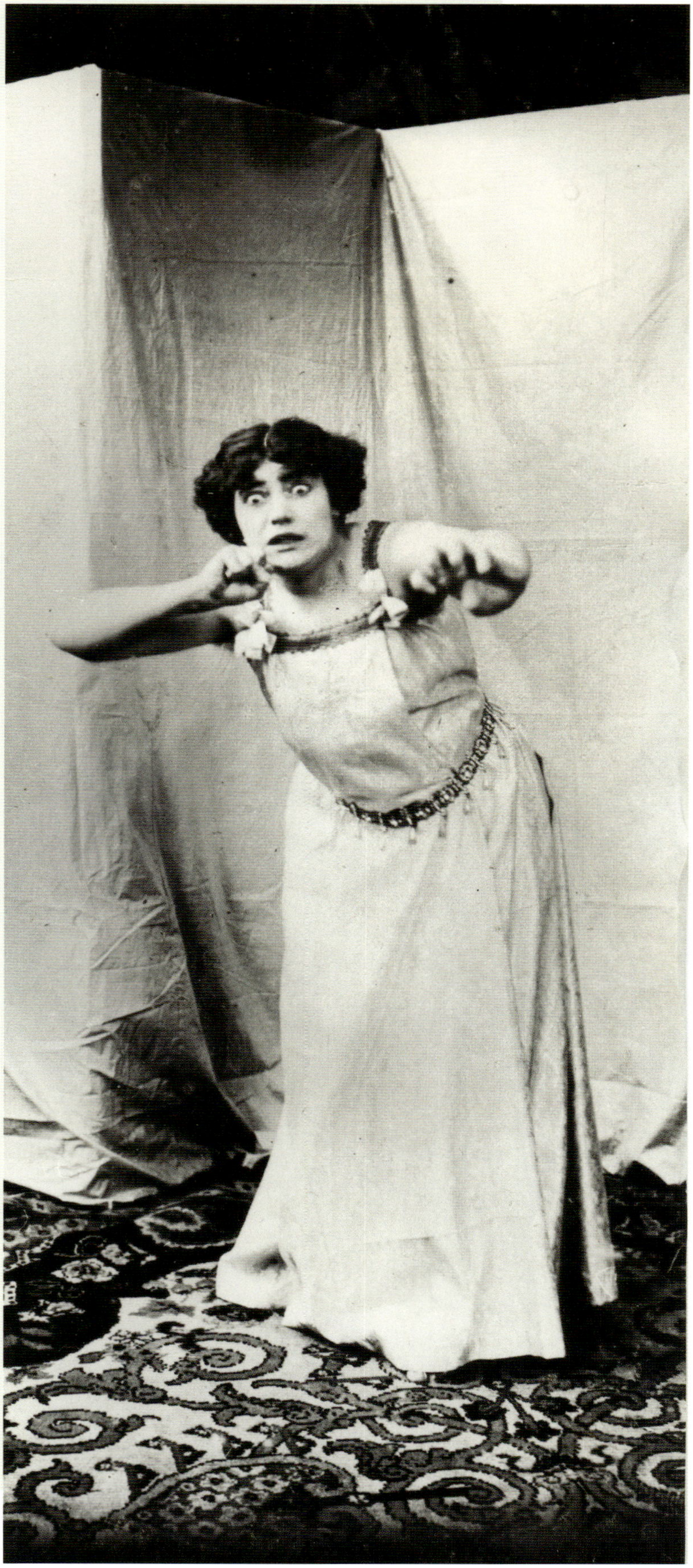

Fig. 3
LINA DE FERKEL, THE MEDIUM, IN MUCHA'S STUDIO, PARIS
Photographed at a psychic experiment conducted by Albert de Rochas in 1898.

published in 1902 with Mucha's pedagogic aspirations to contribute 'towards bringing aesthetic values into the arts and crafts'.[15] Compiling numerous samples of his work in every branch of decorative and applied arts, it was regarded as an invaluable textbook for future designers and was used by art schools in France and abroad, including Russia and the United States.

In parallel with his involvement in social art, Mucha was drawn to Spiritualism, especially the Theosophical doctrine promoted by Helena Petrovna Blavatsky (1831–1891), the Russian Spiritualist who founded the highly influential Theosophical Society in New York in 1875. With the motto 'There is No Religion Higher than Truth', the society advocated spiritual enlightenment through the pursuit of Truth (Divinity) by studying the 'ancient wisdom' (religion, philosophy and science) of the East and the West such as Christian mysticism, Buddhism and Kabbalism, as well as Neo-Platonism and Hermeticism/Occultism. During Mucha's time in Paris, Blavatsky's publications were widely read and discussed at salons and literary gatherings.[16]

Mucha's Spiritualism is rooted in his tendency towards mysticism nurtured by his upbringing in Moravia. His mother Amálie (1822–1880) was a devout Catholic, also, thanks to his gift for singing, Mucha spent many years of his youth as a choirboy in Ivančice and a chorister at the prestigious Cathedral of St. Peter and Paul in Brno. The various impressions of the church from his religious experience – the grand edifice of the cathedral, its frescoes, statues, ornaments, burning candles, the intoxicating fragrance of incense and flowers, bells and music – stayed with him throughout his life,

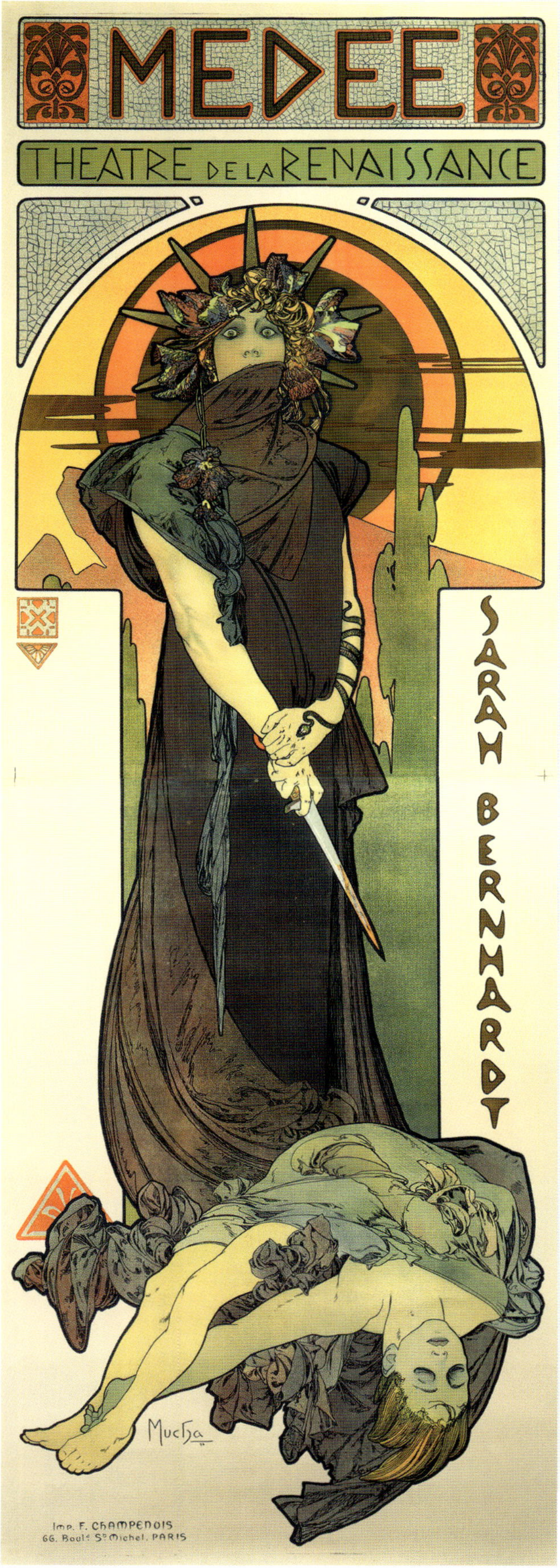

POSTER FOR SARAH BERNHARDT'S PRODUCTION, *MÉDÉE*
1898
Colour lithograph
206 x 76

laying foundations for his aesthetic and mystic taste. Mucha wrote later:

> *'For me, the notions of painting, going to church, and music are so closely knit that often I cannot decide whether I like church for its music or music for its place in the mystery which it accompanies.'*[17]

In Paris Mucha's mystical tendency was particularly deepened under the influence of August Strindberg, who joined Madame Charlotte's artists' colony in early 1895. At the time the Swedish writer was going through the 'Inferno Crisis' known from the title of his autobiographical novel *Inferno* (1897). In his spiritual struggles Strindberg was powerfully drawn to Mysticism and Occultism and Mucha became Strindberg's regular companion for philosophical discussions. Through this friendship Mucha was profoundly influenced by Strindberg's notion of the 'mysterious forces' that guide a man's life. This notion was later to contribute to Mucha's own idea of 'unseen powers'[18], which is manifested in his work as the recurring motif of a mysterious figure appearing behind the subject (see p.137).

During the latter half of the 1890s, following the success of *Gismonda* in 1895, Mucha consolidated his fame as a poster artist and it was during this period that he developed distinctive design formulas known as *'le style Mucha'*. There are two major factors that contributed to this development. Firstly, Mucha formulated his style primarily for advertising posters. Secondly, in his design strategies he began to take into account new scientific knowledge, especially psychological effects on the viewer.

Although Mucha's goal at that time was to work for his homeland using his art, especially through his major project, *The Slav Epic*, his intensive experience in the field of advertising in Paris was indispensable for his artistic development as a whole. The inherent function of the advertising genre – message making and communication with the wider public – combined with Mucha's own definition of the purpose of art, provided Mucha with an ideal testing ground to explore effective methods of communication.

It was in this context that Mucha was particularly benefitted by new scientific ideas introduced by Albert de Rochas (1837–1914), a parapsychologist,

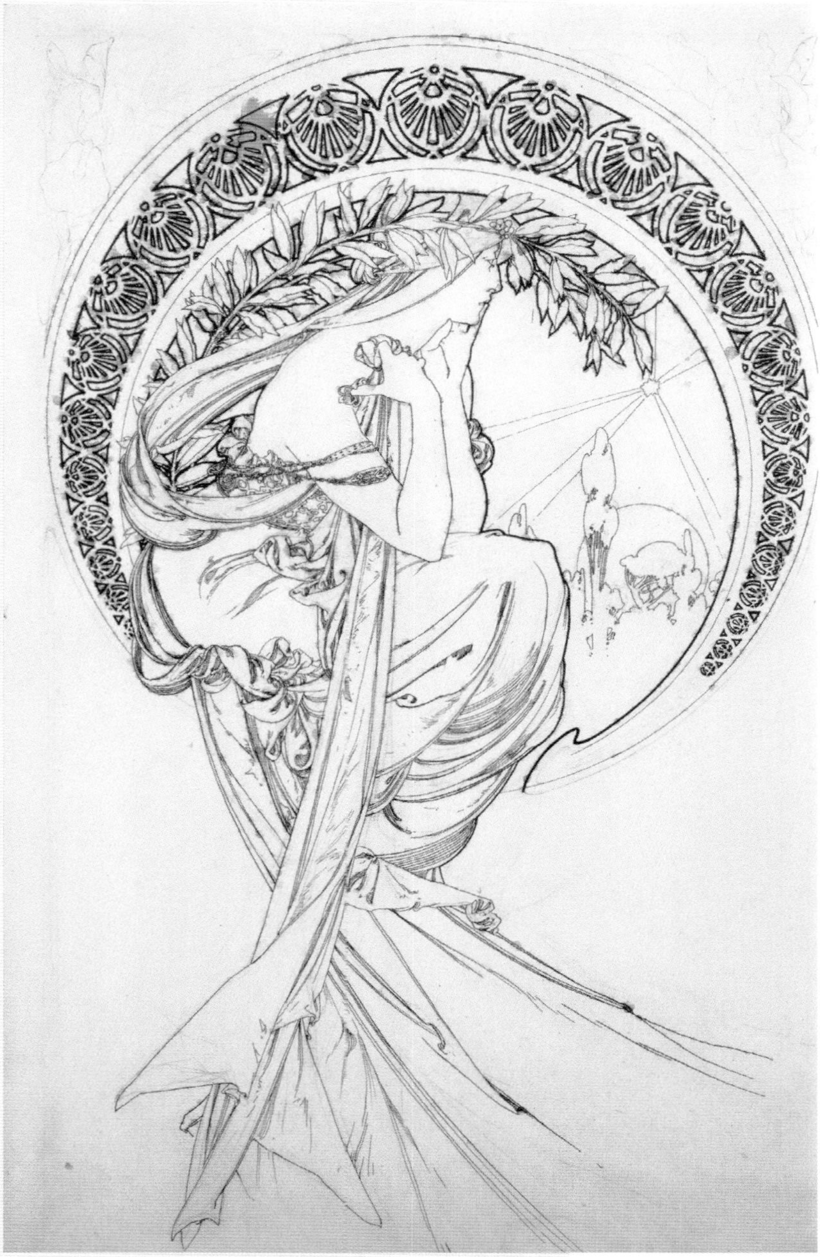

Fig. 4
OUTLINE SKETCH FOR *THE ARTS: POETRY*
1898
Pencil and ink on paper
78 x 58

and Camille Flammarion (1842–1925), an astronomer and scientific writer. Mucha formed friendships with these eminent scientists through Theosophical gatherings between 1896–1897. De Rochas and Flammarion approached Theosophy using scientific methods, exploring the scientific basis for occult phenomena, especially extra-sensory perception. Studying hypnotism and the role of the medium, they investigated 'mystical psychic forces' – the working of the subconscious mind as well as the impact of visual arts and music on emotions and senses[19] – studies recognised today as neuroaesthetics or psychological aesthetics. Mucha regularly participated in their meetings and psychic experiments using a medium, for which Mucha's studio was used occasionally (Fig.3). Of such experiences, Mucha wrote enthusiastically:

> *'Science knows no limits…Man in his curiosity is lifting the edge of the veil [covering Truth] and can only marvel!'* [20]

Fig. 5
FRONTISPIECE FOR *CLIO* BY ANATOLE FRANCE
Book published in 1900 by Calmann-Lévy, Paris, with illustrations by Mucha
33 x 25

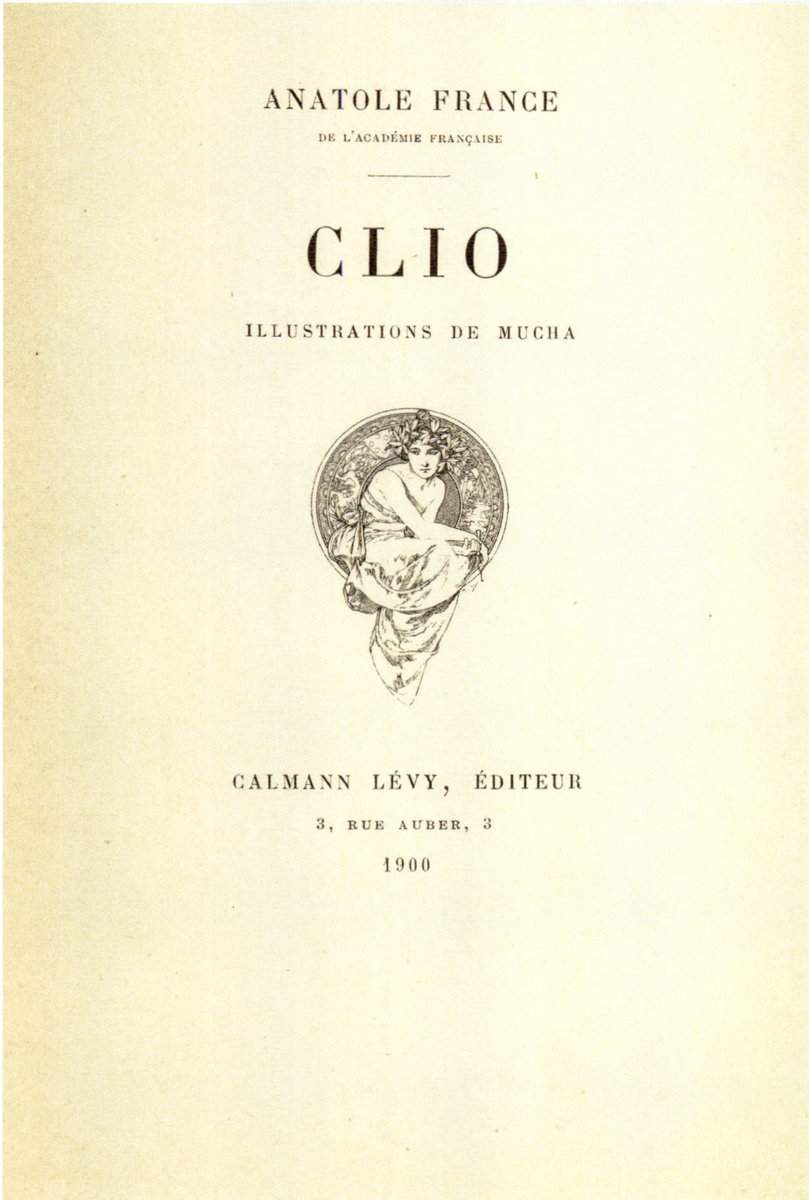

Mucha applied his new scientific knowledge to his design strategies for posters, which were to be articulated as his 'how-to-charm' theories in his *Lectures on Art*. In these Mucha particularly stressed the importance in understanding the mechanism of visual perception (eye-nerve-brain) when following the contours of the forms and the visual forces created by lines. Accordingly, he suggested that curvilinear forms (circles, ovals, concentric circles and spirals) and sinuous lines, which would cause reciprocating actions in the ocular muscles, would make a pleasing effect on the viewer's eyes and mind and consequently be perceived as beautiful. In determining such pleasing forms and lines, Mucha also suggested learning the law of harmonious proportions from organic forms in nature. Mucha wrote:

> *'Visible nature, seen through our eyes, surrounds us with rich and harmonious forms. The marvelous poem of the human body, those of animals, and the music of lines and colours emanating from flowers, leaves and fruits are the most obvious teachers of our eyes and taste.'* [21]

Between late 1896–1898 Mucha consolidated his design formulas with the features widely known as *le style Mucha*: the use of a female figure (the idealistic beauty) as the communicator of a sublime message and sumptuous decorative motifs incorporating circles, whiplash lines and other geometric patterns, which would bring aesthetic pleasure and navigate the viewer to the focal point of the picture or the central message (see p.42). These individual forms were then arranged in carefully calculated, harmonious compositions using his system – 'the law of proportion of II to III' and 'the three principal points' – to determine individual forms and their relationships within the overall composition. Mucha wrote that the 'exterior form is a language which appeals to the (viewer's) sense'[22] and that the 'composition is the speech which the artist uses to translate his emotions (thoughts)'[23].

One of the archetypes of the Mucha Style was the 'Q-formula', the term coined by Brian Reade in 1963[24]. As exemplified by the decorative panels series *The Arts* (see pp.86–87), this composition incorporated a seated figure in a circular or horseshoe motif with a tail of drapery hanging down, forming the letter 'Q' (Figs.4,5). With its emblematic simplicity, this formula and its variations became a hallmark of Mucha's style and its enduring influence is still seen in today's graphic art.

In January 1898, Mucha was initiated into Freemasonry in Paris. While the Masonic philosophy shared ideals similar to Madame Blavatsky's Theosophy – especially a belief in the progress of humanity through enlightenment (the quest of Truth and Beauty) as well as mystic symbolism – Masonry also provided Mucha with 'the power of brotherhood, the power of love and the power of enthusiasm', which would enable him to work for 'the liberation and advancement of the Czech nation'[25]. With this 'power' Mucha maintained the artistic aspirations of his youth, which ultimately developed into *The Slav Epic.*

In 1928, when Mucha presented the complete cycle of *The Slav Epic* to the City of Prague on the occasion of the 10th anniversary of the formation of the Czechoslovak state (see p.137 right), he spoke about his ideas behind this work.

> *'I wanted to talk in my own way to the soul of the nation, to its eyes, which convey thoughts instantly to the consciousness. A picture, I believe, acts aggressively. Unhindered, it penetrates through the viewer's eyes into his soul...Seduced by its exterior form, he would stop in front of it, and perhaps he would search its content and significance, eventually finding its essence – Beauty or Truth – for which a work of art is created... The purpose of my work was to build, to create bridges; because we must all nurture our hope that humanity will draw together, and the easier it will be the more they understand each other. I will be happy if it falls to my lot to have helped with my modest strength towards this understanding, at least in our Slav family.'*[26]

Thus, through his spiritual journey in quest of Beauty, *le style Mucha* evolved into a powerful language, which became the means to express Mucha's philosophical ideas, like the languages of Petr Chelčický (c.1390–c.1460; Fig.6) and Leo Tolstoy (1828–1910).[27]

NOTES

(1) This figure is based on Jack Rennert and Alain Weill, *Alphonse Mucha: The Complete Posters and Panels* (Uppsala, Sweden, 1984).
(2) The Mucha Archive forms part of the Mucha Trust Collection.
(3) Alphonse Mucha, *Alphonse Mucha: Lectures on Art* (London/New York, 1975). The book collects a series of Mucha's lecture notes, originally written in Czech, compiled and edited by Jiří Mucha, the artist's son and biographer.
(4) Alphonse Mucha, 1975, op. cit., p.9.
(5) Alphonse Mucha, Mucha Archive (MSS No. 675.1).
(6) The Battle of the White Mountain (Bílá Hora) of 1620, when the Protestant Bohemian army was defeated by the combined Catholic forces led by the Habsburg monarch, is widely regarded as being decisive in securing Habsburg rule of the Czech lands for the

following 300 years until the dissolution of the Austro-Hungarian Empire in 1918.
(7) Jana A. Brabcová-Orlíková, 'Mucha: Bohemia and Paris' from Victor Arwas, Jana Brabcová-Orlíková and Anna Dvořák, *Alphonse Mucha: The Spirit of Art Nouveau* (Alexandria, Virginia 1998), p.16.
(8) Alphonse Mucha, Mucha Archive (MSS No. 638.1).
(9) Alphonse Mucha, op. cit. (MSS No.674.1).
(10) Jiří Mucha, *Alphonse Maria Mucha: His Life and Art* (London, 1989), p.49. Frederick Delius was born to the family of a wealthy German textile merchant in Bradford, a boomtown of the Industrial Revolution in West Yorkshire. He grew up in the city's highly cultured community where the work of Morris & Co. was much admired, especially with their stained-glass windows installed at Bradford Cathedral in 1863–64.
(11) Located at 13, rue de la Grande-Chaumière, Madame Charlotte's Crèmerie was a famous artists' colony in the Latin Quarter. Mucha lived in this street until 1896.
(12) Jiří Mucha, 1989, op. cit., pp.123–125.
(13) Ibid.
(14) *The Mucha Museum Guide: Alphonse Mucha* (Prague, 2009).
(15) Jiří Mucha, 1989, op. cit., p.138.
(16) Anna Dvořák, 'Le Pater – Alphonse Mucha's Illustrated Lord Prayer: History and Interpretation', from *Alphonse Mucha – Paris 1900: Le Pater/The Lord Prayer* (Obecní dům, Prague, 2002), pp.12–13.
(17) Jiří Mucha, *Alphonse Mucha: The Master of Art Nouveau* (Prague, 1966), p.13.
(18) Jiří Mucha, 1966, op. cit., p.56.
(19) One of such experiments took place in 1898 at Mucha's studio in the rue du Val-de-Grâce as reported in the article, 'L'Expression des sentiments dans les Arts' by Albert de Rochas, featured in *Revue Dauphinoise* (Grenoble, 1898), pp.1–9.
(20) Jiří Mucha, 1989, op. cit., p.114.
(21) Alphonse Mucha, 1975, op. cit., p.12.
(22) Alphonse Mucha, 1975, op. cit., p.13.
(23) Alphonse Mucha, 1975, op. cit., p.45.
(24) Brian Reade, *Art Nouveau and Alphonse Mucha* (London, 1963), pp.18–20.
(25) Alfons Mucha, 'Br. Alfons Mucha (25 ledna 1898)', in *Stavba* (Prague, 1932), p.36.
(26) Alfons Mucha, *Slovanská Epopeje* (Prague, undated), pp.3–4.
(27) Jiří Mucha, 1966, op. cit., p.280. The South-Bohemian philosopher Petr Chelčický was one of the most influential spiritual leaders in the Czech reformation movement. His idea of non-aggression principles influenced modern Pacifist thinkers including Leo Tolstoy, Mahatma Gandhi (1869–1948) and Martin Luther King (1929–1968) as well as Mucha, who featured Chelčický in the cycle No.12 (1918) of *The Slav Epic* with his teaching: 'Do not repay evil with evil.'

Overleaf
Fig. 6
THE SLAV EPIC (CYCLE No.12)
PETR CHELČICKÝ AT VODŇANY:
DO NOT REPAY EVIL WITH EVIL
1918
Egg tempera and oil on canvas
405 x 620
City Gallery, Prague

Drawing its subject from one of the episodes of the Hussite Wars, Mucha paid homage to the influential Czech pacifist thinker, Petr Chelčický. The scene shows the aftermath of the raid of the Taborites on the town of Vodňany in 1420. In the centre of the composition Mucha depicted Chelčický catching hold of an angry villager's arm and dissuading him from seeking vengeance.

The arrangement of the semi-circle, formed by the dead and injured laid on the ground and the plumes of black smoke rising in the background, navigate the viewer to the central message of this work.

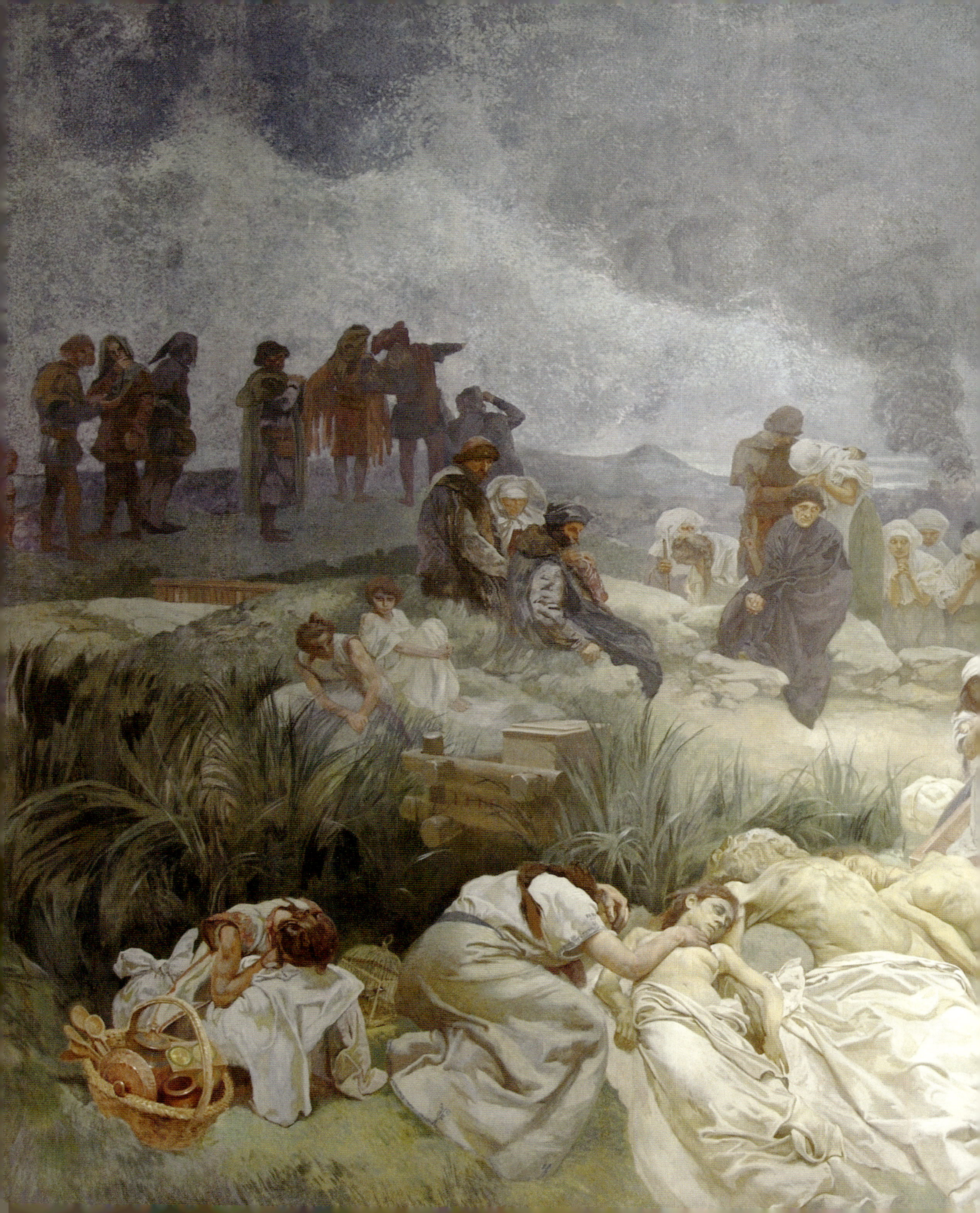

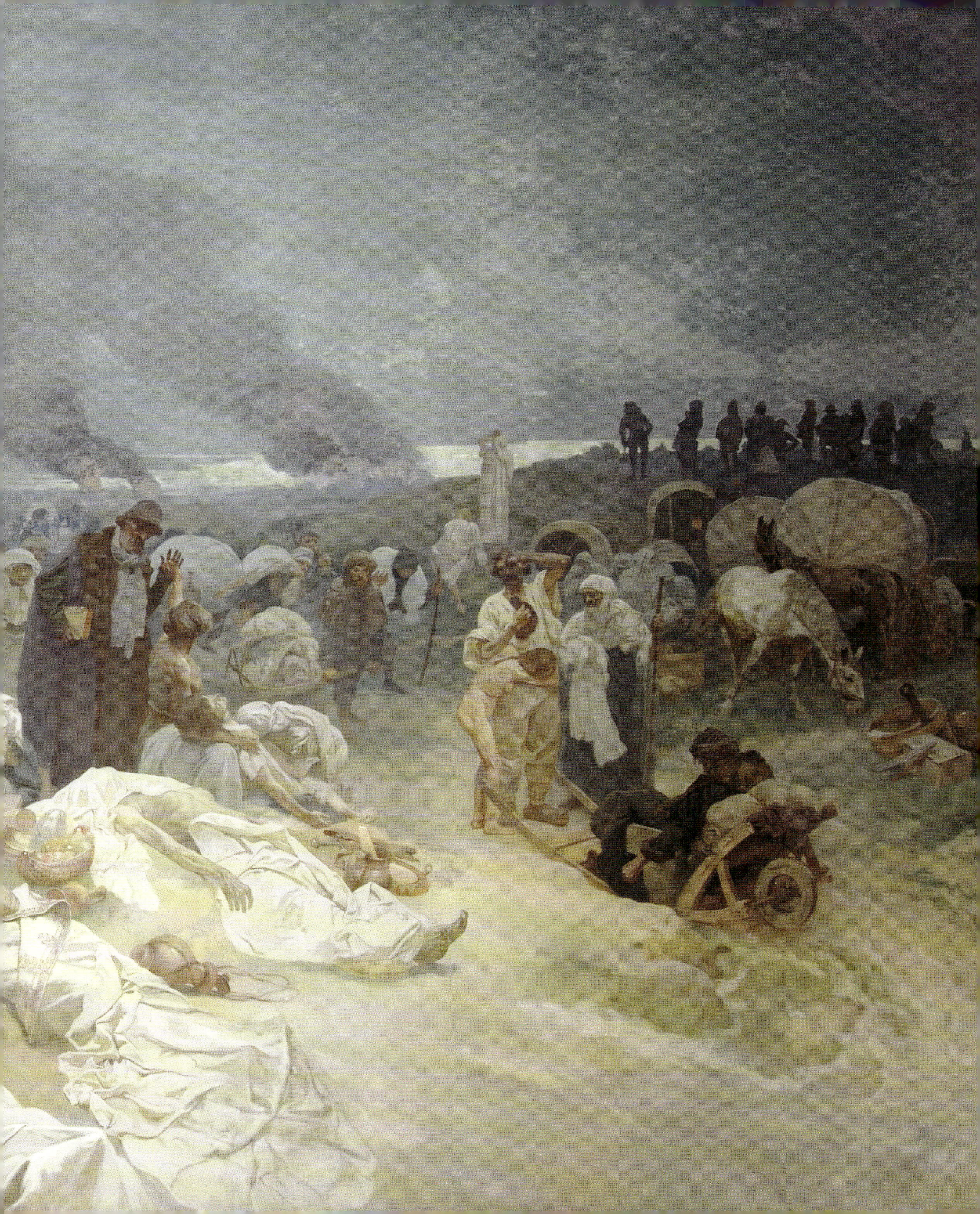

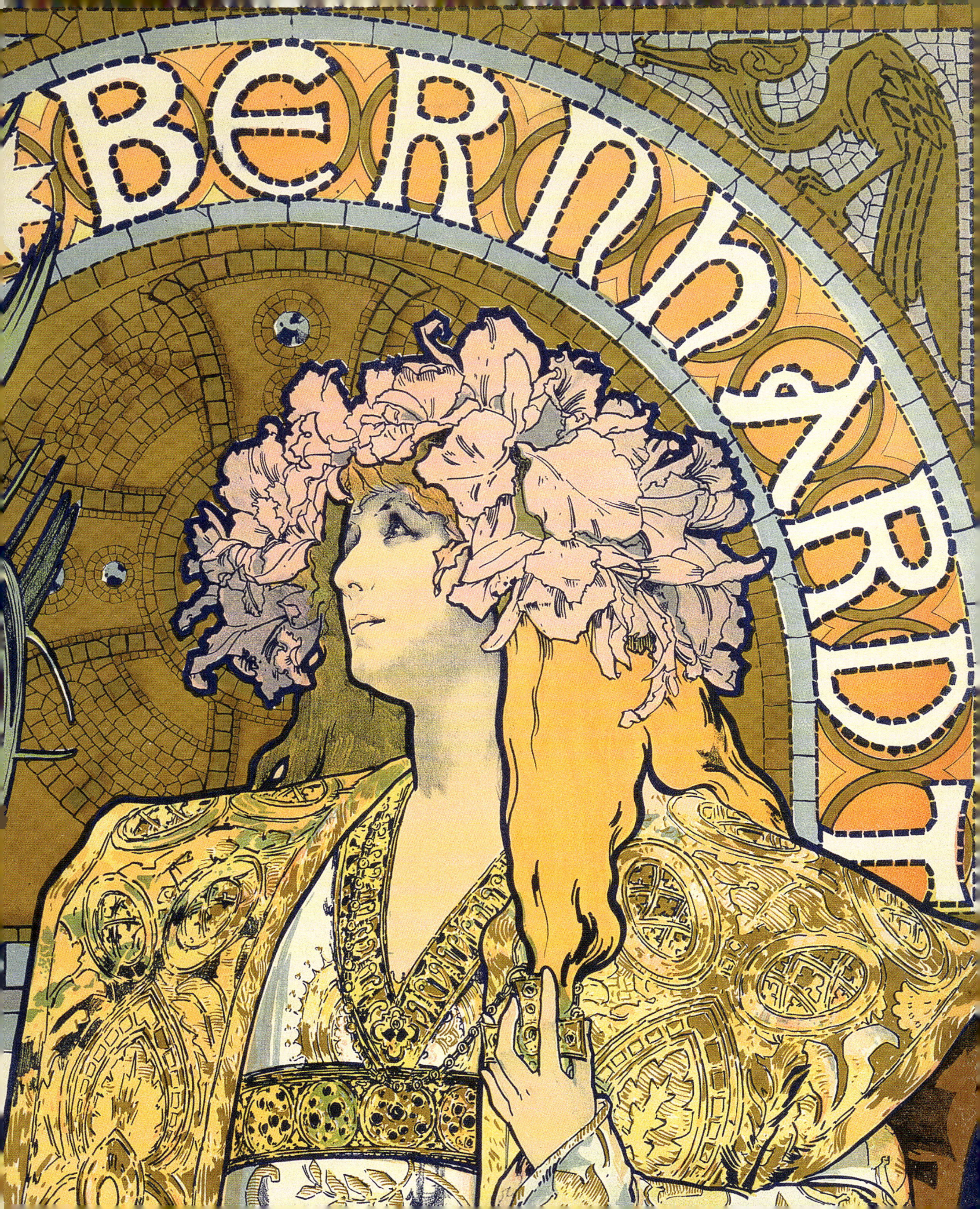
BERNHARDT

I

WOMEN – ICONS AND MUSES

Women form the central part of Mucha's style. Beautiful, wholesome, sensuous yet innocent, they allure viewers with their magnetic charms, yet their serene eyes and benevolent expression are comforting. Mucha's women are the antithesis of the images of decadent, dangerous women represented by other late nineteenth-century artists, such as Félicien Rops (1833–1893), Toulouse-Lautrec (1864–1901) and Aubrey Beardsley (1872–1898). As he wrote later, for Mucha women were 'creative forces to bring forth new beings', and in the creation of his artistic style it was Sarah Bernhardt (1844–1923) – the Parisian superstar actress who earned the nickname 'the Divine Sarah' – who catalysed this force.

Mucha met this great actress towards the end of 1894 through the commission of a poster for her production of the play *Gismonda*. Mucha was then a moderately successful book illustrator but completely unknown in the field of the poster, a new art form taking centre stage in Parisian streets and magazines. Despite Mucha's inexperience in the genre, Bernhardt was struck by the novelty of Mucha's design, which featured her impressive life-size figure in an unusually tall format rendered by elegantly flowing outlines and delicate pastel colours. Furthermore, Mucha's portrayal of the actress *en rôle* – 'the soul' of her art itself, rather than her likeness – matched her aesthetics and the ideal image of herself that Bernhardt aspired to project onstage.

Revealed on Parisian hoardings on New Year's Day 1895, Mucha's first poster for 'the Divine Sarah' electrified Paris. This success prompted Bernhardt to offer Mucha a six-year contract to do more work for her and her theatre, serving not only as a designer but also as an artistic director. Under this contract, Mucha designed Bernhardt's costumes, jewellery and stage sets, as well as six further posters for her productions, which created an enduring image of Sarah Bernhardt as a stage icon.

GISMONDA
(detail)
see p.22

Mucha began to receive commissions for advertising posters and in 1896 he signed an exclusive contract with the Parisian printer/publisher F. Champenois. A large majority of Mucha's poster work from his Paris period resulted from his collaboration with Champenois, and it is this group of posters that established Mucha's international fame as a master of Art Nouveau.

In designing these posters, Mucha used two types of formats: the *Gismonda* prototype, tall with a ratio of 3:1; and an oblong format with a ratio of 3:2, which he considered the most harmonious proportion. With these formats Mucha established a consistent composition style, featuring female figures as icons or muses carrying alluring messages, combined with a variety of decorative and symbolic motifs. Recognisable, engaging and accessible, Mucha's posters were popularly called *'le style Mucha'*, and the characteristic elements of his style became key features of the emerging Art Nouveau style.

> *'Posters were a good way of enlightening the wider public. They would stop and see the posters on their way to work, deriving spiritual pleasure from them. The streets became open-air art exhibitions.'*
>
> *Alphonse Mucha*

GISMONDA
1894
Colour lithograph
216 x 74.2

Set in mediaeval Greece, *Gismonda* was the first of Victorien Sardou's (1831–1908) work that Sarah Bernhardt produced, directed and starred in herself. Here, Mucha portrayed her as an exotic Byzantine noblewoman wearing a splendid gown, with an orchid headdress and a palm branch in her hand. The pose was taken from Gismonda's Palm Sunday procession, the climax of the play.

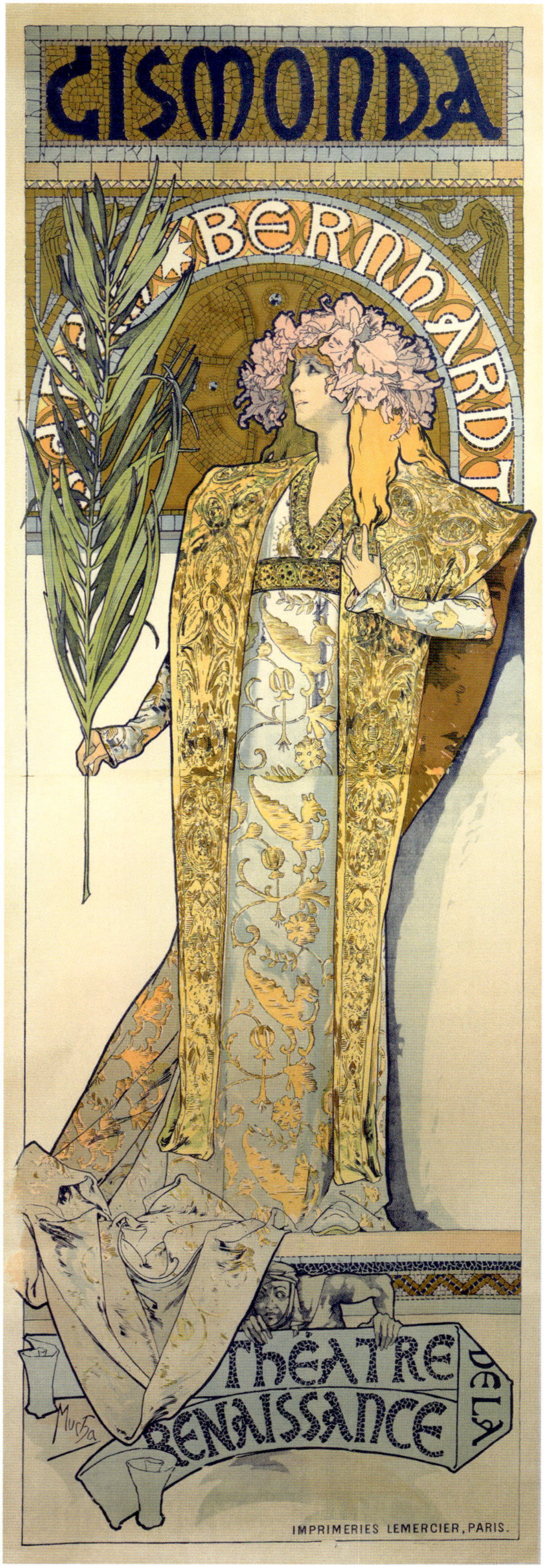

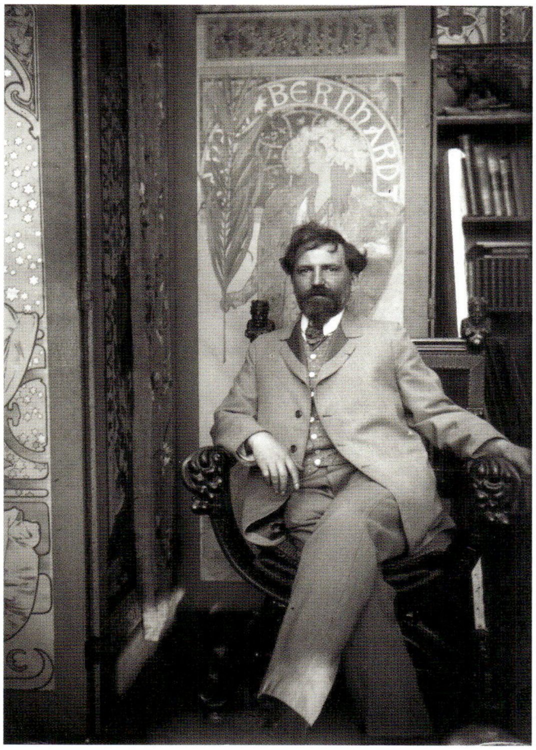

MUCHA WITH SARAH BERNHARDT POSTERS IN HIS STUDIO IN RUE DU VAL-DE-GRÂCE, PARIS
c.1901
Modern print from original glass plate negative

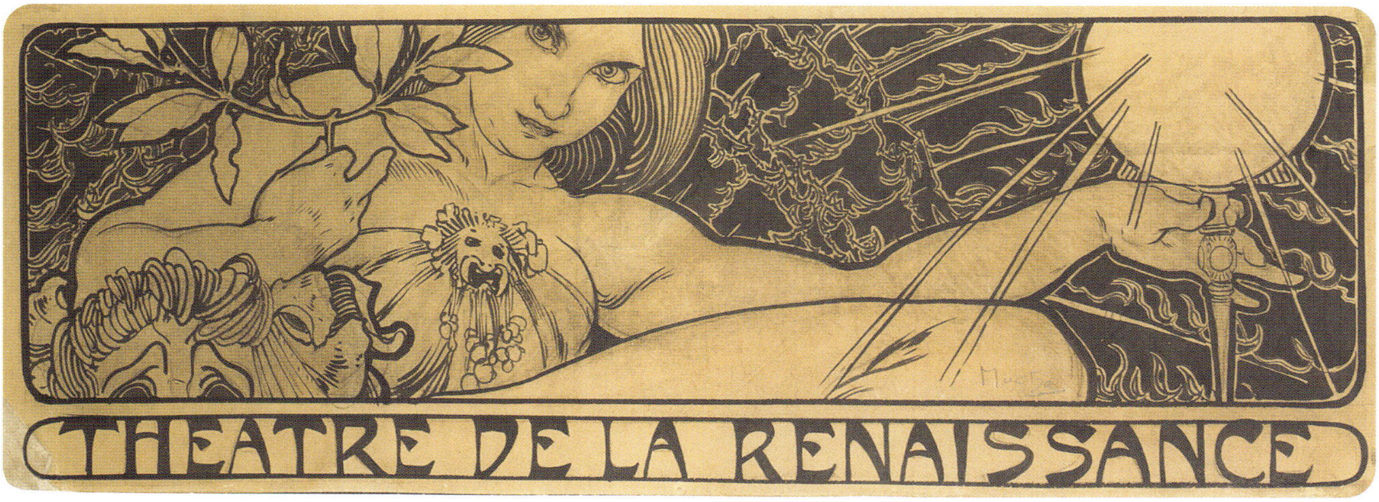

THÉÂTRE DE LA RENAISSANCE: DESIGN FOR A THEATRE BILLBOARD
c. 1895
Pencil and ink on card
29 x 79

Founded in 1873, the Théâtre de la Renaissance was a Parisian theatre company based in the boulevard Saint-Martin, which is still active today.

During the 1880s, the theatre went through a series of management problems, but in 1893 Bernhardt bought the lease and ran it as actor-director-producer until 1899.

SARAH BERNHARDT: STUDY OF HER FULL-STANDING FIGURE
c. 1896
Pen and ink on paper
41.5 x 26

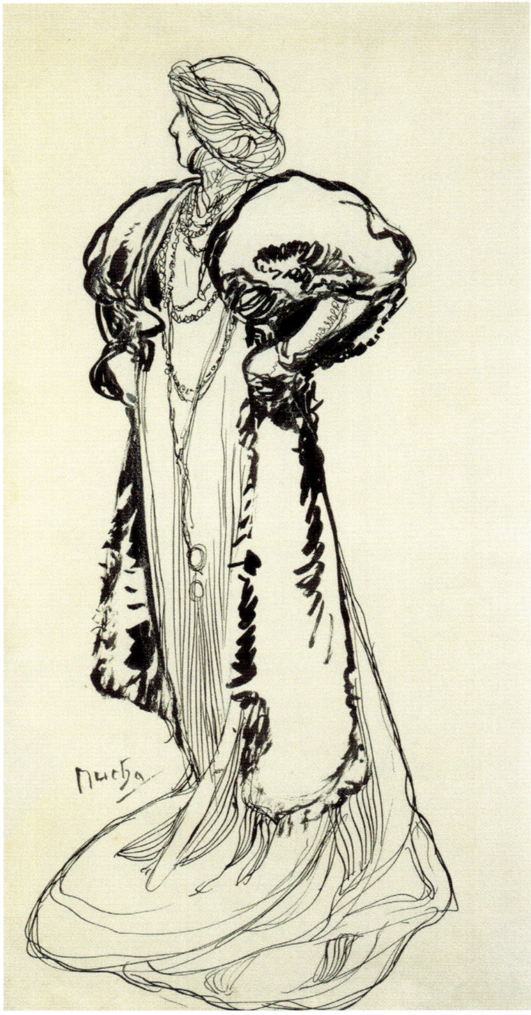

La Dame aux Camélias was originally written as a novel by Alexandre Dumas, *fils* (1824–1895), and subsequently adapted for the stage in 1852. This poster was prepared for Bernhardt's new production of the play, which was premièred on September 30 1896. Presenting the tragic heroine Camille as a modern Parisian woman in a chic dress designed by Mucha, the poster not only renewed the old-fashioned image of the play but also influenced contemporary fashion.

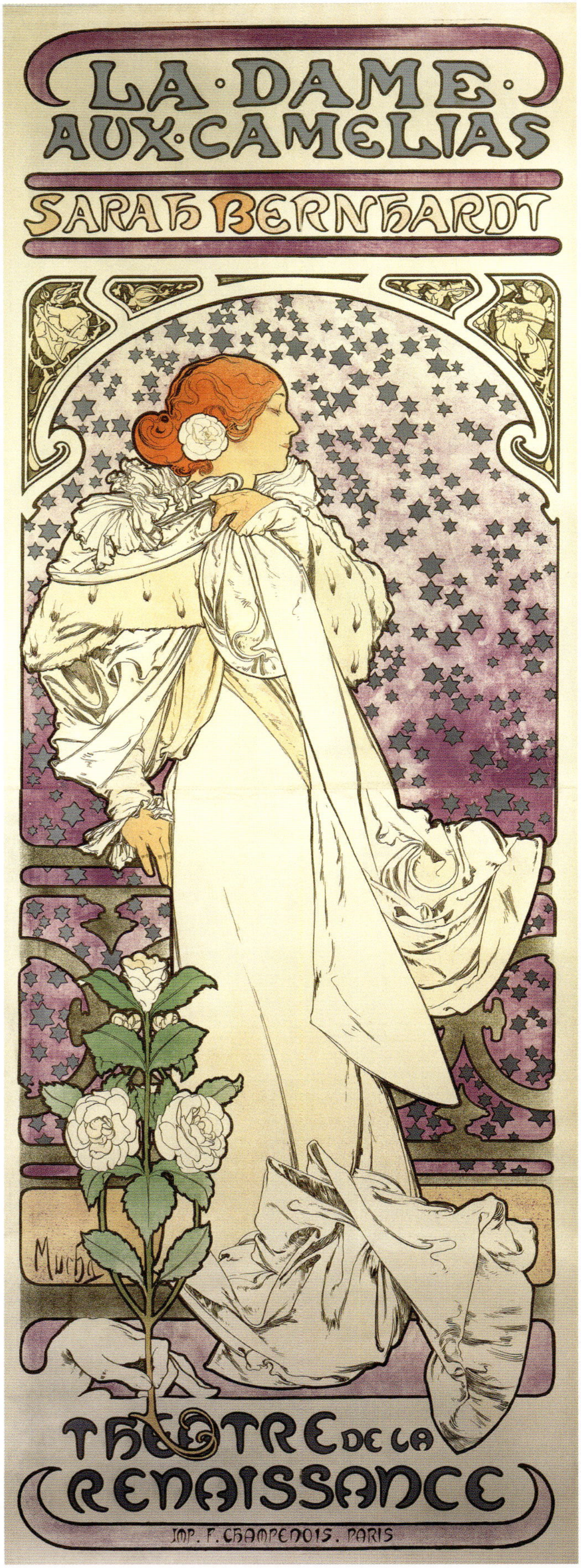

LA DAME AUX CAMÉLIAS
1896
Colour lithograph
207.3 x 76.2

LORENZACCIO
1896
Colour lithograph
203.7 x 76

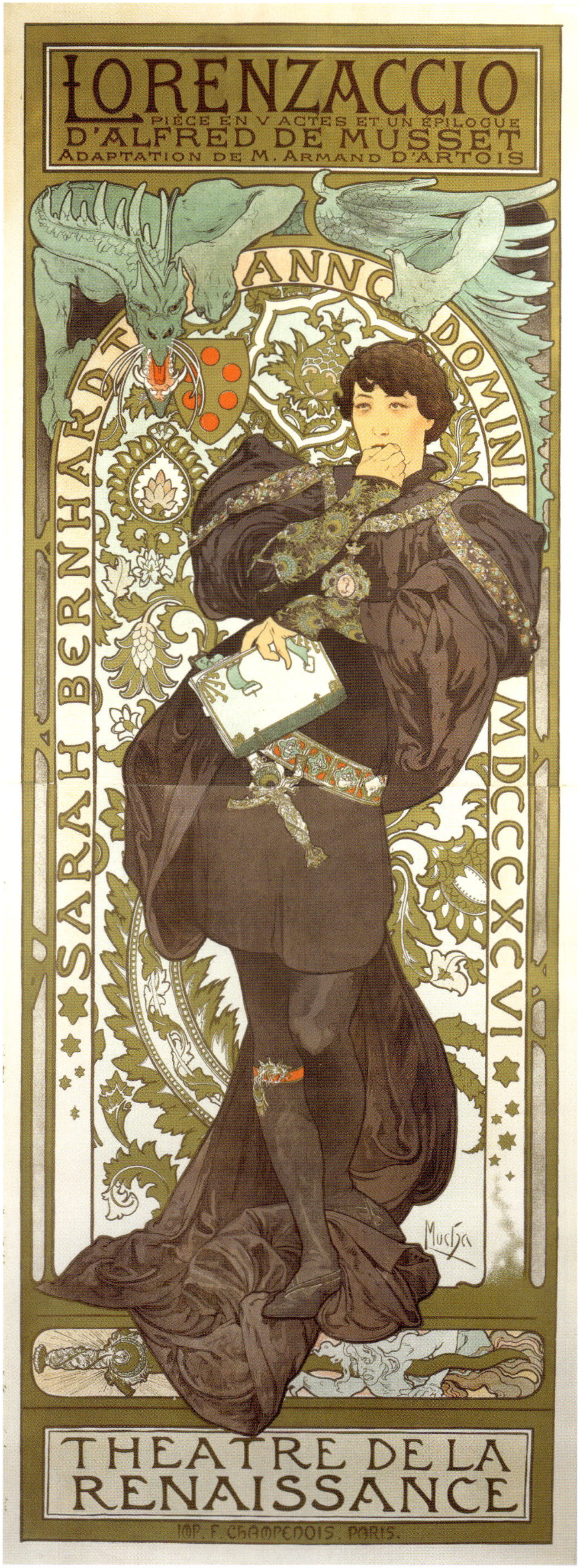

Premièred on December 3 1896, *Lorenzaccio* was a revival of the play written by Alfred de Musset (1810–57) in 1834. Set in 16th-century Florence, Bernhardt played the male hero, Lorenzaccio, who assassinated his cousin Alessandro de' Medici, the tyrant duke of Florence. While presenting Lorenzaccio as a dashing young man, whose elegantly S-curved figure is silhouetted against an arched window, Mucha focused at the same time on Bernhardt's facial expression to portray the hero's contemplation of murder.

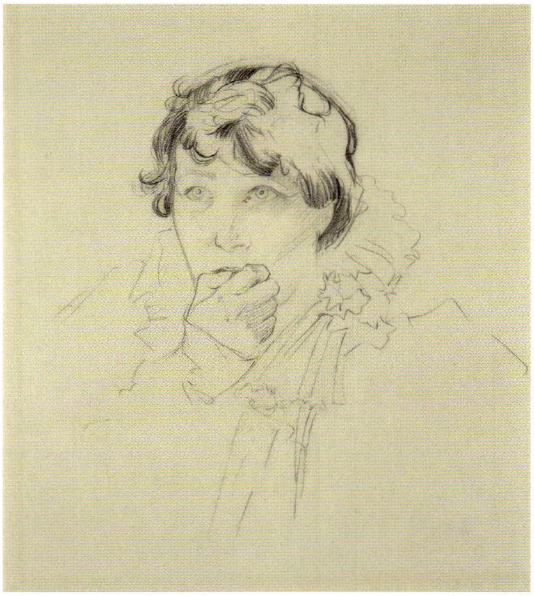

HEAD OF SARAH BERNHARDT:
STUDY FOR LORENZACCIO
1896
Pencil on paper
25 x 21.5

As a collaborator and friend of Sarah Bernhardt, Mucha had an intimate knowledge of her features and theatrical expressions. Of his impressions of the actress on stage, he later wrote:

> *'One can say that rarely has someone's soul been more faithfully exteriorised. Every feature of her face and every movement of her clothing was profoundly conditioned by her psychological needs.'*

LA SAMARITAINE
1897
Colour lithograph
173 x 58.3

Written by Edmond Rostand (1868–1918), *La Samaritaine* drew on a theme from a Biblical episode about Photina, the Samaritan woman (John 4:1-30). The poster shows Bernhardt as Photina carrying a large water jar, alluding to her encounter with Jesus at the well, which led to her conversion to become one of his followers. Behind her head is a halo decorated with Hebrew letters (reading 'Jehovah') and the words 'Sarah Bernhardt' in the style of Hebrew script, which heighten the character of the play.

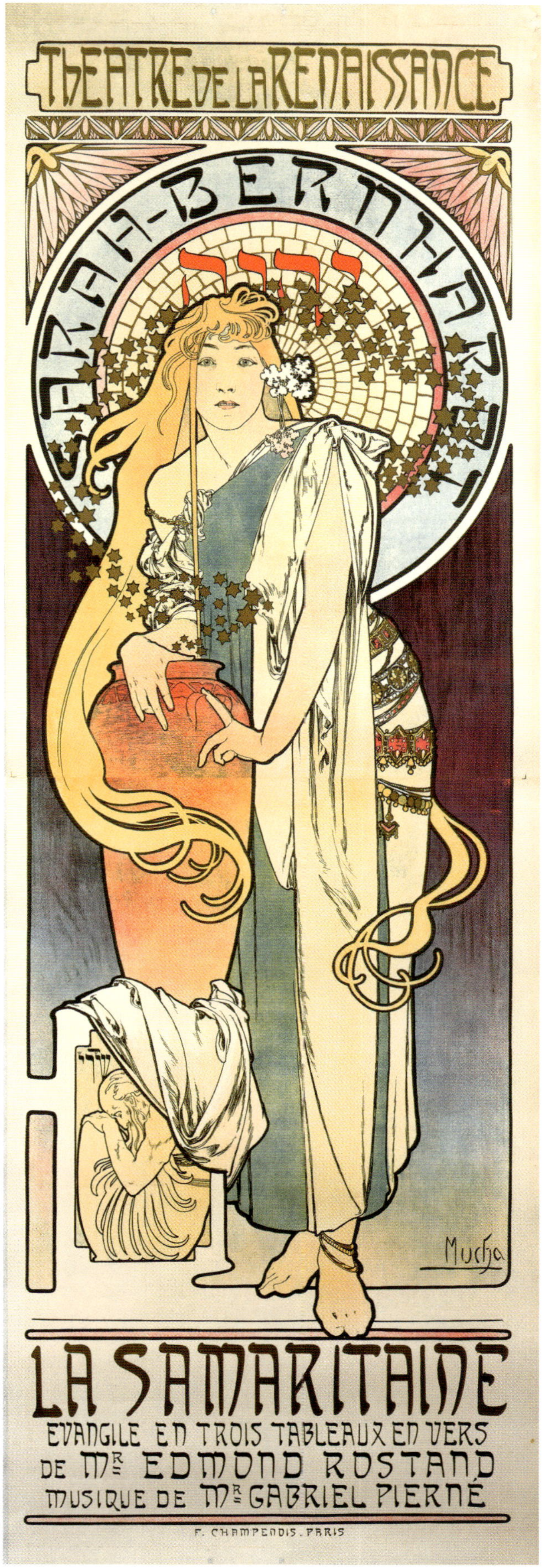

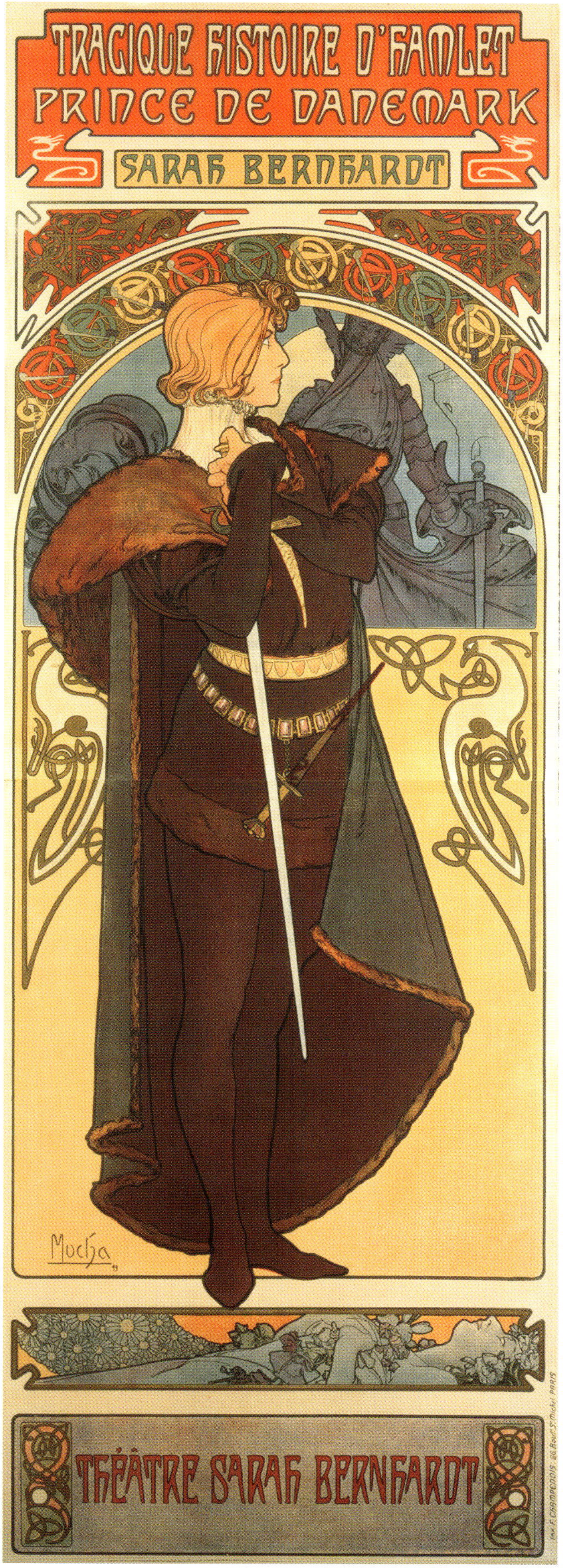

HAMLET
1899
Colour lithograph
207.5 x 76.5

Premièred on May 20 1899 at Bernhardt's new theatre, Théâtre Sarah Bernhardt, this French adaptation of Shakespeare's famous play starred Bernhardt in the title role. In this poster, Hamlet's solitary figure is presented against an arched background richly decorated with Celtic motifs. Hamlet's psychological relationship with his murdered father is emphasised here with the latter's ghost appearing in the lunette behind him. The figure of the drowned Ophelia is also included in the composition, encased in the coffin-like narrow strip under Hamlet's feet. This was the last poster Mucha produced for Bernhardt.

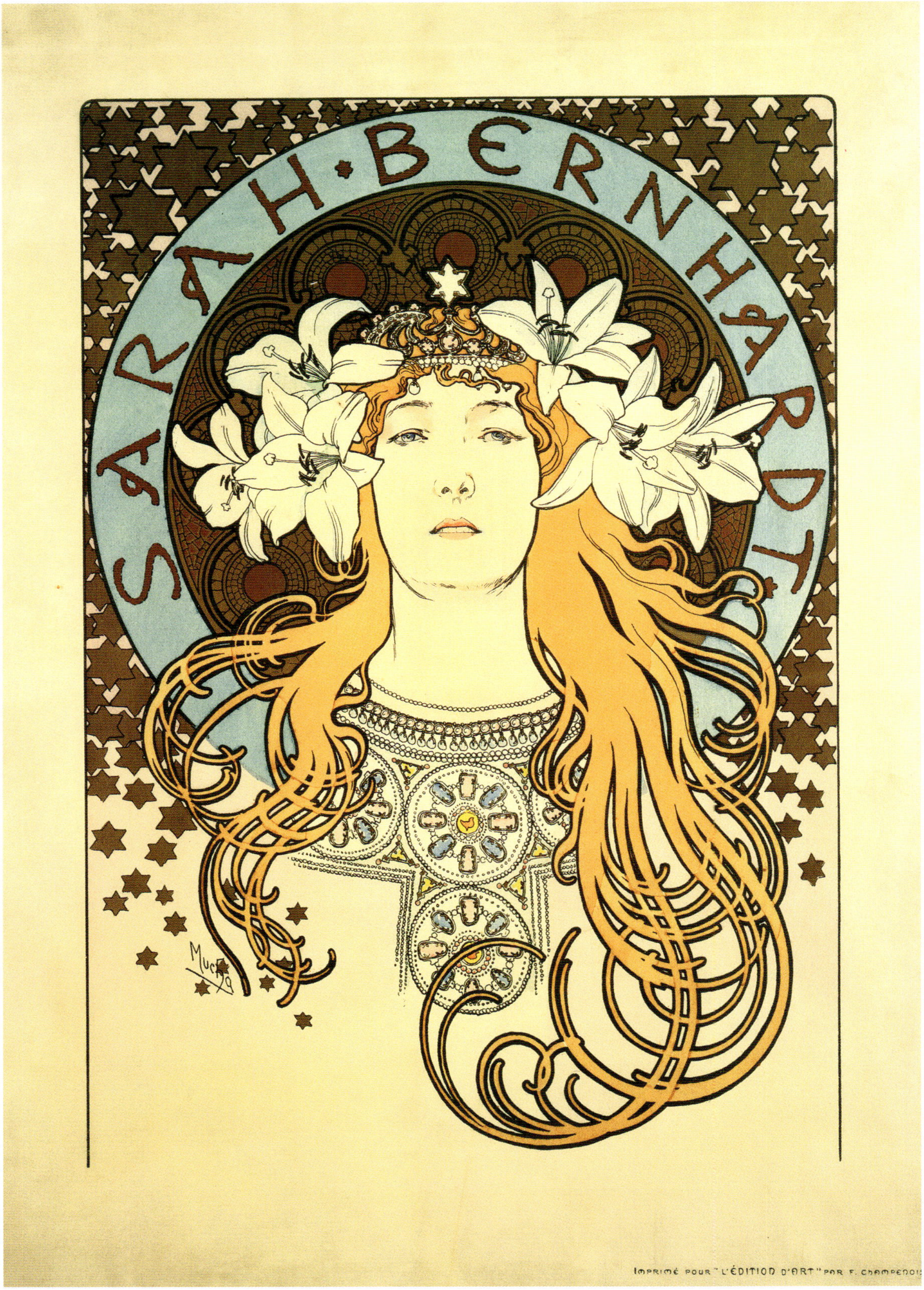

SARAH BERNHARDT: 'LA PLUME ART EDITION' POSTER
1897
Colour lithograph
69 x 51

In this poster Bernhardt is portrayed in her role of the heroine, Mélissinde, in the play *La Princesse lointaine* written for her by Edmond Rostand and premièred in 1895. When Mucha was asked to design a poster with the dual purpose of announcing a banquet to be held on December 9 1896 in honour of the leading actress and also publicising a forthcoming article about her in *La Plume* magazine, he portrayed her in this role. The poster proved a great success, prompting Mucha's publisher, F. Champenois, to recycle the design for a collectors' edition poster without the text, as seen here, and for a postcard.

ADOLPHE ARMAND TRUFFIER (ACTIVE c.1899–1937)
AFTER MUCHA
PRINCESSE LOINTAINE LIGHT FITTING
c. 1900
Gold patina bronze; cabochons of malachite, amethyst and lapis lazuli; mounted on original, curved panel in tinted pear tree wood
42 x 27 x 11
(base) 5 x 36 x 13

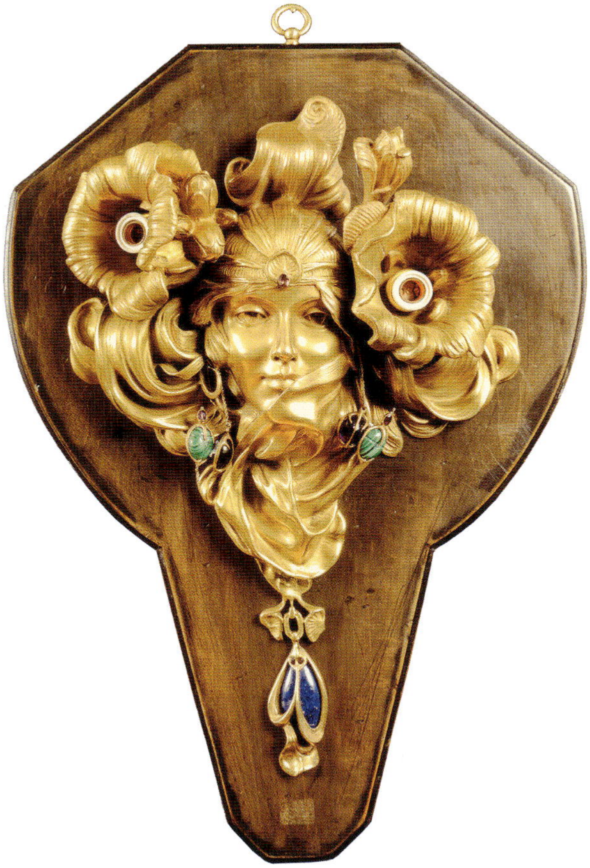

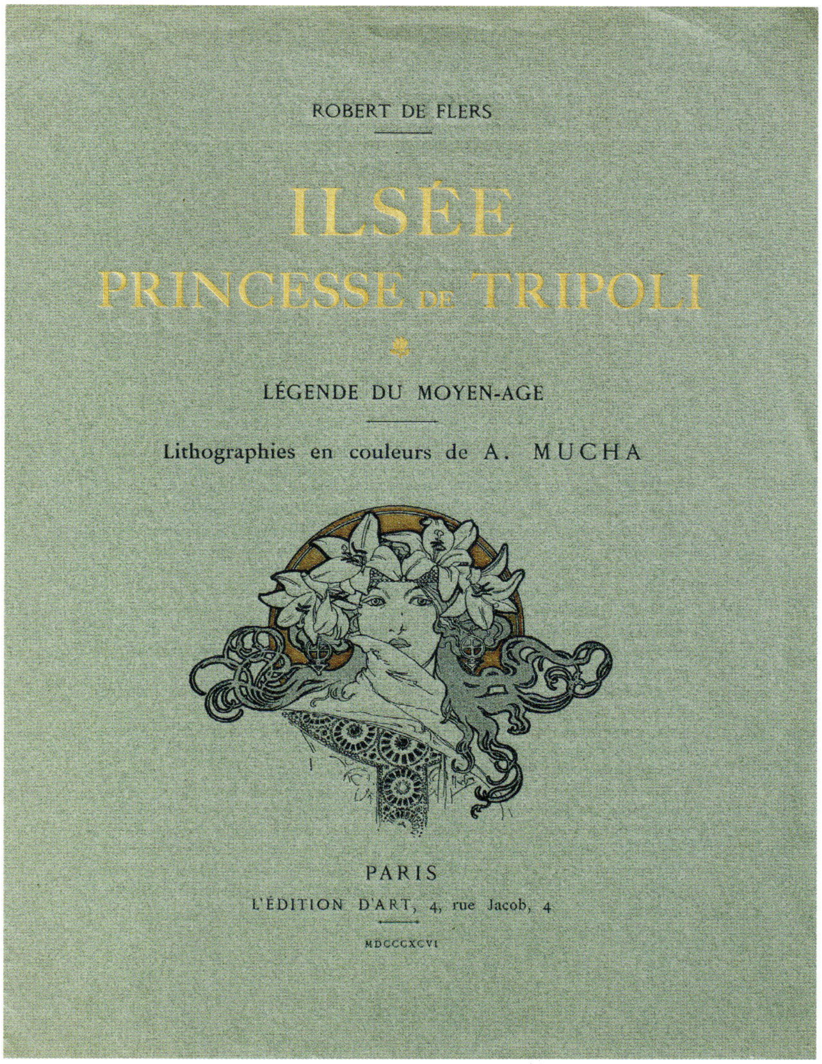

ILSÉE, PRINCESSE DE TRIPOLI: LÉGENDE DU MOYEN-AGE
1897
Cover of the promotional prospectus of the book by Robert de Flers (1872–1927) with colour lithographs by Mucha, published by H.Piazza & Cie, Paris
34 x 25.7

The great success of the play *La Princesse lointaine* led to the publication of a novelised version under the title, *Ilsée, Princesse de Tripoli*, in 1897. From the Sarah Bernhardt poster (see facing page), Mucha created a stylised image of the actress's head with a diadem of lilies, and used it as an emblem on the title page of the book as well as on the cover of its promotional prospectus shown here. This iconic image of the actress was later to inspire Adolphe Armand Truffier's design for a light fitting.

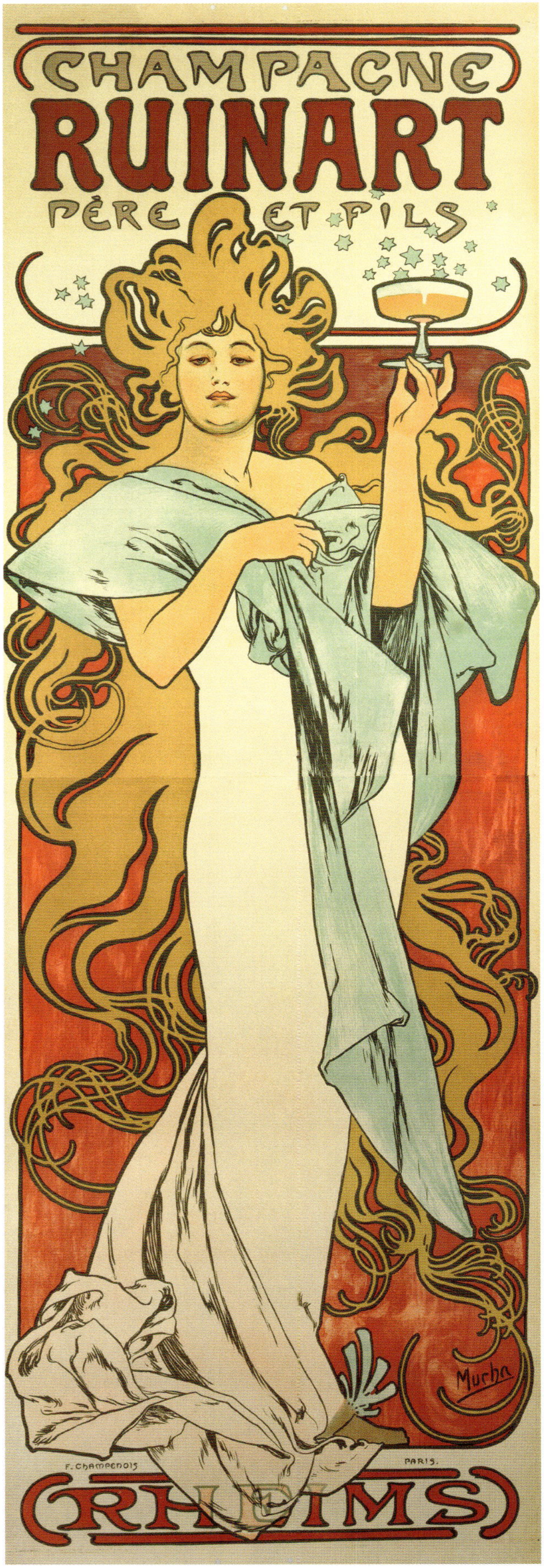

CHAMPAGNE RUINART
1896
Colour lithograph
173 x 59

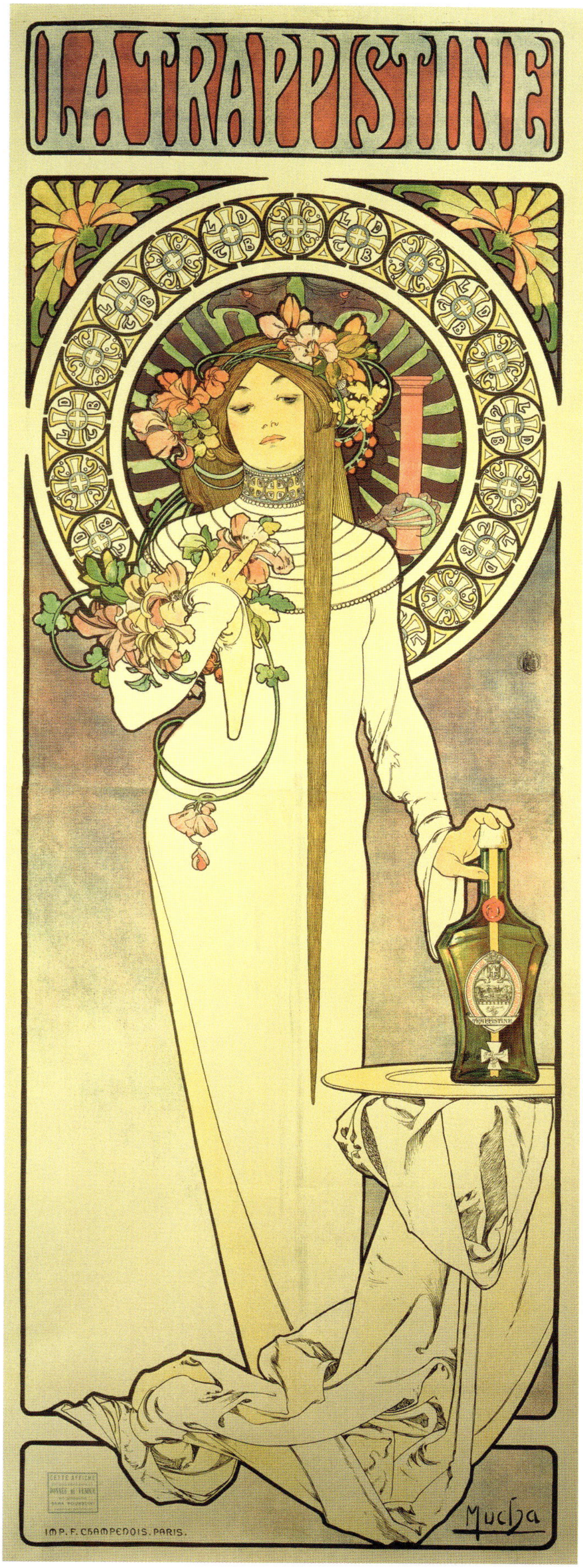

LA TRAPPISTINE
1897
Colour lithograph
206 x 77

La Trappistine was a liqueur made by Parisian distillers, Legouey & Delbergue, from a recipe inspired by Trappist monks. In designing this poster, Mucha used the same design formula as that of the *Gismonda* prototype with its tall format and the single figure of a woman on a raised platform. Mucha used a prominent halo decorated with circular motifs adapted from the Maltese cross to reference the religious order, thereby emphasising the mysterious source of this beverage. Furthermore, Mucha also introduced an idea of visual navigation here, with the use of a long strand of the woman's hair that hangs down to guide the viewer's eyes to the subject – a bottle of La Trappistine.

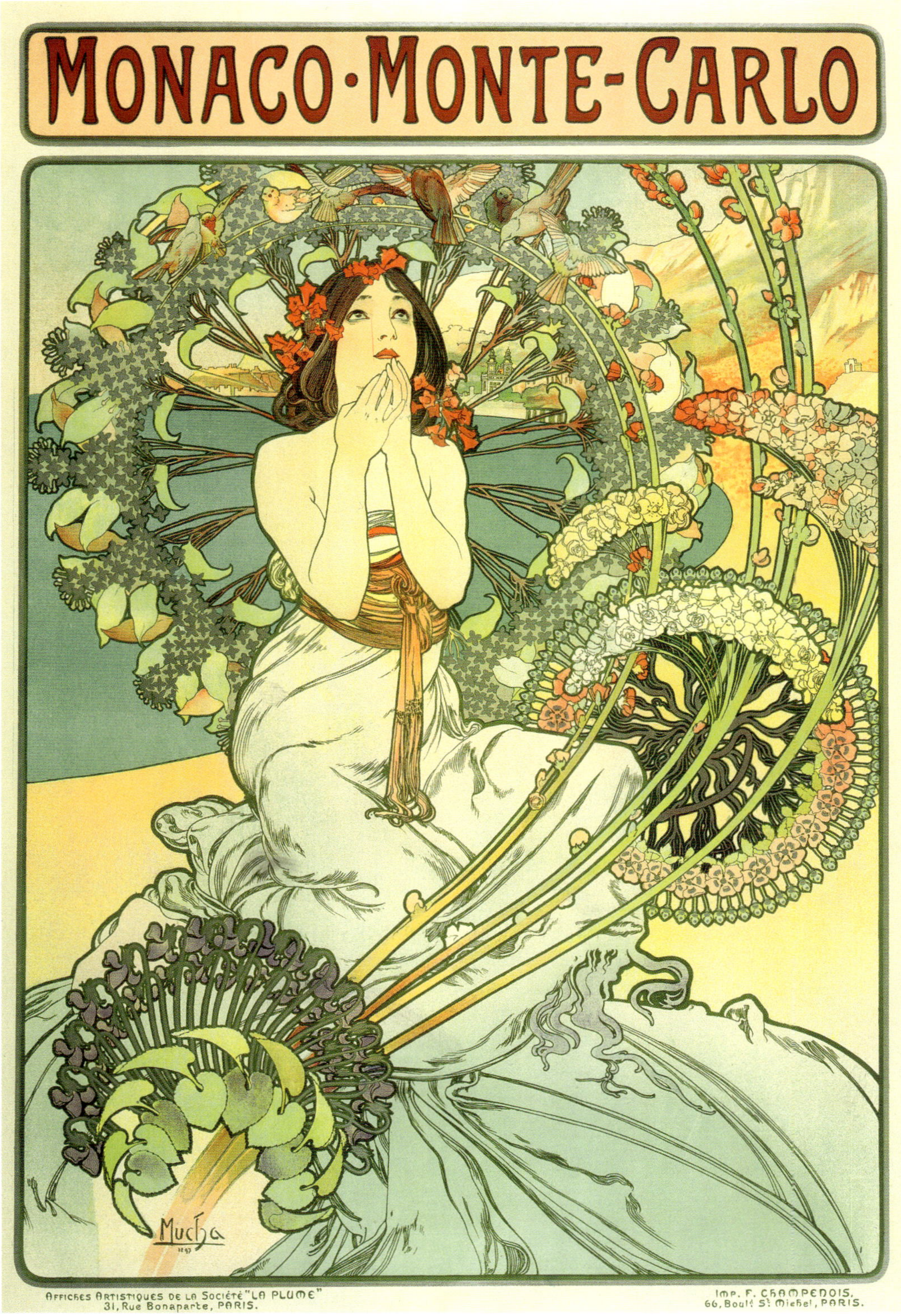

MONACO•MONTE-CARLO
1897
Colour lithograph
110 x 76.5

Designed for the railway company Chemins de Fer P.L.M., which offered a trip from Paris to Monte-Carlo in 16 hours by luxury train, this poster shows a girl daydreaming about the pleasure of Monte-Carlo. The joy of tourism is emphasised by the sumptuous garlands and curving stems of flowers, which possibly allude to the wheels of the train and the tracks, as well as by the view of the Mediterranean coast in the background.

JOB
1898
Colour lithograph
149.2 x 101

Mucha produced two versions of posters for JOB cigarette papers – one in 1896 (see *Les Maîtres de l'Affiche* p.37) and the other in 1898, shown here. Both posters feature the prominent figure of a sensuous woman against a background patterned with the 'JOB' monogram (a trademark for the Joseph Bardou Company). In this design, the woman is seated against an enormous circle, while the arabesques formed by her abundant hair and the swirling smoke rising from her cigarette create a richly decorative effect.

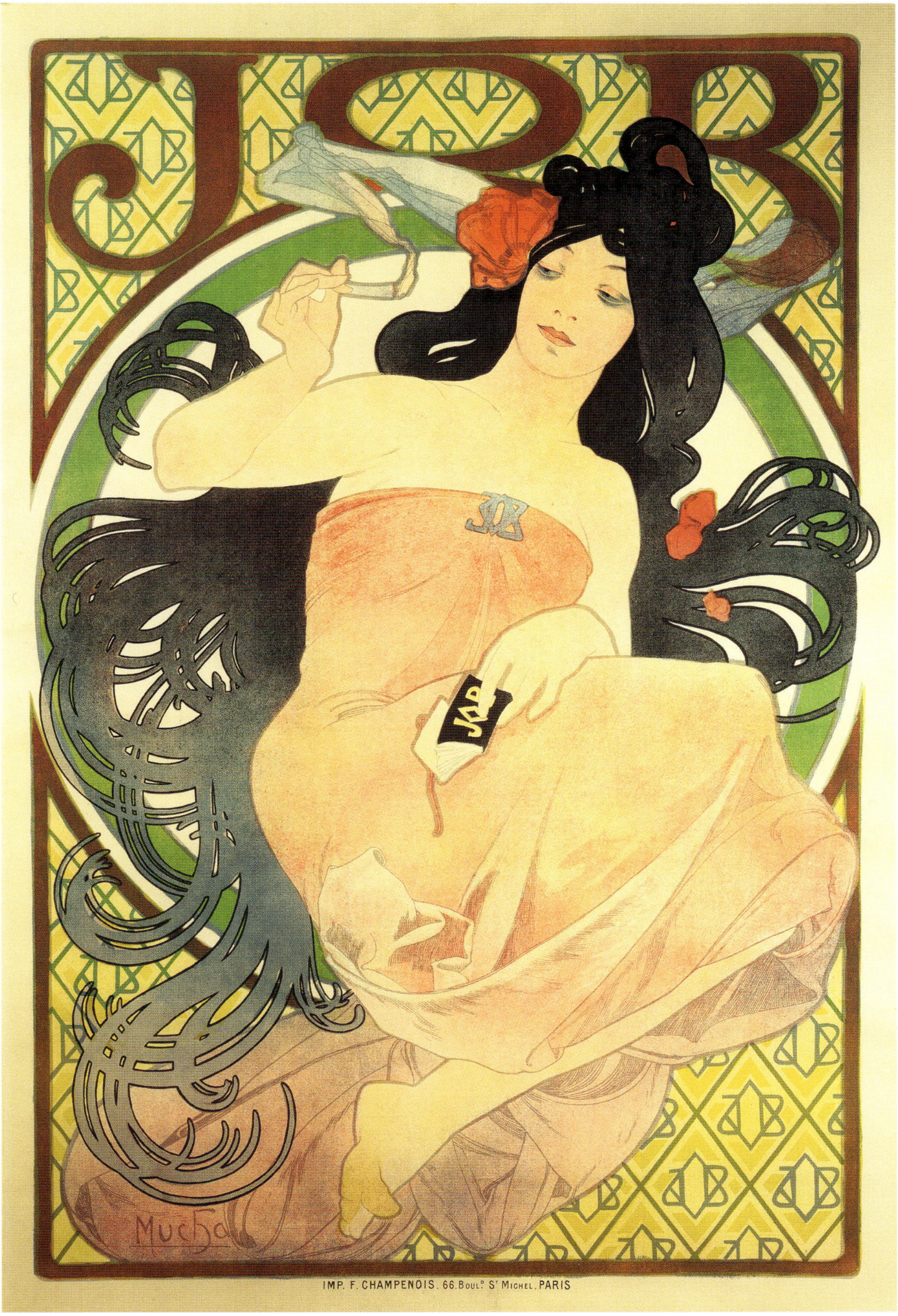
JOB
Mucha
IMP. F. CHAMPENOIS. 66.Boulᵈ Sᵗ Michel. PARIS

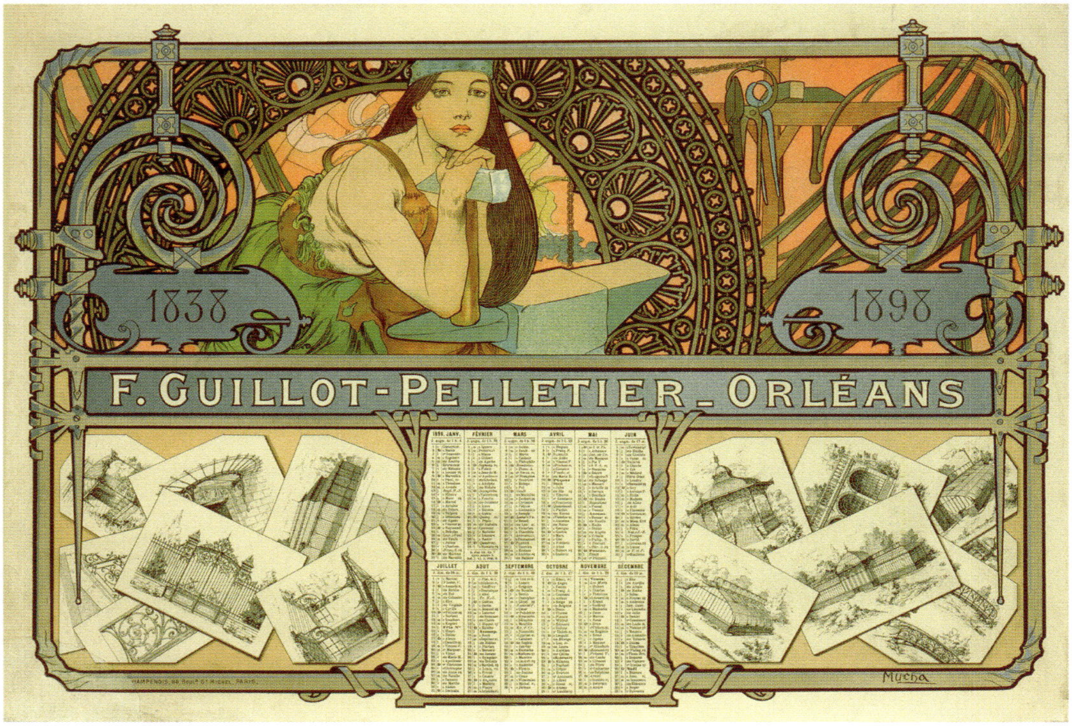

F. GUILLOT PELLETIER-ORLEANS 1838–1898: CALENDAR FOR 1898
1897
Colour lithograph
37 x 53.5

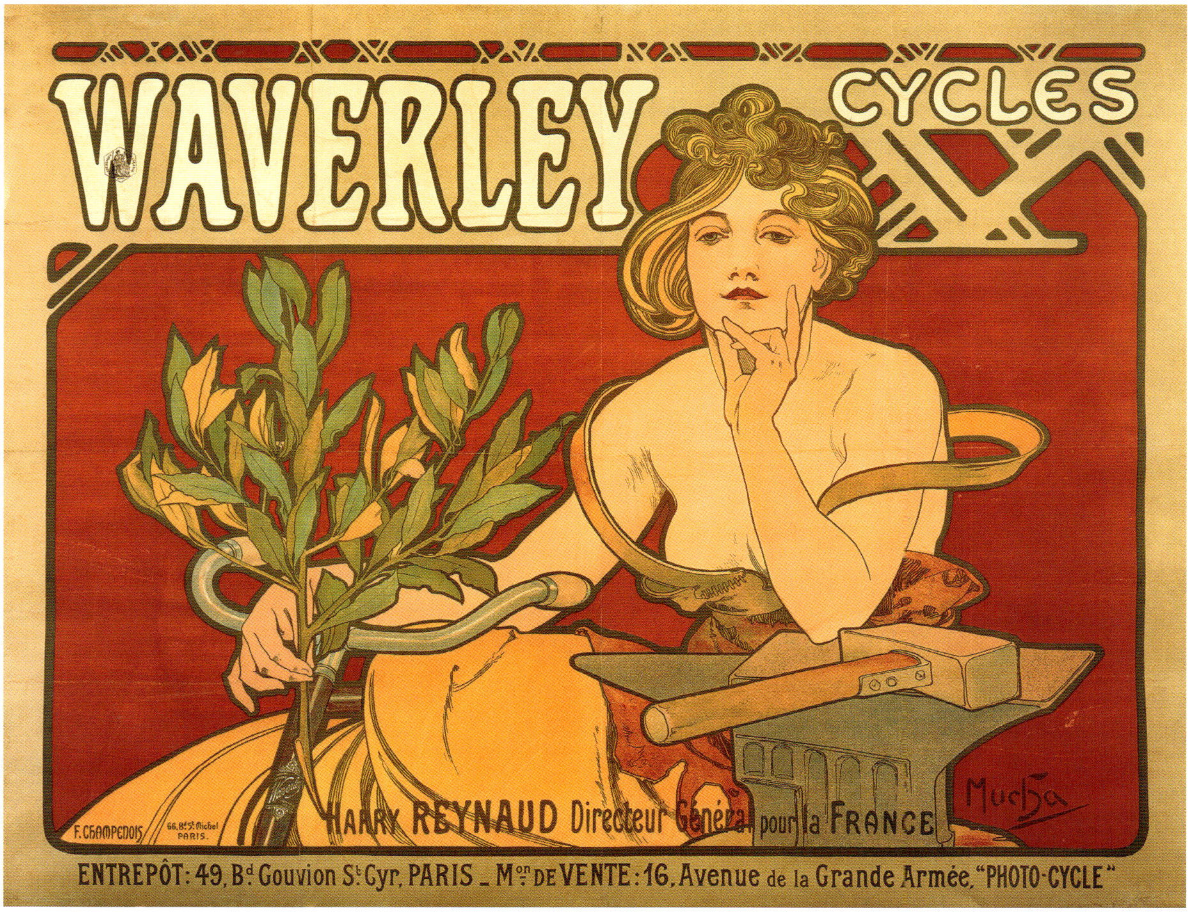

WAVERLEY CYCLES
1898
Colour lithograph
88.5 x 114

LES MAÎTRES DE L'AFFICHE

Les Maîtres de l'Affiche (Masters of the Poster) was a folio of reproductions of posters by leading graphic artists of the day, which was published monthly by Imprimerie Chaix, Paris, from December 1895 to November 1900. Each issue contained four plates featuring the works of international artists selected by Jules Chéret (1836–1932). Seven of Mucha's posters were reproduced in this periodical: *Gismonda* (Plate 27, June 1896), *Lorenzaccio* (Plate 114, April 1898), *La Dame aux Camélias* (Plate 144, November 1898), *La Samaritaine* (Plate 166, May 1899) and the three plates shown here.

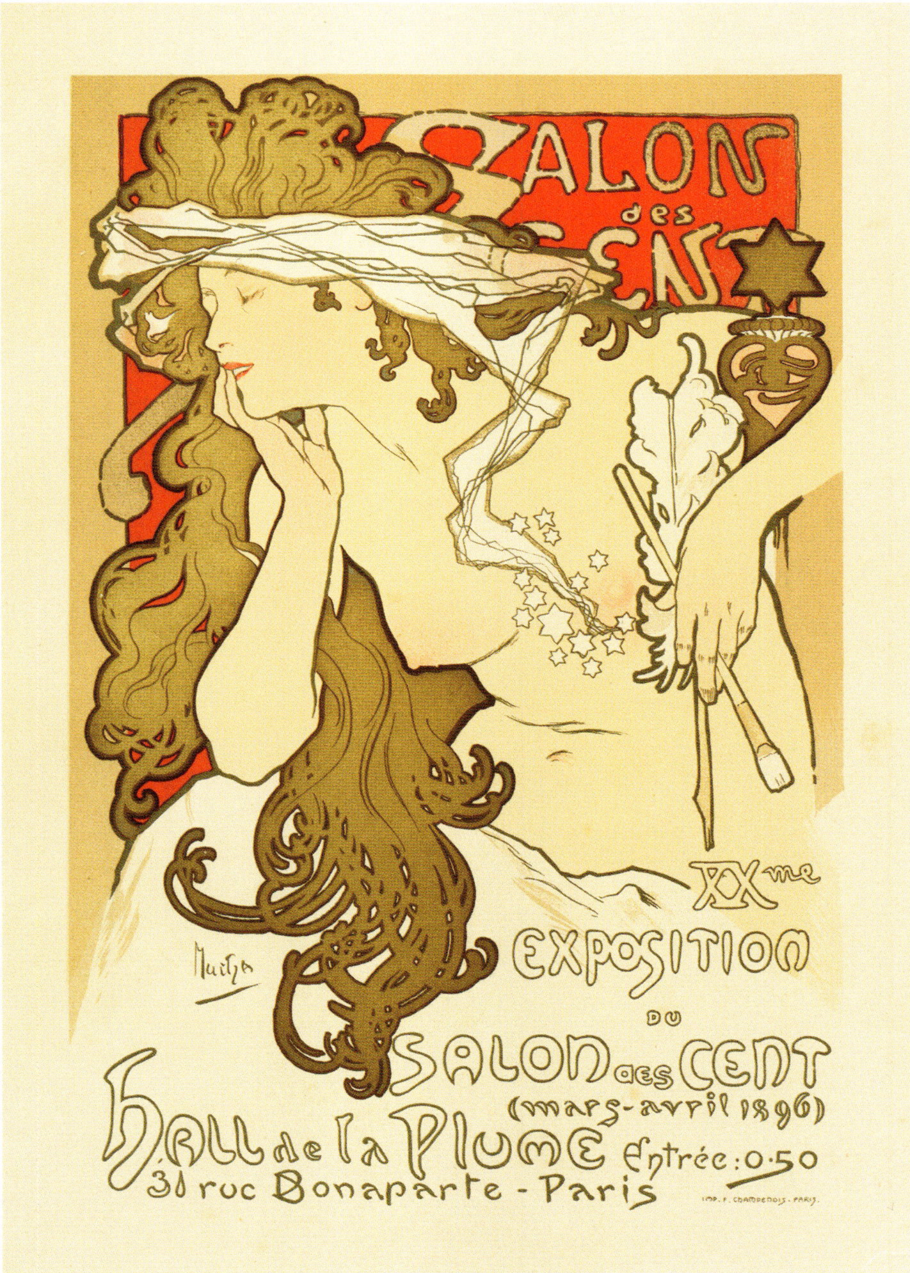

SALON DES CENT 20th EXHIBITION: REPRODUCTION OF MUCHA'S POSTER (1896)
Plate 94 from *Les Maîtres de l'Affiche*, November 1897
Colour lithograph
40 x 29

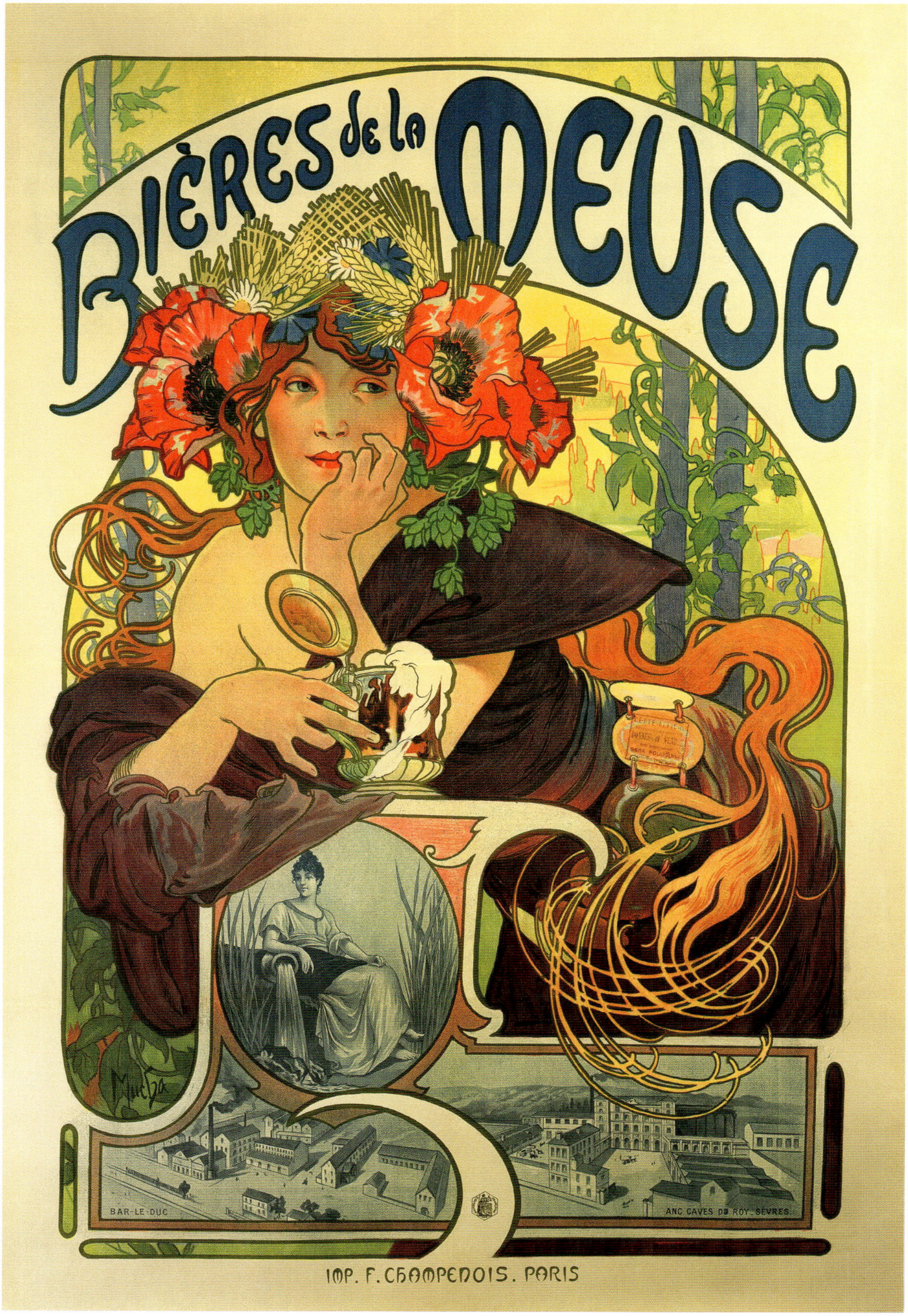

BIÈRES DE LA MEUSE: REPRODUCTION OF MUCHA'S POSTER (1898)
Plate 182 from *Les Maîtres de l'Affiche*, September 1899
Colour lithograph
40 x 29

JOB: REPRODUCTION OF MUCHA'S POSTER (1896)
Plate 202 from *Les Maîtres de l'Affiche*, February 1900
Colour lithograph
40 x 29

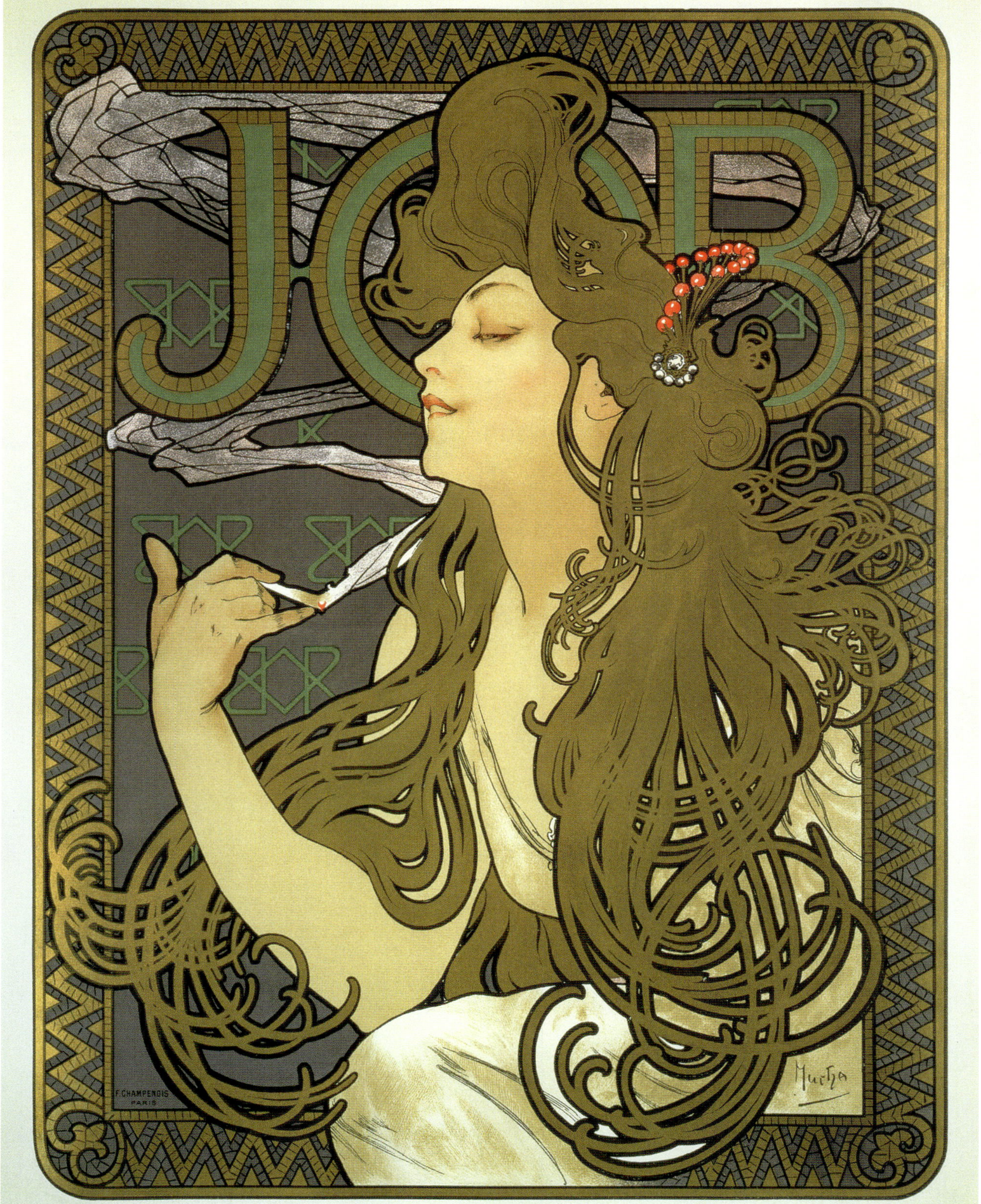
JOB
F. CHAMPENOIS
PARIS
Mucha

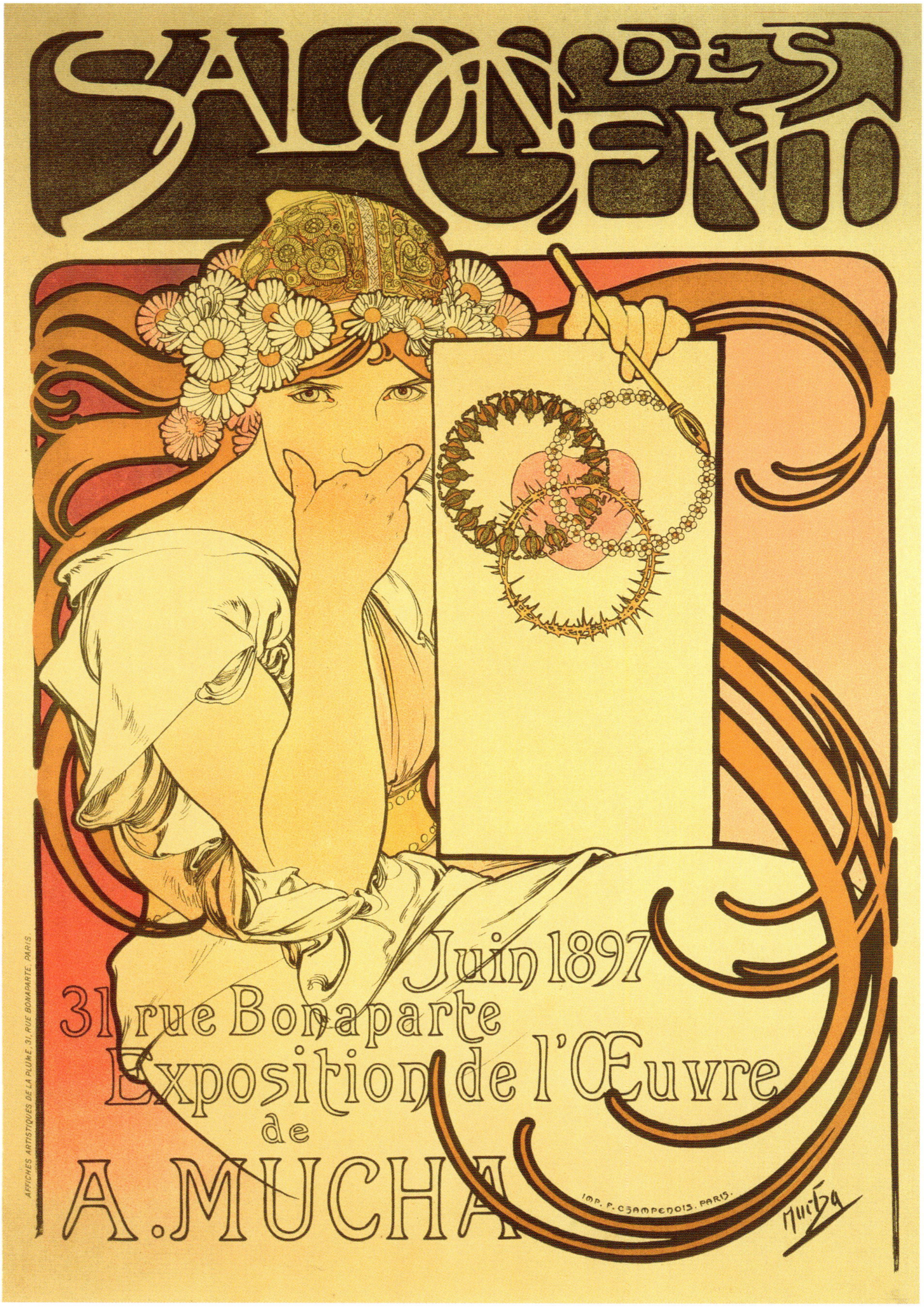
SALON DES CENT
Juin 1897
31 rue Bonaparte
Exposition de l'Œuvre
de
A. MUCHA
AFFICHES ARTISTIQUES DE LA PLUME, 31, RUE BONAPARTE, PARIS.
IMP. F. CHAMPENOIS. PARIS.
Mucha

THE SALON DES CENT

The Salon des Cent was an exhibition venue run by the poet Léon Deschamps (1864–1899), editor of the influential avant-garde magazine *La Plume*. Opened in 1894, the Salon promoted works by artists associated with the magazine including Jules Chéret, Eugène Grasset (1845–1917), Toulouse-Lautrec, Georges de Feure (1868–1943) and the Nabis. Mucha was invited by Deschamps to join this group in 1896 and, in appreciation of this invitation, he designed a poster for the Salon's 20th exhibition of the same year as his debut gift (see p.7). The following year Mucha was given a major retrospective at the Salon des Cent (see facing page), where he showed a staggering 448 works.

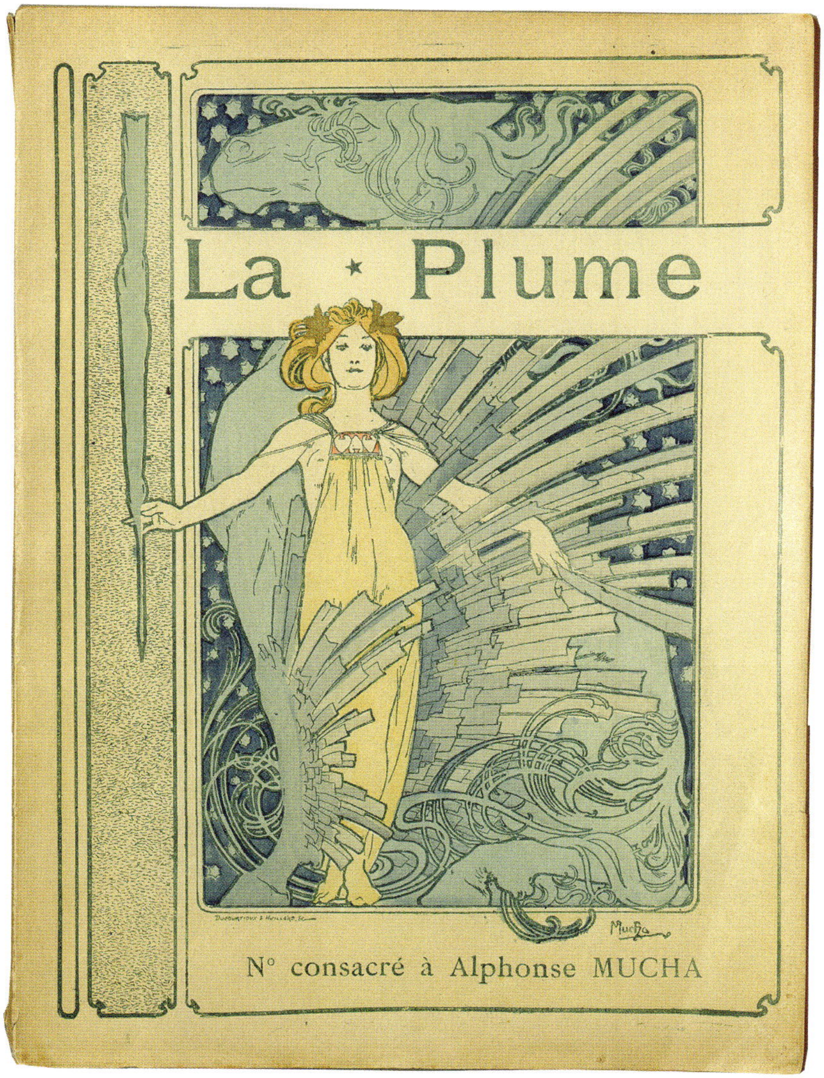

SALON DES CENT:
EXHIBITION OF THE WORK OF A. MUCHA
1897
Colour lithograph
66.2 × 46

In the course of designing this exhibition poster, Mucha incorporated various Moravian elements into his decorative motifs, such as the embroidered folk cap worn by the girl and the daisy crown that evokes the meadows of his homeland. Additionally, the girl holds a pen and a picture displaying a heart in the middle of three intersecting garlands composed of thorns, flowers and fruit, alluding to the fate of Mucha's homeland.

LA PLUME (No.199, 1 AUGUST 1897):
SPECIAL NUMBER DEVOTED TO MUCHA
1897
Magazine, published by Société Anonyme La Plume, Paris
24.5 × 18

Coinciding with Mucha's exhibition, *La Plume* published this special issue devoted to Mucha, which served as the exhibition catalogue. The cover was designed by the artist himself and the design was used for many subsequent issues of the magazine. *La Plume* went on to organise a travelling exhibition from this retrospective, which went on to Vienna, Prague, Munich, Brussels and New York, promoting Mucha internationally.

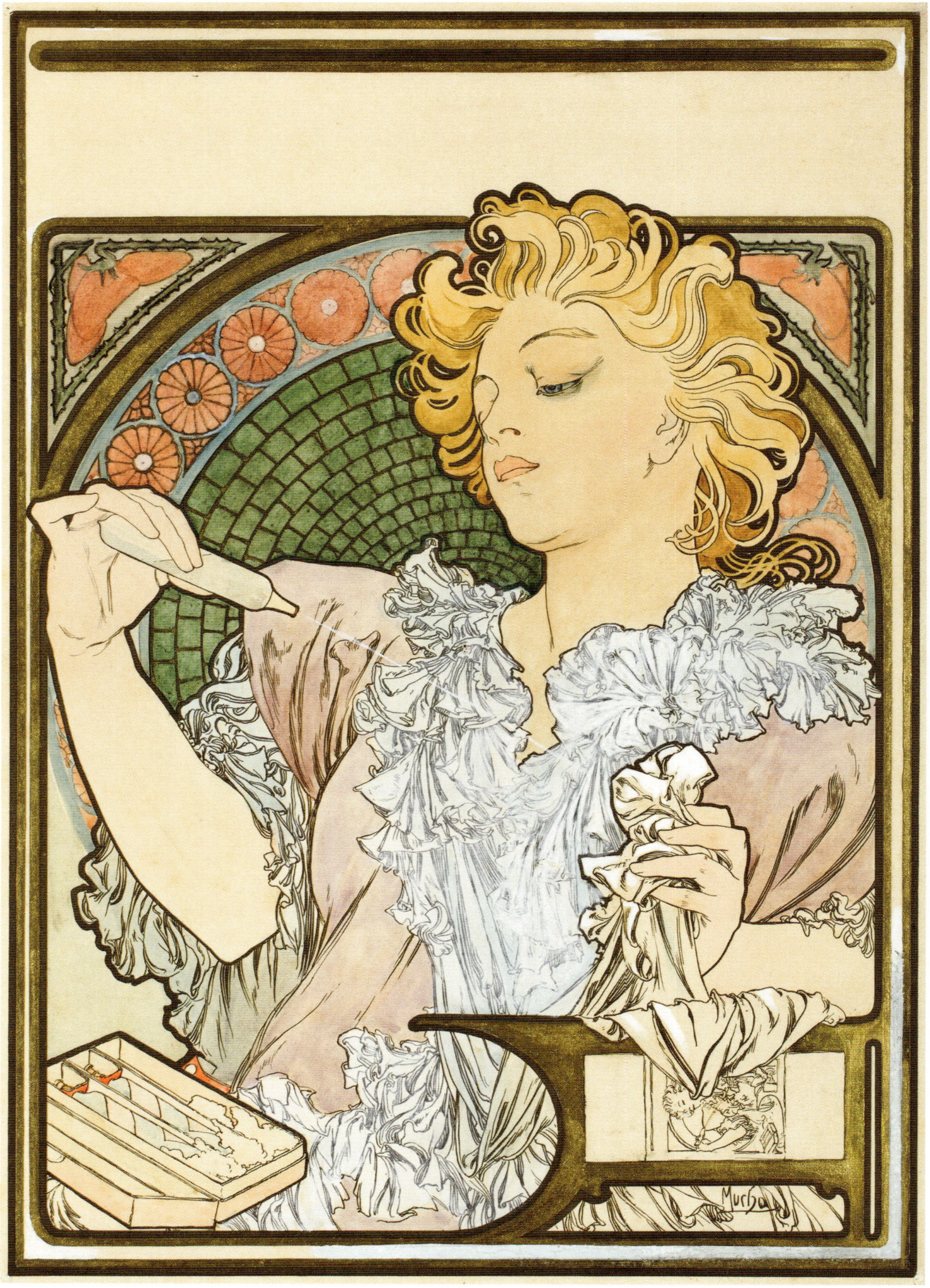

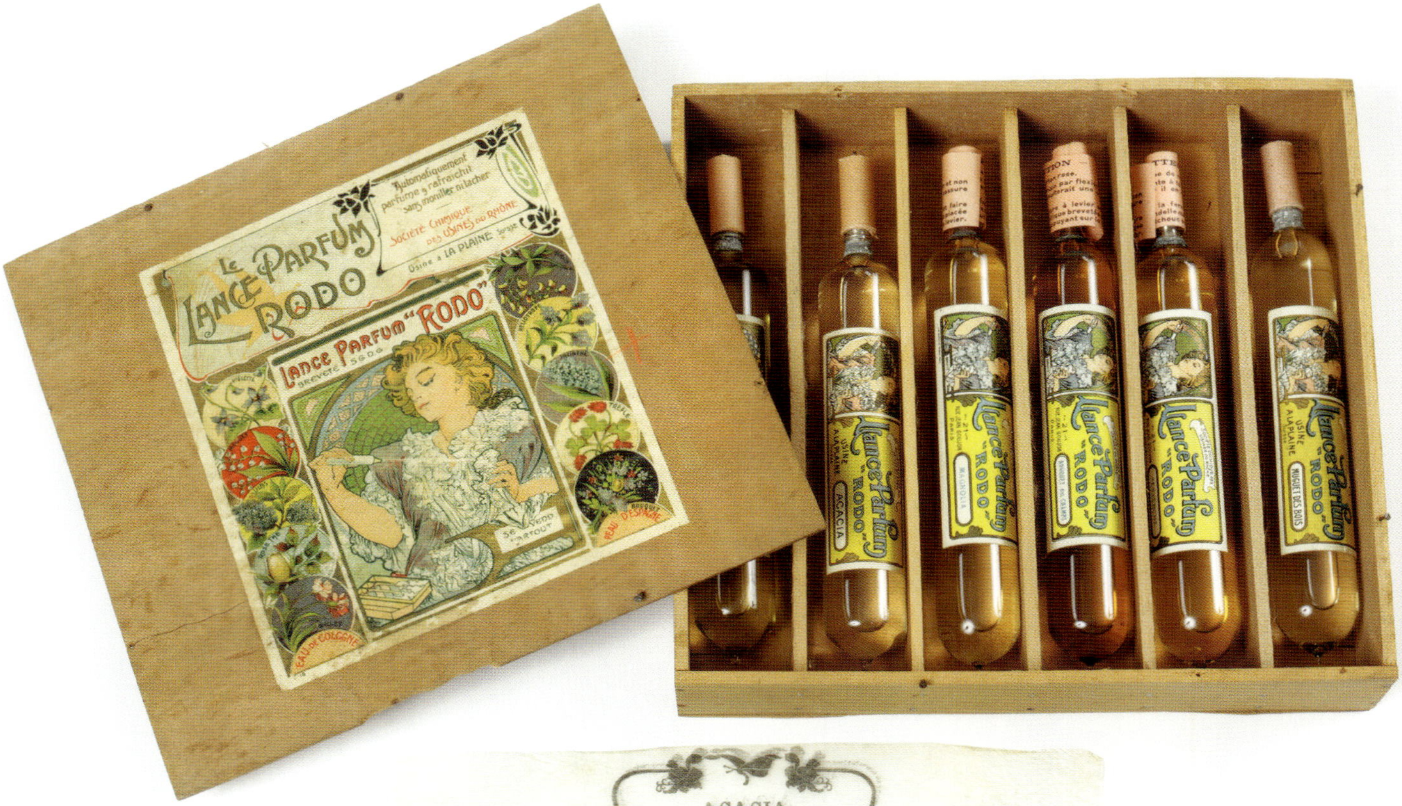

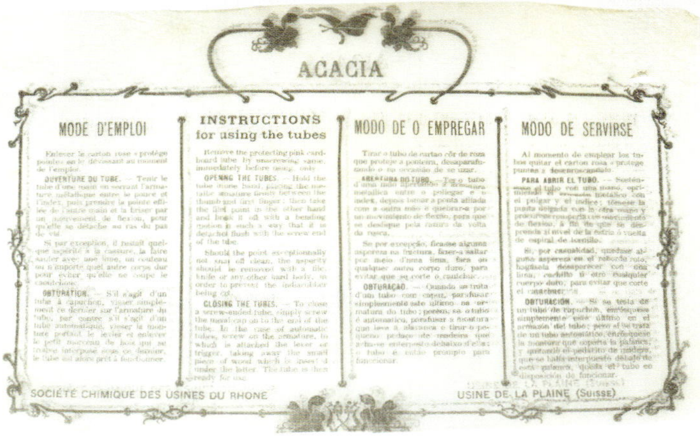

SET OF LANCE PARFUM "RODO" BOTTLES IN THEIR ORIGINAL PACKAGING
c. 1896
Glass perfume filled phials in plywood box with colour-lithographed label
Box: 18 x 19 x 4

STUDY FOR THE POSTER FOR LANCE PARFUM "RODO"
1896
Ink, watercolour, gouache and gold on paper
48.4 x 35.2

Mucha's popularity as a poster artist led to commissions for packaging designs. In 1896, while he was working on the poster for *Lance Parfum "Rodo"*, he was also asked to design the label and packaging for the perfume bottles.

Lance Parfum "Rodo" was a new brand of perfume manufactured by La Société Chimique des Usines du Rhône, which appeared on the market in 1896. Mucha's composition here shows a woman squirting the perfume onto her handkerchief from the spray bottle, the key feature of this product and a novelty at the time. Behind her is a circular motif decorated with a mosaic and floral pattern.

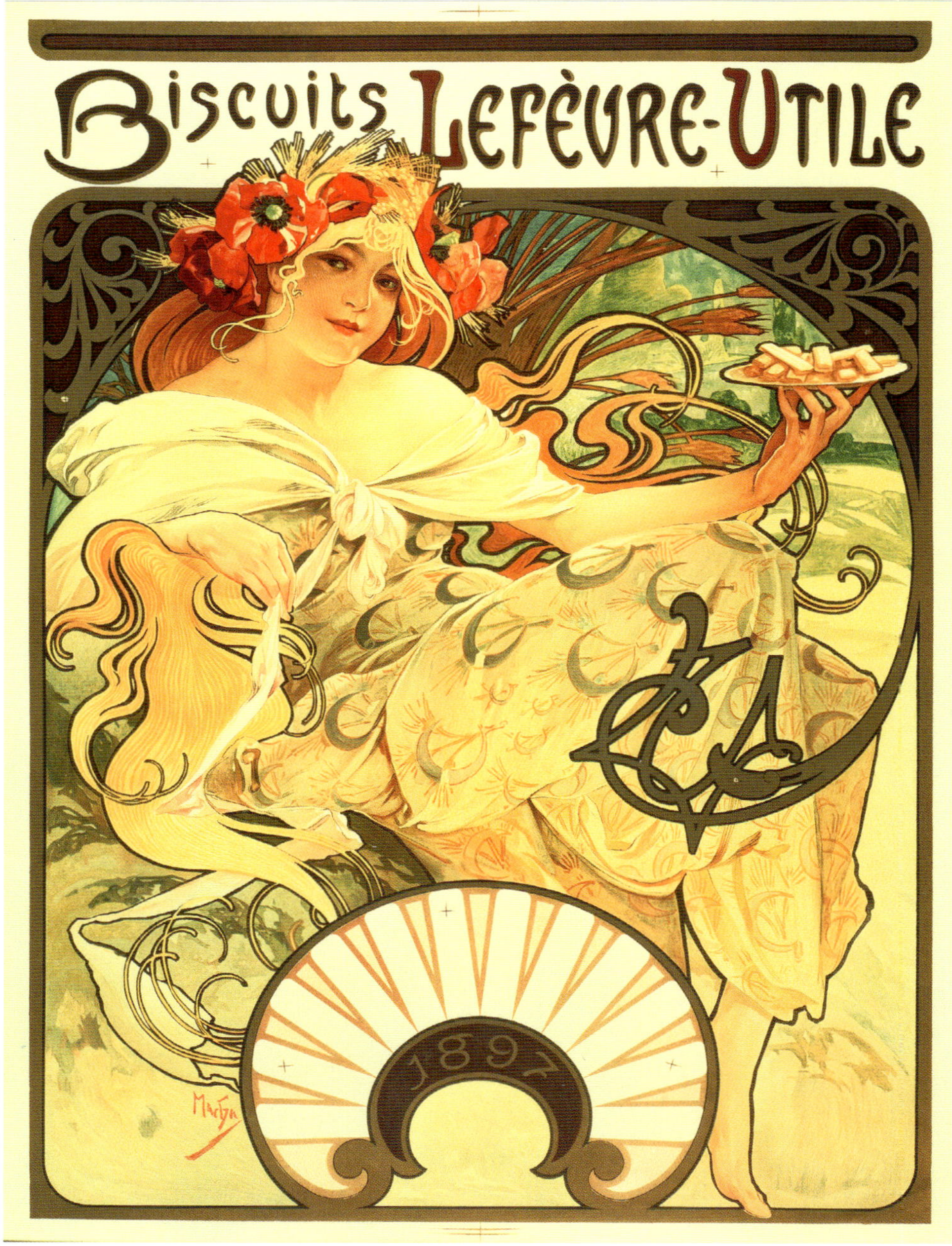

BISCUITS LEFÈVRE-UTILE: CALENDAR POSTER FOR 1897
1896
Colour lithograph
44 x 32.5

In 1896, Mucha began to work for the famous French biscuit company Lefèvre-Utile. As their regular artist, he contributed a number of designs for the company's promotional materials and packaging; this design was produced originally for the company calendar for 1897. The composition shows a girl wearing a wreath of wheat and red poppies who offers a plate of wafers. The subject is further emphasised by the motifs of sickle and wheat emblems decorating her dress. Moreover, Mucha utilised the company logo 'LU' as a decorative motif, integrating the initials in a highly stylised form into the whiplash curve, which extends from the decorative boarder and encircles the girl's hand, thus highlighting the subject.

Mucha was conscious about linking his packaging designs and his posters by using the same images of women to characterise the products and the same styles of lettering for the texts. Consequently, his designs conveyed consistent visual messages about the products, thus enhancing their brand images.

LABEL FOR LEFÈVRE-UTILE
GAUFRETTES VANILLE
c. 1900
Colour lithograph
20.5 x 17.8

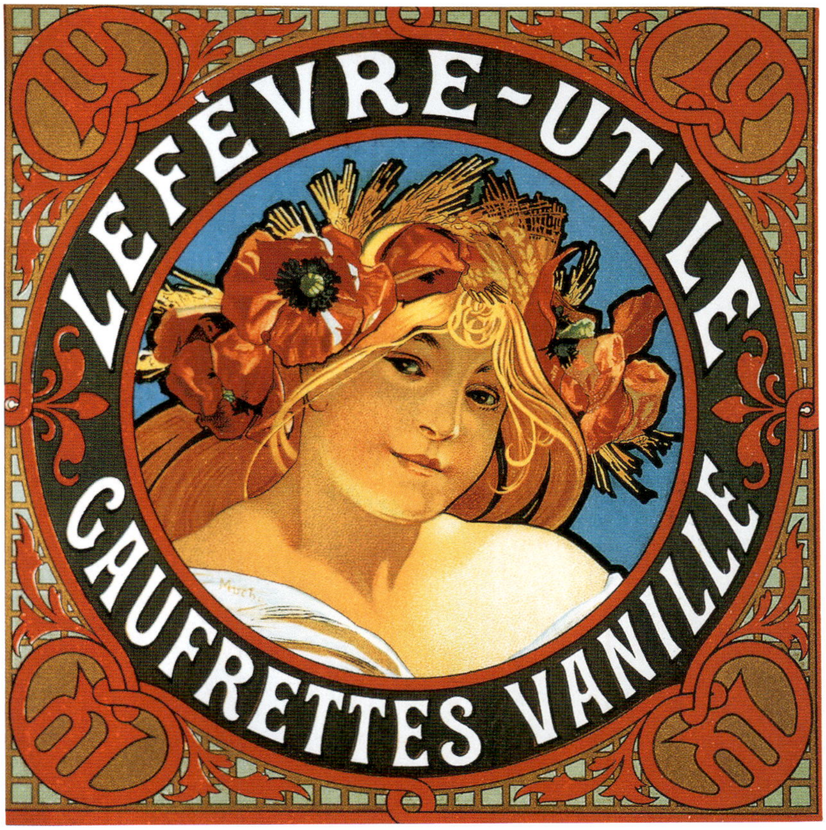

WRAPPER FOR BISCUITS
LEFÈVRE-UTILE: BOUDOIR
1901
Colour lithograph
28 x 20.4

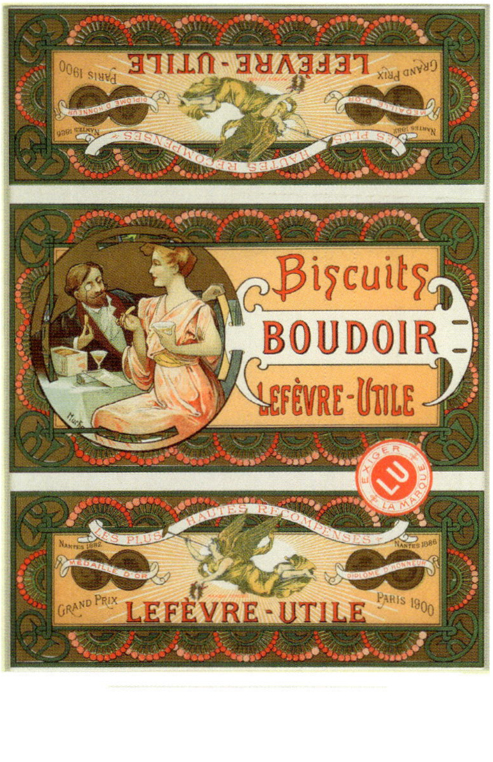

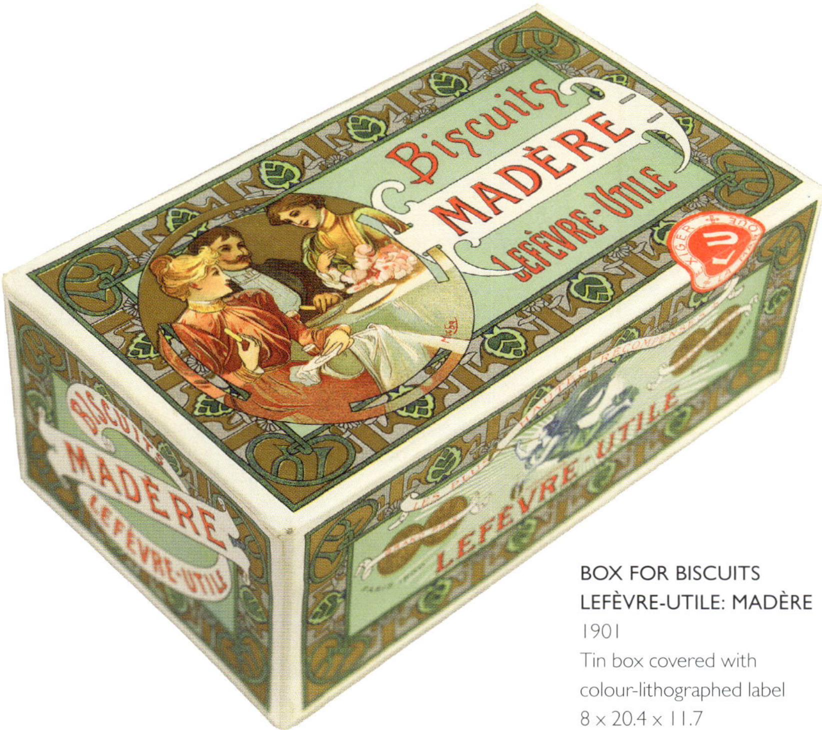

BOX FOR BISCUITS
LEFÈVRE-UTILE: MADÈRE
1901
Tin box covered with
colour-lithographed label
8 x 20.4 x 11.7

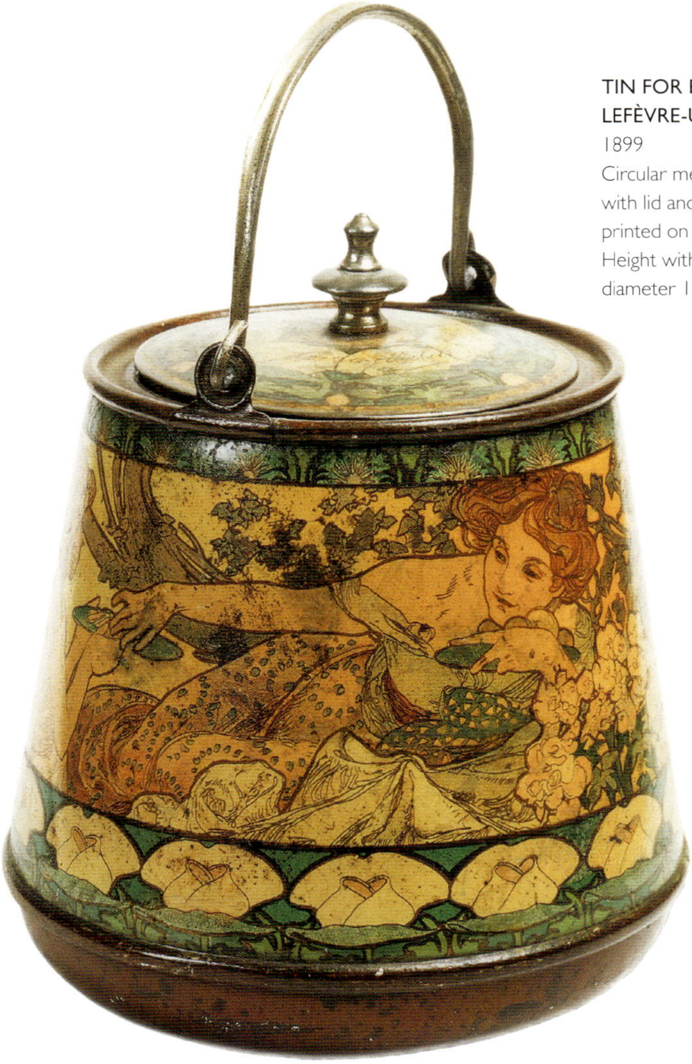

TIN FOR BISCUITS LEFÈVRE-UTILE
1899
Circular metal container with lid and handle; printed on metal
Height with lid 16; diameter 14.5

THE APPLICATION OF ART TO DECORATION

Mucha believed that 'art and its form should serve as a language to the object or to the forms to be decorated' and that the ornament should express the character and the function of the object. In Mucha's decorative designs, one of the most characteristic elements was the prominent border. He considered the border equivalent to the columns or other supporting elements of classic architecture – the essential parts providing strength and solidity to a building and harmoniously unifying all ornamentation. Mucha's design for a circular biscuit tin (shown left) exemplifies his use of such an architectural language assimilating its form to the structure of an entablature, which is emphasised by the bands at the base and the top.

PRINTER'S PROOF FOR BISCUIT LEFÈVRE-UTILE TIN
1899
Lithograph
34.8 x 49.9

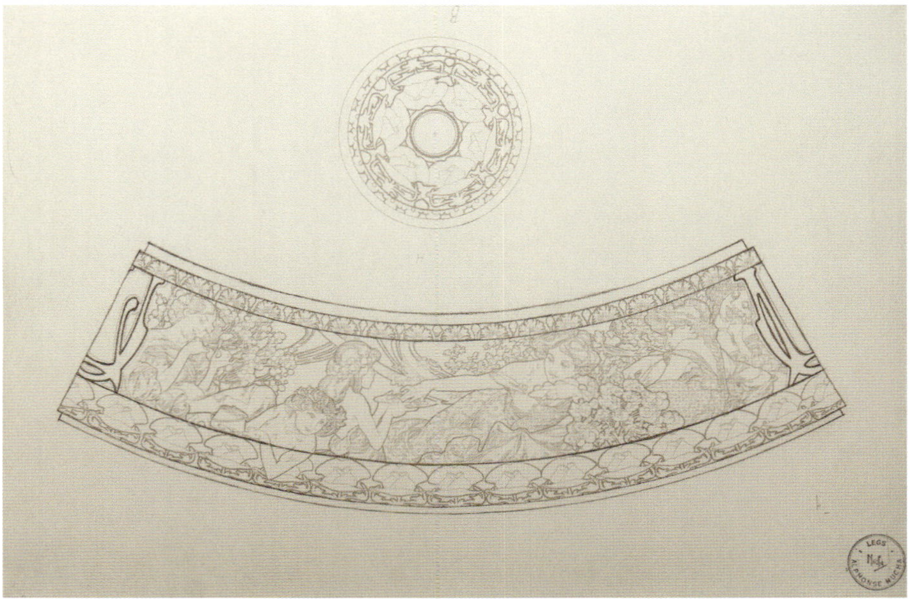

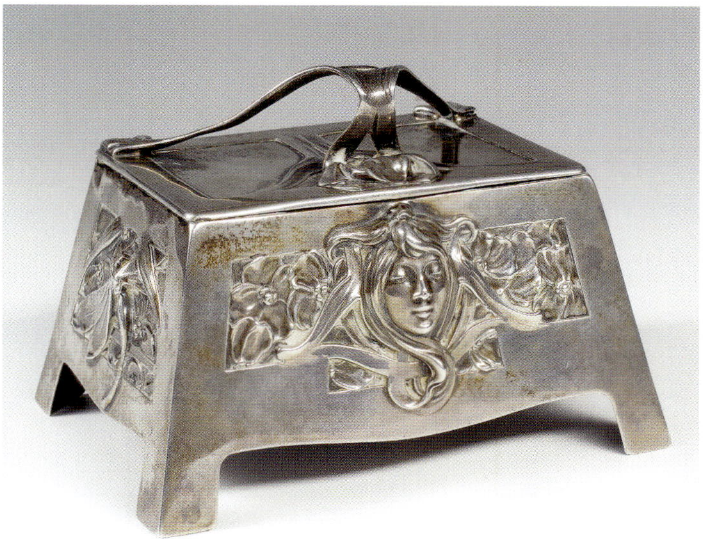

BOX DECORATED WITH A GIRL'S HEAD AFTER MUCHA
c. 1900
Silver
11 x 14 x 11 cm

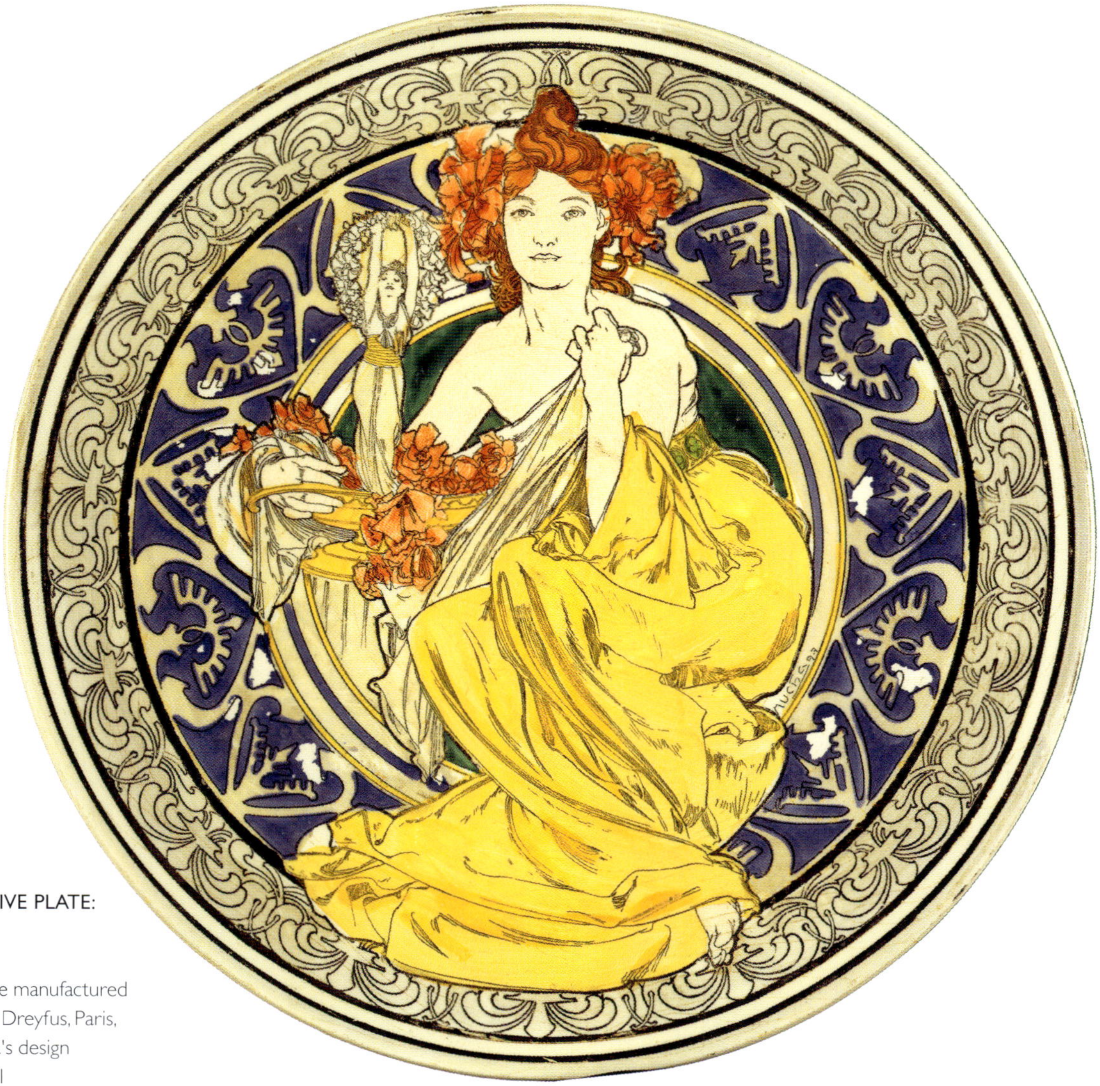

DECORATIVE PLATE: AUTUMN
1897
Earthenware manufactured by Georges Dreyfus, Paris, after Mucha's design
Diameter 31

MUCHA AND BRITAIN

Mucha never visited Britain but he was aware of contemporary English art, in particular Pre-Raphaelite paintings and the Arts and Crafts ideology of William Morris (see pp.11–12), which were well known in Paris in Mucha's time. A further source of inspiration for his decorative motifs was Owen Jones's (1809–1874) seminal book, *The Grammar of Ornament* (1856) – Mucha owned the French edition published in 1865. Mucha's own works were also well known in Britain through posters produced for his English clients such as *The West End Review*, a new literary periodical that appeared in London in 1897, and reproductions featured in numerous art magazines, including *The Magazine of Art* and *The Poster: An Illustrated Monthly Chronicle.*

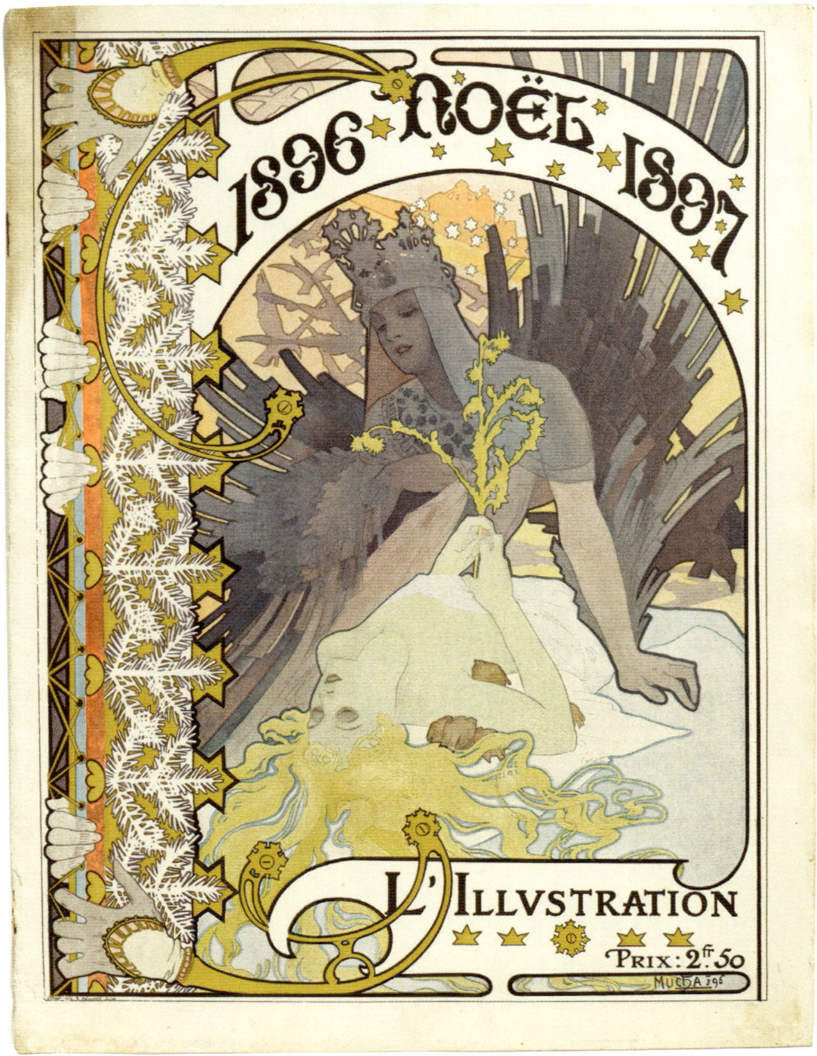

L'ILLUSTRATION:
NOËL 1896/1897
1896
Cover of the magazine published by Rédaction, Paris
38 x 26.5

Mucha's cover design for this French magazine was among the images familiar to British public. It was reused as the cover of three issues of *English Illustrated Magazine* in 1899; this use probably prompted the design of a bookplate, shown here.

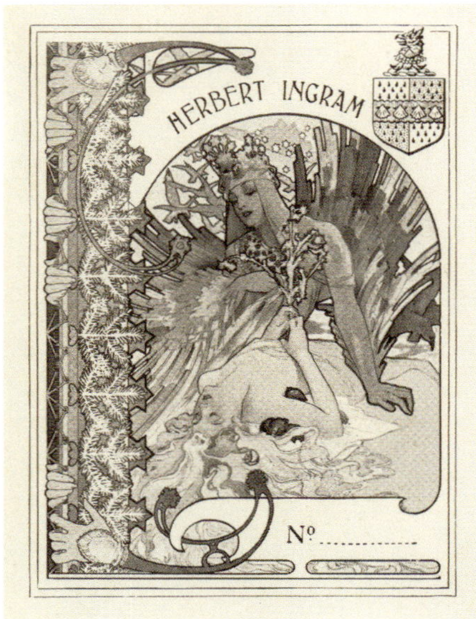

BOOKPLATE FOR HERBERT INGRAM, THE 2nd BARONET OF SWINESHEAD ABBEY, FEATURING THE COVER IMAGE OF *L'ILLUSTRATION* MAGAZINE, CHRISTMAS 1896/1897, BY MUCHA
c. 1897
Monochrome lithograph
N.B. Inside *The Badminton Library of Sports and Pastimes* by H.Cox and G.Lascelles (1892)

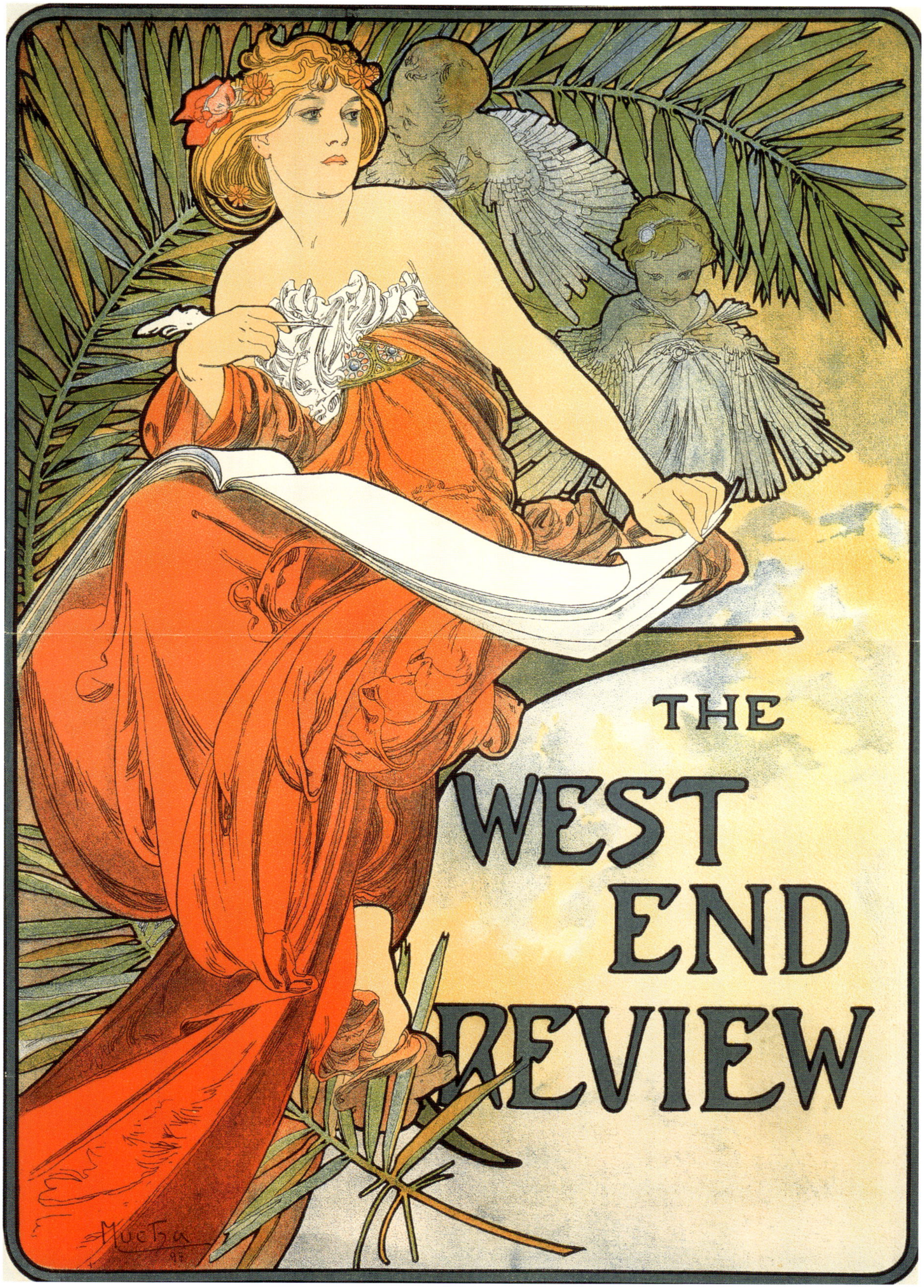

THE WEST END REVIEW
1898
Cover of the promotional copy
36.3 x 25.5

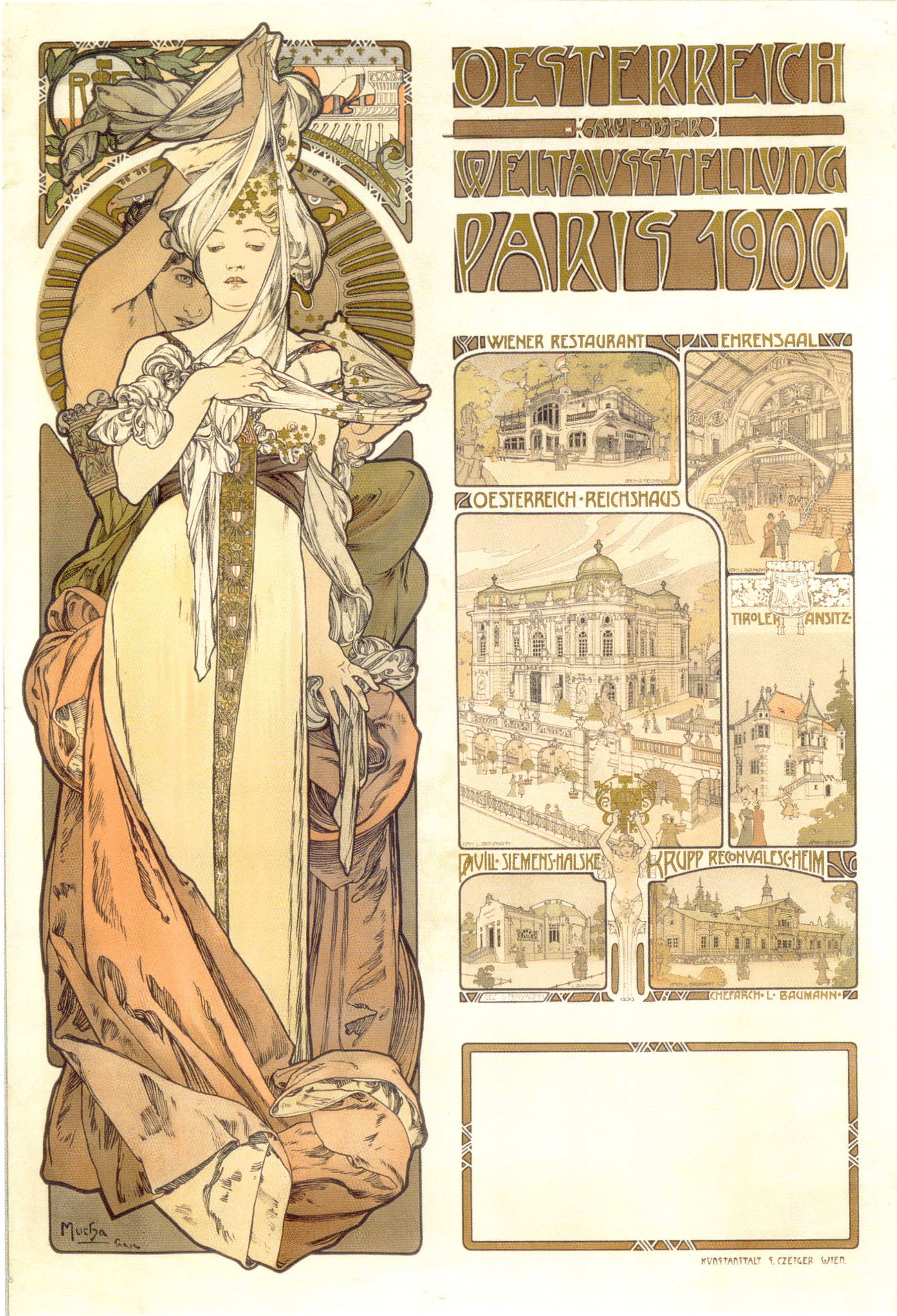
OESTERREICH
WELTAUSSTELLUNG
PARIS 1900
WIENER RESTAURANT
EHRENSAAL
OESTERREICH · REICHSHAUS
TIROLER ANSITZ
PAVILL · SIEMENS-HALSKE
KRUPP RECONVALESCHEIM
CHEFARCH · L · BAUMANN ·
KUNSTANSTALT J. CZETGER WIEN.
Mucha

PARIS 1900: OESTERREICH AUF DER WELTAUSSTELLUNG
1900
Colour lithograph
145 x 73.5

In designing this poster, Mucha was responsible only for the left-hand section and the lettering above the images on the right of the six Austrian buildings presented at the Paris Exposition Universelle of 1900. Mucha's allegorical composition features two figures, with Austria personified as the woman at the front being unveiled by Paris behind her, thus representing the theme of the poster: 'Paris presents Austria to the world.' Mucha's customary circular motif here incorporates a double-headed eagle, the emblem of the Austro-Hungarian Empire.

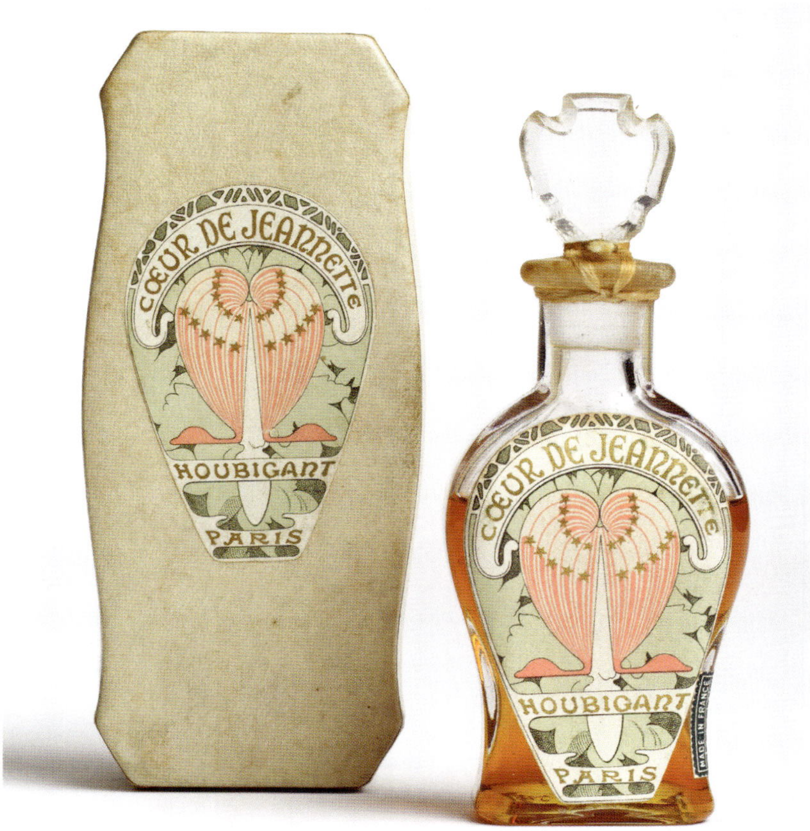

COEUR DE JEANNETTE: HOUBIGANT PERFUME BOTTLE AND CASE
1899
Lyre-shaped glass bottle with Mucha label and cardboard box
(bottle) height 13

THE PARIS EXPOSITION UNIVERSELLE OF 1900

Held in the final year of the 19th century, the 5th Paris Exposition Universelle was a celebration of the progress of humanity over the past hundred years and the arrival of the 20th century. Participated by 58 nations and visited by over 48 million people during a period of 7 months (15 April–12 November), it was considered to be the 'greatest event of the century'.

Mucha contributed towards a wide range of projects at varying levels. As an official artist representing the Austro-Hungarian Empire (Czech division), he was responsible for the decoration of the Bosnia-Herzegovina Pavilion – one of the three pavilions exhibited by the empire – along with designs for promotional materials. As a leading 'Parisian' artist, Mucha worked for prestigious French manufacturers such as Houbigant, one of the oldest perfumeries in France, as well as the leading Parisian goldsmith and jeweller Georges Fouquet, who commissioned Mucha to design an entire collection of jewellery for the Paris Exposition of 1900.

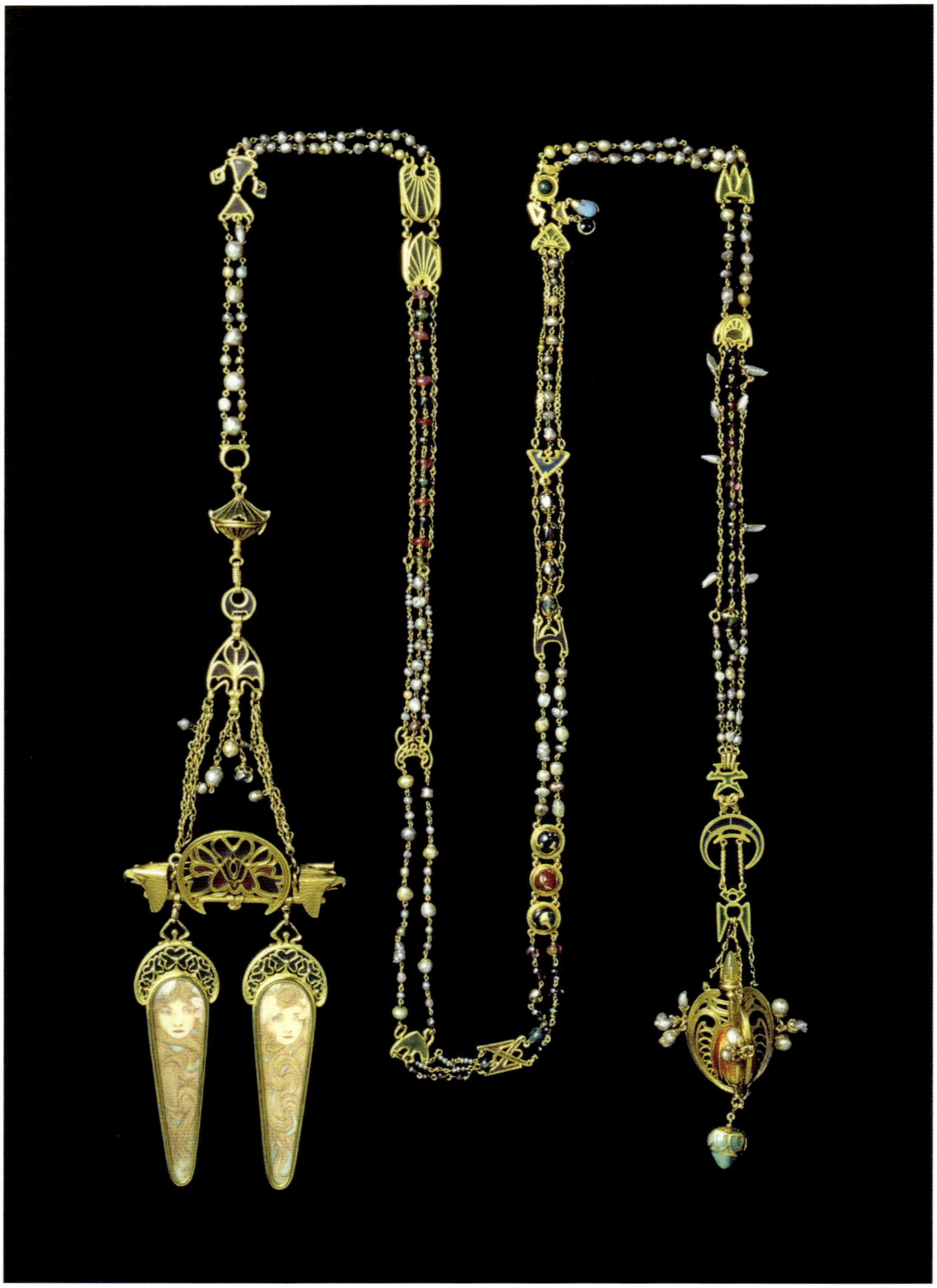

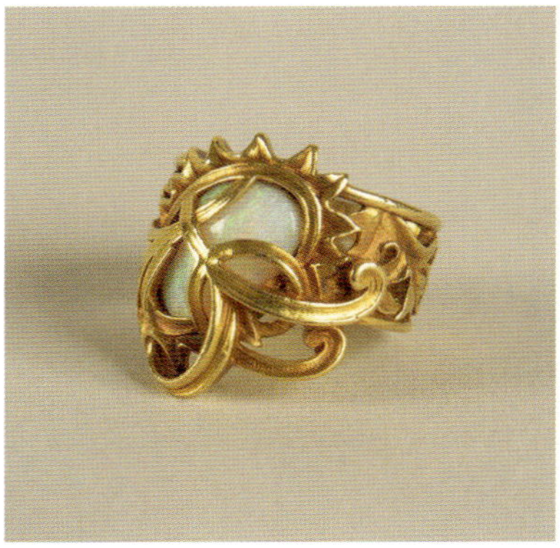

GEORGES FOUQUET
(1862–1957)
AFTER MUCHA'S DESIGN
'PEACOCK' RING
1900
Opal and gold
Diameter 1.8

HEAD OF A GIRL
1900
Bronze, silver and parcel gilt
29 x 22 x 10

GEORGES FOUQUET
(1862–1957)
AFTER MUCHA'S DESIGN
ORNAMENTAL CHAIN
WITH PENDANTS
1900
Gold, enamel, fresh-water pearls, mother of pearl and semi-precious stones
Length 159

Designed by Mucha for Georges Fouquet, this ornamental chain was exhibited on the jeweller's stand at the Paris Exposition. Here Mucha demonstrated his innovative approach to jewellery design, synthesising decorative motifs from Islamic, Egyptian, Byzantine and European art with the abundant use of pearls and gems.

This is one of the ornamental statuettes designed for the Houbigant stand at the Paris Exposition. It presents the bust of a girl with a meditative expression, wearing an arched coronet decorated with lilies and gems, and was designed to embody the soft floral scents of Houbigant perfumes (see p.49). At the Exposition, the bust was installed high above a wreath of irises, roses and violets, in the centre of the display.

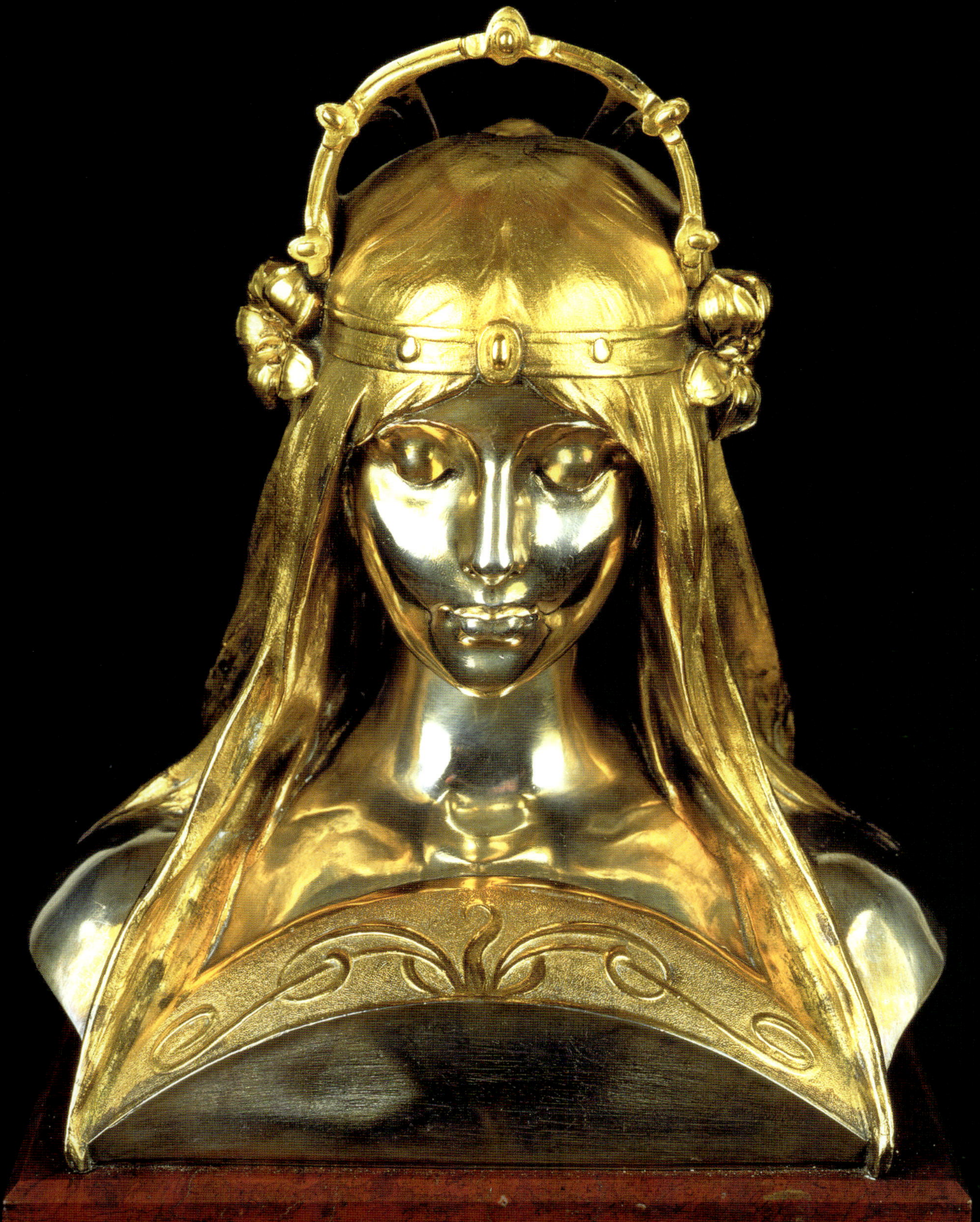

VERVE AND LOGIC: THE LINEAGE OF ART NOUVEAU

PAUL GREENHALGH & CLAIRE ALLERTON

If we were to simplify the aesthetic ethos of Art Nouveau down to its essential components, we might say that more than anything else it is to do with the use of line. There are exceptions of course – and some of them very considerable ones as in the case of Antoni Gaudí (1852–1926) – but looking at the style as a whole, especially among the northerly European nations, the line, on flat surfaces or in architectural space, defined the style in its greatest moments. Certainly, by the time the style attained 'mass' status by 1910, the countless Art Nouveau-inspired designs on posters, fire-places, biscuit tins, tea-caddies, chocolate wrappings and terraced house interiors were essentially linear. This is not a retrospective observation. At the time writer Herbert Croly (1869–1930), among others, identified the role of line and tried to characterise it:

> *I should say that from my own impressions of "Art Nouveau" that perhaps its most salient technical motive was a noticeable liking for continuity of line. This tendency prevails at once in the architectural forms used, in those connected with interior decoration, in its furniture, and in its metalwork. Many influences seem to have contributed to make this motive dominant.*[1]

What Croly was describing was the unbroken asymmetric line and its tendency in Art Nouveau to embrace and dominate whatever object or image it was used in, and its insistence on symbolising movement – flow – rather than stasis. We can understand part of this at least to refer to the iconic 'whiplash' line, brought in to existence by the embroidery of Hermann Obrist (Fig.7: 1862–1927). And, while Obrist's original statement of the *coup de fouet* line acts as a pattern for that which would take hold of Art Nouveau, the line that would follow in works such as Aubrey Beardsley's illustrations of Oscar Wilde's (1854–1900) *Salome* was a more passionately determined force (Fig.8). With the unyielding and weighty sense of steel and yet decidedly organic, the Art Nouveau line simultaneously grows and restricts. Contrasting those sometimes delicate forms offered up by the artists of the time and containing the bright colours used in billboard advertising, the line leads the eye, winding around to create its subject; an unapologetically distinctive device of a commercial product. More than just a border, the contours of the whiplash line provide an instantly recognisable image: the maker's mark of the Art Nouveau artisan.

As suggested by Croly (and a number of others), the Art Nouveau linearity is felt to be *a priori* anti-classical, and he notes three core inspirations behind the style: use of plant forms and especially the leaf; Japanese art; and Mediaeval art and architecture. Croly was shrewd but not especially unusual in his discussion of Art Nouveau and its sources. It was

Fig. 7
HERMANN OBRIST
Whiplash (Peitchenhieb)
c. 1895
Textile
Stadtmuseum, Munich

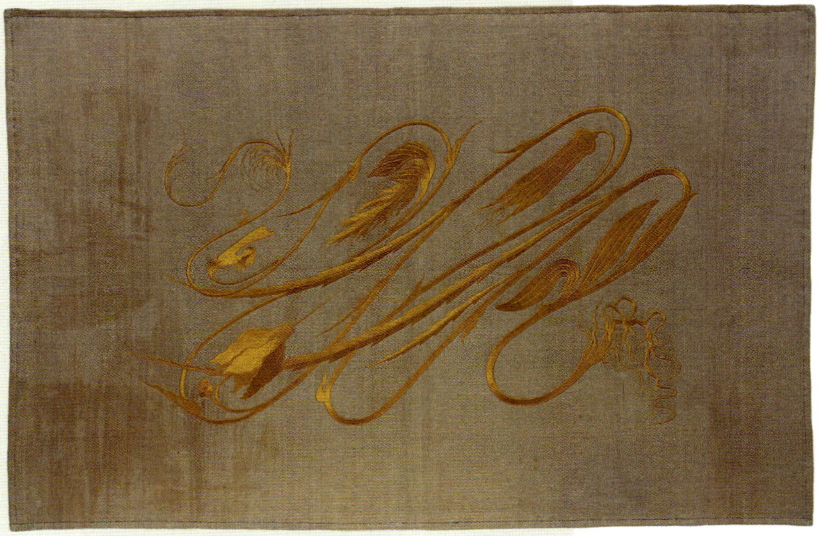

Fig. 8
AUBREY BEARDSLEY
J'ai baisé ta bouche Iokanaan
Illustration for 'The Climax' from Oscar Wilde's *Salome*
1894
Line block print
Victoria and Albert Museum, London

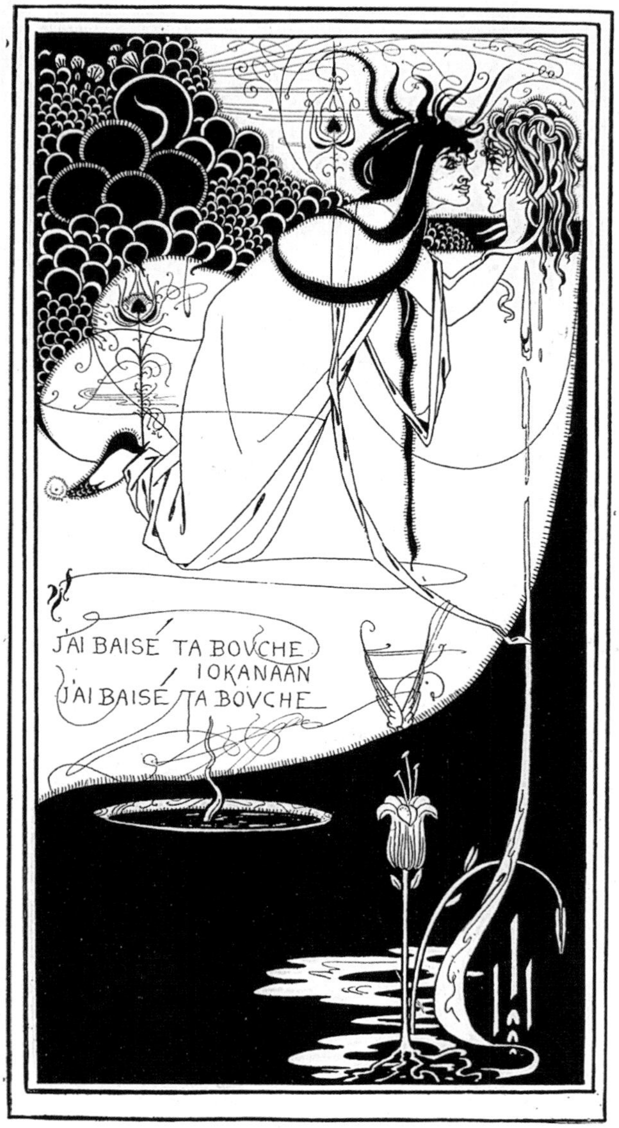

meanings, composition and merit.

In pondering Art Nouveau line, the aim here is not simply to agree with or to summarise the writer of 1902 but to attempt to answer a question which he and most writers after him did not broach: *why* did so many talented young artists and designers use line in this way? What was the motive? What did they see in it? What exactly does this linearity mean in the bigger context of modernity? As the young and ambitious Czech artist Alphonse Mucha began to make his definitive contribution to the Art Nouveau style from the mid-1890's, what exactly was the wider significance of the taut, dynamic line he used to depict the figures and forms in his graphic art? What did Mucha's line mean?

The *fin de siècle* was an especially important moment for line, not simply as a vehicle for disinterested artistic expression – as a component in the artistic process – but also from a wider intellectual and even ideological perspective. First of all the *fin de siècle* saw the final resolution of a process that had been in train for generations, whereby in painting line had broken out of its role as sketch or preparatory

widely talked about at the time and the style itself was unusual in that it self-consciously named and described itself. In 1894 Henry Van de Velde (1863–1957) was (arguably) the first to use the name in relation to the new style[2] and in the following year Siegfried Bing (1838–1905) opened his shop the *Maison de l'Art Nouveau*: from that point a considerable literature emerged that continually stated the claim to being modern. Art Nouveau has been accompanied then, through its life and after-life, by an on-going commentary on its origins,

activity into the work proper. Debates about 'finished' and 'unfinished' work largely resolved in the period. Toulouse-Lautrec, Edgar Degas (1834–1917), Honoré Daumier (1808–1879), Auguste Rodin (1840–1917) in his two-dimensional work, Paul Gauguin, Edvard Munch (1863–1944) and many others in the wider Impressionist and Post-impressionist circles, routinely and uncontroversially allowed line a spontaneous, undisguised life as part of the finished painting in recognition of the shifting parameters of

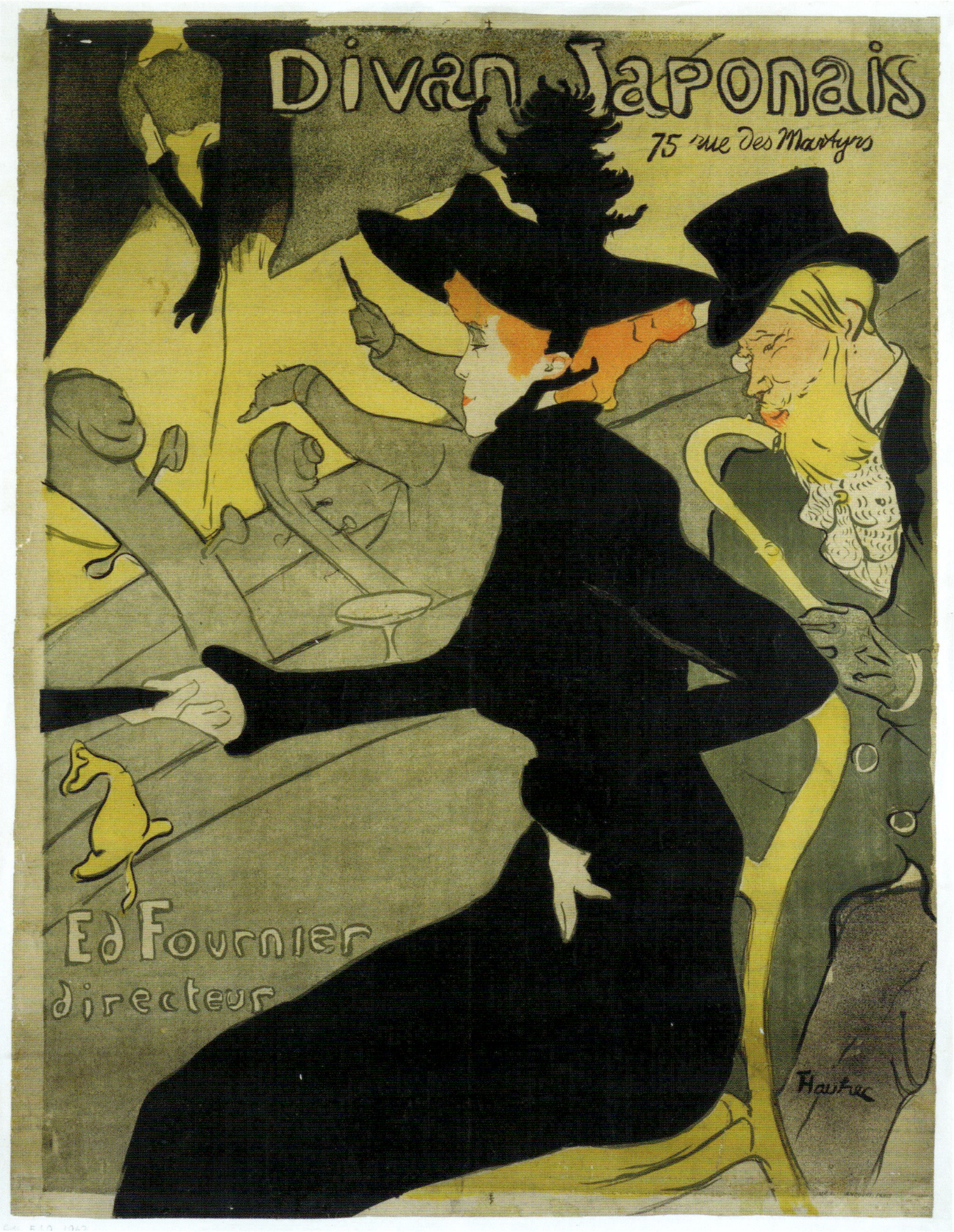
Divan Japonais
75 rue des Martyrs
Ed Fournier
directeur

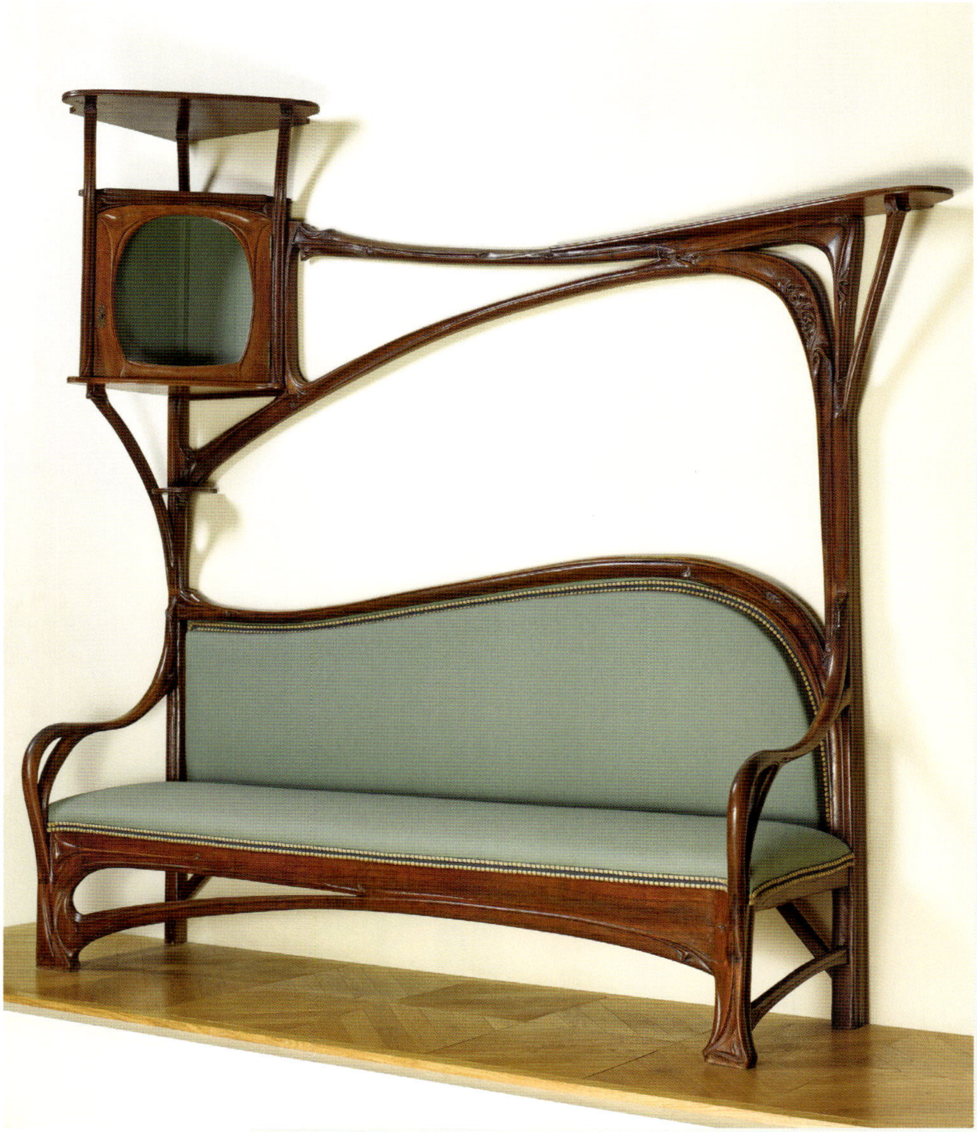

Fig. 10
HECTOR GUIMARD
Bench for a smoking parlour
1897 (OAO 340)
Jarrah, chased metal, modern upholstery
Musée d'Orsay, Paris, acquired 1979

were brought up with; a major visual resource was Japan, the new (for the Europeans), exotic and somewhat mysterious culture that underpinned much recent practice; nature was a main vehicle of most artists trying to generate fresh and novel forms; and Mediaevalism was at the heart of the aesthetic, social and political thought of a wide range of radical thinkers from William Morris to Eugene Emmanuel Viollet-le-Duc (1814–1879). All implied a radical departure from normative academic practice. In short, Art Nouveau literally had a radical *lineage* and this permeated all images and objects in which it had a presence.

Additionally, those sources mentioned were all susceptible to a further distinctly Modern approach, one alluded to by Croly, that a style should be capable of moving effortlessly across all forms of art and design. In the Wagnerian sense, they facilitated the notion of *gesamtkunstwerk*, or a total work of art, that understood art as being to do with the creation of a complete environment. This implied a breaking down of barriers between the high and 'lesser' arts and a commitment to reach a wider public. The line then that drifted across the arts, pulling them into proximity, by definition had a transformation agenda. In his essay for the catalogue of the seminal

representation (Fig.9). Partly as a consequence of this liberation, by 1890 a wide public understood the linear presence in contemporary painting as a signifier of the Modern. The signification spread into the wider world of graphic and product design.

In Art Nouveau there were a number of things going on beyond this liberation of the individual from academic process. Most importantly, the use of the Art Nouveau line was eclectic and the sources of its eclecticism implied modernity. A cursory glimpse at those inspirations identified by Croly says a great deal. Pointedly, it was anti-Classical and alien to the training regimes all Western practitioners

Fig. 9
HENRI DE TOULOUSE-LAUTREC
Divan Japonais
1892
Colour lithograph
Victoria and Albert Museum, London

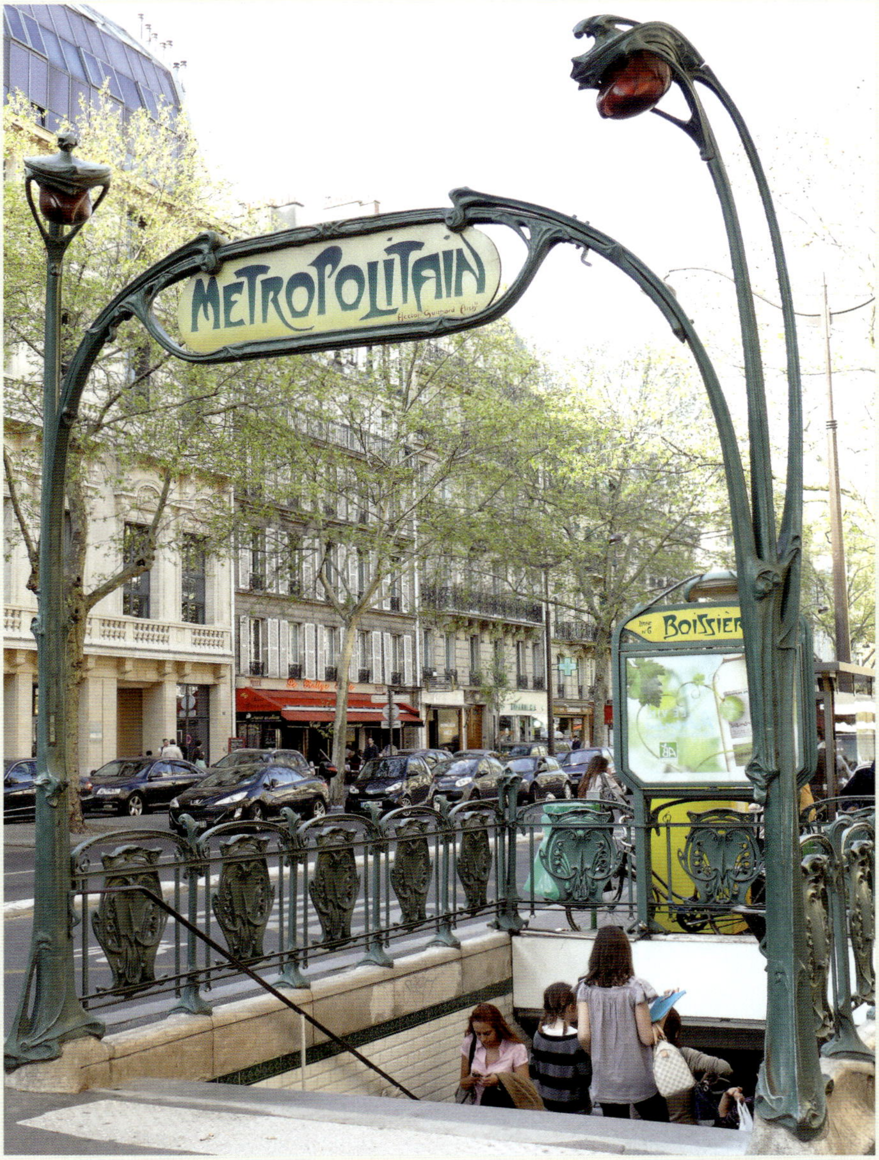

Fig. 11
HECTOR GUIMARD
Entrance to the Paris Metropolitain, Boissière station
c. 1900

Art Nouveau exhibition at the Museum of Modern Art, New York, in 1960 (in which one radical decade recognised another), the great curator Peter Selz, noted that:

> *Historically Art Nouveau fulfilled the liberating function of an "anti" movement. It discarded the old, outworn conventions and set the stage for the developments which followed with such extraordinary rapidity in the twentieth century.* [3]

For Selz the style *a priori* had a radical pedigree and this largely explained its role during and after its turbulent life. In this scenario, Art Nouveau line becomes the *enfant terrible* of normative art and design, the serpent that coiled and slid viperously across the face of accepted practice.

While the notion carries undoubted truth, the style was more than this; it wasn't only a breakaway from earlier movements, a youthful revolt, or an eclectic agglomeration of feisty sources adding up to a Modern look. Art Nouveau was more than simply 'anti'. It was also a fundamental reflection of the urban conditions and aspirations it was born into;

Fig. 12
HECTOR GUIMARD
Entrance to *Castel Béranger*, Paris
1894-95

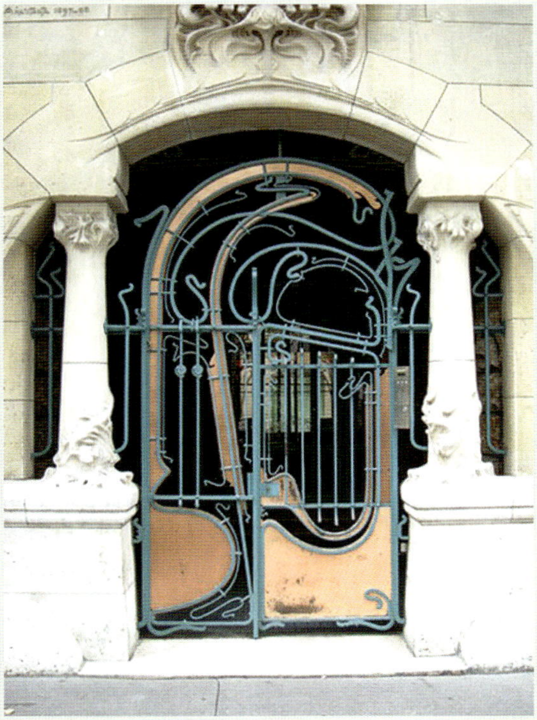

the way it framed and formed compositions had something to say about the material and intellectual outlook of the *fin-de-siècle* generation. And it said it largely through the language of the line.

If we take the literature surrounding Art Nouveau as a whole, produced both then and since, and extrapolate from it what we might call the style's historiography, a major but underlying theme emerges as a constant presence: contradiction. Interestingly, contradiction has been identified as a major flaw in the aesthetic of the style and has provided ammunition for critique through the decades, but in reality it epitomises *fin-de-siècle* life. The period was wracked with paradoxical inconsistencies, in which opposing value systems came to occupy the same spaces: the newly organised urban framework was largely inhabited by subjective and superstitious populations who harboured older, archaic views of life. Within this age the ambiguities abound: the old and the new; the secular and the religious; the ascetic and the erotic; and the public and the private. The artistic practice of this generation had a choice; to resolve these tensions or to remove themselves from it.

Most powerfully in this light was the understanding of Art Nouveau both as a rational approach to design based on Enlightenment logic and its status as an irrational, Romantic product of Symbolism. On the one hand, major practitioners and theorists themselves – and many since – saw it as being centrally concerned with utilitarian logic. In 1895 Henry Van de Velde could angrily proclaim that 'Life is utilitarian – a truth that no-one can regret, save only those who are good for nothing'.[4] Less passionately, but perhaps more surprisingly, critic Fernand Mazade (1861–1939), writing about architect Hector Guimard (1867–1942), determined that:

> *Although M. Guimard's style is puzzling at times, he shows a grasp as rare as it is meritorious of the necessities of the present day. He is eminently rational, and possesses verve and logic.* [5]

Van de Velde evolved into a leading International Style designer, giving his utilitarianism an eventual synergy with his design, but his words sat very uncomfortably with the twining, sensuous and sensual physicality of his metal and wood-work made at the time of his statement (Fig.10). And when Mazade wrote, Guimard's work appeared to be anything but rational but appeared rather to be an expression of late Romanticism and the spawn of Symbolism.

Interestingly, later historians such as Henry Lenning seminally saw the style as an expression of rational public practice. [6] But others, committed to Modernism as an expression of Enlightenment logic like J.M. Richards (1907–1992) and Nikolaus Pevsner (1902–1983), struggled to see Art Nouveau as an example of this value-system: their 1973 publication dedicated largely to Art Nouveau architecture was titled unequivocally *The Anti-rationalists.* [7]

The apparent need to dress Art Nouveau in

rationalist clothing wasn't by any means shared by all. Having proudly gone under the banner of Decadence, there were those who understood the artist and designer in a powerfully Romantic light. Poet and critic Arthur Symonds (1865–1945), for example, writing in 1898, understood the motive force behind art to be anything but utilitarian:

> *Every artist has his own secret, beyond the obvious one, of why he works. So far as it is not the mere need of earning one's living, it is generally some unhappiness, some dissatisfaction with the things about one, some too desperate or too contemptuous sense of the meaning of existence. At one period of his life a man works at his art to please a woman; and then because he is tired of pleasing her. Work for work's sake it always must be, in a profound sense.* [8]

Hardly the stuff of a Five Year Plan. It is difficult to position Symonds, Mazade, Van de Velde, and many others in the same camp, but they were. This is because in reality the apologists for Rationalism and Romanticism are both essentially valid, and are flawed only their separatist failure to recognise that an architect like Guimard *simultaneously* embraced Rationalism and Romanticism. The use of new technology and materials and the concern for functionality are evident throughout his oeuvre. He built apartment blocks and subway stations that function comfortably a century after he designed them, yet standing in front of the twisted, tense, and bulbous sepals and stems of the Paris Metro entrances, or the symmetric gothic darkness of his Castel Béranger decked out with cats, dragons and gargoyles, a rationalist worldview is not the first one to spring to mind (Fig.11 and 12). Guimard was a product of the new engineering *and* the Symbolist poets. Like so many other practitioners within the Art Nouveau canon, he was comfortable with Gustave Eiffel (1832–1923) and Edgar Allen Poe (1809–1849): with a simultaneity that powerfully impacted the next generation of avant-garde practice, his work brought together two key icons of the age, the engineer and the vampire.

The other major contradictory tension within the style was between the natural and the artificial. In this regard, there is a clear irony within the style. While nature is constantly promoted as the key inspiration, for so many designers nature is deliberately and carefully transformed into an artifice, a pattern system that represents not nature as such but its transfiguration into another form. This is a new vision of natural form, which embraces the notion that the urban environment is a manufactured construct, a giant artifice. The city is an artificial construction occupied by natural beings. Art was a means of mediating between the two. Hence, the conventionalisation of nature in Art Nouveau is a recognition of the new conditions of existence, a reconciliation of the artificial and the real, a humanisation and celebration of these conditions.

The style also embodied the duality of art and design, and the new economic reality of the impact of consumerism on practice. The term 'designer' began to gain its modern meaning in the period, giving rise to structural tensions within the visual arts that survive until today. For example, historian of the graphic arts Alain Weill noted that poster production in the period was divided between those artists who made posters for personal reasons and those who embraced it as a means of mass communication within the parameters of marketing and advertising:

> *Most of the salon posters are high-quality lithographs, the work of painters of designers whose one aim was to advance their ideas... they were publicity only by chance. Even Lautrec, the most productive among these artists, made only thirty-one posters in his lifetime, a good number of them for his*

friends, and the case was the same for many of the Belgians. [9]

Mucha was an interesting figure in all this, in that he came to prominence and fame as a graphic designer before committing wholly to painting in his later career. Toulouse-Lautrec, Pierre Bonnard (1867–1947), and others were painters first, and turned their hands to graphic design when invited to do so. Unlike these artists, Mucha embraced the full possibilities of the poster as a means of communication and is one of the grand figures for the making of mass imagery in the Art Nouveau style. The young Mucha, we know, found his distinctive style under some pressure when the actress Sarah Bernhardt requested a poster for her portrayal of *Gismonda* (see p.22) shortly after Christmas 1894. Mucha made the decision to represent Bernhardt in an elongated format, life-size to the viewer, presenting the 'ethereal, ageless sorceress' she would become on stage. Gone were the bright colours of Mucha's contemporaries, and instead an emphasis on striking, bold outlines and a tasteful selection of pastel shades. He is a seminal figure in the history of design.

The reconciliation of opposites abounds in his magnificent poster *Job* 1896 (see p.37). The image alludes to but laughs at the Classical frieze, because this is no timeless celebration of gods and heroes but an encouragement to purchase cigarettes. And it is in examples such as these that we see the contradictions of the age come together through the use of line. Compositionally, the artist has deliberately forced together two dimensional flat planes and three dimensional form and space: the woman has naturally modelled facial features but aggressively linear and flat hair; her body is provocatively rounded, but bursts through decorative borders and type that sits in no space; her cigarette smoke has acquired the substance of fabric and her hair could be a metal grate. She is a fascinating fusion of nature and mechanisation and takes great pleasure in this identity, appearing voluptuously energised because of it. She is at the same time real and unreal, a celebration of artifice as being at the core of artistic practice. The imagery is heavily outlined with black line, making the whole quintessentially linear, and an exercise in the use of line to transform nature into Modern pattern-forms.

In many ways the Modernity of Art Nouveau is to do with the reconciliation of opposites, with the recognition that urban life in 1900 embodied and embraced many contrary and contradictory forces and that these cohabited in a condition of on-going, mobile flux. Art Nouveau is to do with movement in both the aesthetic and the metaphysical senses; it was a celebration of Heraclitus, not Plato. And more than anything else, it was about the use of line as an explanation of the modern world.

NOTES

(1) Herbert Croly, 'The New World and the New Art', *Architectural Record*, June 1902, Volume XII, No.2, p.146.

(2) Henri Van der Velde, *Déblaiement d'Art*, 1894, p.15.

(3) Peter Selz, in *Art Nouveau: Art and Design at the Turn of the Century*, 1960, MOMA, p.17.

(4) From 'Observations Toward a Synthesis of Art', in Isabelle Frank (Ed), *The Theory of Decorative Art*, 2000, Yale, p.198.

(5) Fernand Mazade, 'An "Art Nouveau" edifice in Paris', *Architectural Record*, May 1902, Volume XII, No.1, p.62.

(6) *The Art Nouveau*, 1951, The Hague.

(7) *The Anti-rationalists*, J.M. Richards and Nikolaus Pevsner, Eds, 1973, London, Architectural Press.

(8) Arthur Symonds, written in 1898, from *Aubrey Beardsley*, 1966, London, Pall Mall, p.14–15.

(9) Alain Weill, 'The Art Nouveau Poster', in *Art Nouveau Belgium/France*, 1976, Rice University, p.95.

(10) Victor Arwas, 'Mucha and Sarah' in: Sarah Mucha Ed. *Alphonse Mucha*, 2000. p.44. Mucha Ltd: Czech Republic.

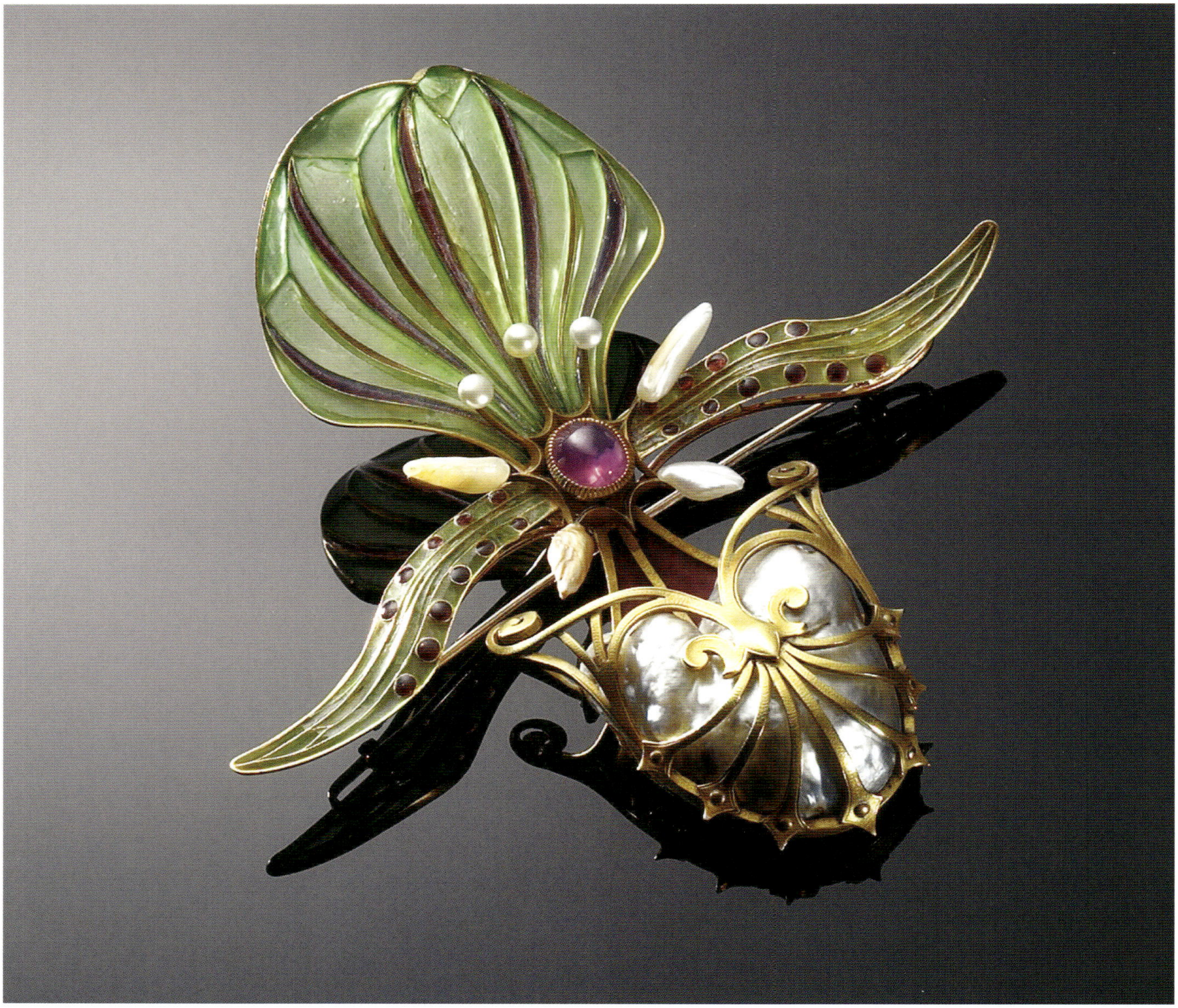

GEORGES FOUQUET (1862–1957)
ORCHID BROOCH
c. 1898–1901
Gold, ruby, pearl and enamel
10 x 10.5 x 2.5
Anderson Collection of Art Nouveau,
Sainsbury Centre for Visual Arts,
University of East Anglia
UEA 21149

One of the most important jewellers working at the *fin de siècle,* Georges Fouquet (see p.50) used nature to develop wholly innovative forms. This dramatic brooch is modelled in the form of a paphiopedilum lawrenceanum orchid. Comprised of gold and pearl, and rendered in deep purple and green *pliqué à jour* enamel, the ornament is sumptuously rendered and quite deliberately decadent, an exploration of the dark side of nature.

EMILE GALLÉ (1846–1904)
CRISTALLERIE DE GALLÉ
LA FLEUR DE GENTAINE VASE
c. 1890–1900
Glass
19 x 9.6 x 9.6
Anderson Collection of Art Nouveau, Sainsbury Centre for Visual Arts, University of East Anglia
UEA 21064

EMILE GALLÉ (1846–1904)
CRISTALLERIE DE GALLÉ
VASE
c.1900
Glass
30.5 x 11 x 11
Anderson Collection of Art Nouveau, Sainsbury Centre for Visual Arts, University of East Anglia
UEA 21025

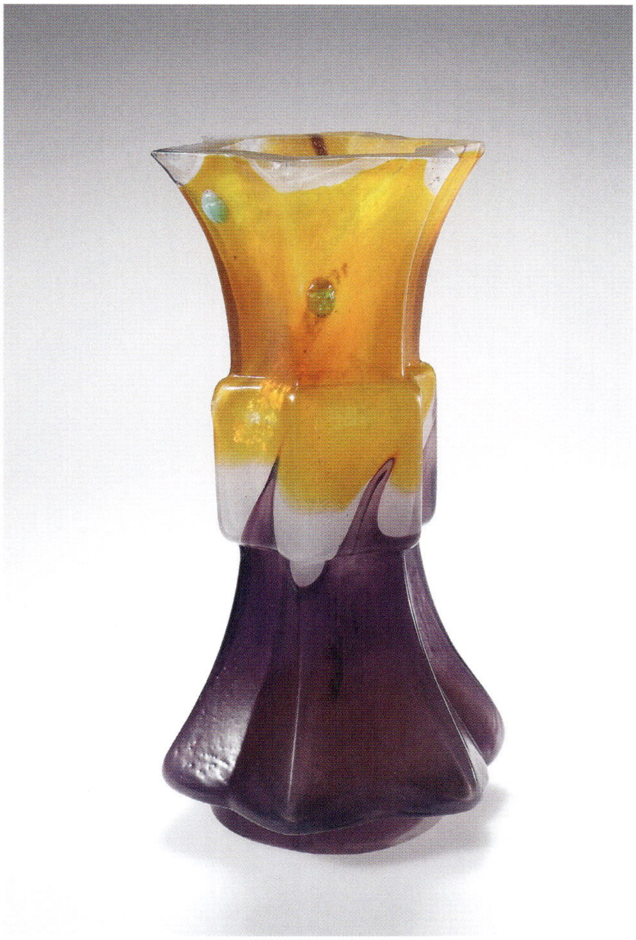

The form of this exceptional glass vase is thought to be inspired by that of a Ku vessel of the Chinese Shang dynasty (c.1600 BC – c.1046 BC). It has the feel of a piece of rock crystal. Dramatic in appearance, the piece is comprised of a heavy orange, mauve and white glass, decorated with applied cabochons which take the form of carved scarabs with metalic foil.

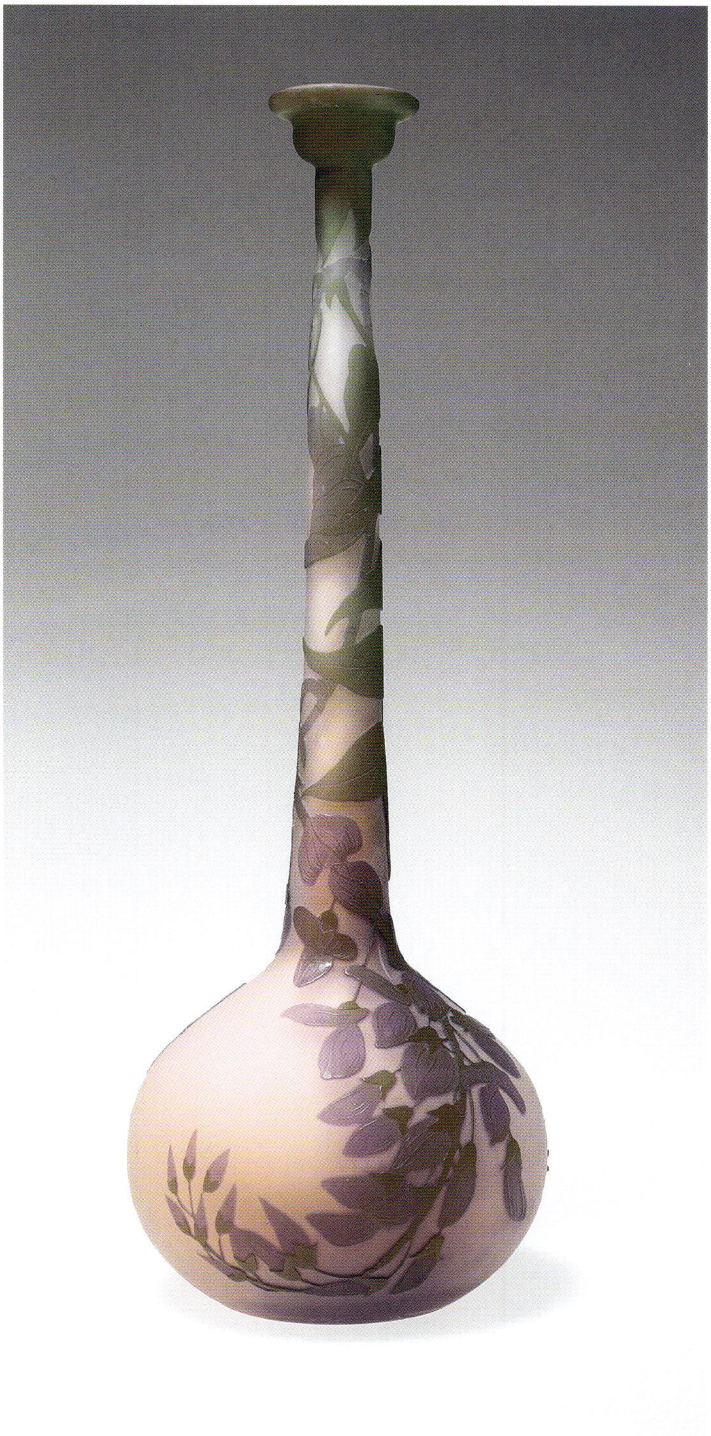

Both the decoration of this vase and the shape of the vessel itself are indicative of Gallé's fascination with botany. Simultaneously romantic and scientific, rational and emotional, the pink and grey glass is sensitively overlaid with green and mauve and etched with decoration of wisteria.

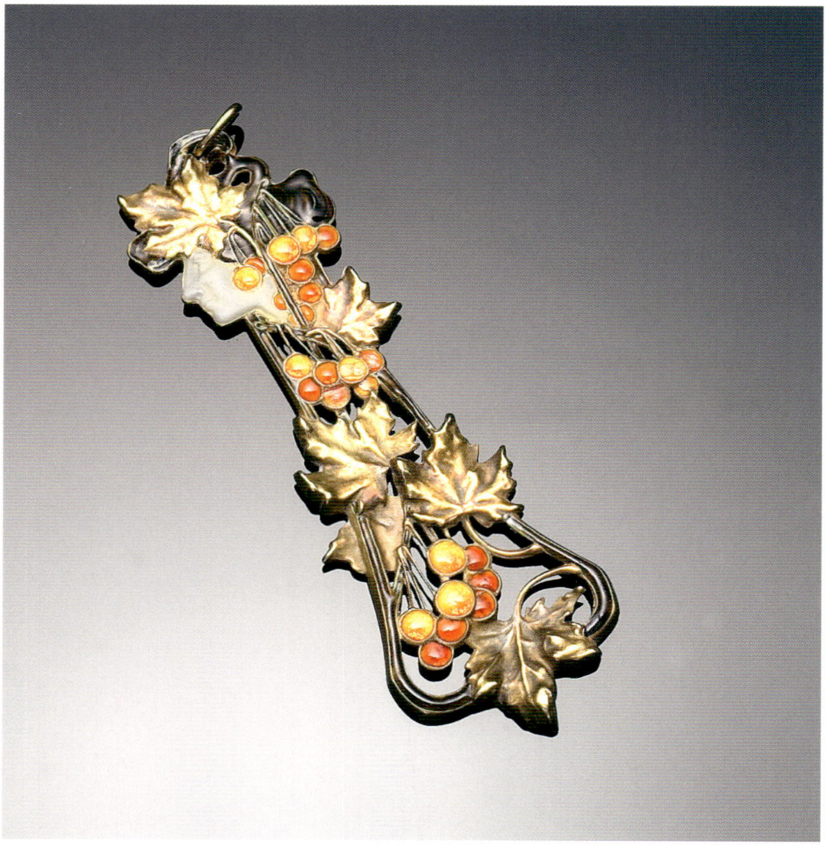

RENÉ LALIQUE (1860–1945)
PENDANT
c.1898–1900
Gold and enamel pendant
11.5 x 3.5 x 0.8
Anderson Collection of Art Nouveau,
Sainsbury Centre for Visual Arts,
University of East Anglia
UEA 21123

This work sees Lalique engaged with Symbolist imagery. Crafted in gold and enamel, a woman's face emerges from a draped frame of golden leaves and orange berries within this 'Autumn' pendant. Female images such as these appear in the Classicist tradition; women are depicted as fairies and nymphs, spirits of the flora and fauna that surround them.

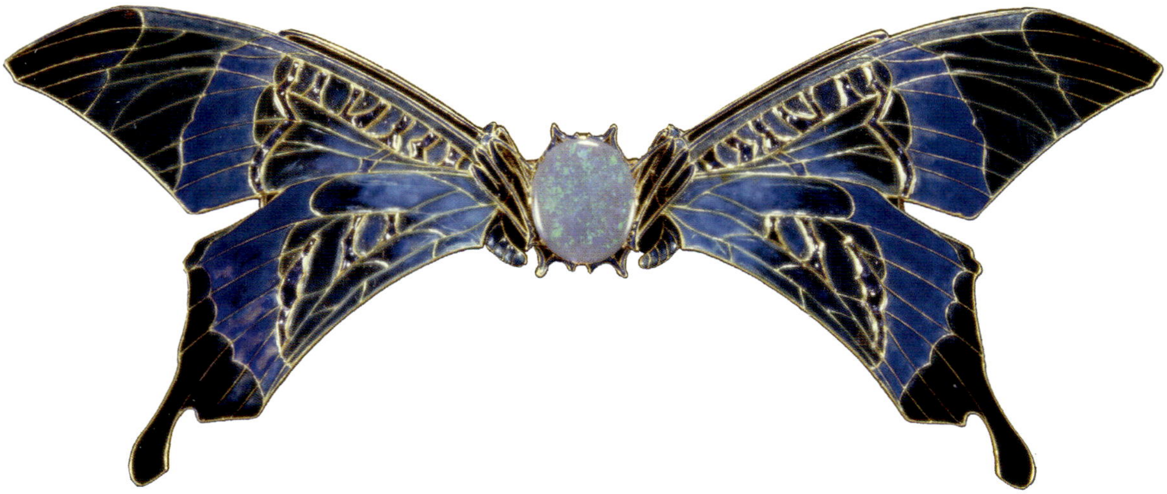

RENÉ LALIQUE (1860–1945)
BUCKLE
c.1903–1904
Gold, enamel, opal and sapphire
18.2 x 7.2 x 2.5
Anderson Collection of Art Nouveau,
Sainsbury Centre for Visual Arts,
University of East Anglia
UEA 21122

In 1892 Lalique renounced his previous accomplishments and began relentless technical research to create 'something completely new'.[1] Pre-eminent among the virtuoso jewellers of the period, he embraced the *pliqué à jour* enamelling technique across a range of accessories. The method is exploited to great poetic effect in this masterful double swallowtail butterfly buckle.

(1) Lalique quoted in Vever 2001, p. 1222. Vever, Henri. 2001. *French Jewellery of the Nineteenth Century*, translated from the original editions of 1906–08 by Katherine Purcell, London.

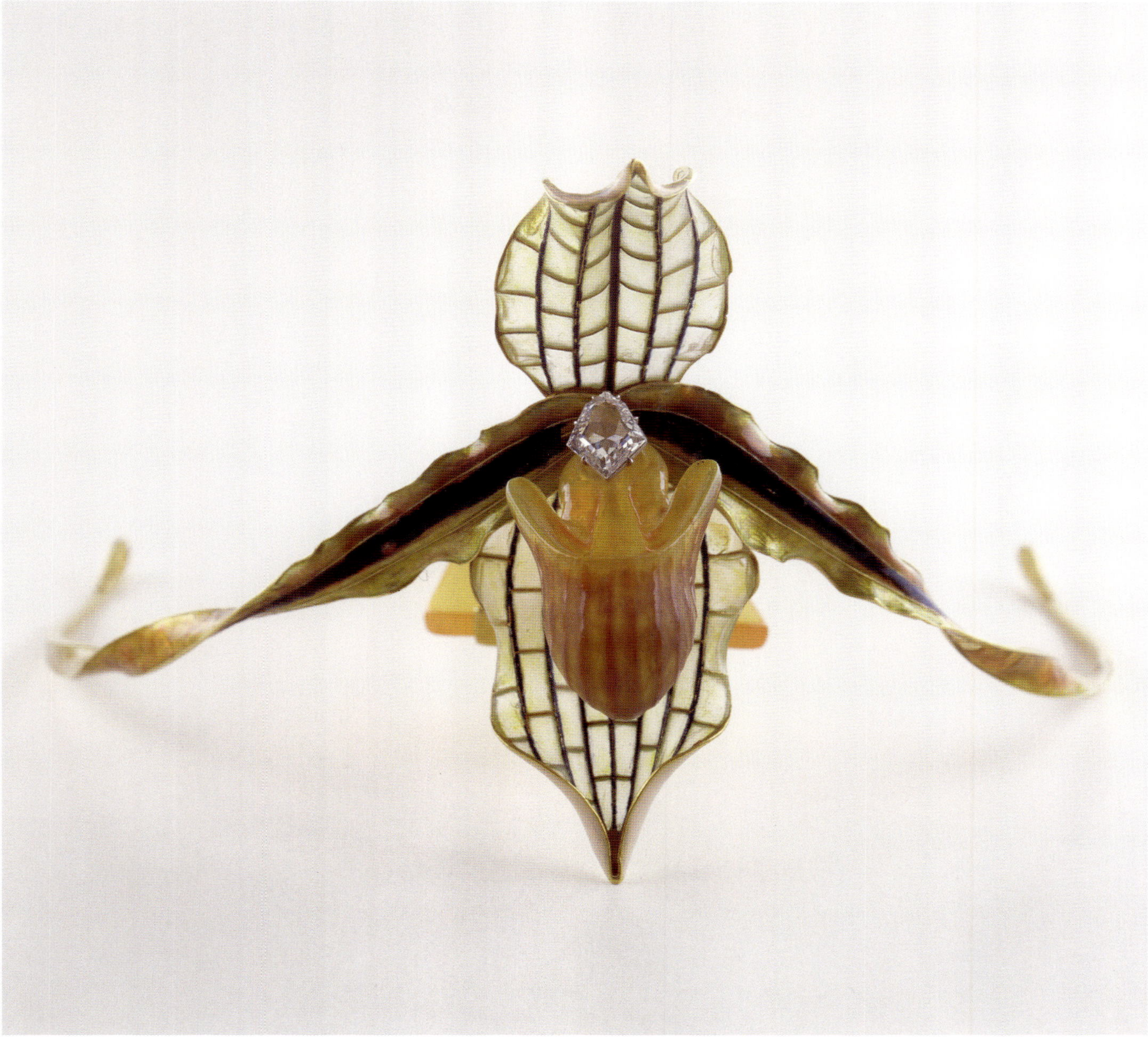

RENÉ LALIQUE (1860–1945)
HAIR ORNAMENT
c.1902
Gold, diamond, glass, horn and enamel
19 x 9 x 6
Anderson Collection of Art Nouveau,
Sainsbury Centre for Visual Arts,
University of East Anglia
UEA 21125

Lalique was interested in crossing boundaries within the arts. Designed to crown a generous chignon, this expressive and modern hair ornament is precisely rendered in the form of a cypripedium orchid. The petals are created with yellow and brown enamels and the centre is completed with a trapeze-cut diamond. The piece characterises the conception of Art Nouveau jewellery as 'bijoux de peintre', or artists' jewels[1].

(1) Gere quoting Meusnier 1901, p. 111. Gere, Charlotte, 'Les créateurs parisiens' in Les Fouquet, 20, n. 19.

LOETZ WITWE GLASSWORKS
VASE (LEFT)
ROSEWATER SPRINKLER (RIGHT)
c.1900
Silver and glass
Vase 12.7 x 14 x 14
Rosewater sprinkler 25.8 x 12.5 x 12.5
Anderson Collection of Art Nouveau,
Sainsbury Centre for Visual Arts,
University of East Anglia
UEA 21033 & 21041

Similar in form to antique Persian rosewater sprinklers, the larger glass vessel is attributed to the Loetz Glassworks. A dimpled, iridescent body with a fine cylindrical neck, the piece has a delicate overlay of silver in scrolling stylised stems and flowers. The smaller vase is comprised of a bulb-shaped bowl atop a tall, slender stem, with a similar silver decoration.

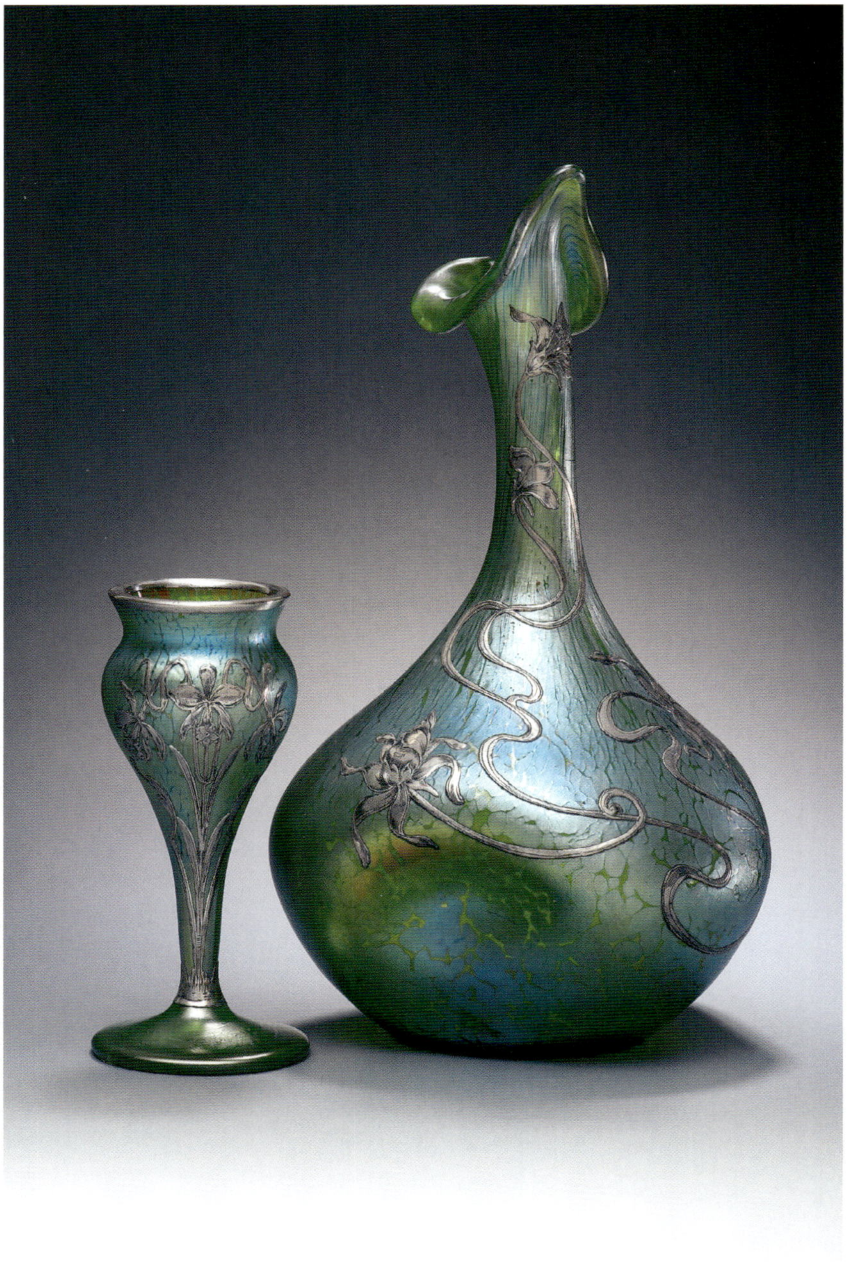

RIESSNER STELLMACHER UND KESSEL
FIGURE OF LOÏE FULLER
c.1900
Earthenware
49.5 x 44 x 20
Anderson Collection of Art Nouveau,
Sainsbury Centre for Visual Arts,
University of East Anglia
UEA 21016

This ceramic figure of Loïe Fuller (1862–1928) depicts the American dancer in full relief with swirling draperies, as if in motion. Fuller performed at the infamous Folies Bergère and in her own theatre at the Paris Exposition Universelle of 1900, becoming an icon of femme fatale beauty. Designed by Reissner, Stellmacher und Kessel, the figure follows the archetypal Art Nouveau 'whiplash' line; skirts like veils that circle the contours of the body.

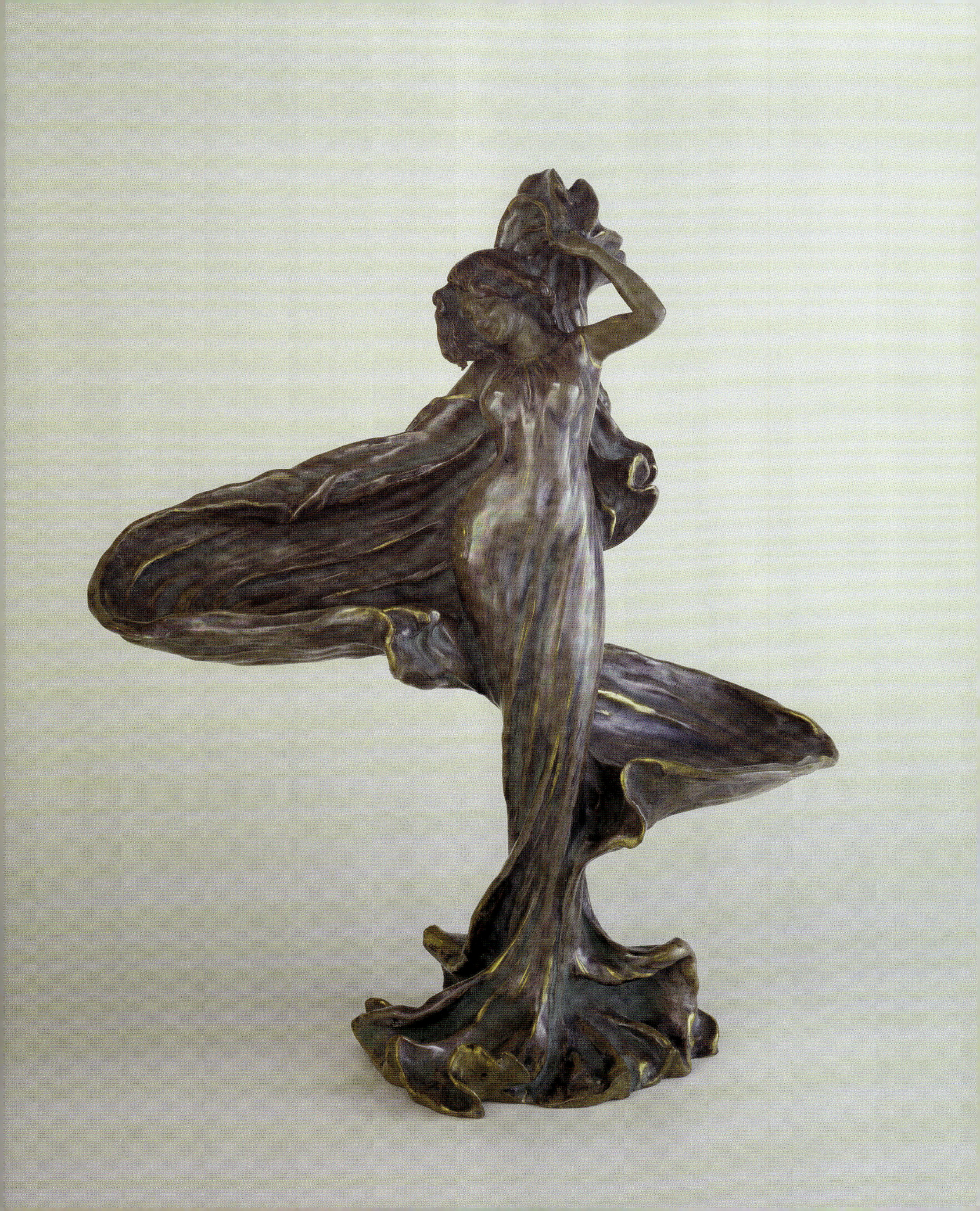

THE GLASGOW STYLE, THE FOUR, AND THE CONTROVERSIAL POSTER GHOULS

ALISON BROWN

> *'The influence of the Mackintosh group is far-reaching. Its influence in its native city is already so generally obvious that Mackintosh's repertoire of forms may almost be said to have created a local style.'*
>
> Hermann Muthesius, *Das Englische Haus*, 1904[1]

'The Glasgow Style' is the collective title now given to the distinctive design and decorative arts produced in Glasgow from the early 1890s until about 1920. It is centred around the work of teachers, students and graduates of The Glasgow School of Art, and embraces a wider number of talented professional designers working commercially in the city's many trades and craft-based manufacturing industries. This creative outpouring makes Glasgow the only place in Britain that can be classed as an Art Nouveau centre.

At the core of the Style are the distinctive ideas and imagination of 'The Four': the architect, designer and artist Charles Rennie Mackintosh (1868–1928), his future wife Margaret Macdonald (1864–1933), her younger sister Frances Macdonald (1873–1921) and Frances' future husband James Herbert McNair (1868–1955). Their influential works drew upon ideas prevalent in Symbolism and Aestheticism – the work of writers, poets and artists – imbued with an edgy personal language and executed with a very distinctive attenuated line.

There was a fifth member of The Four. Talwin Morris (1865–1911) arrived from London in May 1893 to become Art Manager for the Glasgow-based publisher Blackie & Son. Morris shared many of the same interests as the group and quickly became a close friend. Through his book cover designs sold across the British Empire and beyond, Morris would be highly influential in the spread of the Glasgow Style and its motifs (see p.76).

The rise of the Glasgow Style is synonymous with the establishment of the Technical Art Studios. In 1891–82 a new government excise duty on alcohol distributed income specifically to the Art Schools of the largest British industrial cities to create centres for technical instruction. Day and evening classes were taught in the Studios – day

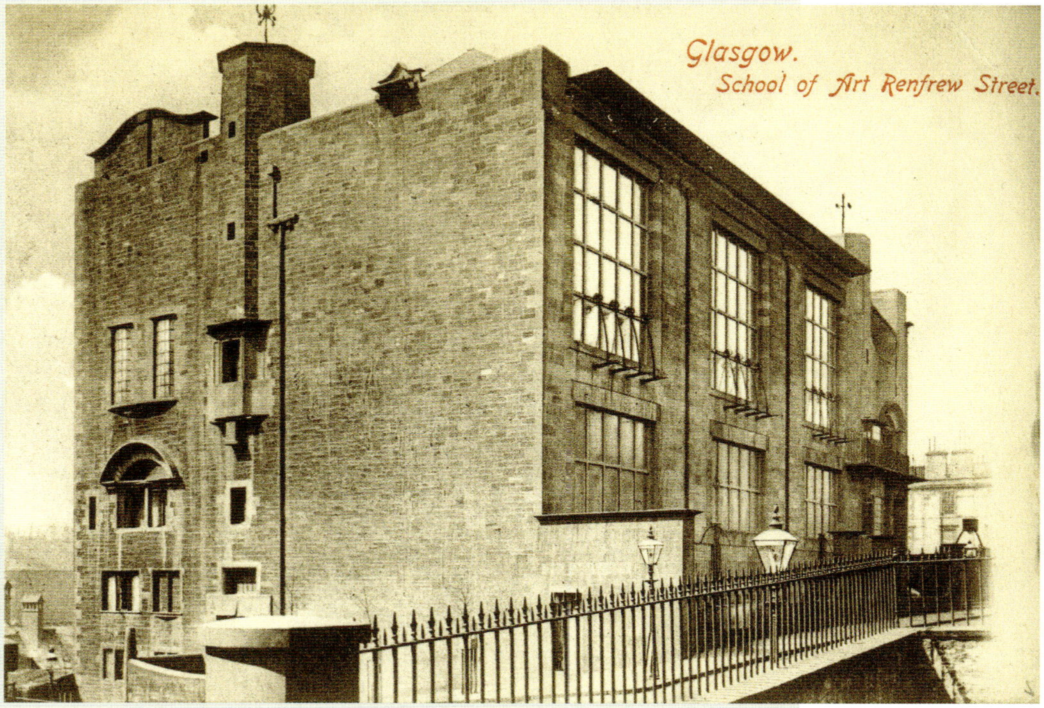

Fig. 13
Postcard showing The Glasgow School of Art, phase 1 (1897–1899), pasted into page 29, Volume 15, of William Young's Glasgow Scrapbooks.

classes for full-time students, evening classes for those already in work, with a particular focus on the industries and trades – to refine students' knowledge of materials and the understanding and application of good design. The Glasgow School of Art established workshops to teach glass staining, pottery, repoussé and precious metalwork, poster design, gesso work, wood carving and bookbinding: 'a complete cycle of technical artistic education to the city of Glasgow'.[2] This initiative responded to the findings from a country-wide and grassroots review of industrial and technical education during the mid-1880s. The over-riding ambition was to create a skilled workforce – of both men and women – to raise the quality of design and product and improve Britain's standing in the international export market.

The political desire to see more women receiving art school training was positively encouraged in Glasgow. Since the Technical Instruction Act of 1884, girls of all economic and social backgrounds – not just those attending high schools – received art instruction through the elementary education system. Such progress in educational equality coupled with the formation of the Technical Studios led ultimately to the flourishing of 'The Glasgow Girls' – our collective title for the women who studied and taught at the Art School at the time. A number of the women who graduated from the day classes at the Technical Studios successfully set up their own workshops and teaching studios and sold their work at craft fairs and art exhibitions. Such ventures were often in partnership with a sibling, leading to another title: 'The Sister Studios'. The work favoured by these ladies was relatively small scale and domestic: painted ceramics and glassware, repoussé metalwork, needlework, leatherwork and illustration. The Macdonald Sisters set up their studio in Glasgow's Hope Street in 1894–85.

At the time the Studios were established, the Art School was long ensconced in rented rooms attached to the Corporation Art Galleries on Sauchiehall Street – a good location for students to study the City's growing art collection and special exhibitions, but not for suitable studio and workshop space, especially for technical instruction. By the mid-1880s, both institutions – the Art School and the Art Galleries – were championing the need for bespoke buildings to meet their respective expansion needs. The new municipal galleries opened in Kelvingrove Park in May 1901, initially as part of Glasgow's second International Exhibition. Its rooms included displays of the Arts and Crafts with many of the key female teachers from the Technical Studios – including Jessie Newbery (1864–1948), Ann Macbeth (1875–1948) and Jessie M King (1875–1949) – exhibiting. The adjoining large temporary building was the Industrial Exhibition Hall. Here two Glasgow furnishing and decorating companies presented critically praised pavilions showcasing their New Art room designs: George Walton & Co.[3] and Wylie and Lochhead.[4]

The Art School moved into their spacious new premises two years earlier in 1899 (Fig.13). They did not move far – just up one street diagonally north onto Renfrew Street. Designed by Charles Rennie Mackintosh, the School was, for funding reasons, built in two phases: 1897–99 and 1907–09. While we may now associate all things Glasgow Style with this building, Mackintosh's architectural masterwork, it should be remembered that the important, dynamic formative years of the Glasgow Style took place when the Art School occupied those early anonymous, dark and cramped rooms.

Francis Newbery (1855–1946), the Director of The Glasgow School of Art, was the catalyst who spotted the talented, like-minded individuals at the Glasgow Art Club[5] and so introduced the English-born Macdonald sisters – day-time students – to McNair and Mackintosh, two young apprentice draughtsmen at the architectural practice of Honeyman and Keppie and evening-class students

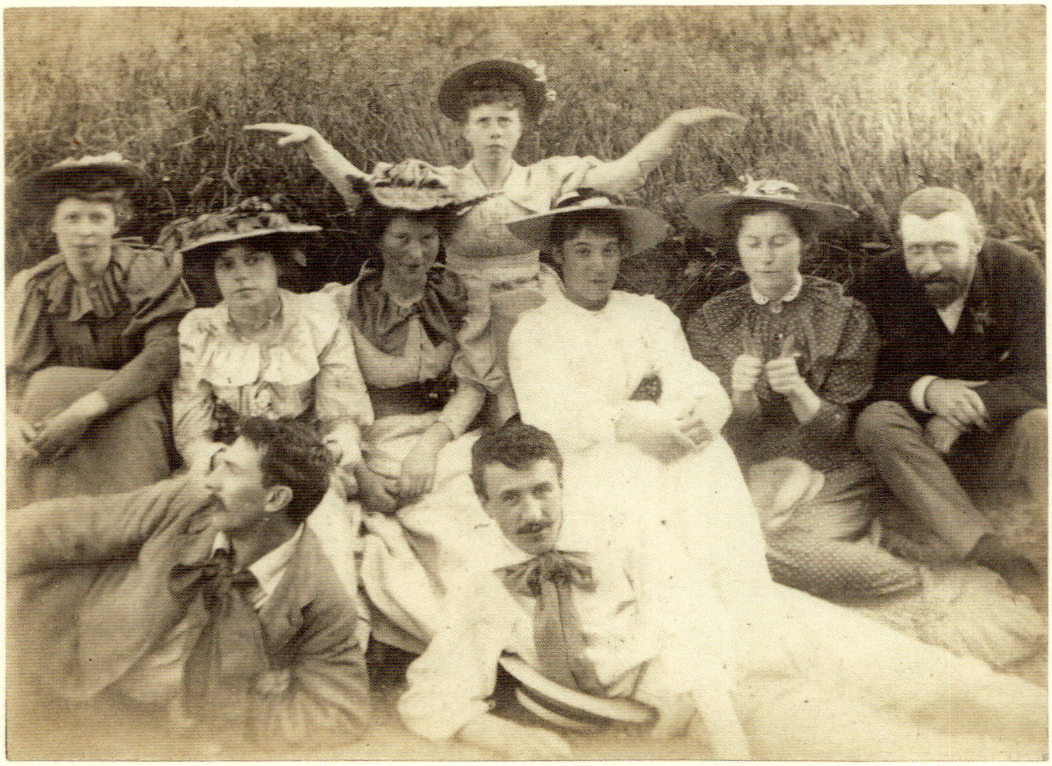

Fig.14
The Immortals at Dunure, Ayrshire, about 1893. From left to right: Back: Frances Macdonald; Middle: Margaret Macdonald, Katherine Cameron (1874–1965), Janet Aitken (1873–1941), Agnes Raeburn (1872–1955), Jessie Keppie (1868–1951), John Keppie (1862–1945); Front: James Herbert McNair and Charles Rennie Mackintosh.

at the School. The rest, as they say, is history. The Four, in turn, became 'members' of 'The Immortals' (Fig.14) – a self-titled group of artistic friends who first gathered for weekend socials in the 1893–84 academic year.

The Immortals all contributed to *The Magazine*.[6] The four volumes that survive dating between 1893 and 1896[7] are a compendium of the abstract and highly symbolic watercolours and drawings from the formative period of The Four. These works establish the organic, sinuous, taut attenuated lines, the formal organisation of the picture plane and the mysterious eerie figures and unearthly plant forms which are unmistakeably Glasgow Style. When exhibited at the School of Art Club Exhibition in November 1894 their work was dubbed 'ghoul-like' and derided as 'hideous' and 'The Spook School' by detractors. It was the Macdonald Sisters' work 'fearfully, wonderfully, weirdly "now"'[8] that was singled out for criticism. Amid this furore Francis Newbery came to the defence of his students: 'For our School then I claim it has thrown overboard the old conventions and is bravely struggling to uphold a new standard in Art... it is in the pursuit of ideals, however mystic or erratic they may seem, that the future of Art is assured.'[9] The large-scale printed poster designs by The Four and other unnamed students exhibited at *The Glasgow Institute of Fine Arts* further down Sauchiehall Street the following February proved as controversial.

It is the lithographic medium of the poster that links, parallels and contrasts the work of The Four with that of Alphonse Mucha. In the months straddling 1894 to 1895 the designs they produced set each of them on the trajectory that forged their respective artistic identities and individual styles. Deliciously, there are only four degrees of separation between these, now towering, individuals of Art Nouveau, linked by three of the most controversial and colourful artistic figures of their time: the actress Sarah Bernhardt, the playwright Oscar Wilde and the illustrator Aubrey Beardsley.[10]

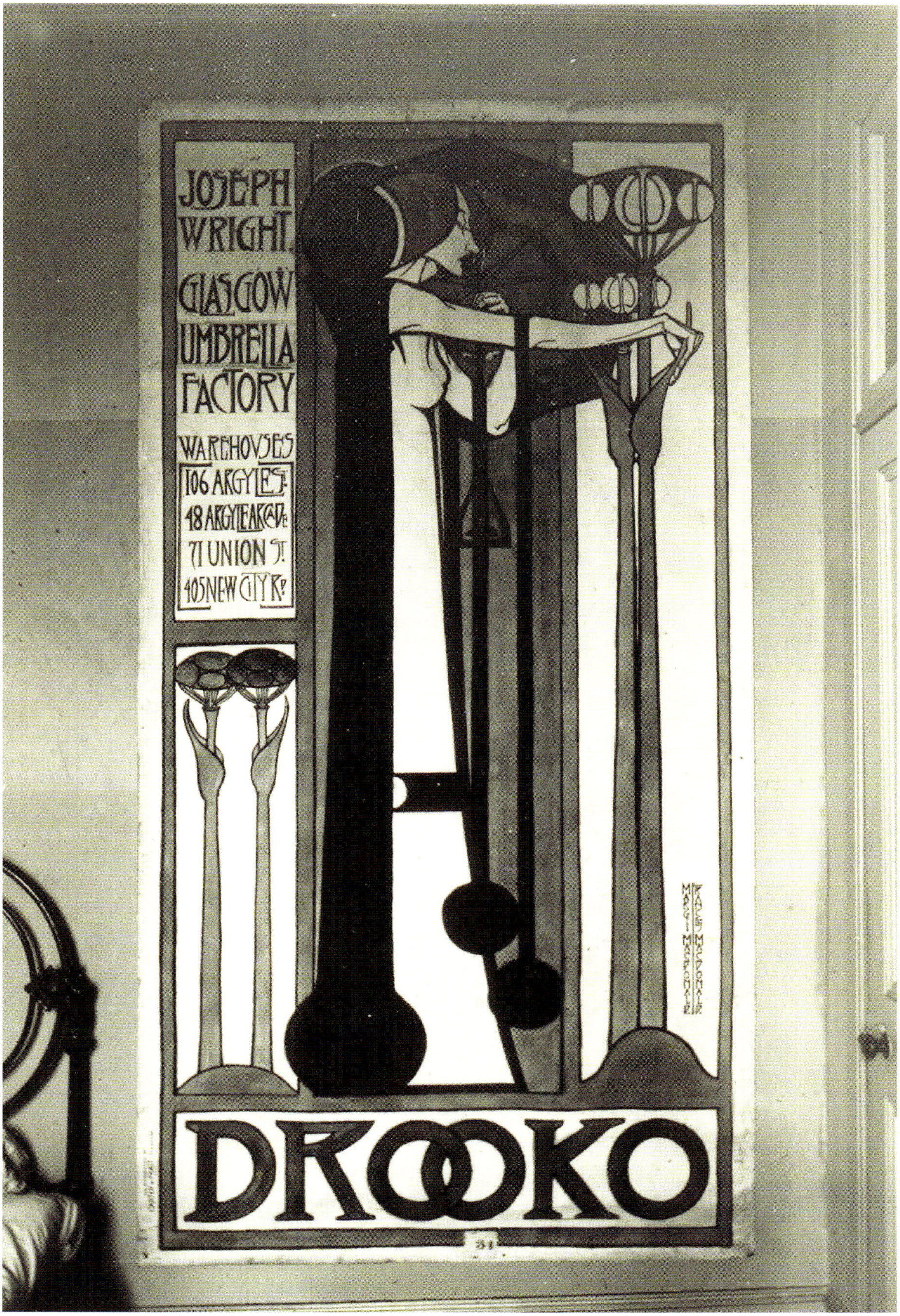

Fig.15
Photograph of a *Drooko* poster, designed by Margaret and Frances Macdonald, printed by Carter and Pratt, Glasgow, about 1894–5.

Mucha's career-starting poster was for Sarah Bernhardt's production of *Gismonda* (see p.22), designed in 1894 for the performances of January 1895. It portrays feminine grace personified, with an exotic opulence of pattern and detail. The Macdonald Sisters' poster design for *Drooko*, a Glasgow umbrella manufacturing company, designed and exhibited around that same time[11] (Fig.15) could not be more different. Dramatic, severe and slightly unnerving, this poster compositionally and stylistically shows the clear influence of Beardsley's androgynous, even menacing, black and white figurative illustrations for the English translation of Oscar Wilde's *Salomé*, published in 1894.[12]

Paris was considered ten years ahead of London in its approach to poster design, and London ten years ahead of Glasgow.[13] In January 1895 the Glasgow art dealer Alexander Reid (1854–1928) – a champion of the French Impressionists – hosted a poster exhibition at his city centre gallery La Société des Beaux Arts at 124 St Vincent Street, Glasgow. Parisian designs – now classics to our eyes – by Henri de Toulouse-Lautrec, Jules Chéret and Théophile Steinlen (1859–1923) – were displayed alongside British artists including Beardsley and Dudley Hardy (1867–1922). 'The Misses Macdonald' were also exhibited – 'the only "new" poster designers who have yet arisen in Glasgow, and whose rather weird adaptation of the human form to decorative purposes at the recent exhibition of the School of Art will be remembered.'[14] It is likely the Macdonalds were represented here by *Drooko*. These 'ghoulish' posters by The Four would be exhibited and published alongside works by their French and English contemporaries during the next few years.[15]

Drooko provides insight to the Macdonalds' grounding in plant study, received as part of their art school training. The tall stylised plant forms beside the figure are derived from study of the *Umbelliferae* plant family – aromatic plants with hollow stems and the multi-spoke flat-topped flower heads – including fennel, hemlock and giant hogweed.[16] Knowledge of the plants' seeds is also incorporated decoratively into the design. The Four devised a distinctive approach to the application, and symbolic application, of plant forms to their designs, often showing all stages of plant growth – from germination, to flowering, to seed – all within the same composition. As the years progressed the abstraction and symbolism of these integral organic forms became more sophisticated.

This is seen to great effect in Mackintosh's large-scale and dramatically abstract poster for the *Scottish Musical Review*, 1896 (see p.75). The source sketch, a drawing titled *Autumn*, dates to November 1894.[17] The composition of these designs can be formally compared with Mucha's *Gismonda*. Both designers employ the focal point of a halo to frame the head of the central figure.[18] Both use a raised ground line for the figure to stand upon. Below this line Mackintosh adds a sprouting seed from which his plant-human hybrid figure grows. The proportional divisions and arrangement of the pictorial plane, the relationship of this large, framing ring to the borders of the design and the overall figurative composition is striking. Did the two men have a common source or were they responding to ideas in circulation at that time from which they both drew to create their visual language – the study of geometry and proportion, the art of Japan, Aestheticism or religious iconography, perhaps? We know through the accounts of Mackintosh's close friend James Herbert McNair that a pastime in the architect's office was to place tracing paper over illustrations of interest and then improve upon and evolve the original design with their own lines. Through such beginnings – an excellent exercise for the study of proportional harmony – the elegant simplicity of *Glasgow Style* emerged.[19]

In early 1895 the reaction of the general public in Paris and in Glasgow to these two styles of poster could not be more different! In Paris the public

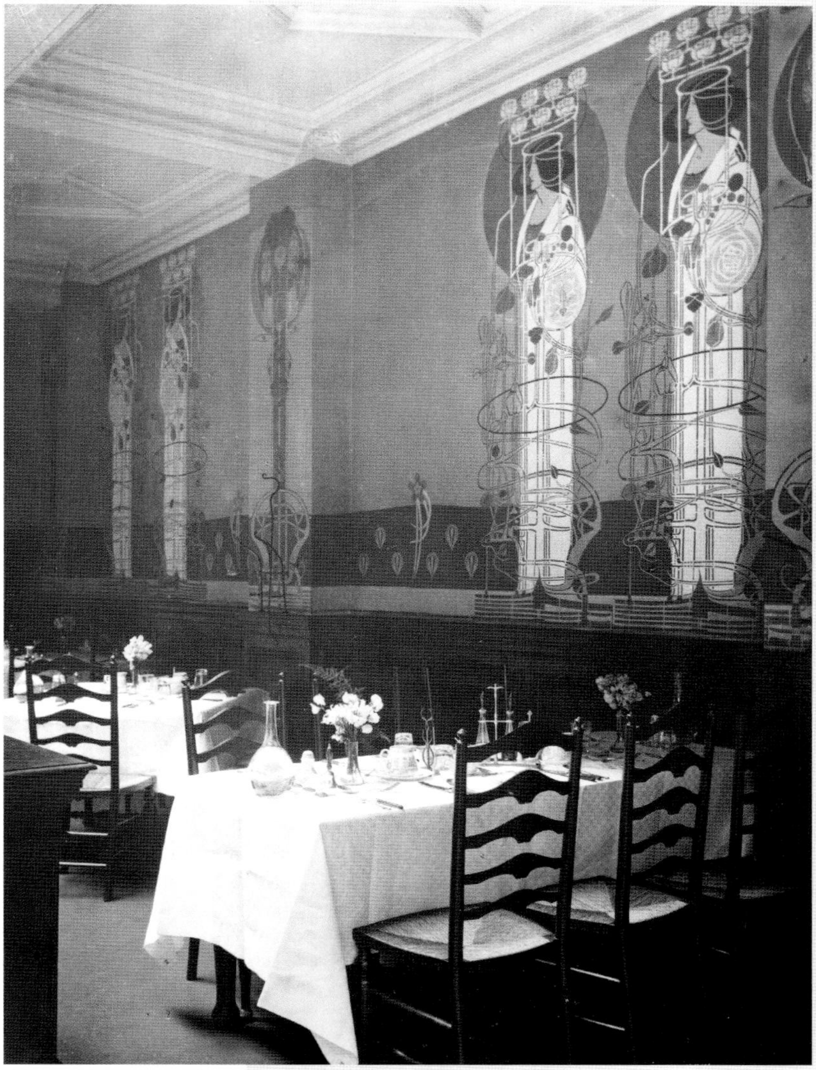

Fig.16
Photograph of the Luncheon Room at Miss Cranston's Buchanan Street Tearooms, mural by Charles Rennie Mackintosh, furnishings by George Walton, about 1897.

clamoured to obtain copies of *Gismonda*. Some people bribed the poster hangers and others stripped posters from the hoardings.[20] In Glasgow when The Four exhibited their posters at The Glasgow Institute of Fine Arts exhibition the reaction was largely hostile and the work described as 'ghoul-like'. One review commented how 'It has caused the hair of the Philistine to curl and provoked that amiable personage to the use of "language" '.[21]

There were critical comments in the letters pages of the local newspapers, and even humorous, mocking poems: 'One day as I gazed at a hoarding – My soul was filled with dread – For I looked on an Art School Poster – A poster comprised of a head – With lines attached that seemed to fall – In somewhat aimless ways – It was the crazy Aubrey Beardsley – No – the Aubrey Beardsley craze.'[22] The effects of alcohol were equated regularly with the mental upset caused by looking at these works. All the more ironic given the significant role the Temperance Movement-associated Glasgow tearooms would play in Charles Rennie Mackintosh's design career.

Miss Cranston's Buchanan Street tearooms became the first permanent home for these Glasgow Style figures of bill-poster proportions. Around the time of Mackintosh's participation in the 5th Exhibition of the Arts and Crafts Exhibition Society, London, in 1896, Miss Catherine Cranston (1849–1934) commissioned him to design mural schemes for three floors of her new tearooms, including the Luncheon Room (Fig.16). This frieze showed a procession of Japanese-attired Art Nouveau ladies with billows of black hair emerging from rose-briars. 'The Spook School' imagery lingered in the form of sinister eyes peering from behind tall totemic trees. The architect Edwin Lutyens (1869–1944), a frequent visitor to the building after it opened on 5th May 1897, described the decoration as 'all very elaborately simple on very new school High Art Lines. The result is gorgeous! and a wee bit vulgar!' The latter remark possibly reserved for Mackintosh's top floor stencil scheme for the gentleman's smoking room which overtly drew on 'Beardslian' imagery: a sad looking moon – the face taken directly from *The Woman in the Moon* in *Salomé* – and entwined decorative lines of stencilling that occasionally resembled an erect phallus.[24]

The work by The Four softened as they married and moved into the 20th century. The McNairs relocated to Liverpool, The Mackintoshs stayed in Glasgow. Though less controversial, the figure continued to play an important symbolic focal role, particularly in Mackintosh's furniture and interior designs. Only two further Glasgow tearoom interiors – the Room de Luxe at the Willow Tea Rooms, 1903,

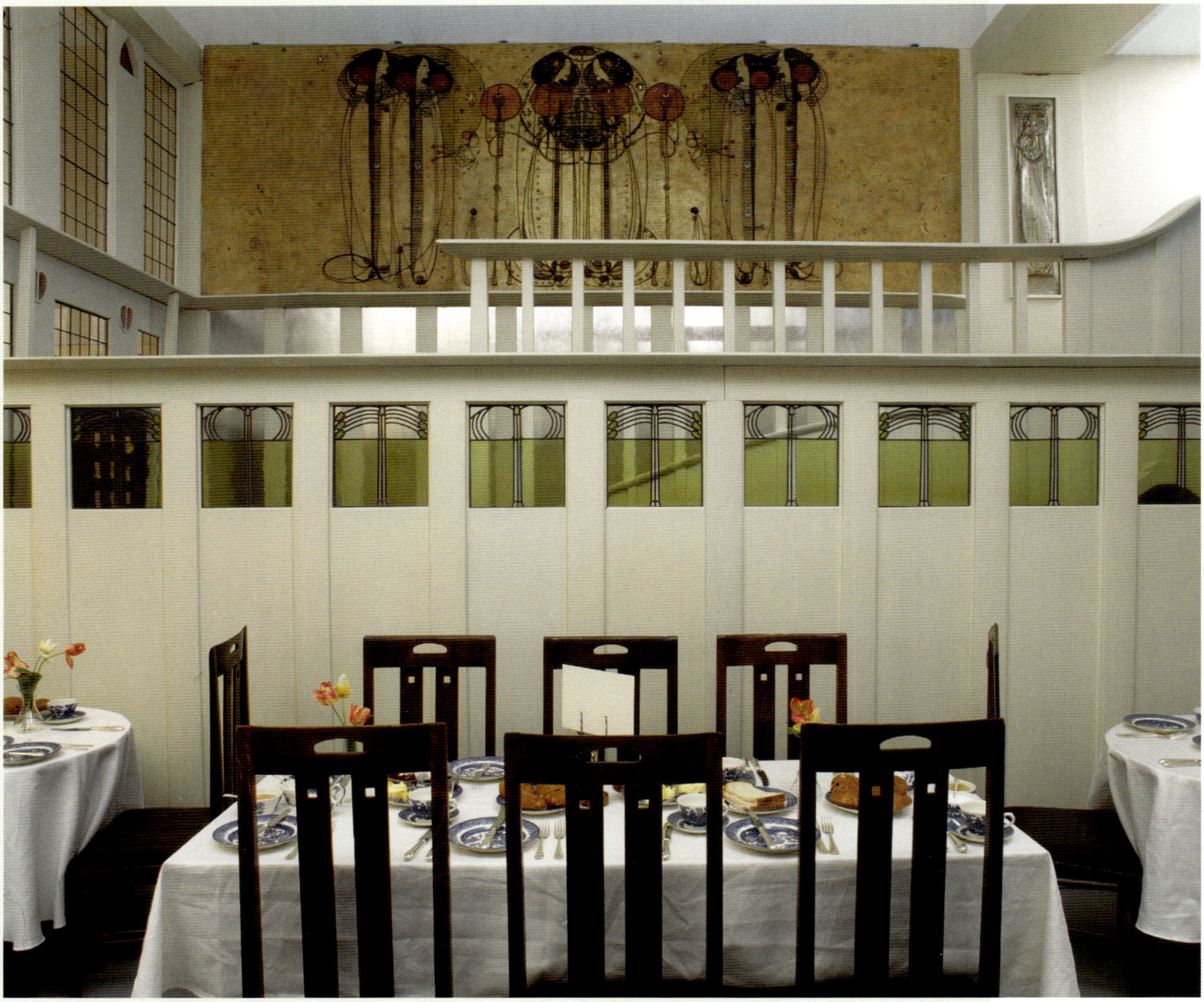

and The Ladies Luncheon Room at Ingram Street, 1900–01, (Fig.17) have a figurative focus within their design. Here large gesso panels provide the symbolic focus and narrative of the rooms. Only one, *The Wassail*, is made by Mackintosh's hand; the others, *The May Queen* and *Willowwood*, are by Margaret Macdonald, his wife. The humans are gentler, feminine. Sometimes their bodies and clothes are formed merely by an abstract tangle of looping lines and curves – a device drawn from early ideas in Beardsley but now distinctly forged as the Mackintoshs' own.

Through architecture and interior design, Mackintosh pursues his preoccupation with geometry and proportional and spatial harmony. But look through his oeuvre and you see that the underlying construction, organisation, motif and line of those posters by The Four from the mid 1890s are, in effect, the personal manifesto that continues to inform his beautiful, harmonious language and symbolism of increasingly complex three-dimensional forms for the rest of his design career.

Fig.17
The Ladies Luncheon Room, 1900–1 from the Ingram Street Tearooms looking across to *The Wassail* gesso panel by Charles Rennie Mackintosh. Room conserved and restored by Glasgow Museums, 1994–6.

NOTES

(1) *The English House* by Hermann Muthesius. Wasmuth, Berlin, 1904. First English edition edited by Dennis Sharp, translated by Janet Seligman, Lockwood Staples, London, 1979, p.52.
(2) *Glasgow School of Art*, Annual Report, 1892/3, p.7.
(3) George Walton (1867–1933) ran his own interior decoration business, with craftsmen's workshops in Glasgow and showrooms in Glasgow, York and London.
(4) Wylie and Lochhead were cabinetmakers, upholsters and an interior decorating company – for ships, commerce and homes with a five floor showroom on Buchanan Street. Their 1901 Exhibition pavilion displayed a suite of four modern interiors, the product of three designers: John Ednie (1876–1934), George Logan (1866–1939), and Ernest Archibald Taylor (1874–1951).
(5) Francis Newbery, formed the Club immediately after starting as Headmaster in 1885. He wanted to encourage the cross-fertilisation of ideas between students, graduates and practising artists and professionals. The Club allowed free-thinking and creativity as a break from the rigours imposed by the main curriculum.
(6) *The Magazine*, edited by Lucy Raeburn (1869–1952), was like a homemade *The Yellow Book*, the significant Aesthetic Movement publication that printed poetry, short stories and artworks between April 1894–early 1897. *The Yellow Book's* 10th Volume, 1896, published work by the Macdonald Sisters, McNair and a number of the other *Magazine* contributors.
(7) Collection: Glasgow School of Art.
(8) Glasgow School of Art Cuttings Book, The Mitchell Archives, p.48.
(9) *Glasgow Evening News*, 16th November 1894.
(10) Wilde wrote *Salomé* for Sarah Bernhardt. It was to premier in London in 1892, but was banned on the grounds that it was illegal to portray Biblical characters on the British stage. The play eventually premiered in Paris in 1896 with Bernhardt in the lead whilst Wilde was in jail.
(11) Only photographs survive of this poster, Collection: Hunterian Art Gallery, Glasgow University, GLAHA 52932 and 52933.
(12) *J'ai baisé ta bouche*, the frontispiece for *Salomé* was published in a feature on Beardsley in the first issue of *The Studio*, April 1893. Ten months later in 1894 *The Peacock Skirt* was published in a review of Beardsley's illustrations for Wilde's play.
(13) 'Extra Mural Art. Exhibition of Posters'. *Glasgow Evening News*, 24 January 1895, p.2.
(14) Ibid. It has not been possible to determine if Mucha's *Gismonda* poster was exhibited at Reid's exhibition. If included it was not mentioned in reviews.
(15) Their posters were included in the first exhibition of Siegfried Bing's Salon de L'Art Nouveau, Paris, opening 26th December 1895 catalogue entry 627 'affiches anglaises' – fellow exhibitors included Beardsley; Edward Bella's second exhibition of posters at the Royal Aquarium, London, 1896 (see Pamela Robertson, *Doves and Dreams – The Art of Frances Macdonald and James Herbert McNair* p.35); and published in *The Poster, An Illustrated Monthly Chronicle*, July 1899 p.286–7.
(16) The reverse of photograph GLAHA 52933 has written in Margaret's hand: 'Poster for umbrellas/ 'invention' showing the umbilliferae the source of its construction'.
(17) The watercolour sketch *Autumn* appears in the third surviving edition of *The Magazine*, November 1894, p.5. Collection: The Glasgow School of Art.
(18) The Glasgow illustrator and designer Jessie M. King also frequently added a nimbus device around the heads of her figures.
(19) *Charles Rennie Mackintosh and the Modern Movement*, Thomas Howarth, Routledge and Kegan Paul Ltd, 1952/1977, p.18–19.
(20) *Alphonse Mucha – The Message and the Man*, Ronald F Lipp in *Alphonse Mucha*, Mucha Ltd /Malcolm Saunders Publishing Ltd, 2000, p.13.
(21) *Ghouls and Gas Pipes: Public Reaction to Early Work of 'The Four'*, Elizabeth Bird, *Scottish Art Review* 1975 p.13–16, 28; citing *Glasgow Evening News* February 1st 1895.
(22) *The Poster's Mission', or 'Why I signed the pledge*, by 'Jeer Cebone', *Quiz*, February 21st 1895
(23) 17 June 1897, *The Letters of Edwin Lutyens to his Wife Lady Emily*, C.Percy and J.Ridley (editors), Harper Collins, 1985, p.49
(24) Four stencil cards for the Buchanan Street tearoom schemes are in Glasgow Museums collection: E.1984.32.5-8

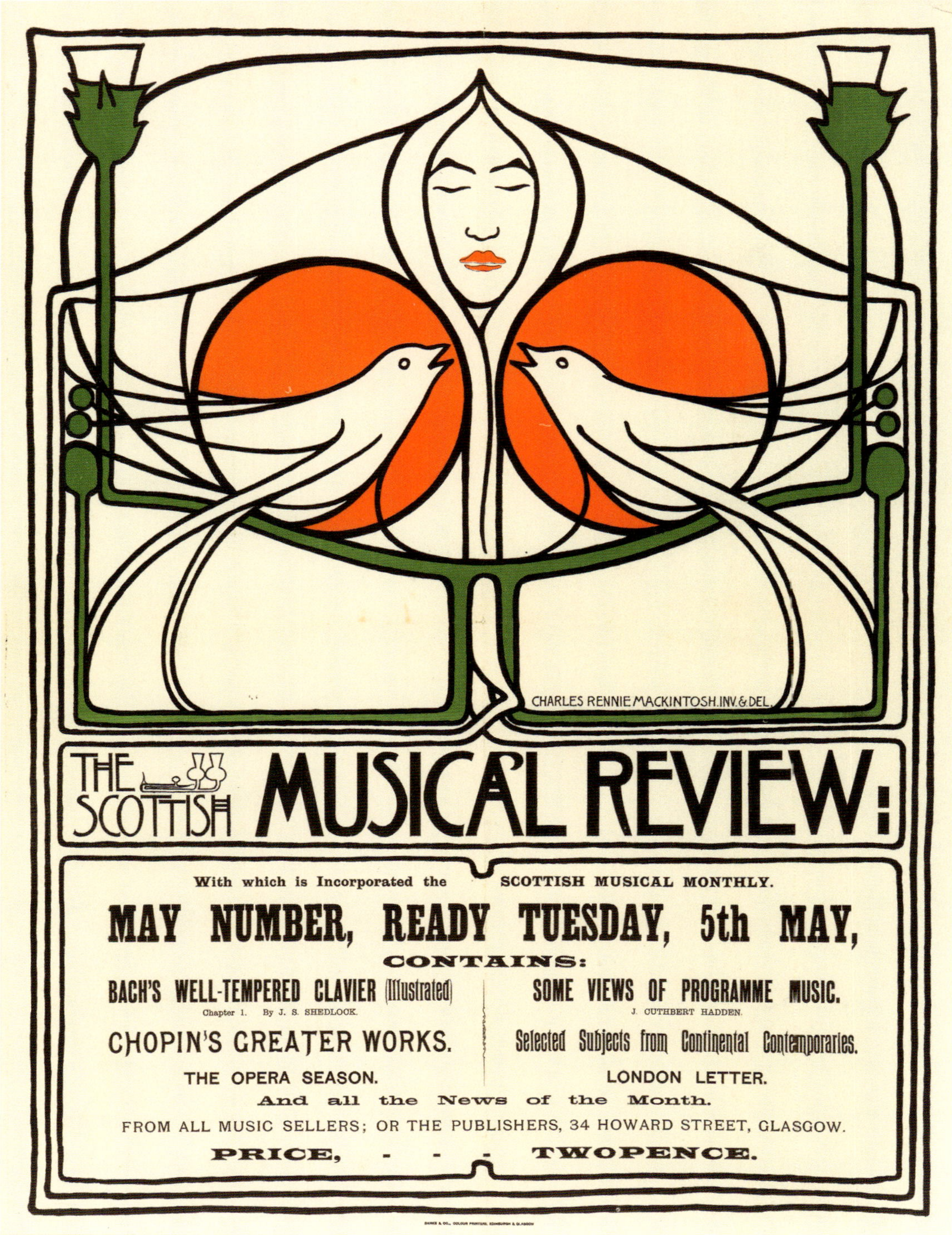

CHARLES RENNIE MACKINTOSH (1868–1928)
POSTER FOR *THE SCOTTISH MUSICAL REVIEW* (MAY 1896 EDITION)
1896
Planographic, lithographic, print on paper
57.6 x 45.1
Given to Glasgow Museums by Alice Talwin Morris, 1939
PR.1977.13.aj

The Scottish Musical Review was a short-lived and modest musical journal launched in October 1894. Published in Glasgow, it aimed to be 'thoroughly representative of the progress of musical art in Scotland.' This is one of two publicity poster designs Mackintosh produced for the title. Surprisingly, his avant-garde designs did not transfer to the *Review's* artwork.

Mackintosh began to experiment with the possibilities of poster design in 1894. These early graphic works establish his mathematical approach to the sub-dividing of a two-dimensional plane for decorative purposes. The kinks in the woman's hair just above the periodical's title and the thistle heads are the only asymmetrical elements in the design.

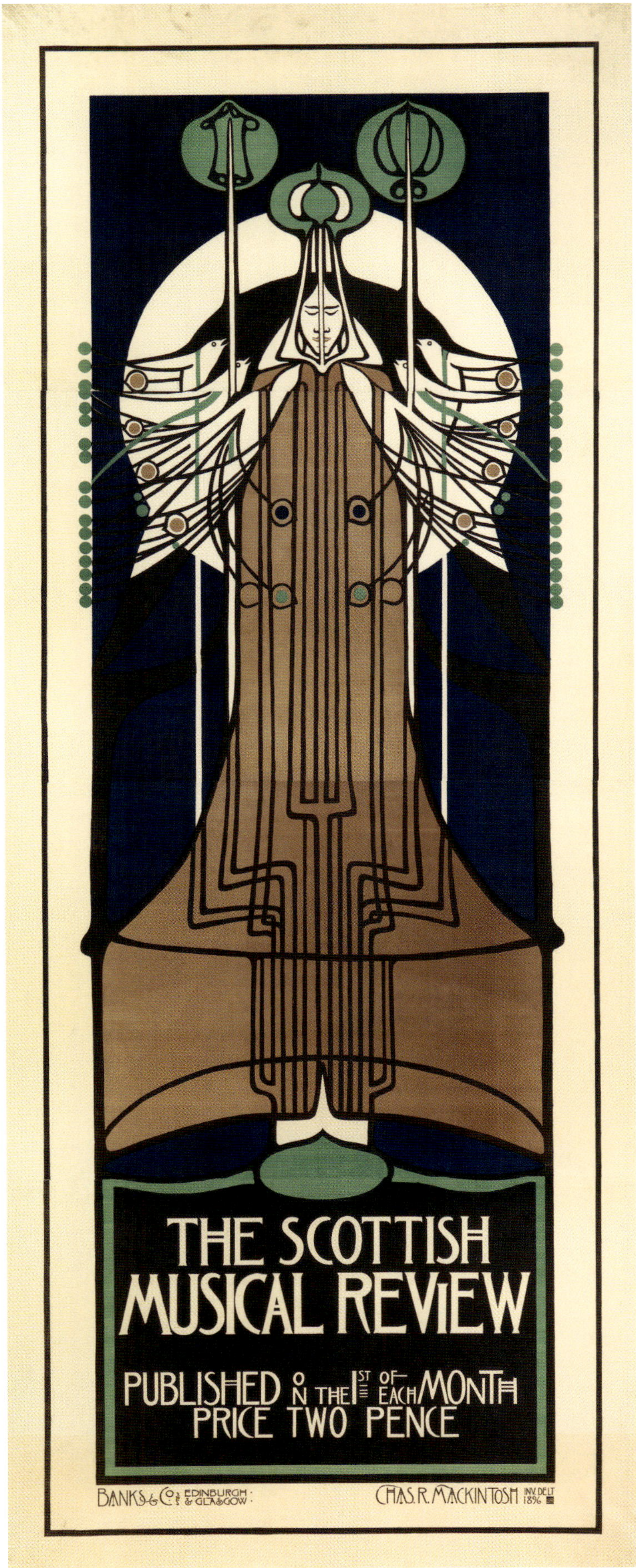

CHARLES RENNIE MACKINTOSH (1868–1928)
POSTER FOR *THE SCOTTISH MUSICAL REVIEW*
1896
Planographic, lithographic, print on four joined sheets of paper
230 × 85.8
Given to Glasgow Museums by Alice Talwin Morris, 1939
PR.1977.13.ar

At the centre of this large poster is the suggestion of an androgynous human figure enclosed within a growing plant, the head set within a stylised flower against a full moon. The human emerging from a tangle of plant forms is a preoccupation for Mackintosh in 1896. It is the focus of his drawing *Part Seen Imagined Part* exhibited that year in London, a work he subsequently developed into a large mural for the Buchanan Street tearooms. The green circular forms at the top of the poster resemble the metalwork Mackintosh would soon design for the railings of The Glasgow School of Art.

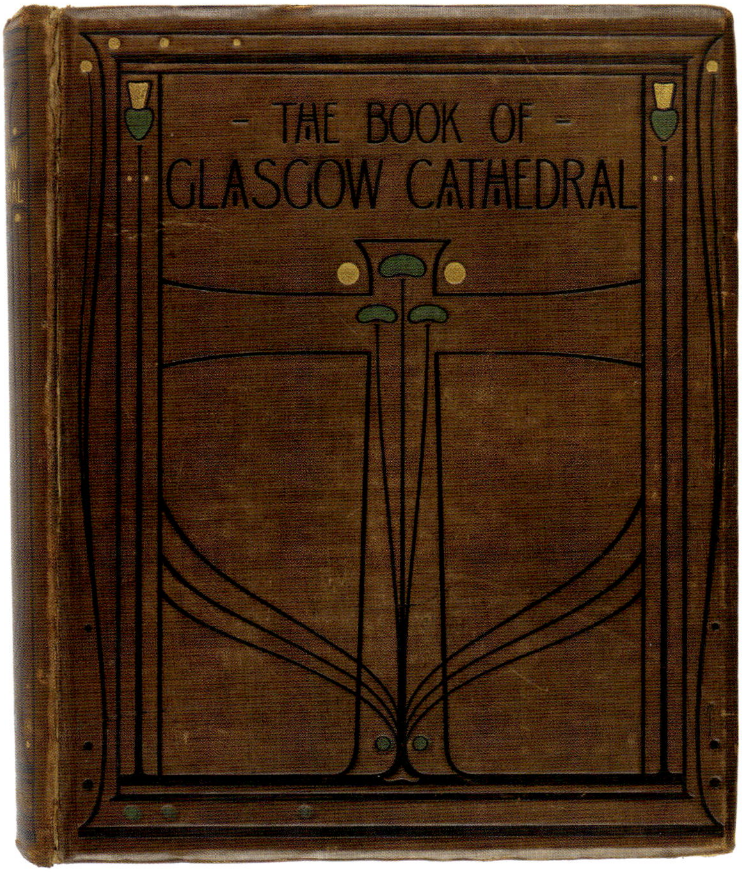

TALWIN MORRIS (1865–1911)
COVER DESIGN FOR *THE BOOK OF GLASGOW CATHEDRAL*
PUBLISHED IN 1898 (EDITION 360/1000)
Printed and debossed buckram hardcover
32 x 27 x 5.3
GML.2011.9

Talwin Morris, the artistic director for Glasgow publishers Blackie and Son, shared his friend Mackintosh's sensibility towards 'New Art' lines. The arrangement of this cover possesses many of the proportional harmonies and taut lines evident in Mackintosh's *Scottish Musical Review* posters. Morris's distinctively simple and stylish book cover designs helped spread the Glasgow Style around the world.

The book's subject matter is cleverly referenced within the design: the crucifix is overlaid with a three-headed and leaved plant form symbolising the Holy Trinity. The thistle – the emblematic flower of Scotland – appears in the inner border, its rigid stem offset by the sinuous curve of the gold-topped reed in the outer margins.

JESSIE MARION KING (1875–1949)
THE DANCE OF THE WHITE ROSE
c.1901
Ink and pencil on vellum
27.6 x 28.7
Given to Glasgow Museums by Messrs T & R Annan & Son, 1960
PR.1960.13.aa

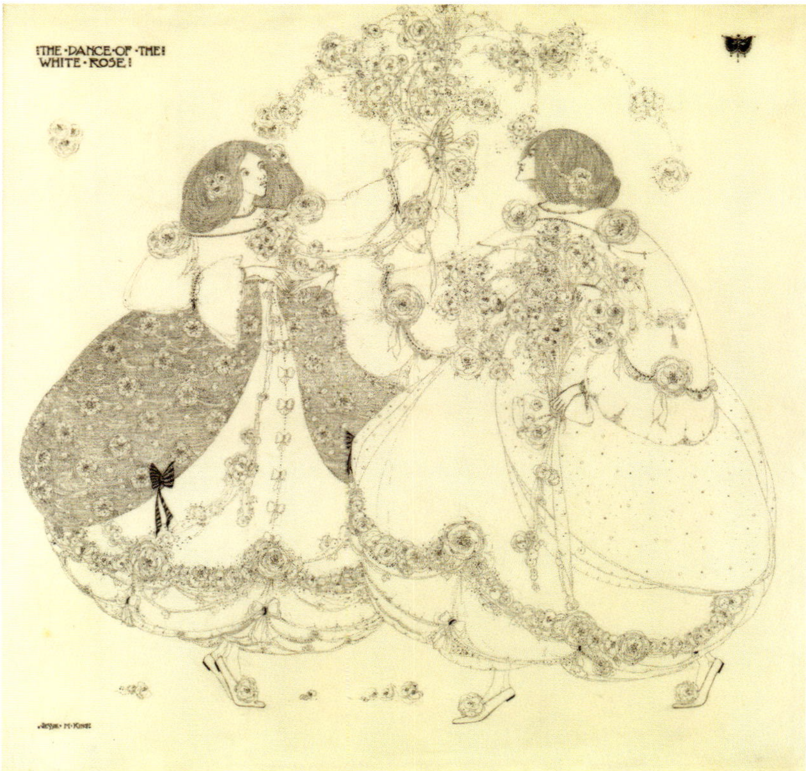

King's fine pen-work illustrations are clever contradictions. They have the appearance of being rapidly executed but close examination shows the detailing is painstakingly applied. Here most lines are formed from minute dots and small circles; it is only the faces, hands and feet that are drawn with a continuous line. The effect throws forward those areas where black is more heavily applied – the ribbons, bows and heels. These act like visual anchors within the swirling, ethereal, composition.

The inclusion of the decorated butterfly at the top right is unusual. Possibly King was making a deliberate reference to the signature of James Abbott McNeill Whistler (1834–1903) and, through that, his *Symphony in White* compositions.

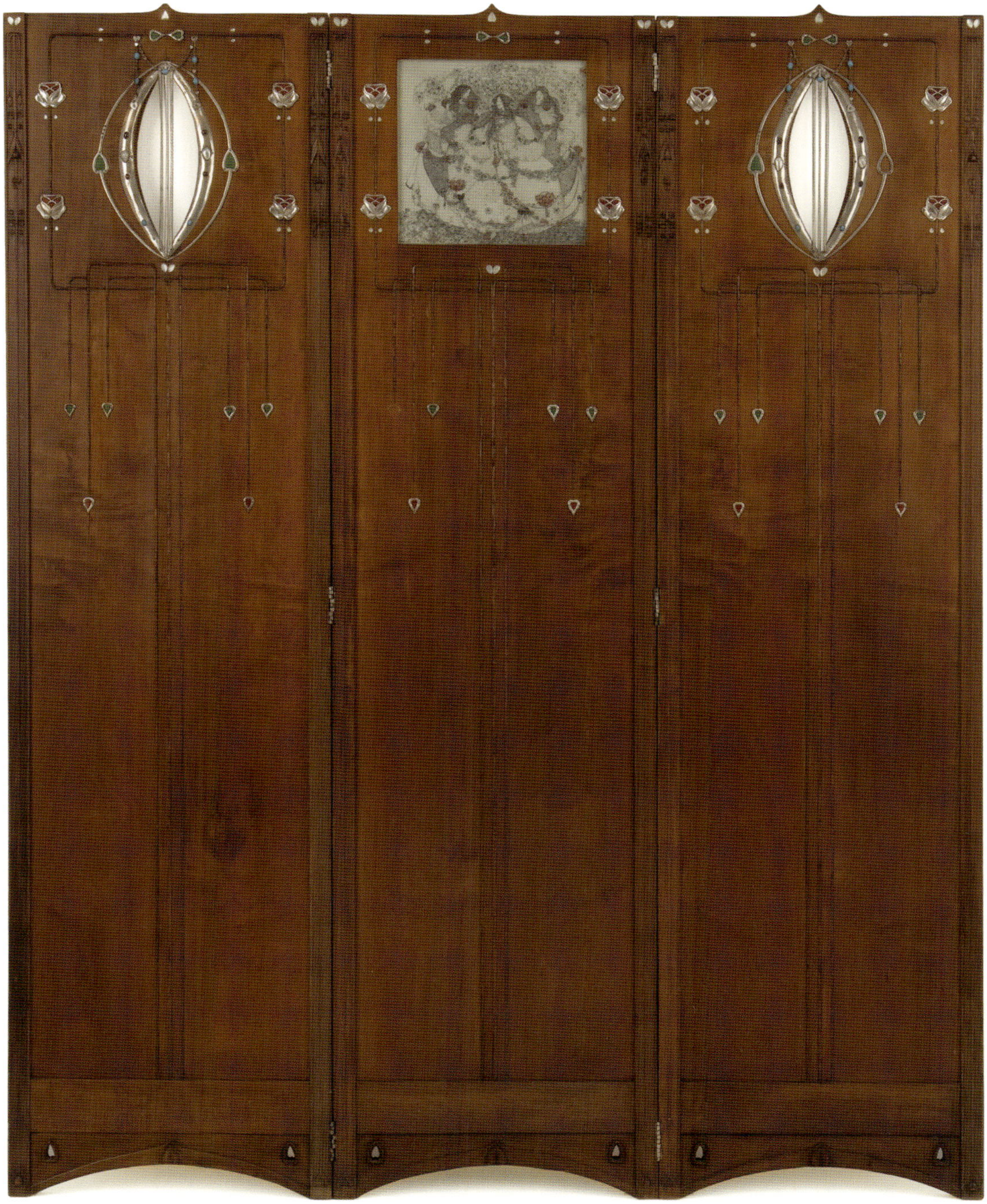

DESIGNED BY GEORGE LOGAN (1866–1939) FOR WYLIE & LOCHHEAD, GLASGOW
FOLDING SCREEN
1901–1902
Satin walnut, silver, mother of pearl, turquoise, red amethyst, white stone, leather, metal, glass, ink, watercolour and vellum
172.1 x 137.2
Purchased with the assistance of the Fraser Family Trust
E.1986.52

This folding screen was exhibited in Turin in 1902. It wears semi-precious embellishments around its three head-height panels in the same way that a woman wears jewellery around her face and neck. There are two ovals for the user to look through, though each silver-framed opening is teasingly barred by three silver vertical rods. Set into the centre panel is an ink and watercolour drawing on vellum entitled *The Princesses of the Red Rose* by illustrator Jessie Marion King (cf. p.76 bottom). The roses and garlands surounding her women are referenced through the decorative details applied to the screen. Leather roses, mother-of-pearl hearts and carved fuschia flowers enrich the screen's surface textures.

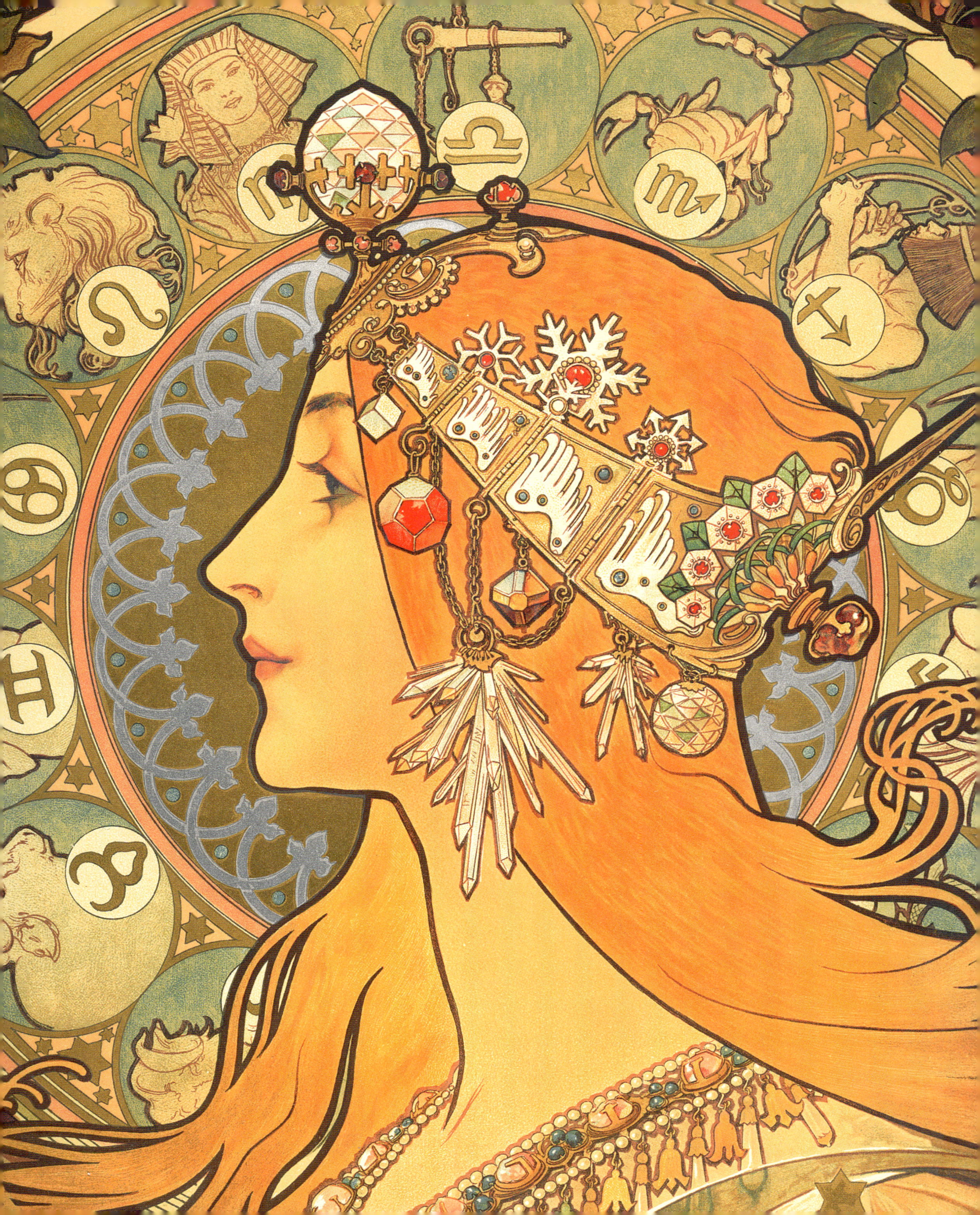

II

LE STYLE MUCHA – A VISUAL MESSAGE

The advent of Modernism brought revolutionary changes to the concept of art in Mucha's time. During his residency in Paris between 1887 and 1906, the French capital, which was also at that time the artistic capital of the world, saw a succession of new artistic doctrines from Neo-Impressionism to Cubism in parallel with the international vogue of the Art Nouveau style. Accordingly the traditional notion of 'beauty' was also challenged and expanded to embrace new ideas. In such a time of change Mucha was one who pursued the unchanging, universal value of art. Mucha wrote:

> *'Art cannot be new. The notion of "modern" art as a passing fashion is an insult. Art is as eternal as man's progress and its function is to guide man's path with light. Therefore art is in a continuous state of development and is always a few steps ahead of humanity'.*

It was Mucha's belief that a beautiful work of art – 'the symbol of goodness' – would help elevate public morale and improve the quality of people's lives, eventually creating a better society. In 1896 when Champenois (see p. 21) conceived the idea of decorative panels or *panneaux décoratifs* (see p. 12) primarily to maximise the business potential of Mucha's designs, Mucha viewed this enterprise as a great opportunity to carry out his artistic mission – to disseminate art among ordinary people as 'a democratic art form'. Mucha's decorative panels were printed on stronger paper than that used for advertising or even on silk satin for collectors' deluxe editions (see *The Arts*), which could then be framed for hanging or used to make folding screens (see *The Seasons*) to embellish ordinary people's households.

For the decorative panels Mucha chose universal themes such as the seasons, the flowers and the times of the day. Celebrating the poetic beauty and the harmonious working of nature, these themes were aesthetically pleasing and inspirational. Mucha created a dynamic tension within a consistent rectangular format, with the graceful forms of female bodies and sinuous lines from nature, often combined with prominent halos or horseshoe motifs, intended to guide the viewer's eyes to focal points in compositions – messages of beauty.

Mucha's designs for decorative panels were recycled in a variety of forms such as calendars, postcards or even as decorative objects and reproduced in numerous art magazines both in France and abroad, thus disseminating *le style Mucha* internationally. Among the earliest to introduce Mucha's decorative panels outside France was *The Poster: An Illustrated Monthly Chronicle*, a London magazine founded in 1898, which reproduced *The Flowers* (see pp. 84–85) and *Zodiac* in its inaugural year.

> *'The marvelous poem of the human body... and the music of lines and colours emanating from flowers, leaves and fruits are the most obvious teachers of our eyes and taste.'*
>
> *Alphonse Mucha*

ZODIAC
(detail)
see p. 80

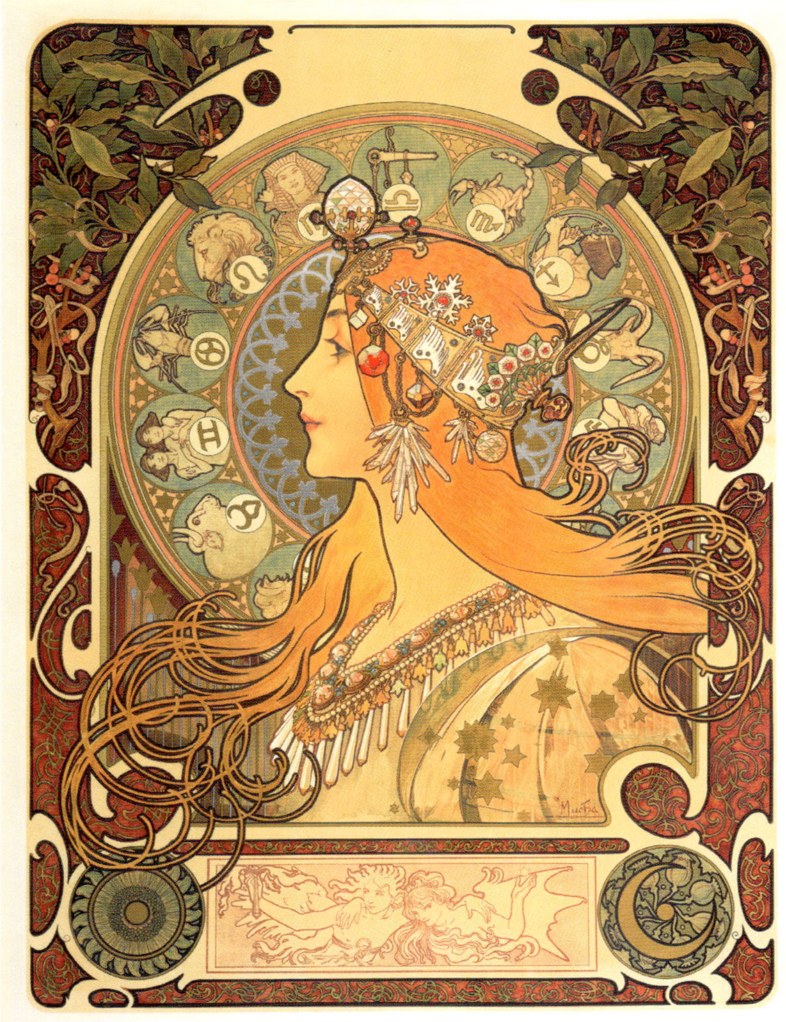

ZODIAC
1896
Colour lithograph
65.7 x 48.2

Featuring the striking profile of a majestic woman against a prominent halo, this design was originally made as a company calendar for Champenois for the year 1897. The theme – the harmonious working of the universe – is reflected in the twelve signs of the zodiac, which are incorporated in the circular band with decorative motifs featuring hexagrams – mystic symbols frequently appearing in Mucha's designs. The distritution rights of this design were soon bought by Léon Deschamps (see p.39) who sold it under the name of his magazine *La Plume* as a calender and a decorative panel as shown here.

SLAVIC ELEMENTS IN MUCHA'S STYLE

Mucha drew inspiration for his designs from the ornamental features of a wide variety of historical cultures ranging from Celtic, Greek, Gothic and Rococo to Islamic, Jewish, Egyptian and Japanese. On the whole, however, Mucha's style evolved organically from his Slavic roots. From 1896 onwards he consciously integrated traditional elements from his homeland into his designs. These manifested themselves as Slavic dresses worn by the subjects, floral and other botanical motifs inspired by Moravian folk arts and crafts, prominent halos evoking Byzantine icons (in Mucha's view Byzantine art was the home of Slavic civilisation), and also the curves and geometric patterns familiar in Czech Baroque churches.

RÊVERIE
1898
Colour lithograph
72.7 x 55.2

Like *Zodiac*, this design was originally made as an image for an in-house calendar for Champenois but its great popularity led to its swift publication as a decorative panel as seen here. The blank spaces at the top were originally used to show the company name and address as wel as the year designation '1898'. The composition features a dreamy young woman in a beautifully embroidered Slavic dress, leafing through the pages of a decorative design book. Her figure is set against a prominent halo – a symbol of universal harmony according to Mucha – which is decorated with an elaborate floral pattern.

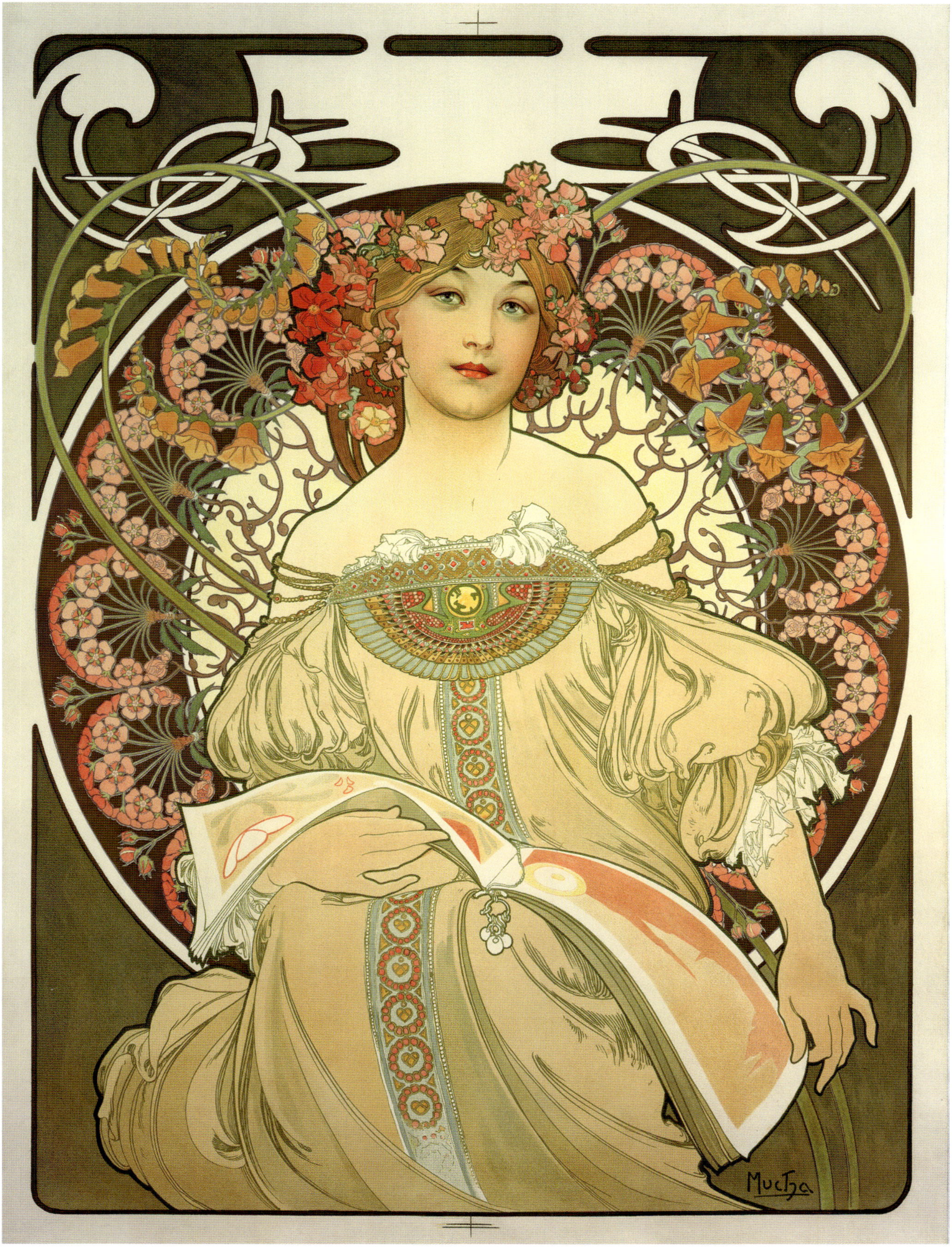
Mucha

THE SEASONS
1896
Colour lithograph
54 x 71.4

The first of Mucha's series of decorative panels was *The Seasons.* Depicting a popular and classic theme, Mucha personified the seasons as nymph-like women in a series of four panels. Each one captures the mood of the season – innocent Spring, sultry Summer, fruitful Autumn and frosty Winter – against a corresponding seasonal landscape; as a whole together they represent the harmonious cycle of nature. The great success of this series led to many variants, including this design incorporating all four panels into a single ornamental frame.

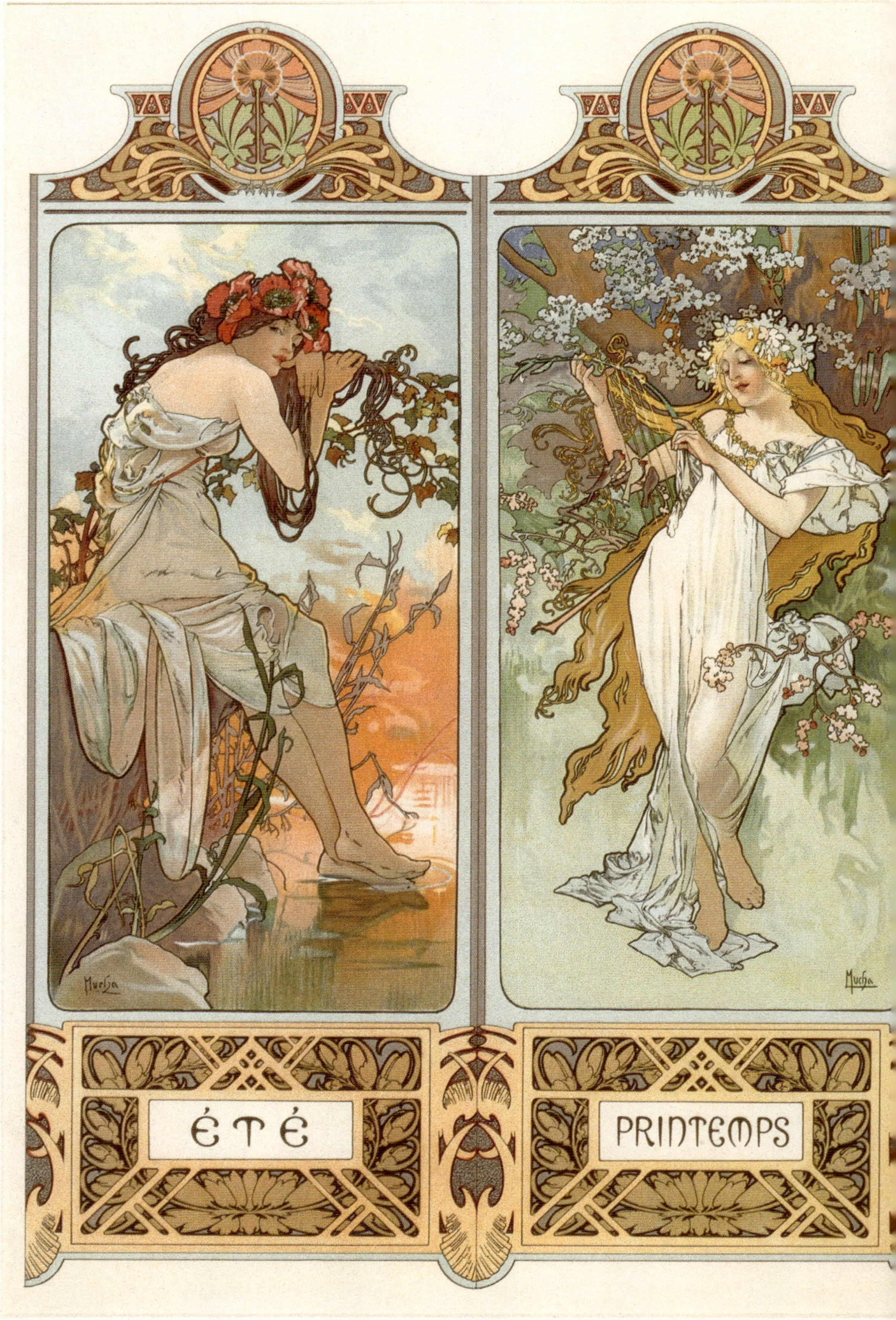

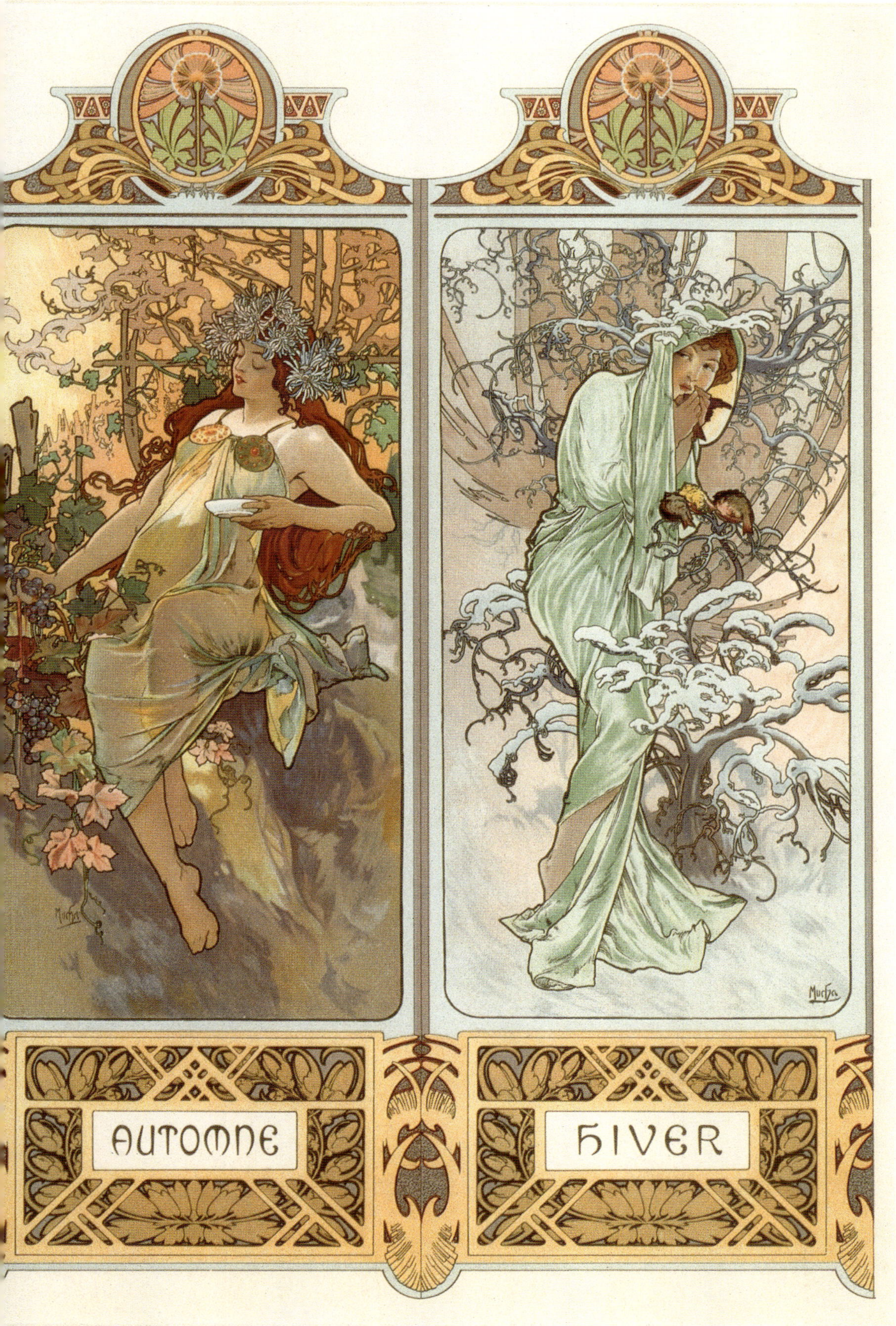
AUTOMNE
HIVER
Mucha
Mucha

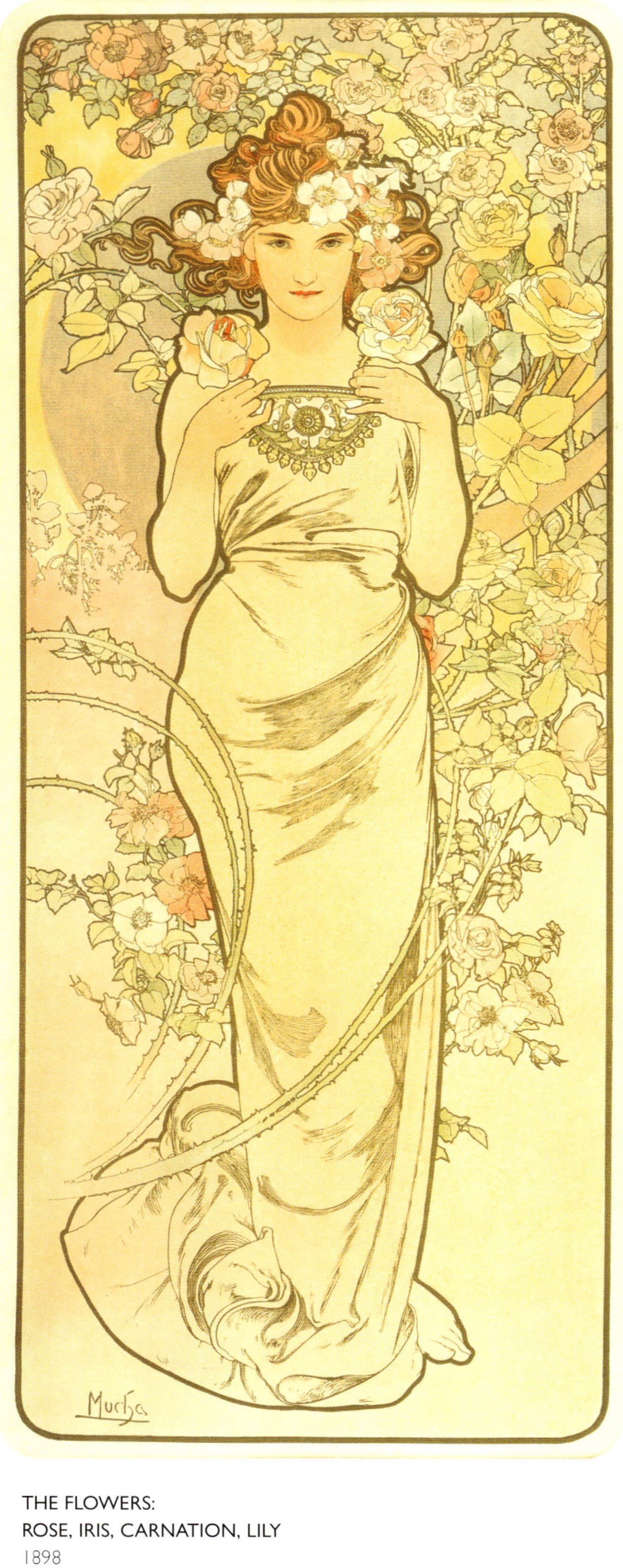

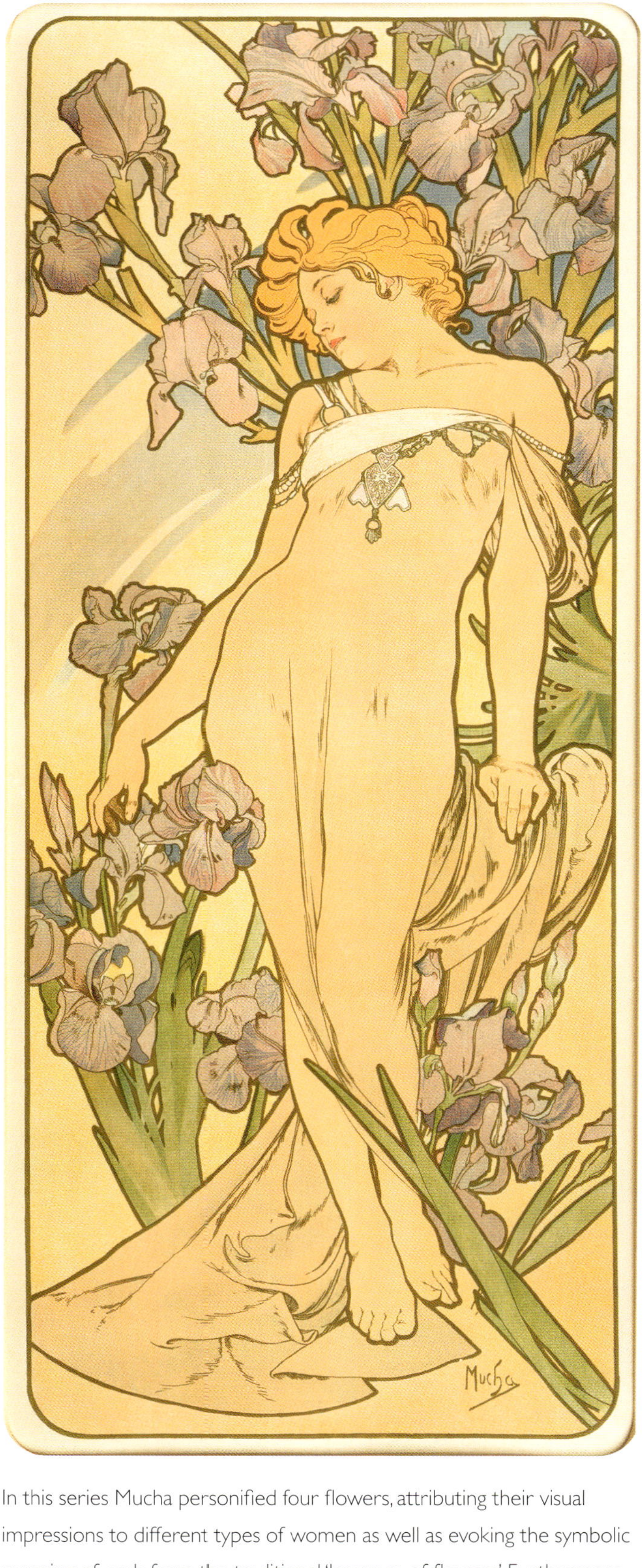

THE FLOWERS:
ROSE, IRIS, CARNATION, LILY
1898
Set of four colour lithographs
103.5 × 43.3 each

In this series Mucha personified four flowers, attributing their visual impressions to different types of women as well as evoking the symbolic meaning of each from the traditional 'language of flowers'. Furthermore, in blending the women and the floral motifs together, Mucha enhanced

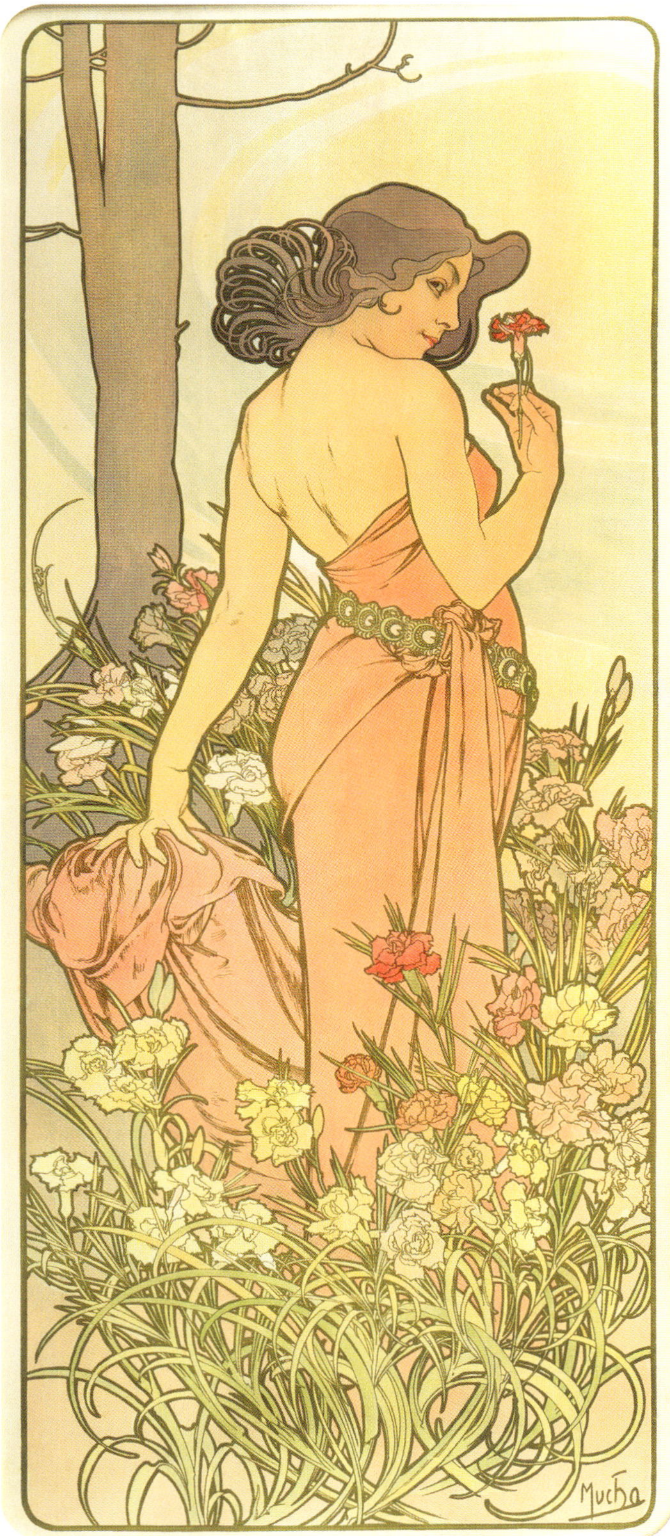

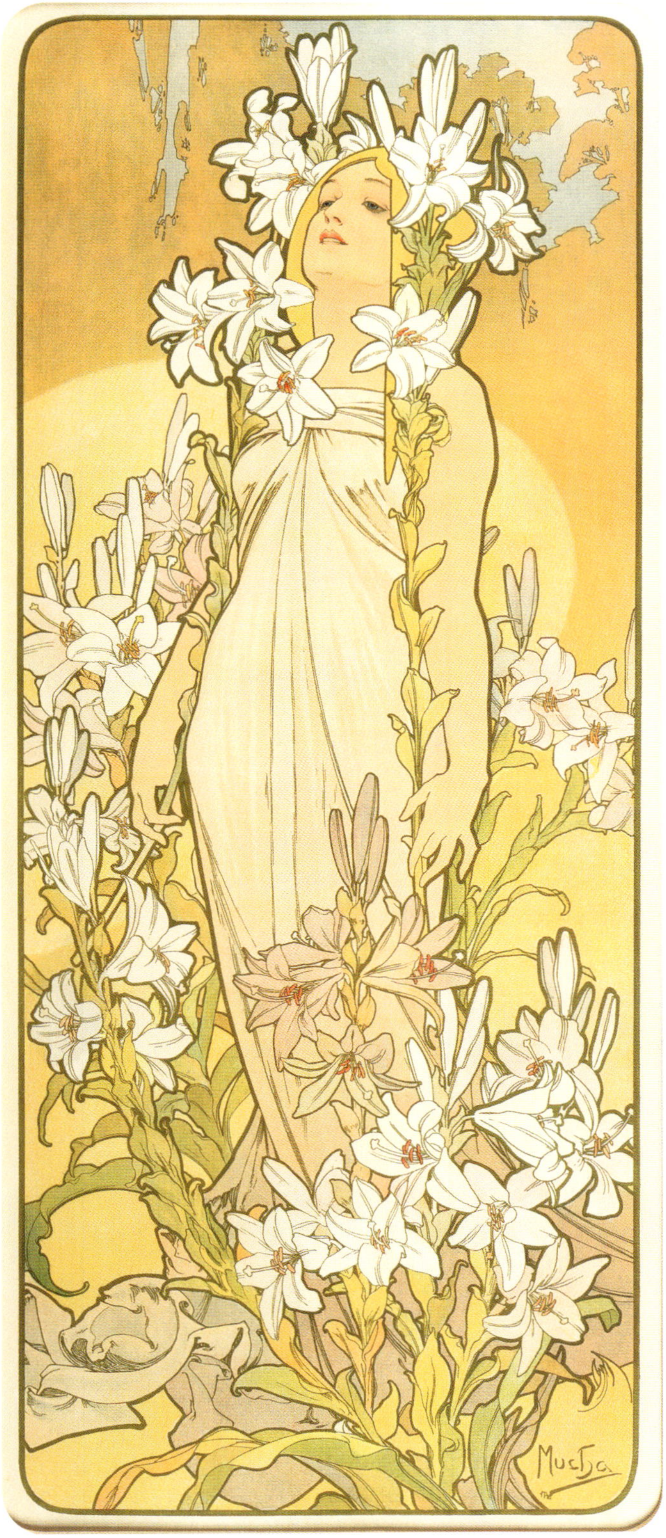

the decorative effect of female figures, which was to be explored further in a design for a fan, *The Passing Wind Takes Youth Away* (see p.89) as well as in *Documents décoratifs* (see p.95) and *Figures décoratives* (see p.101).

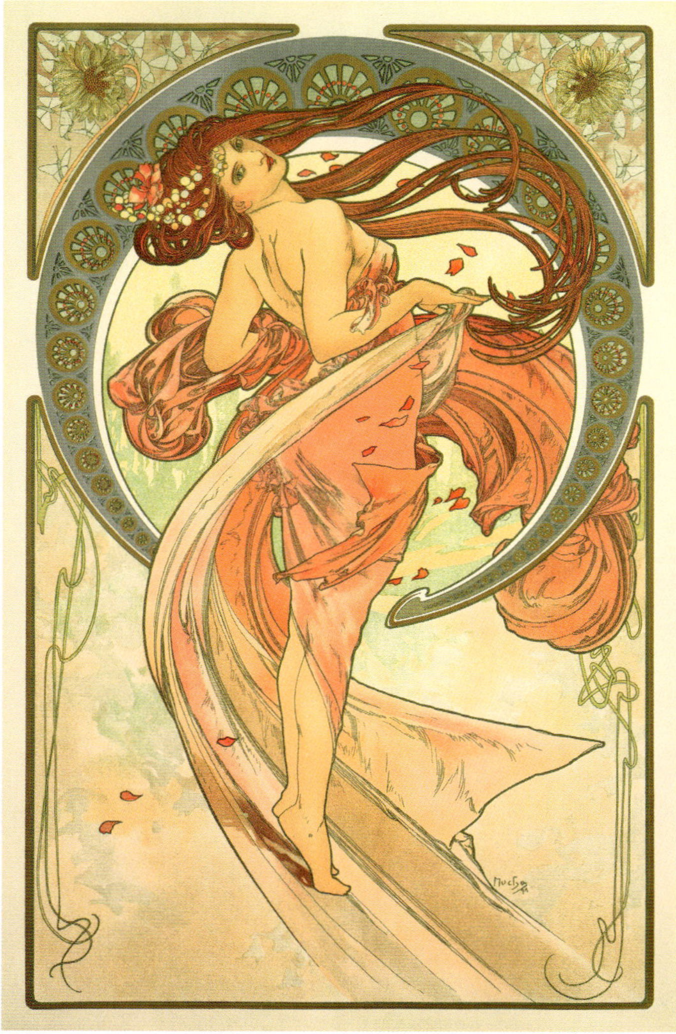

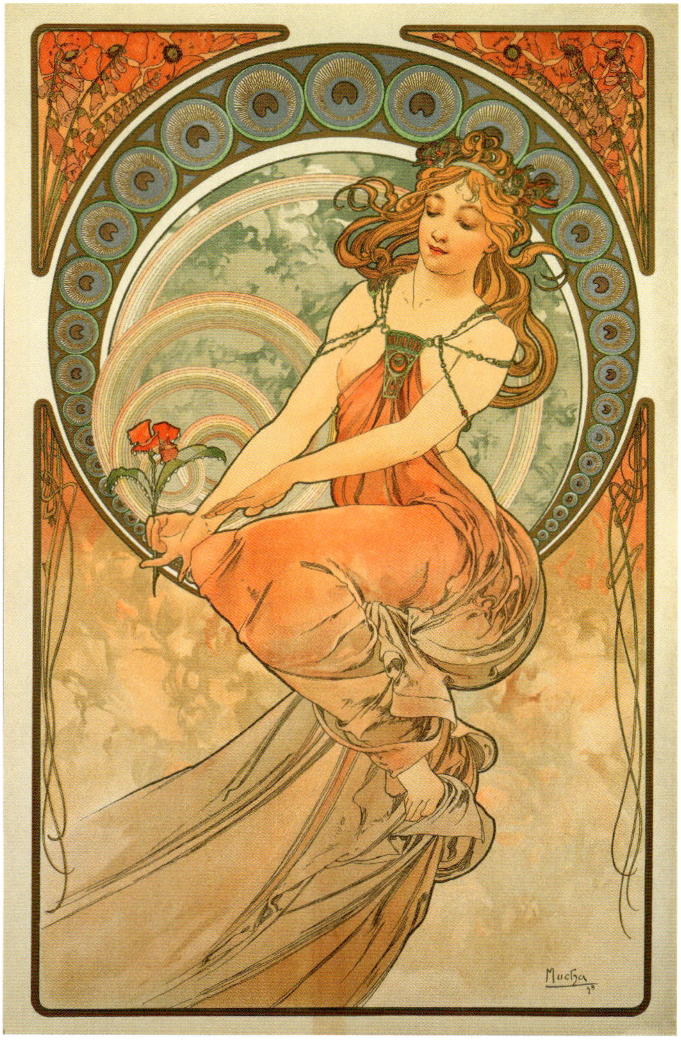

THE ARTS:
DANCE, PAINTING, POETRY, MUSIC
1898
Set of colour lithographs printed on satin
(deluxe edition)
60 x 38 each

In this series celebrating the four arts, Mucha emphasised the contribution of nature to creative inspiration by providing each example with a circular backdrop featuring a motif from nature associated with a particular time of day. Thus, for *Dance*, there are falling leaves blown by a morning breeze; for *Painting*, a red flower beneath rainbows in full daylight; for *Poetry*, the evening star shining in the sky at dusk; and for *Music*, the song of birds at moonrise.

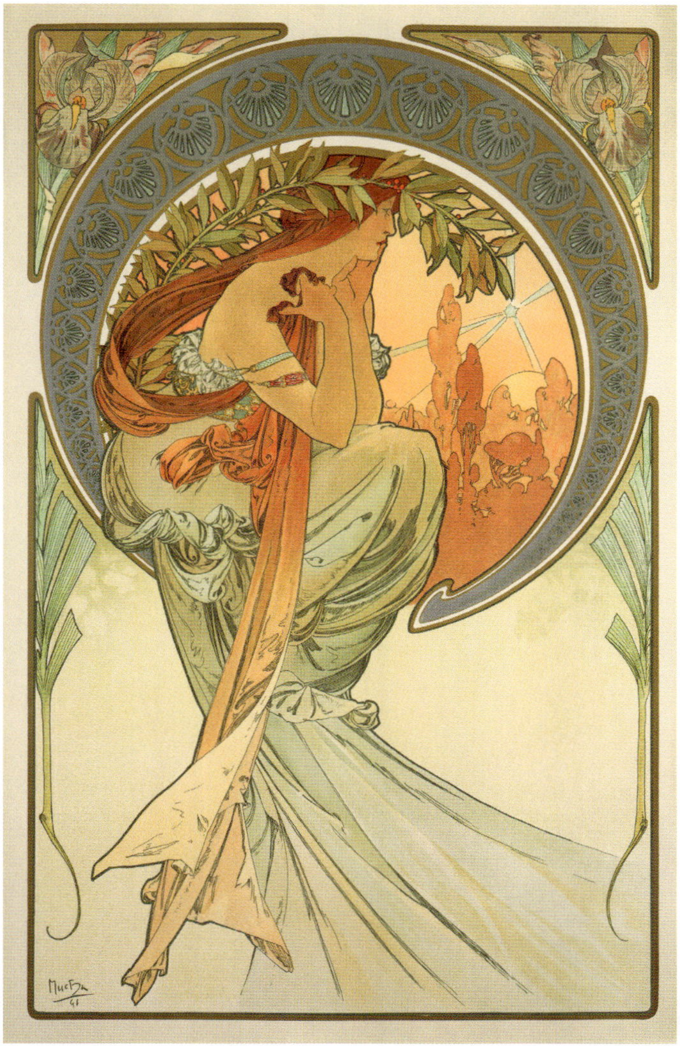

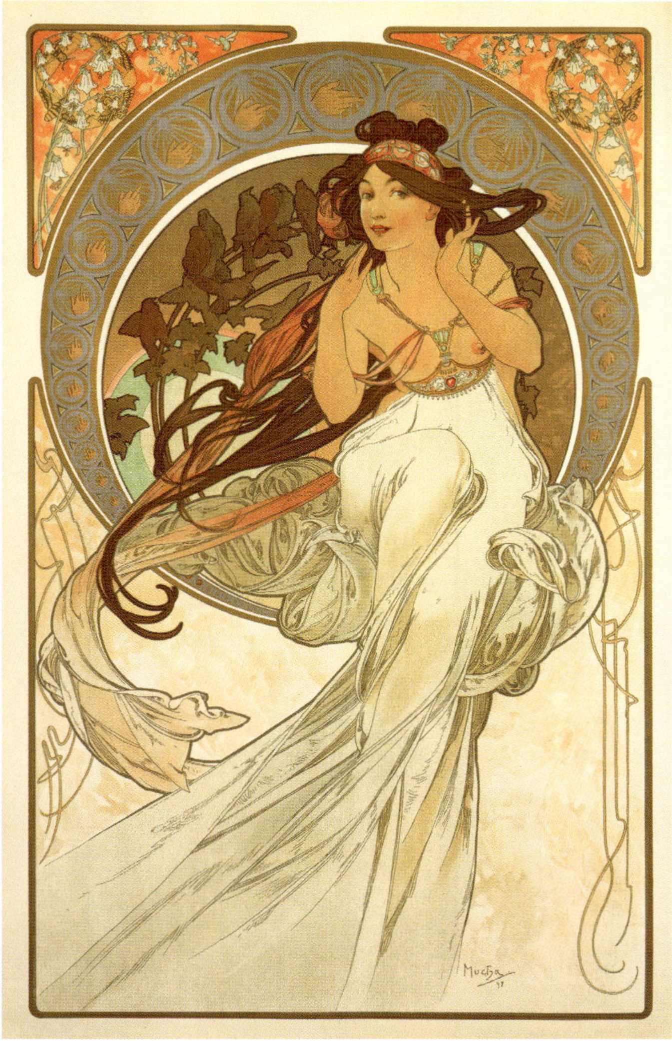

Here Mucha accomplished a harmonious style of composition, which was later called a 'Q formula' (see p.16). Evolving from previous compositions such as *Monaco • Monte-Carlo* (see p.32), this formula incorporates a seated figure into a circular motif with a tail of drapery hanging down. Its swaying movement counterpoints curvilinear forms created by flowing hair and other decorative motifs. This style of composition appears in many works from this period, including *Job* (1898) (see p.33), and it will also be revisited in later years.

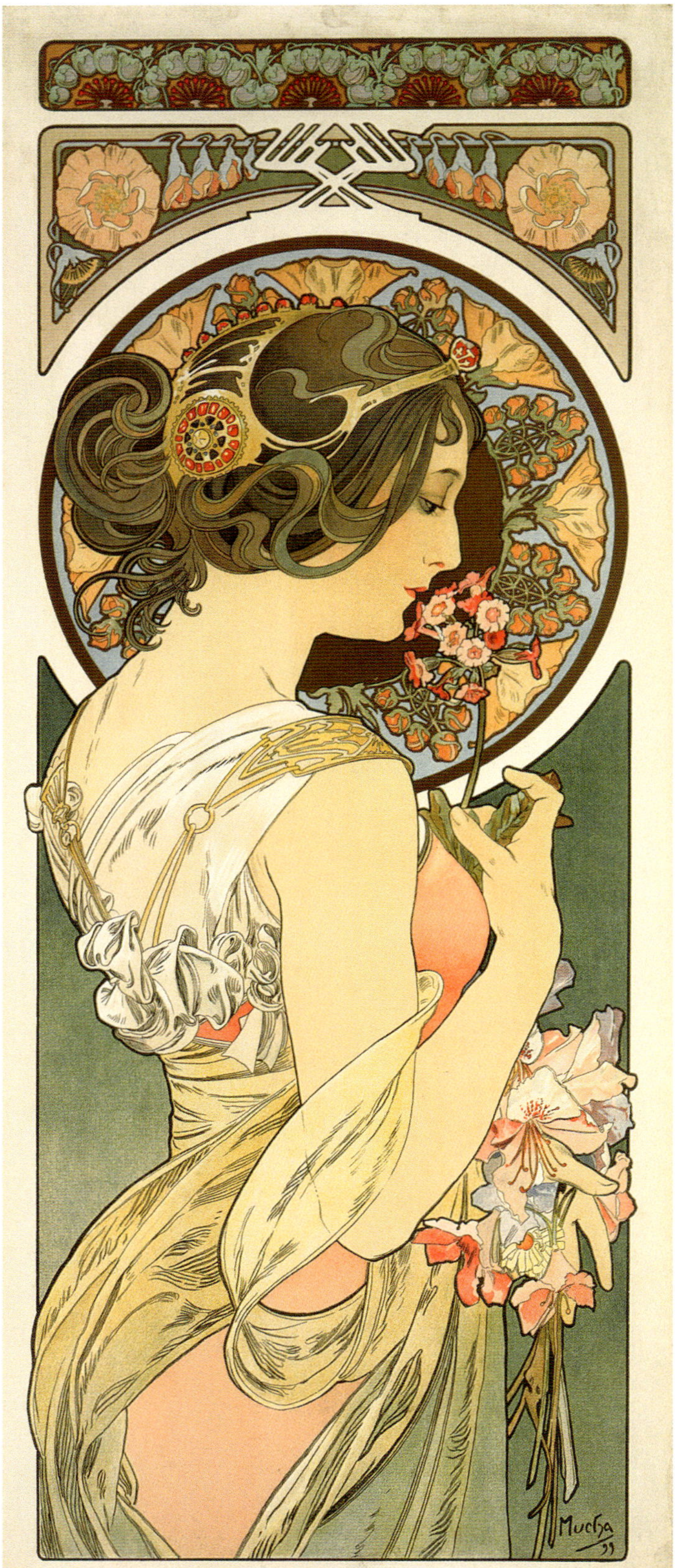
Mucha

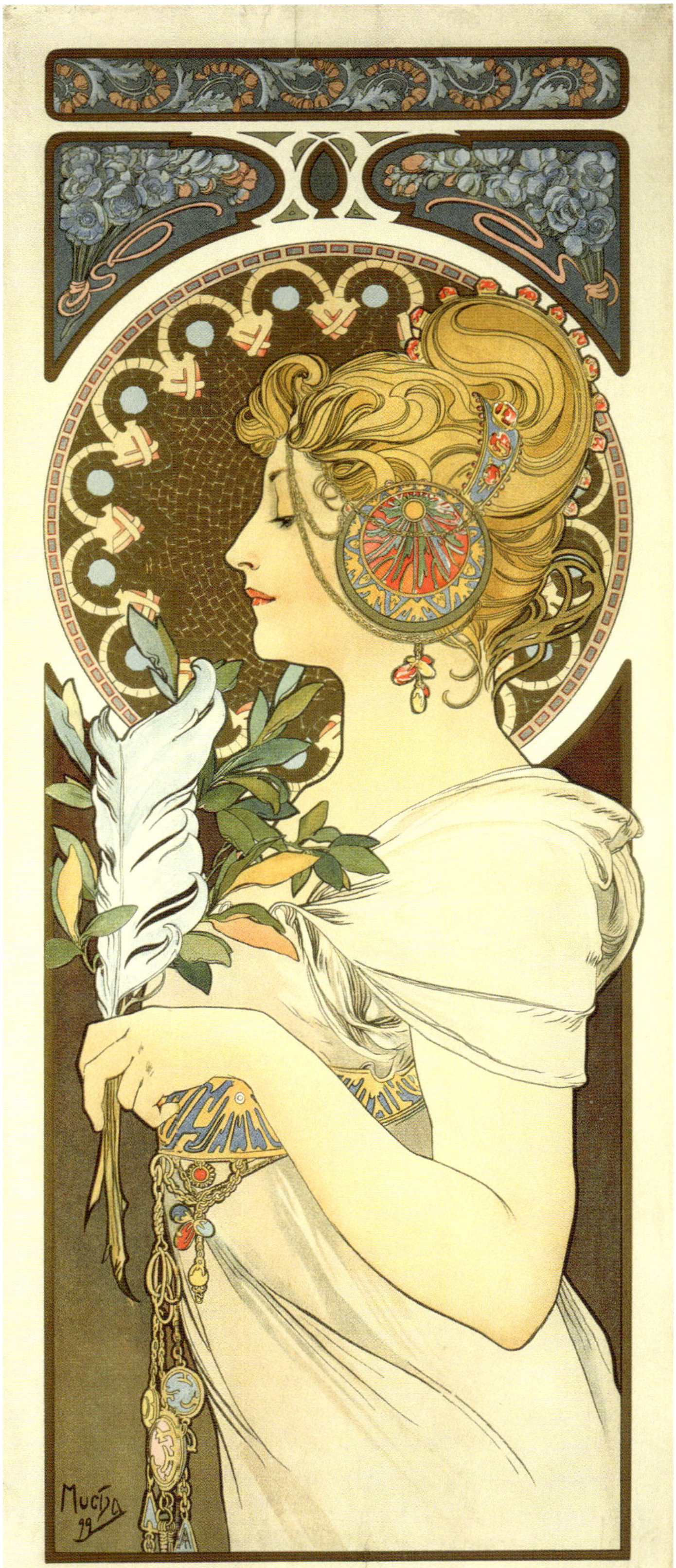
Mucha

PRIMROSE
1899
Colour lithograph
71 x 27.5

FEATHER
1899
Colour lithograph
71 x 27.5

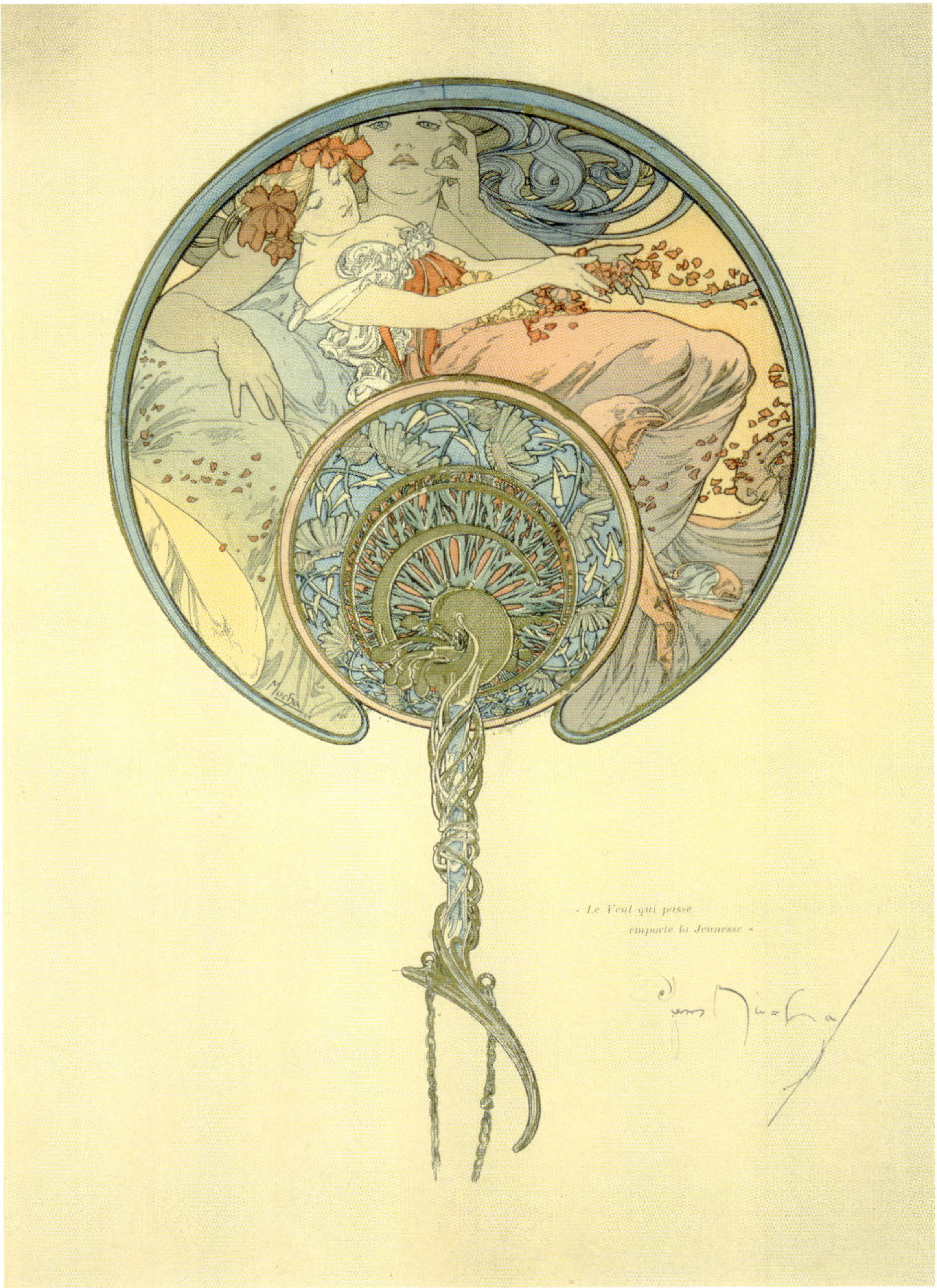

THE PASSING WIND TAKES YOUTH AWAY
1899
Colour lithograph
32 x 24

LANGUAGE OF FLOWERS:
PLATE 35 FROM *L'ALBUM DE LA DÉCORATION* (VOL. II)
1900
Colour lithograph
26.4 x 36.5

Mucha produced several designs for printed fabrics and wallpapers for manufacturers in France and Britain: Atelier C.G. Forrer, Paris; Scheurer, Lauth & Cie, Alsace; and Messrs. Hines, Stroud & Co., London. This design was originally made for an upholstery fabric by C.G. Forrer. It was reproduced in *L'Album de la Décoration*, which was published in Paris in 1900 by the Librairie des Art Décoratifs to present samples of decorative designs by contemporary French graphic artists.

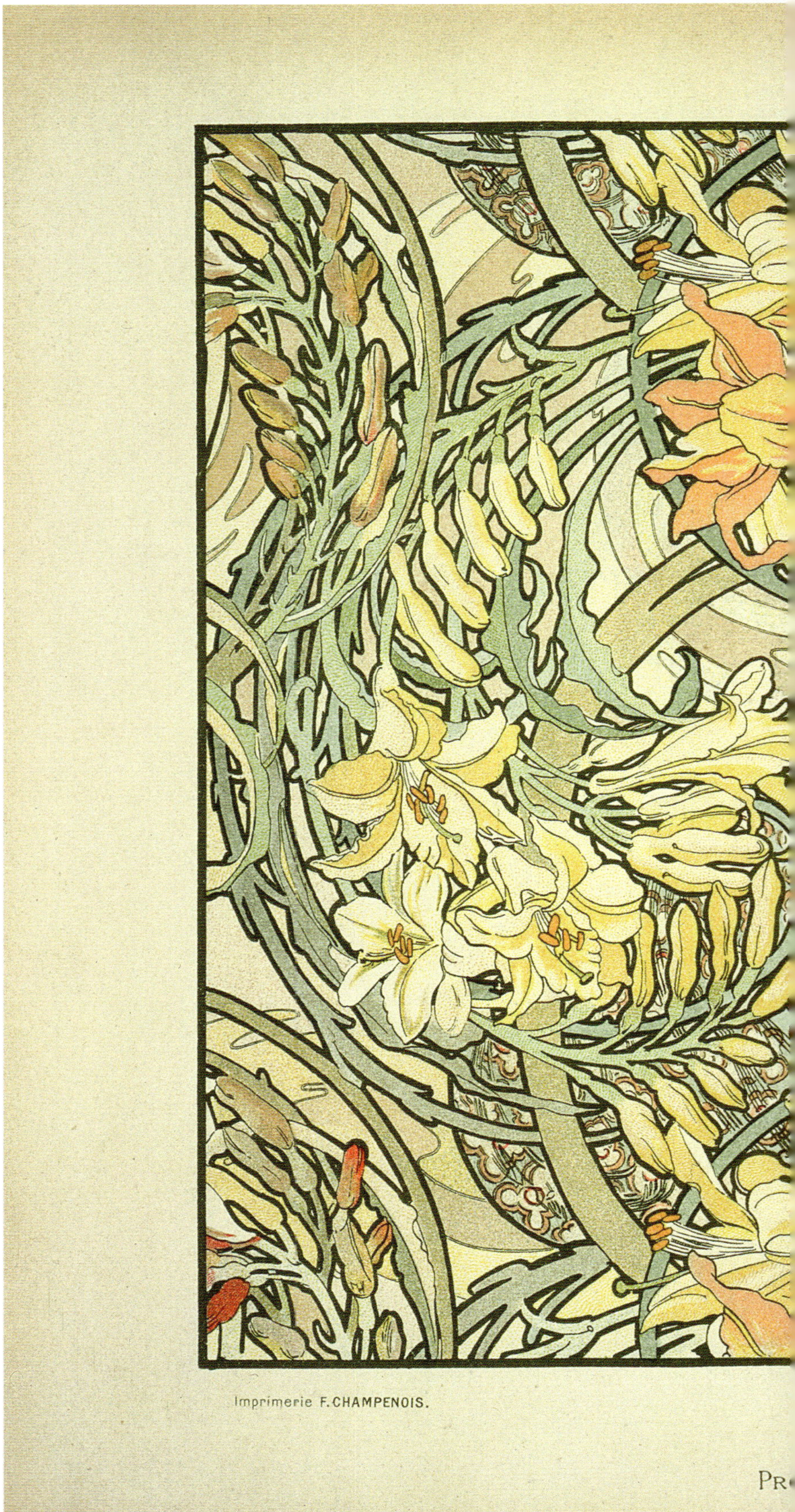

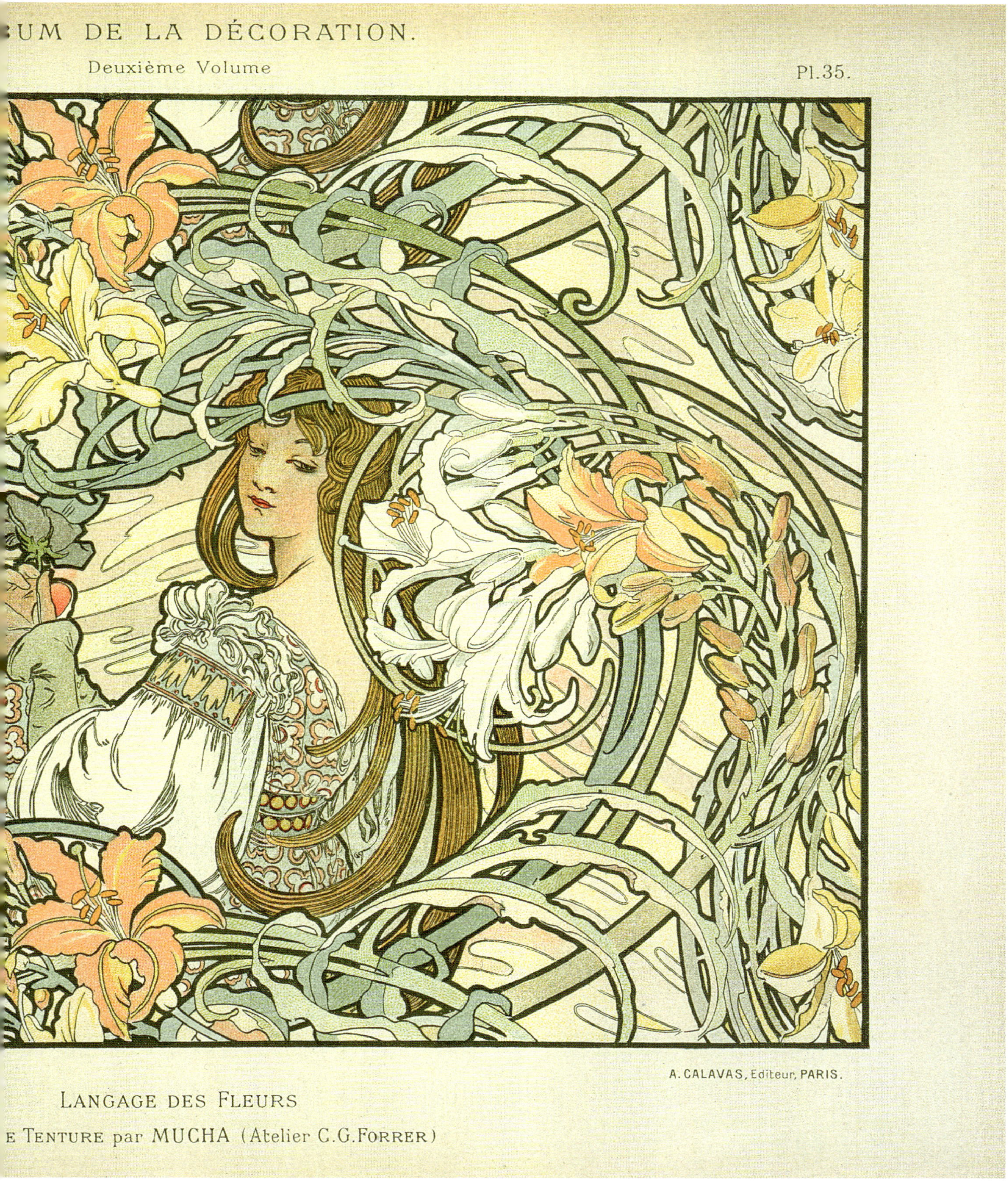
UM DE LA DÉCORATION.
Deuxième Volume
Pl.35.
A. CALAVAS, Editeur, PARIS.
Langage des Fleurs
e Tenture par MUCHA (Atelier C.G.Forrer)

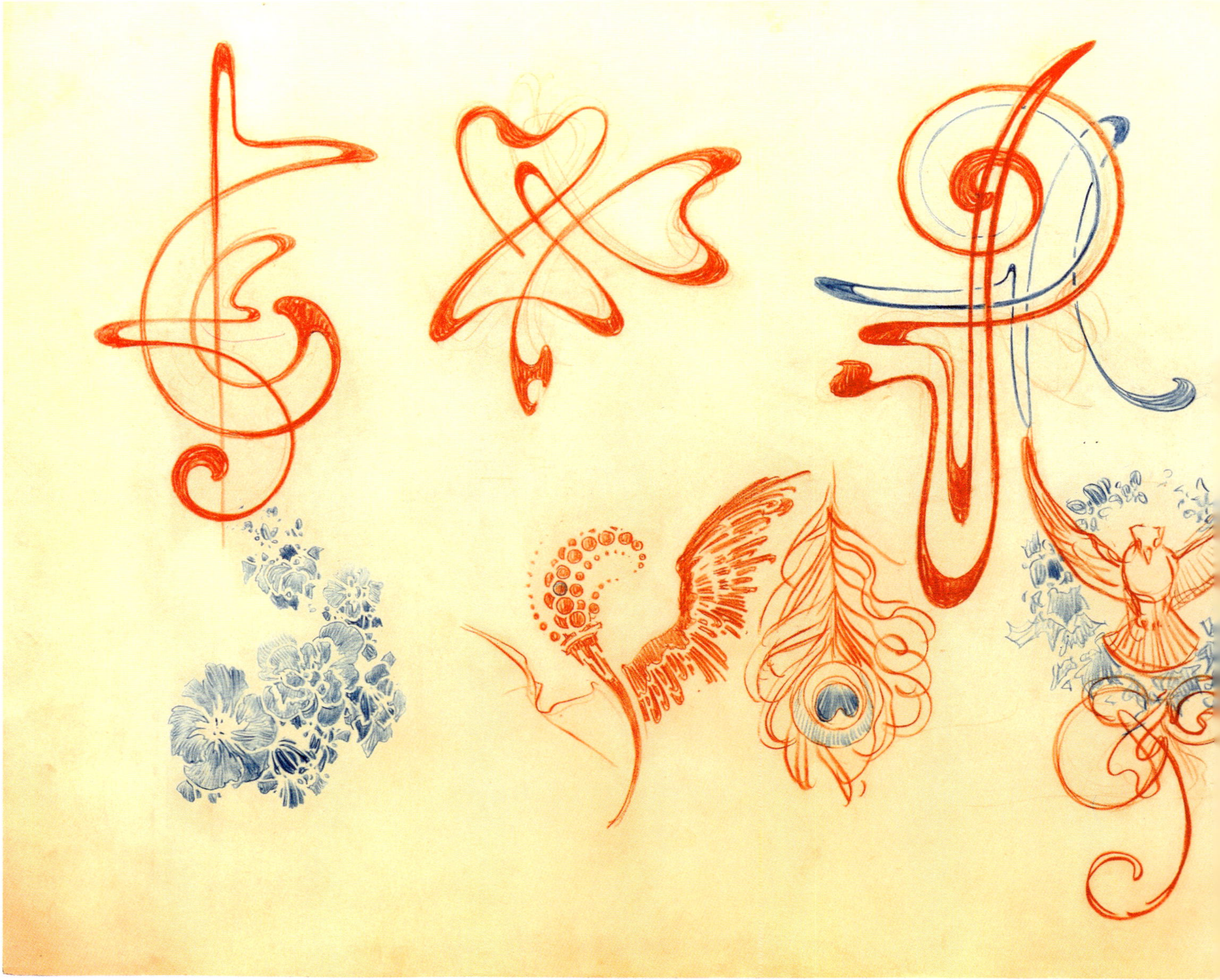

ORNAMENTAL MOTIFS DESIGNED FOR *COMBINAISONS ORNEMENTALES SE MULTIPLIANT À L'INFINI À L'AIDE DU MIROIR*
c.1900
Red and blue pencil on paper
33.6 x 51.7

Combinaisons Ornementales was published as a pattern book for designers, offering a variety of examples of ornamental motifs featuring plants, birds, insects and other forms from nature. As the latter half of its title indicates, viewers were encouraged to look at each plate with two joined mirrors, which would 'infinitely multiply' these motifs like a kaleidoscope, providing fresh inspiration for design. Mucha contributed eleven plates to the book, which included designs featuring abstract linear motifs, as shown here, to create optical vibraticns with rhythmic curves and circular patterns (see also p.15).

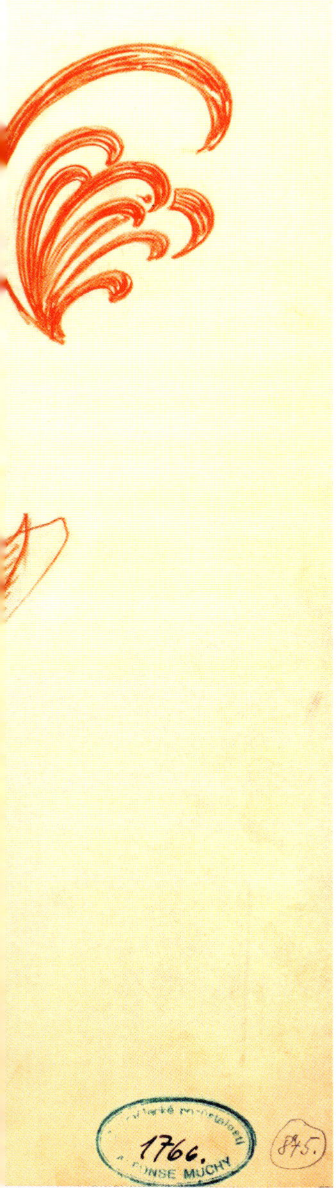

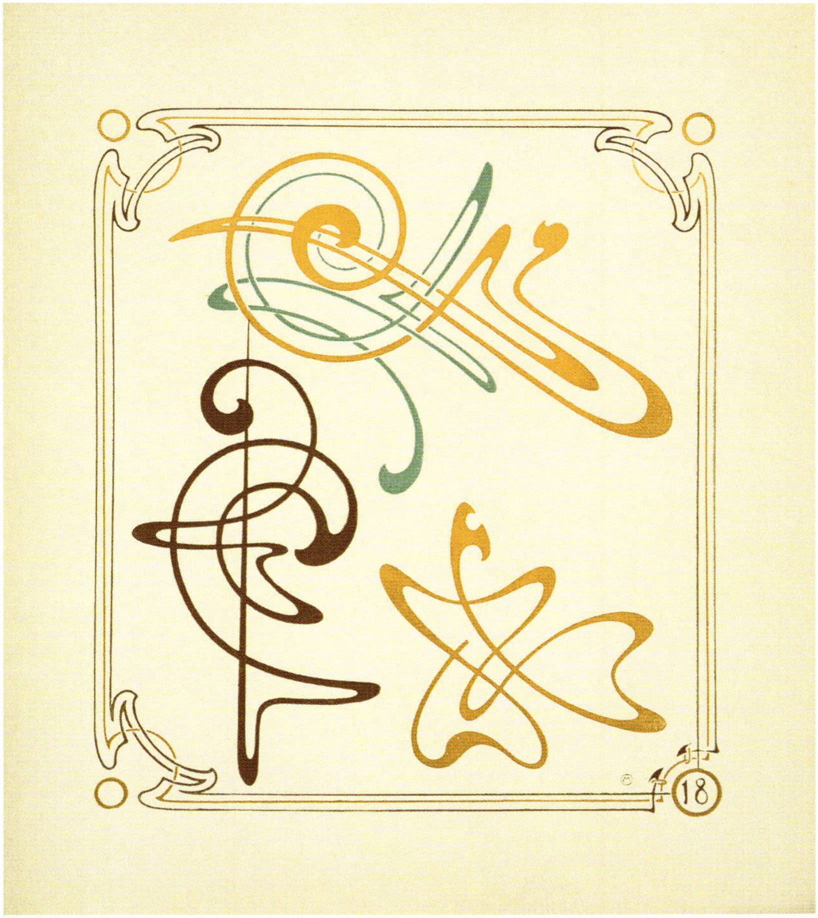

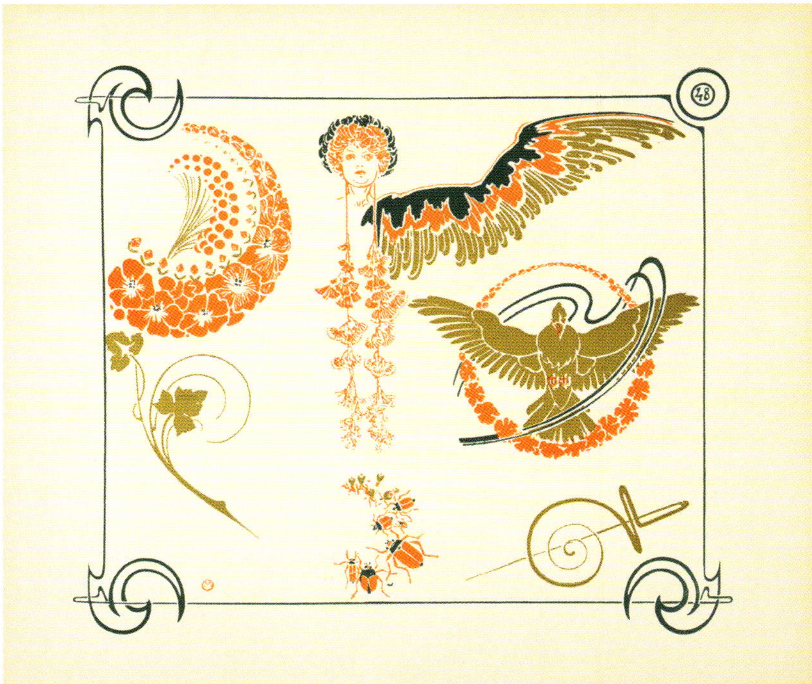

COMBINAISONS ORNEMENTALES SE MULTIPLIANT À L'INFINI À L'AIDE DU MIROIR:
PLATE 18
PLATE 48
1901
George Auriol (1863–1938), Maurice Pillard Verneuil (1869–1942) and Alphonse Mucha
Folio with 60 colour-lithographed plates, published by the Librairie Centrale des Beaux Arts, Paris
25 x 21.6

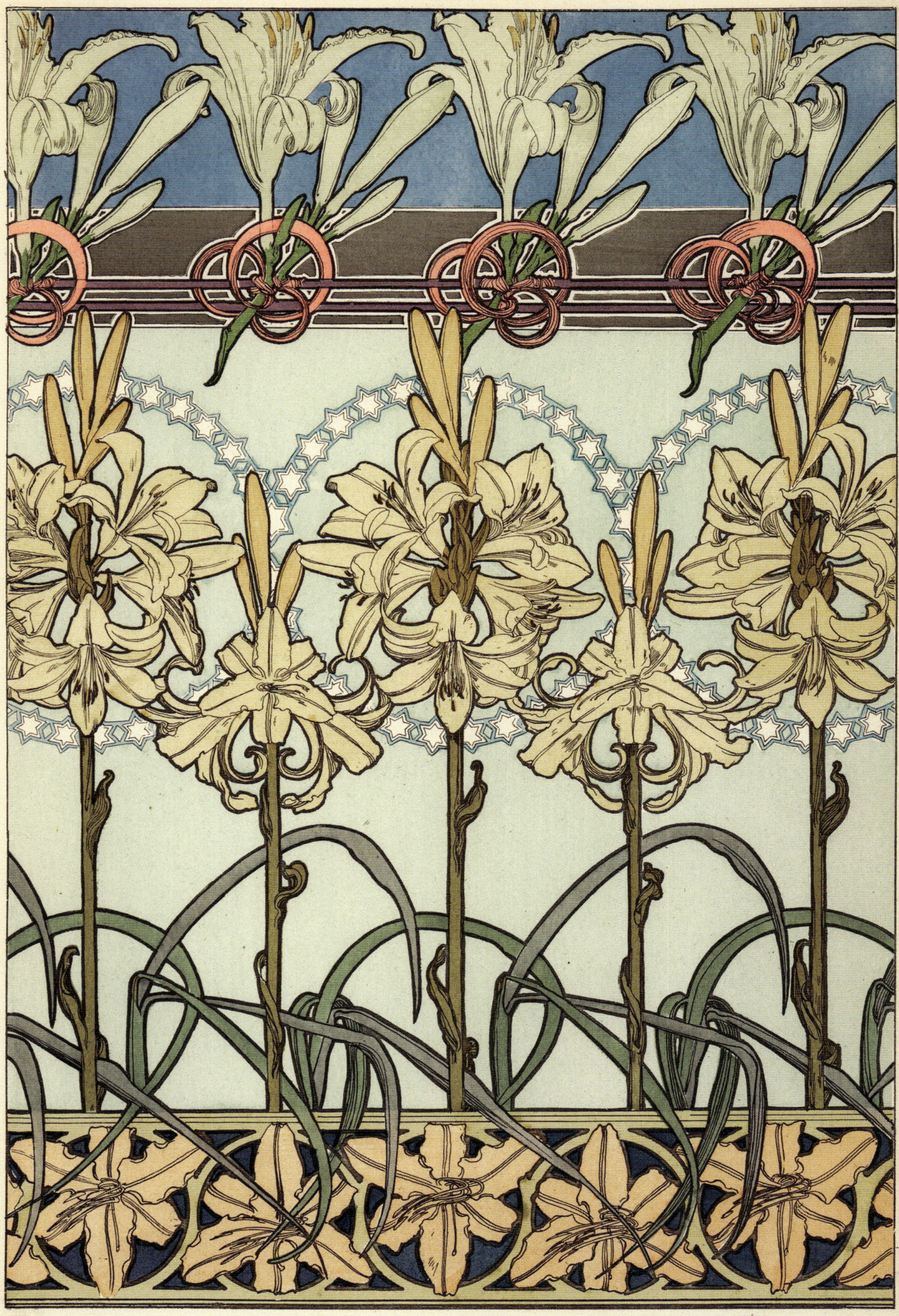

DOCUMENTS DÉCORATIFS: PLATE 33
1902
Colour lithograph
46 x 33

DOCUMENTS DÉCORATIFS: LINE DRAWING FOR PLATE 33
c. 1901–2
Pencil, pen and ink on paper
58 x 44

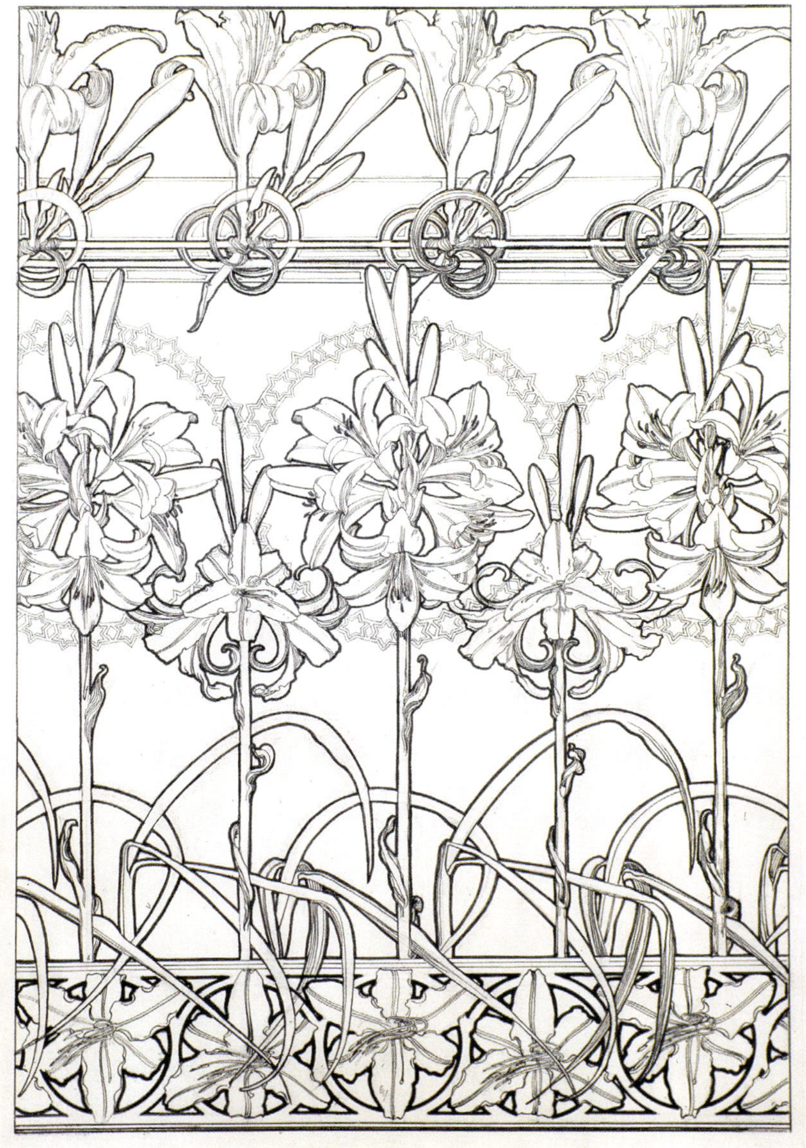

DOCUMENTS DÉCORATIFS

Mucha's *Documents décoratifs* was published in 1902 by the Librairie Centrale des Beaux-Arts, Paris, as a folio with seventy-two plates. Mucha conceived *Documents décoratifs* as a handbook for artisans, designers and art students and presented all aspects of his design work in the publication. It features not only ready-to-use design samples for manufacturers but also a variety of drawings intended to take the designers through the process of stylisation, transforming realistic studies from nature into decorative motifs which can then be applied to manufactured products. Mucha's designs demonstrated his boundless imagination to create new forms from motifs taken from nature and from the human body.

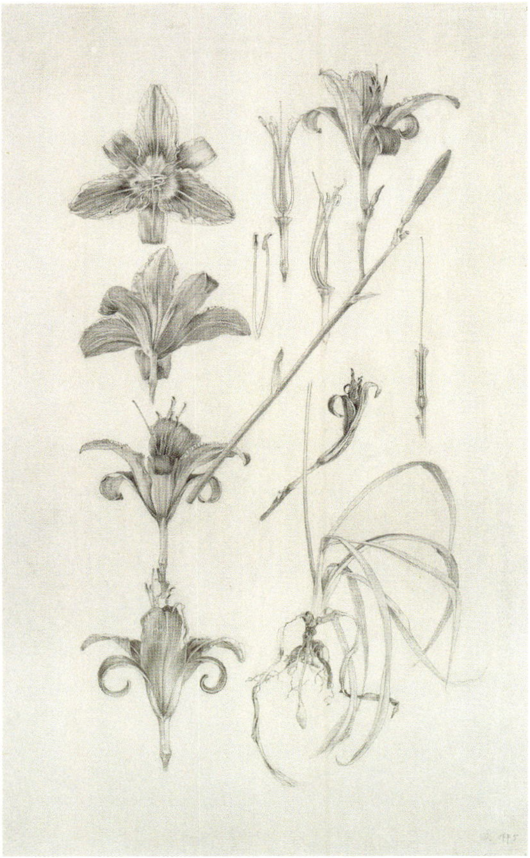

DOCUMENTS DÉCORATIFS: DRAWING FOR PLATE 25
c.1901–2
Pencil on paper
47.3 x 31

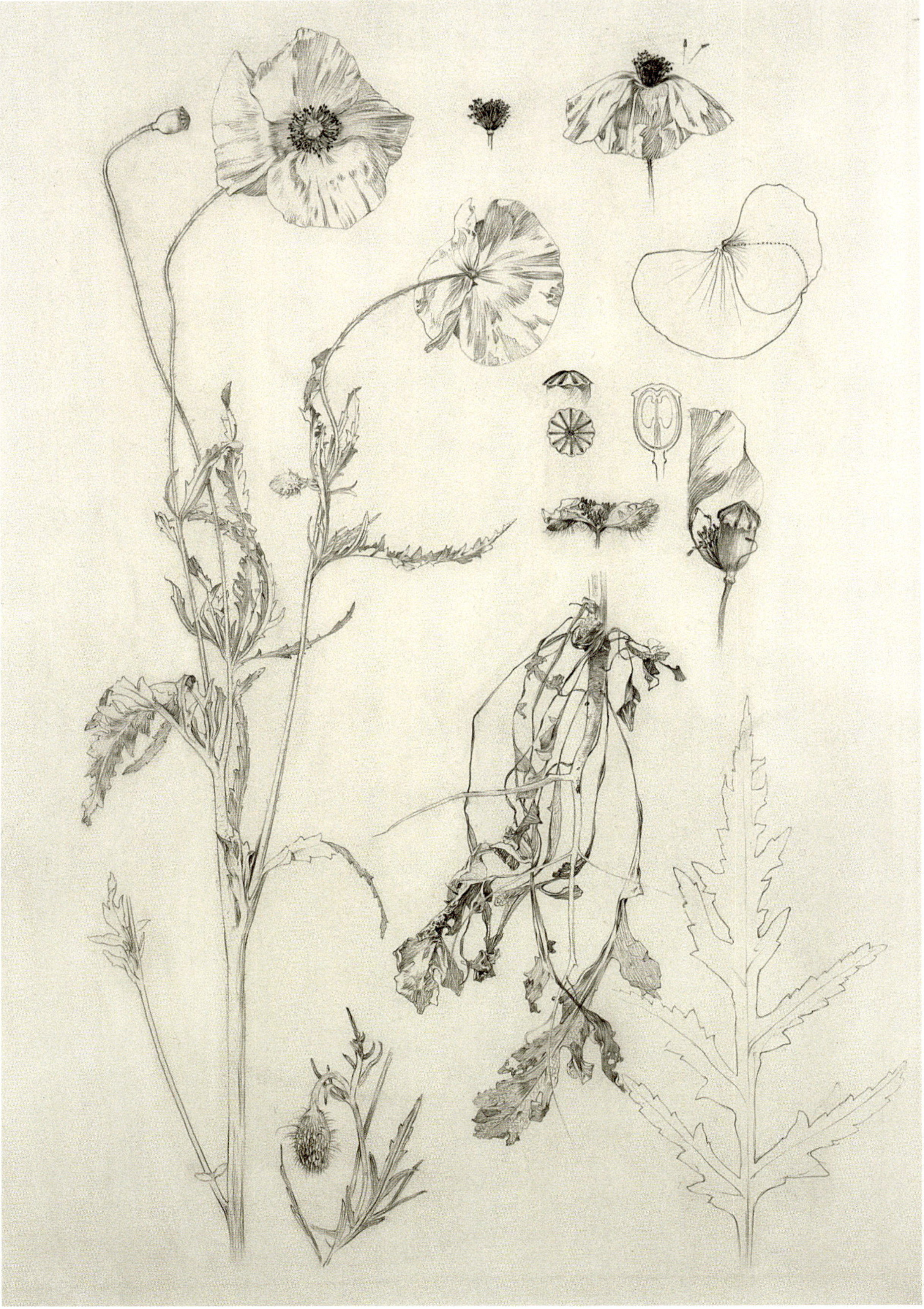

DOCUMENTS DÉCORATIFS: DRAWING FOR PLATE 26
c.1901–1902
Pencil on paper
47.5 x 31

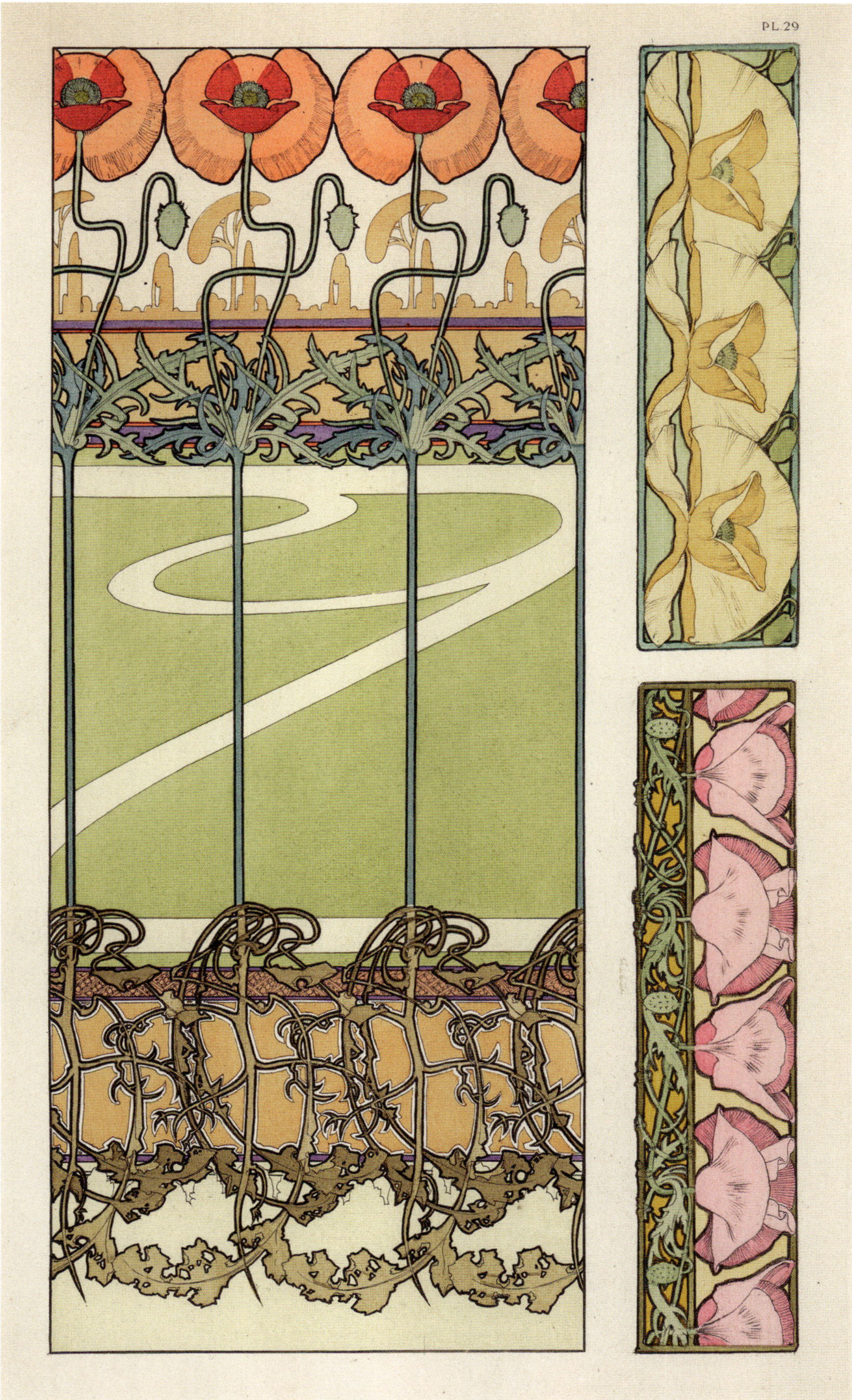

DOCUMENTS DÉCORATIFS: PLATE 29
1902
Colour lithograph
46 x 33

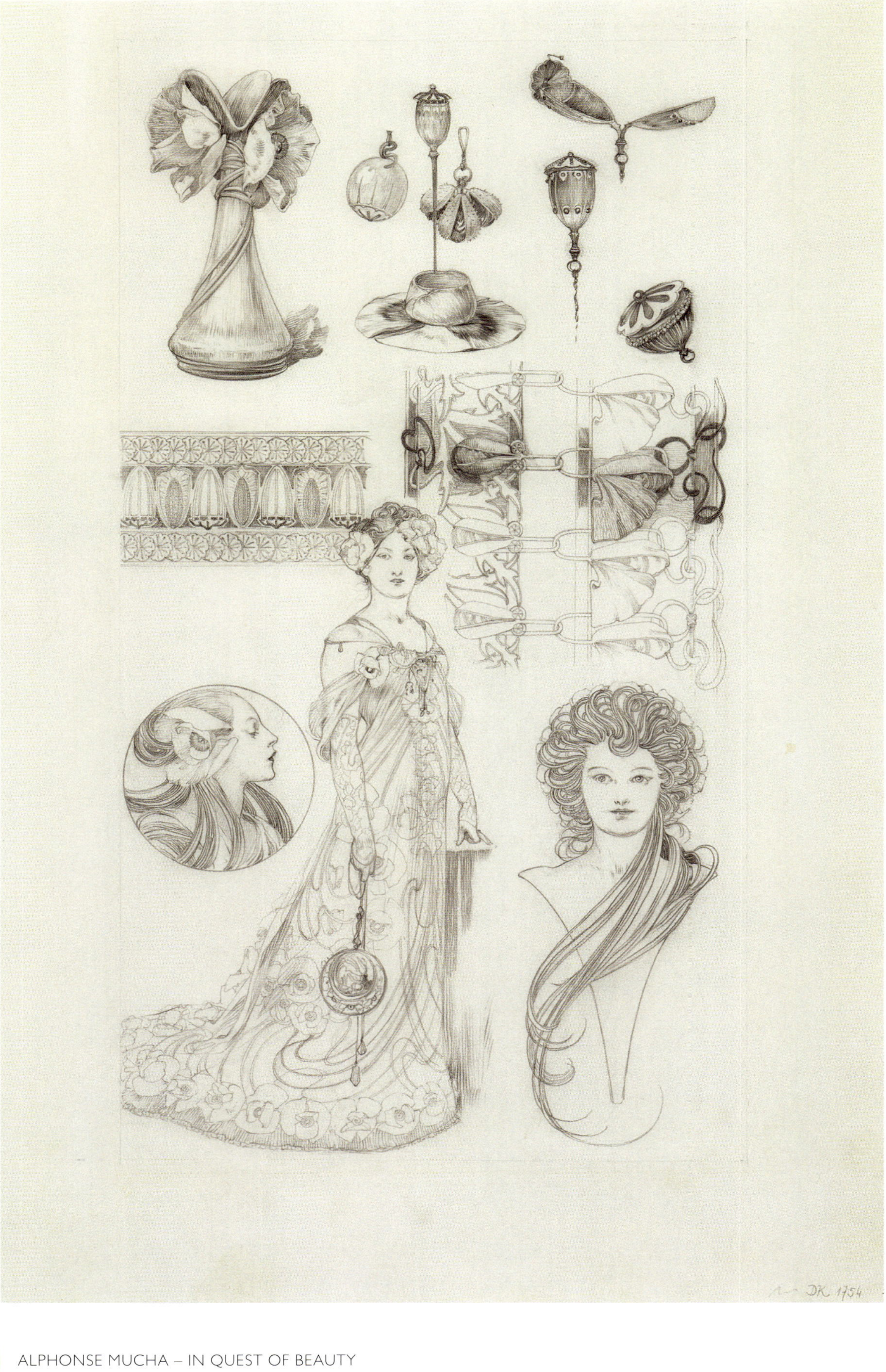

DOCUMENTS DÉCORATIFS: DRAWING FOR PLATE 37
c.1901–1902
Pencil on paper
48 x 31

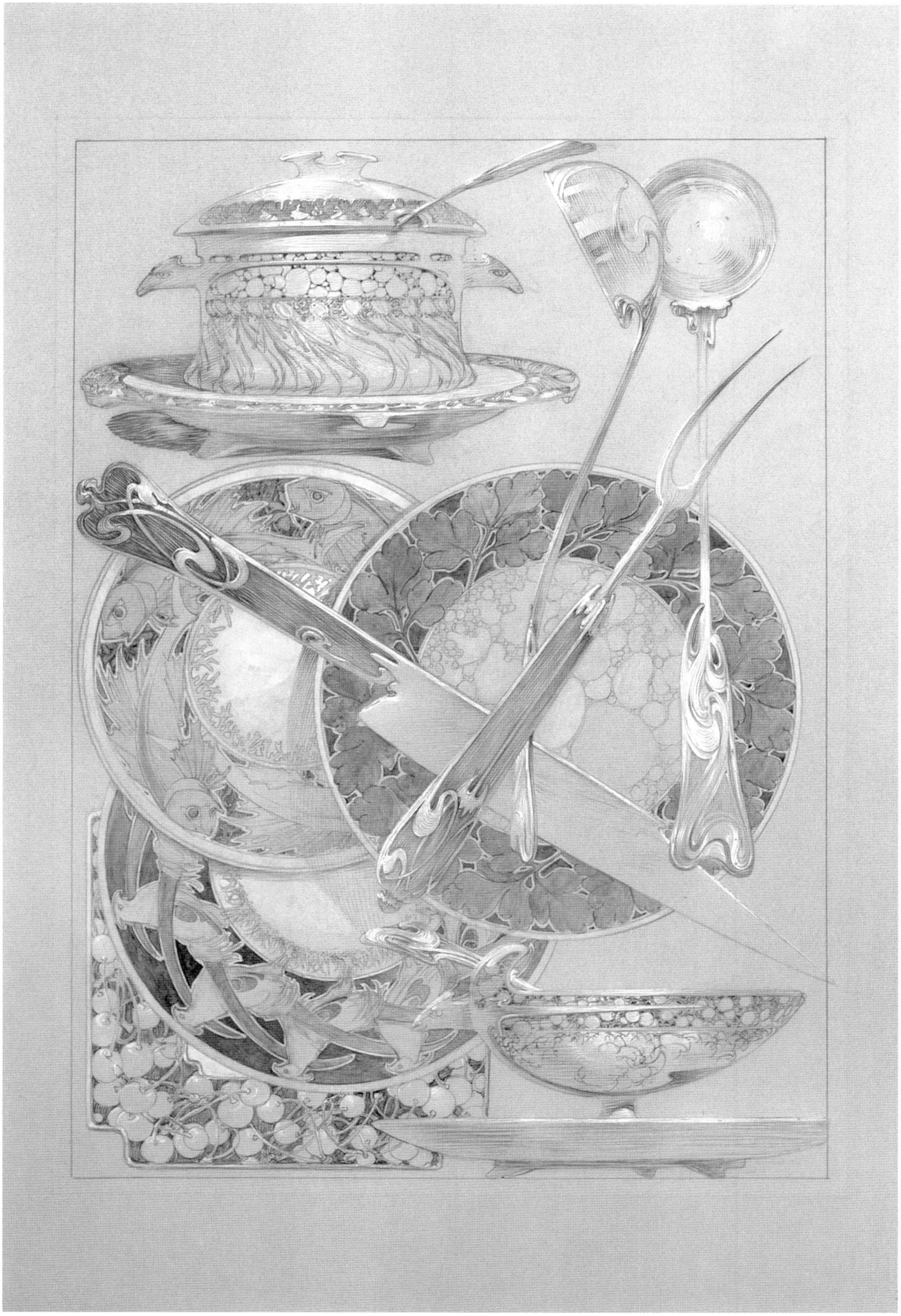

DOCUMENTS DÉCORATIFS: DRAWING FOR PLATE 59
c.1901–1902
Pencil on paper
48 x 31

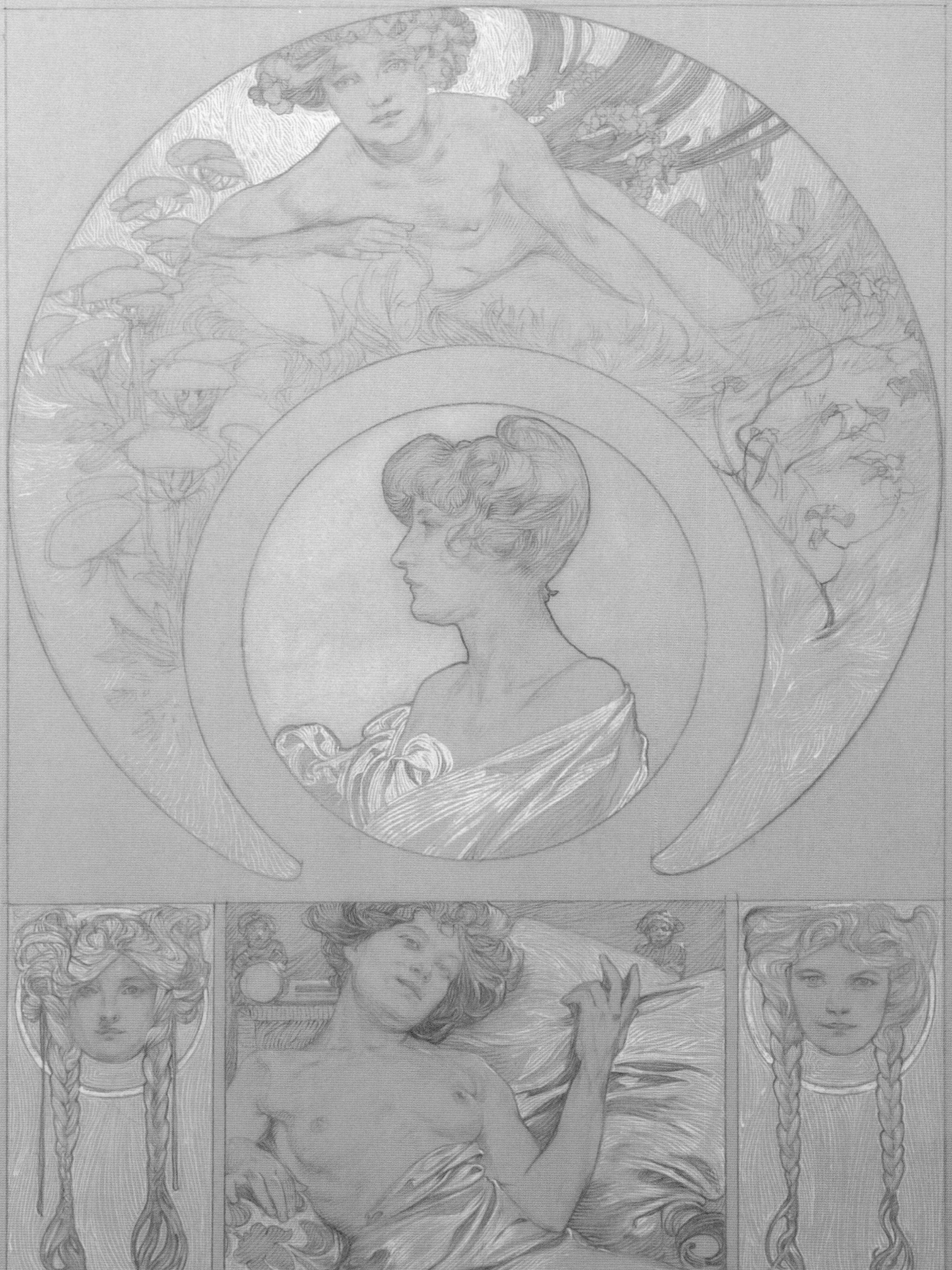

FIGURES DÉCORATIVES: DRAWING FOR PLATE 2
1904
Pencil and white on paper
64 x 49

These drawings were prepared for *Figures décoratives*, which was published to follow on and complement Mucha's *Documents décoratifs* (see p.95). Focussing on the use of the human body as a source of decorative motifs, the folio of 40 plates explored the figures of women, girls and children in a variety of poses integrated into circles, triangles, rectangles and many other geometric forms.

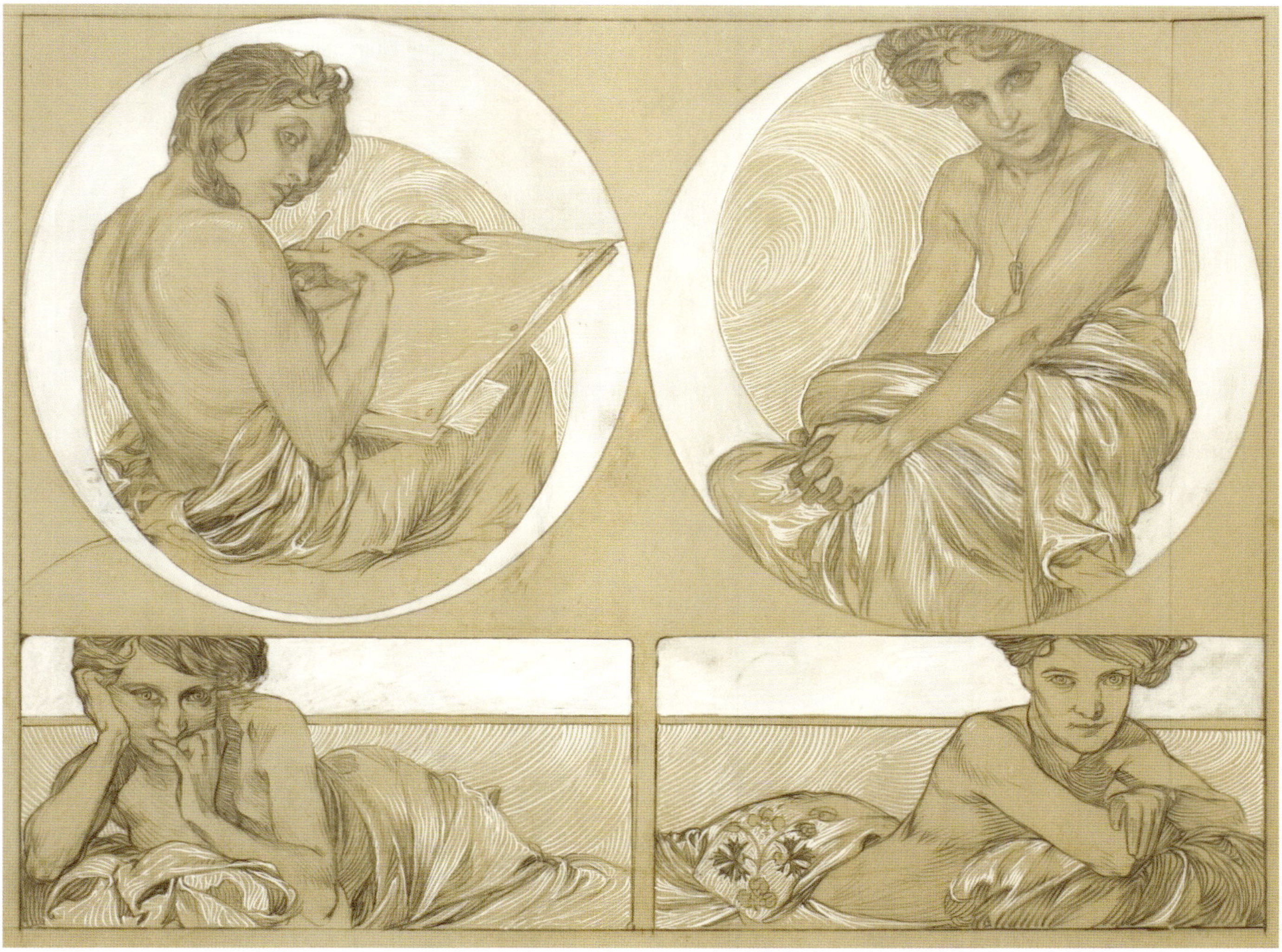

FIGURES DÉCORATIVES: DRAWING FOR PLATE 25
1904
Pencil and white on paper
38 x 58

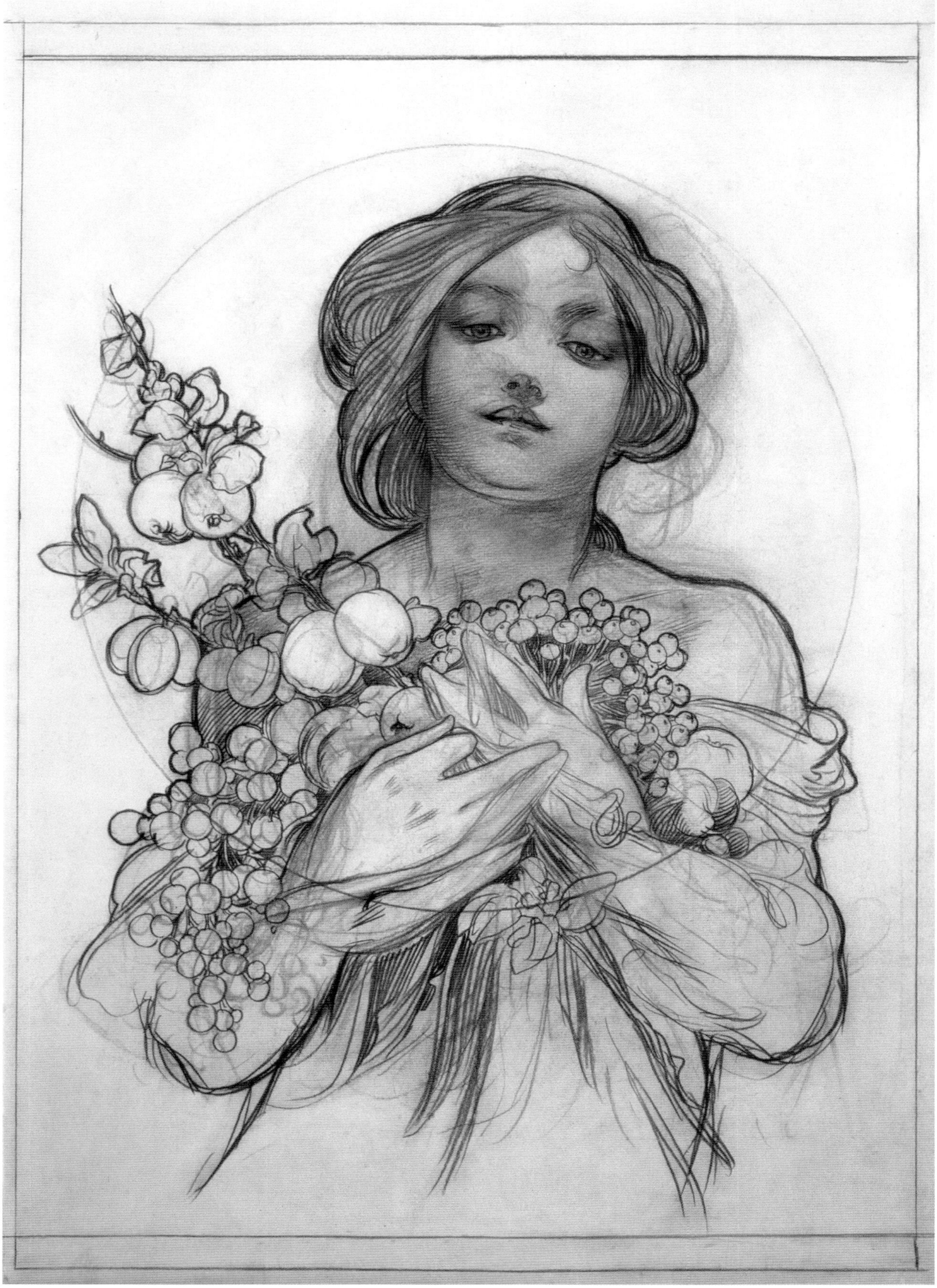

GIRL HOLDING FLOWERS
c.1900
Study for a decorative panel
Pencil on paper
63 x 47.5

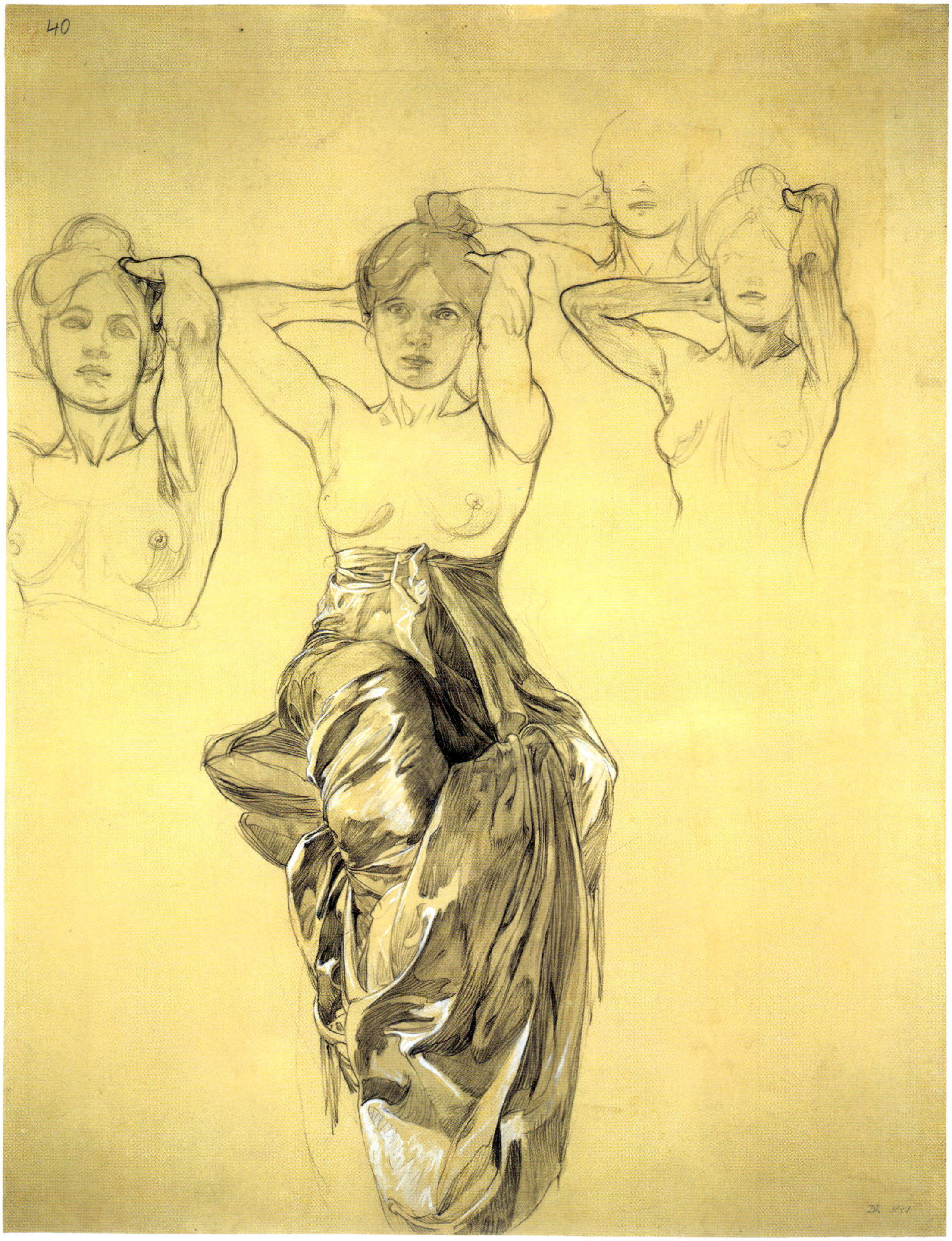

NUDE STUDIES FOR THE DECORATIVE PANEL
'AMETHYST' FROM *PRECIOUS STONES*
1900
Pencil and white on paper
57 x 41.5

MUCHA AND PHOTOGRAPHY

Mucha began taking photographs in the early 1880s while working as an apprentice scene painter in Vienna and he continued this practice throughout his life. At first he used a borrowed camera to take snapshots of his friends and of street scenes but in Paris, after purchasing his first camera that took 10 x 13 cm glass plates, photography became an important part of his creative process. During the latter half of the 1890s photography began to assume the role of a visual notebook and diary, which complemented his sketches and drawings.

Images of studio models form a large part of the numerous photographs taken during this period. Often Mucha had no special plans for specific projects but rather worked spontaneously with the models improvising a variety of poses. Later many of these images were used as parts of studies or as sources of inspiration for his designs and paintings.

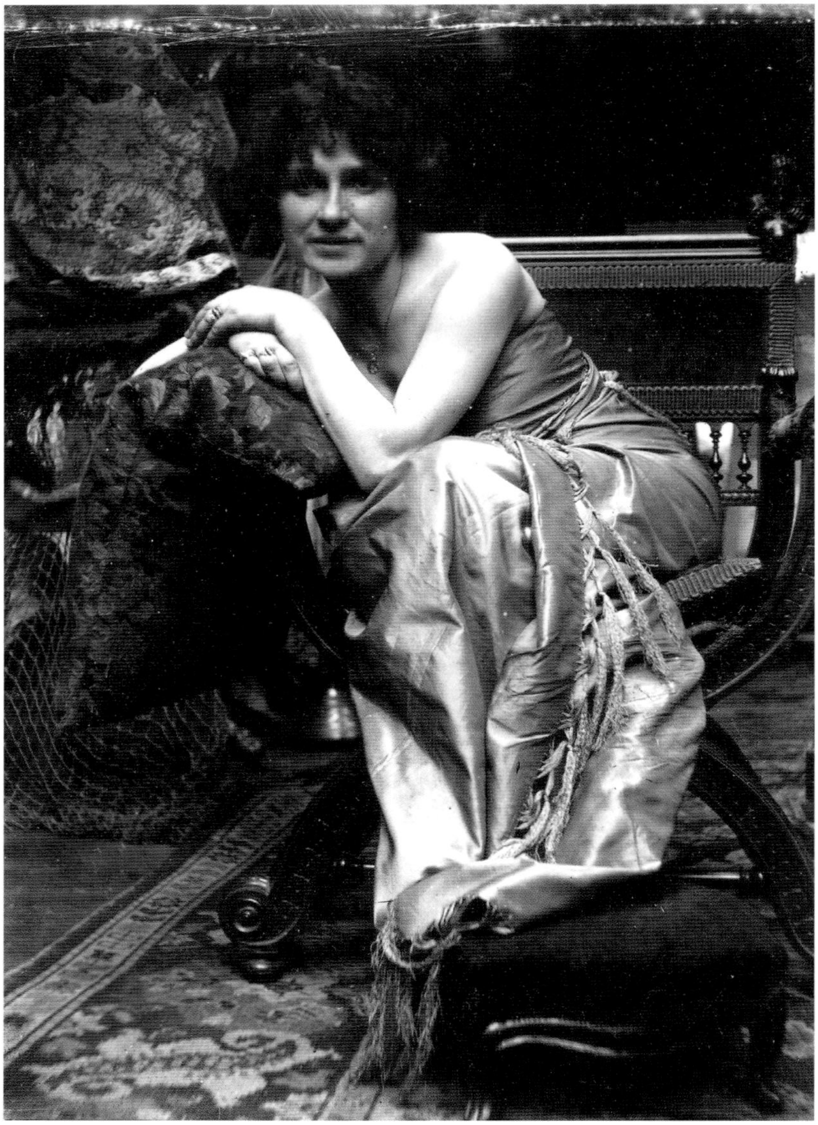

MODEL POSING AT MUCHA'S STUDIO IN RUE DU VAL-DE-GRÂCE, PARIS
c.1899
Modern print from original glass plate negative

MODEL IN A BOHEMIAN FOLK COSTUME AT MUCHA'S STUDIO IN RUE DU VAL-DE-GRÂCE, PARIS
c.1898
Modern print from original glass plate negative

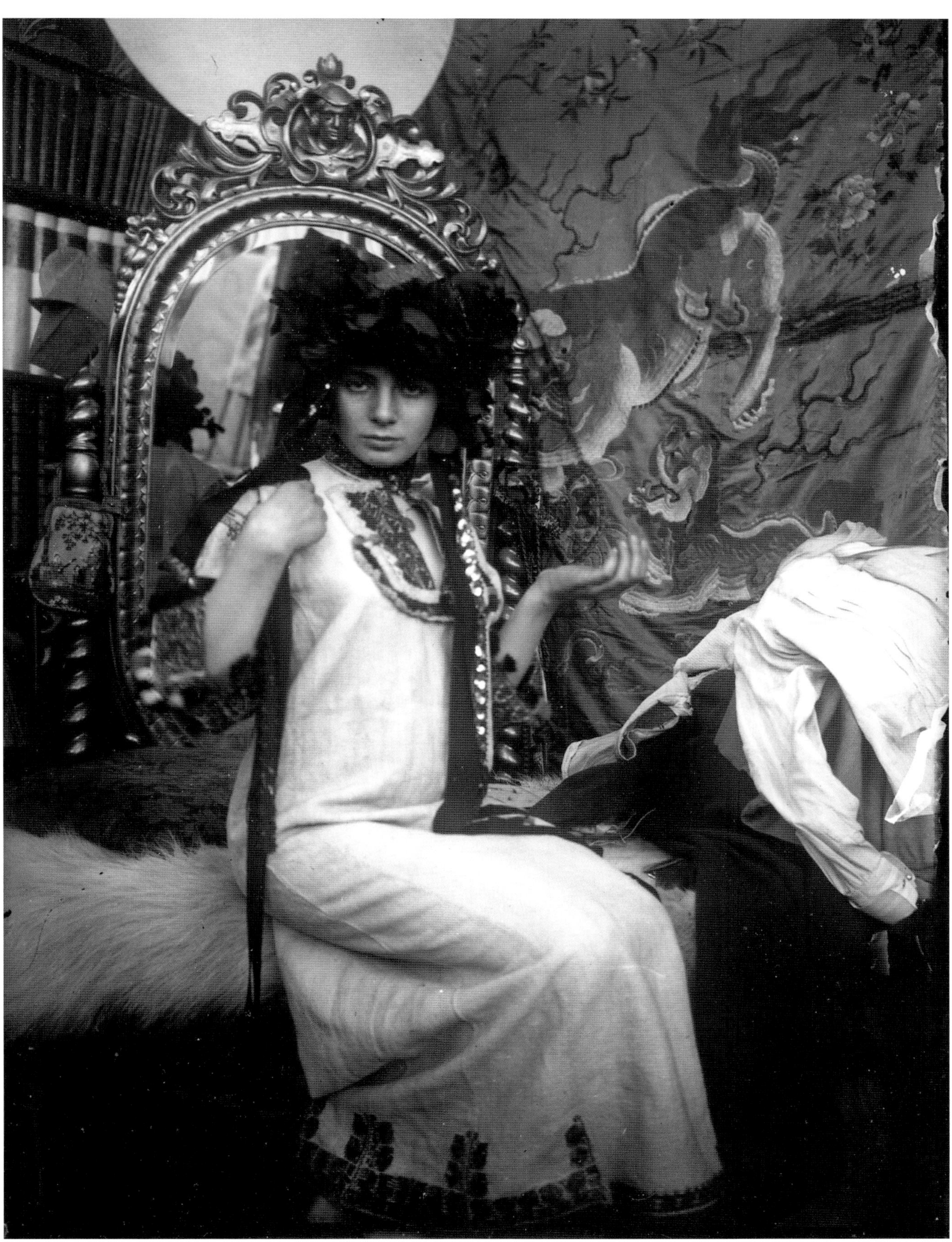

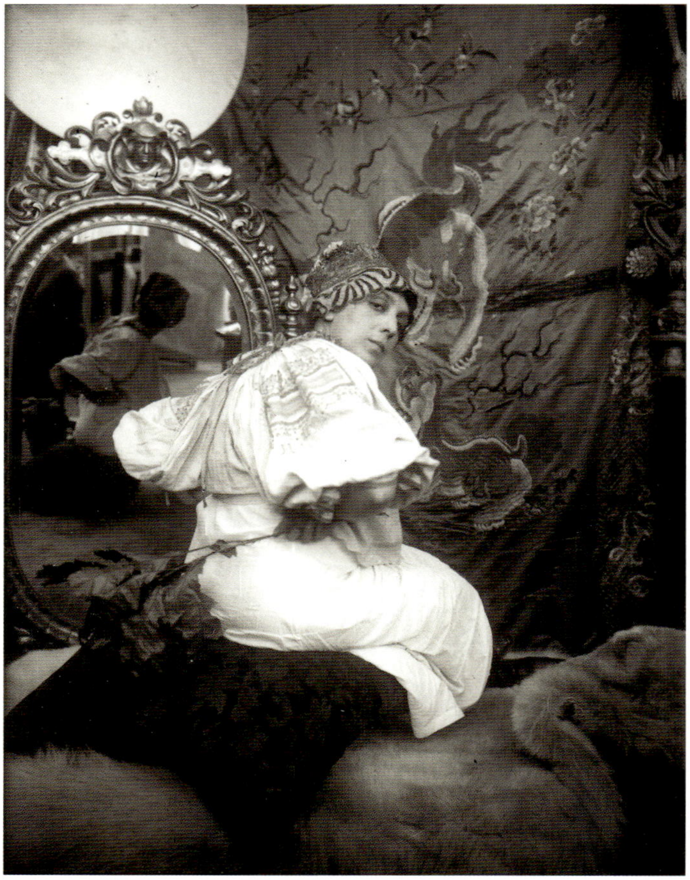

MODEL IN A BOHEMIAN
FOLK COSTUME AT
MUCHA'S STUDIO IN
RUE DU VAL-DE-GRÂCE,
PARIS
c.1900
Modern print from original
glass plate negative

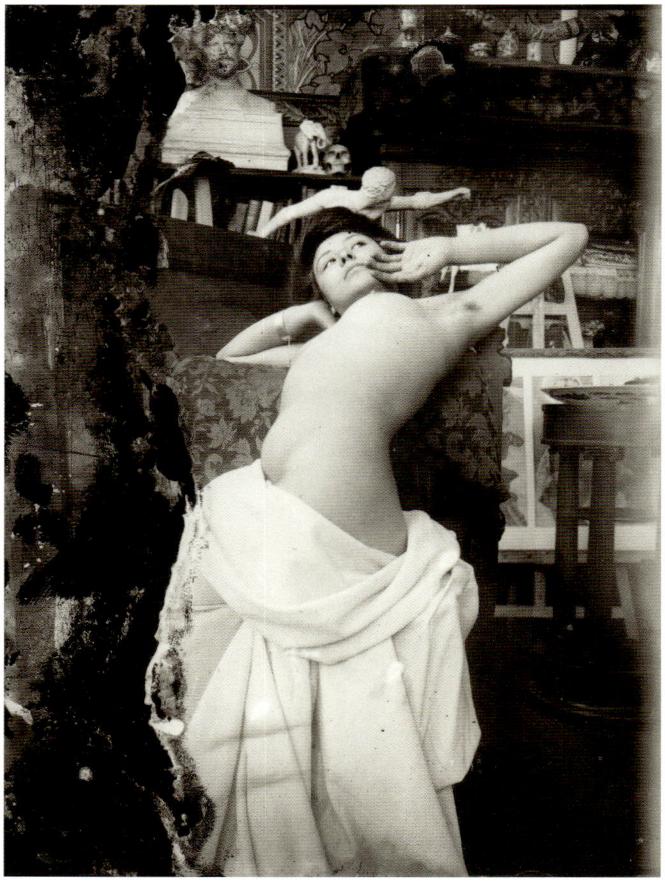

NUDE BENDING
BACKWARDS
c.1902
Modern print from original
glass plate negative

DANCING NUDE
c.1901
Four photographic studies
from a series of five
Modern prints from original
glass plate negatives

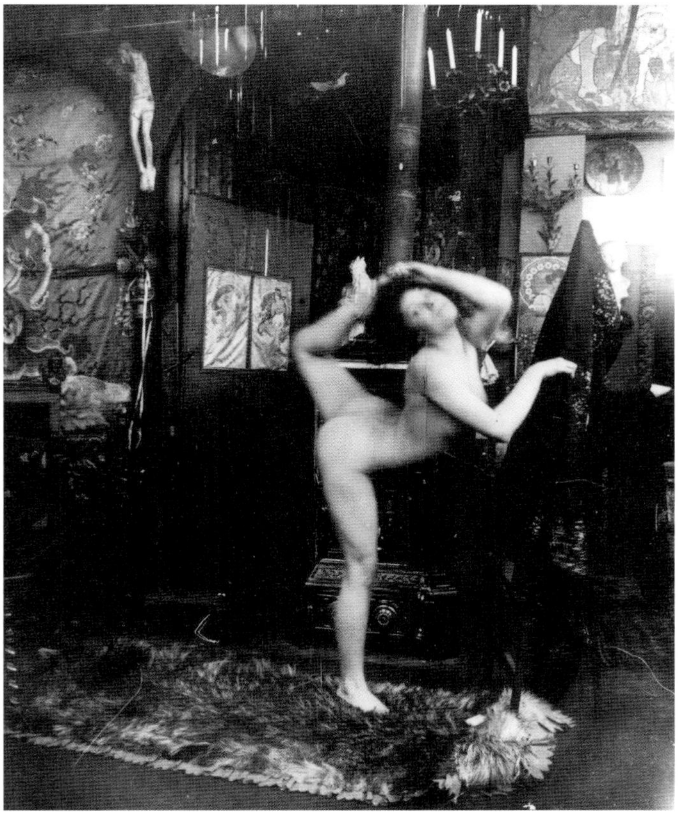
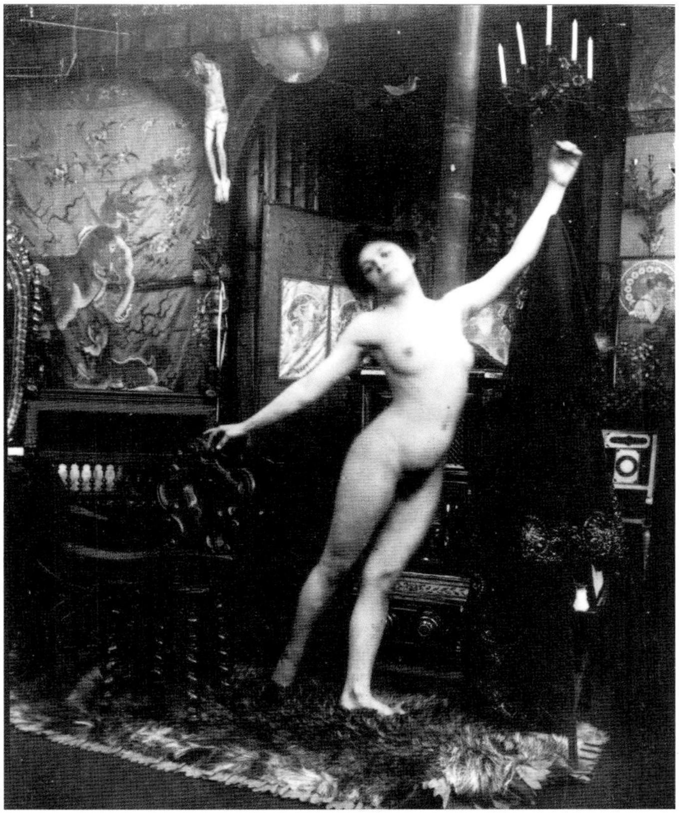
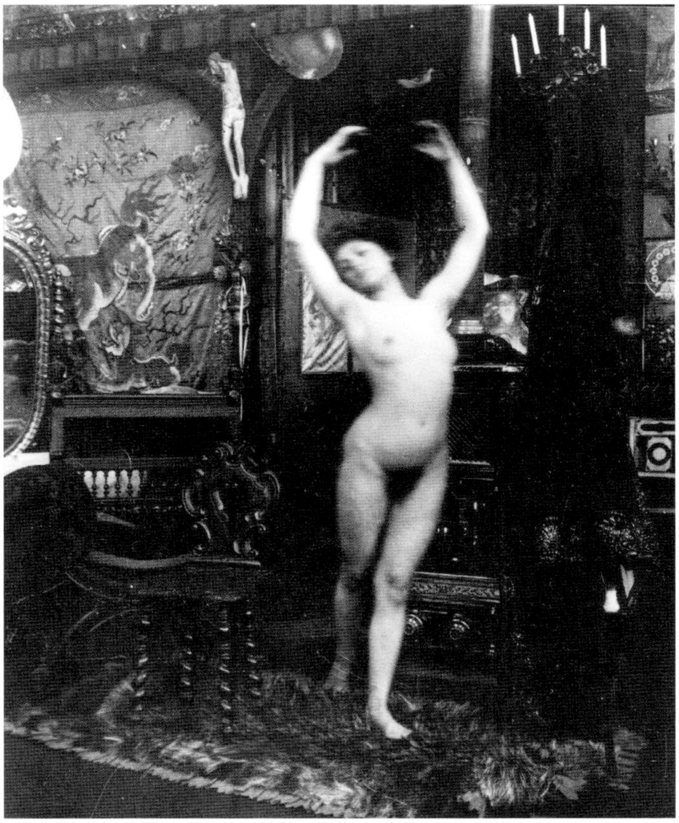
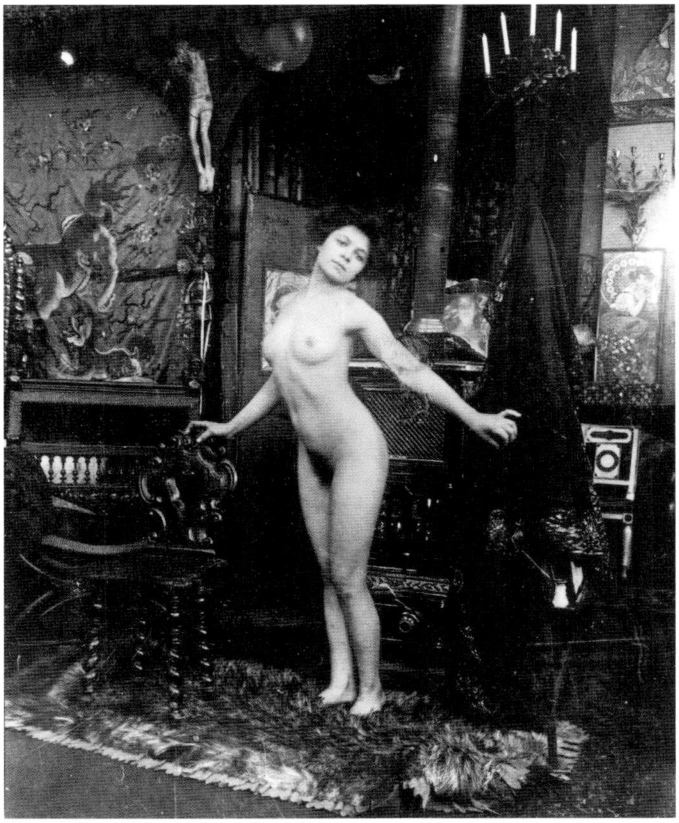

BEGUILING BEAUTY: AESTHETICISM IN BRITAIN AND WORKS FROM THE COLLECTION OF THE NATIONAL MUSEUMS LIVERPOOL

SANDRA PENKETH

In 1867 the art critic Sidney Colvin (1845–1927) wrote an article about contemporary painting.[1] In it he discussed a small group of young artists whose aim 'seems to be pre-eminently beauty'. The names listed in his publication included Frederic Leighton (1830–1896), Albert Moore (1841–1893), Dante Gabriel Rossetti (1826–1882) and Edward Burne-Jones (1833–1893) amongst others. The American artist James McNeill Whistler (1834–1903) was also mentioned. Although he doesn't use the term – its general use came later – essentially what Colvin is describing is Aestheticism. A study of paintings from the collections of National Museums Liverpool by these artists, including their aspirations, the influences that came to bear on their work, and the needs of patrons, demonstrates the characteristics of this fascinating moment in British art history extremely well.

Aestheticism in British art is generally said to have begun in the 1860s and to have lasted until the 1890s. It is difficult to define; there was no written agenda, no formal group of artists and no single style of production.[2] Most simply, as Colvin succinctly explained it, the movement was about beauty. For the Aesthetic practitioner, art did not need to serve any political, religious, or didactic purpose; it could exist for the sake of its beauty alone. Many of the artists noted by Colvin would have been very aware of the more recent writings about beauty, taste and judgment. Considerations of beauty and what it meant had long been explored, but from the eighteenth century German philosophers, including Immanuel Kant (1724–1804), began to consider the subject of aesthetics in greater depth. Their work was much admired by the Oxford don, Walter Pater (1839–1894), who became an influential supporter of the Aesthetic approach to art in Britain. French influence was also important. Early in the nineteenth century, the provocative writer Théophile Gautier (1811–1872) had formulated the concept of *'L'Art pour L'Art'*, that is 'Art for Art's sake', which he elaborated in his novel *Mademoiselle de Maupin* in 1835. Gautier's writings were in turn influential on the poet and writer Charles Baudelaire (1821–1867) and Whistler, who spent some of his formative years in Paris. The young English poet Algernon Charles Swinburne (1837–1909) was inspired by Baudelaire's unconventional writings and discussion of aesthetics. Swinburne, one of Rossetti's closest friends, who sensationalised the Victorian public with his highly sensual *Poems and Ballads* of 1866, believed in the primacy of the artist in influencing style and promoted beauty as a principle consideration in the practice of art. This continuous exchange of ideas across Europe, made all the more possible by easier travel and a more cosmopolitan approach to training, was an important factor in the development of Aestheticism.

Alongside this intellectual consideration of 'beauty' was a growing dissatisfaction with the industrialisation of the Victorian period. In many ways Aestheticism was a reaction to it. The Great Exhibition of 1851 not only highlighted the technical achievements of manufacturing, it also demonstrated all too well the poor level of design of most British mass-produced goods. William Morris was so frustrated by what he saw that he made it his mission to improve design, emphasising the important relationship between the maker and the finished product. His campaign eventually led him

Fig. 18
DANTE GABRIEL ROSSETTI
Sibylla Palmifera
1866–1870
Oil on canvas
98 x 85
Purchased by William Hesketh Lever in 1917
LL 3628

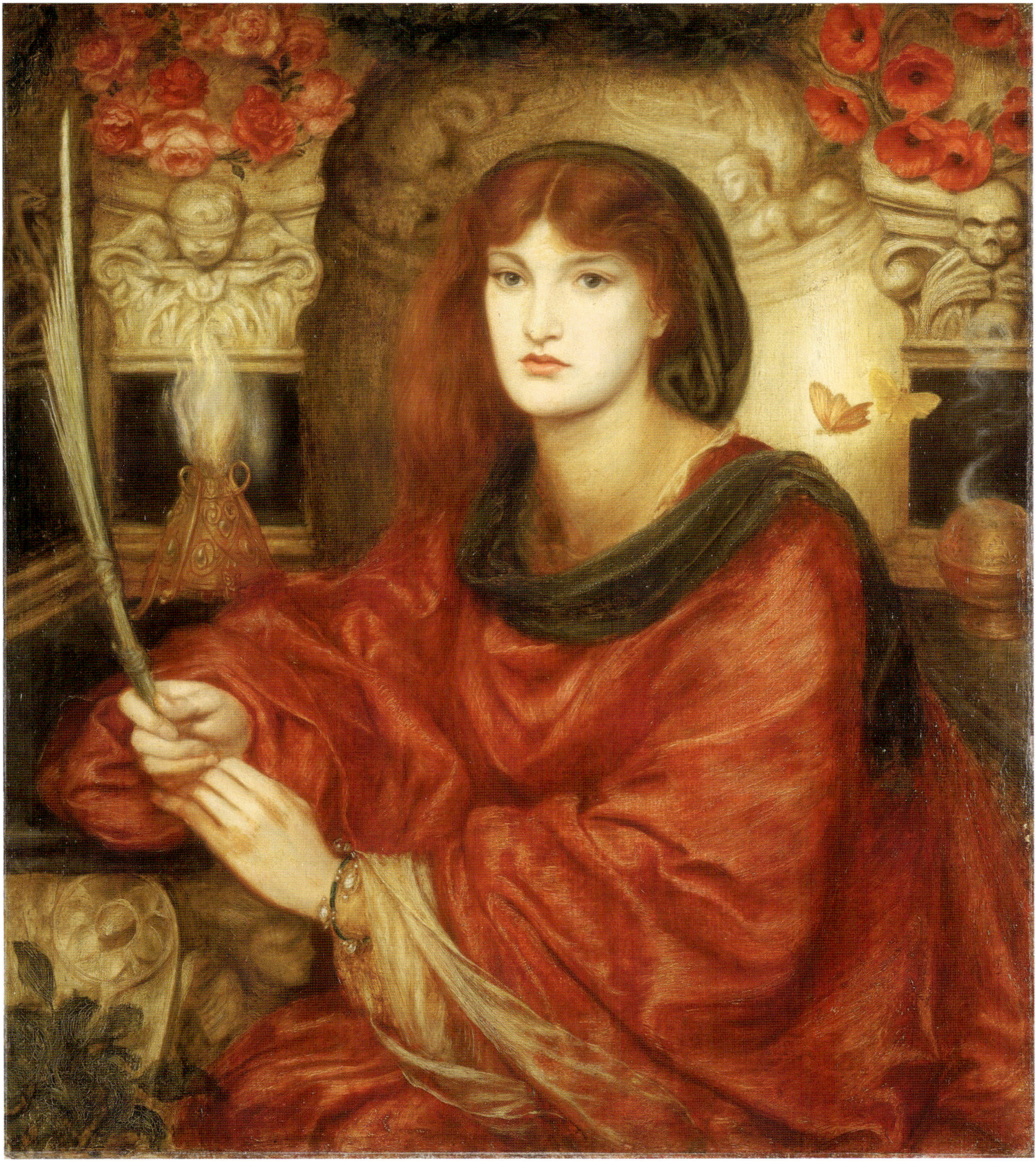

to set up Morris, Marshall, Faulkner and Co. (later to be Morris and Co.) in 1861. In a desire to move away from an emphasis on the functional aspects of an object, makers turned to natural forms for inspiration. Flowers, leaves, birds, and insects were just some of the popular motifs used by the anti-industrial designers. The middle of the nineteenth century was also marked by an ever-increasing number of opportunities to see examples of foreign arts through trade and travel. Oriental art in particular had a profound influence. There was a revival of interest in Chinese art, especially blue and white porcelain of the Kangxi period (1662–1772), and, perhaps even more importantly, there was a new appreciation of the beauties of Japanese art following the opening up of the country to general foreign trade in 1853. The wonderful examples of prints, furniture and textiles now available induced a craze for all things Japanese. The simplicity and elegance of Japanese art was in stark contrast to the often fussy, over-detailed look of early Victorian products. The arts of India and Islamic countries also provided a valuable source of design motifs and colour. Many of these international influences can be seen in the paintings of the artists listed by Colvin in his 1867 article. Also discernable is a renewed interest in classical art and the art of the Renaissance. The painters absorbed these different influences and allowed them and their responses to merge with other art forms such as music and poetry, another hallmark of Aestheticism. The mixing of design elements, the focus on compositional beauty and emotive power and the vagueness of subject was to influence later the methodology of Art Nouveau artists including Mucha.

The work of Aesthetic artists was not always well received by art critics or indeed the public at large. The rather flamboyant characters of some of the movement's leading protagonists (such as the painters Rossetti and Whistler, and the poet Swinburne) led to a characterisation of the Aesthetic artist as amoral and decadent. Their behaviour, their lifestyles, and of course their clothes were lampooned.[3] Art establishments, most significantly the Royal Academy in London, also struggled to grasp the significance of Aesthetic works. The seeming total disregard for the normal academic conventions of subject, composition and painting technique forced the Academy's selection committee to take a hard line with some artists such as its rejection in 1862 of Whistler's painting *Symphony in White, No. 1: The White Girl* (National Gallery of Art, Washington D.C). Sir Coutts Lindsay (1824–1913) was more enlightened. Acutely aware that artists, and indeed patrons, needed a new, more radical exhibiting forum for contemporary work, he took on responsibility for building the Grosvenor Gallery.[4] The venue, sited on New Bond Street in London, opened in 1877. The Gallery became synonymous with Aestheticism. Burne-Jones and Whistler were leading exhibitors along with Walter Crane (1845–1915), Albert Moore and George Watts (1817–1904). Even artists who were loyal Academicians, including Frederic Leighton, ventured to exhibit some works at the Grosvenor. In addition to its more accepting approach to contemporary painting, the Grosvenor aimed to display works in a different way. It avoided dense hangs that occupied walls from floor to ceiling but instead allowed each picture the space to breathe.[5] Pictures either by the same artist or of similar style or tonal value were hung close together. This considered approach to display chimed with the highly considered use of space, theme and colour in Aesthetic paintings. Surprisingly, Rossetti, whose later work might easily be classed as Aesthetic, refused to exhibit in this new 'palace of art'.

Rossetti's self-led exclusion from the Grosvenor Gallery as well as other exhibiting arena meant that at his death in 1882 many of his paintings were little known. The memorial exhibition of his work held in the winter of that year came as a revelation to many apart from his immediate circle of friends and family and patrons. An original founding member of the Pre-Raphaelite Brotherhood in 1848, Rossetti, along with John Everett Millais (1829–1896) and William Holman Hunt (1827–1910), brought about a revolution in painting in Britain. They encouraged a new consideration of the narrative and symbolic strength of early Renaissance painting as well as promoting the importance of the careful observation of nature. They followed the teaching of the art critic John Ruskin (1819–1900) and he in turn supported their ideals. The Pre-Raphaelites also introduced a jewel-like colour to painting, sweeping away the dull-toned regular palette of early Victorian art. Rossetti's empathies with the narratives and moral preaching of early Renaissance and mediaeval art, so implicit in the Pre-Raphaelites' early work, continued into the later 1850s when there was a significant change in his approach to painting.[6] By 1860 the delicate and detailed painting of his earlier period was replaced by an extravagant and luscious style executed in oil paint. The subjects of his paintings also underwent a significant shift. A large proportion of his early work had links to religious and mediaeval writings. Women often played a central role in these images but their qualities were elucidated through the narrative. From the 1860s women became the sole focus of his paintings but their qualities were explained in an abstract way. The meaning of these paintings was, and indeed still is, as much about the viewer's perceptions of the subject as it is the artist's own interpretation.[7]

Sibylla Palmifera (Fig.18), now in the collection of the Lady Lever Art Gallery, Port Sunlight, is typical. The subject is drawn in a confined space, sitting disconcertingly close to the picture plane. The sibyl holds a palm-sceptre and sits on a throne. Above her is a carved marble canopy and at the sides are pilasters decorated with the figures of a blind-folded Cupid with roses (love) and a skull with poppies (death). Butterflies representing the soul fly at the right of the figure. The sibyl was modelled by the classically beautiful Alexa Wilding (c.1845–1884), who had only recently begun to sit for the artist. She is shown with the hallmark auburn hair and red lips of many of Rossetti's beauties. Her expression is enigmatic. The exquisite Pre-Raphaelite detailing of the natural forms (such as the roses and the poppies) is meshed with an Aesthetic concern for pattern and colour harmonies. The intense tones and rich application of paint reflect Rossetti's interest in Venetian painting.[8] This painting was acquired by one of Rossetti's most important patrons, the banker George Rae (1817–1902), who lived in Birkenhead just across the River Mersey from Liverpool. Rossetti first mentioned the subject to him in December 1865 when he was still working on another painting also commissioned by Rae, *The Beloved* (1865–1866: Tate Britain, London). In the correspondence he refers to it simply as *Palmifera* and notes that she is holding a palm-sceptre to mark her as first among his beauties.[9] Later in his career Rossetti gave a slightly different explanation of the meaning of the picture than that first given to Rae. The artist suggested that the work embodied the idea of 'the Principle of Beauty, which draws all high-toned men to itself'. He suggests a relationship with the beautiful object and the viewer's interpretation; this allusion ties in with the intellectual writings on Aestheticism and the belief in 'art for art's sake'.[10] This interpretation was also reflected in a sonnet Rossetti created to accompany the picture (also see *Venus Vertocordia* pp.124–125). Although in his early work Rossetti had based his paintings on literary sources, these female half-length paintings of the 1860s onwards worked in a reverse pattern; the painting came first then the written interpretation. This connectivity between pictorial and literary representation was a key feature of the Aesthetic Movement and indeed much inspired by Rossetti's approach. *Sibyilla Palmifera* was eventually to hang in Rae's home along with *The Beloved* and another picture *Monna Vanna* (1866: Tate Britain, London). Together these celebrations of female beauty and power must have made a startling impression on any visitors to the house.

Rossetti first offered *Sibylla Palmifera* to another

of his patrons, Frederick Leyland (1832–1892), without success. Like Rae, Leyland was local to the city of Liverpool. He had made his fortune in shipping, first as a partner in the shipping company John Bibby, Sons & Co. then as owner of the Leyland shipping line established in 1873. He was a generous patron of the arts and became known as 'the Liverpool Medici'. His first commissions from Rossetti and his other great interest, Whistler, were made in the mid 1860s. This was around the time of his tenancy of Speke Hall, a Tudor mansion located on the outskirts of Liverpool. Although he failed to pick up Rossetti's offer of *Sibylla Palmifera*, Leyland went on to commission numerous works from the artist including portrait studies of his wife. Many of these pictures were eventually shown in Leyland's grand London home at 49 Princes Gate. The interiors of this house reflected perfectly Leyland's interest in Aestheticism and were developed with close input from his preferred artists, designers, architects and art dealers. Notoriously, Whistler took one such commission too far, developing the extravagant homage to Aestheticism, the Peacock Room, without due consultation with Leyland. Photographs taken by Harry Bedford Lemere (1864–1944) of Leyland's home just after the collector's death in 1892 show this room and others in all their splendid detail.[11] In the image of the Drawing Room, there is a breathtaking collection of Rossetti's painted beauties including *The Blessed Damozel* (Fig.19).[12]

In 1850, Rossetti had published a poem in the Pre-Raphaelite journal *The Germ*. He re-issued it with some alterations in his collection *Poems* in 1870. The title of the work was *The Blessed Damozel*. It explored the theme of doomed love. A young woman tragically died leaving her youthful lover behind on earth. From heaven she gazed on him desperate for them to be reunited at his death. Friends and patrons of the artist much admired this work and repeatedly encouraged him to illustrate it in a painting. In 1871, Rossetti finally relented at the behest of his major patron William Graham (1817–1885).[13] In fact, Rossetti worked on three canvases of the subject, and certainly completed two. The largest went to Graham and the slightly smaller version was sold to Frederick Leyland.[14] The format of the picture resembles a Renaissance altarpiece; highly appropriate for a work about devotion, both devotion of the subject for her lover and, arguably, the devotion of the viewer in admiring the subject's faithfulness and beauty. The content of the picture closely follows the text of the poem.[15] The model for this picture, as for *Sibylla Palmifera*, was Alexa Wilding. Again, colour harmonies and the careful arrangement of motifs are key considerations. It was the support of collectors like Graham, Rae and Leyland that allowed Rossetti to explore his interest in poetic feeling, ideal beauty, sensuous colour and womanly attributes with a certain degree of freedom from convention.[16]

Edward Burne-Jones was much influenced by Rossetti's work. His paintings, a legacy of early

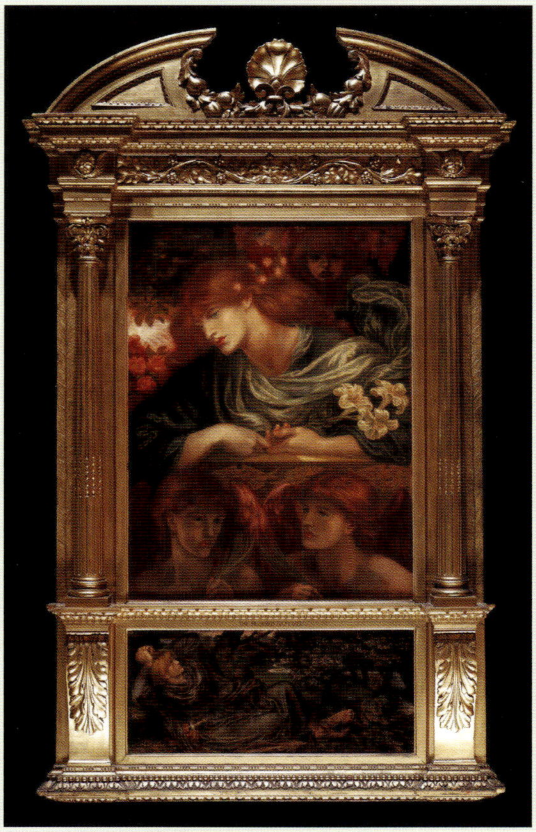

Fig. 19
DANTE GABRIEL ROSSETTI
The Blessed Damozel
1875-79
Oil on canvas
111 x 83 plus predella
36 x 83
Purchased by William Hesketh Lever in 1922
LLAG 3148

Pre-Raphaelite teaching, understandably also found favour with Frederick Leyland. Their themes of female beauty, love and power set within powerfully decorative arrangements were very much to the taste of this leading Aesthetic collector. Unlike Rossetti's later works, narrative was still a major concern for Burne-Jones but he balances this expertly with an impeccable sense of poetic beauty. Any viewer could, and still does, marvel at the works' emotive presence and sublime beauty even if the story seems unfamiliar. In the late 1860s Leyland commissioned the artist to work on an Arthurian subject, *The Beguiling of Merlin* (see p.118), for his Princes Gate house. The work proved a trial for Burne-Jones, taking at least five years to complete. This lengthy gestation was due primarily to technical difficulties, but the personal connotations the picture held for the artist no doubt made its completion all the more torturous. It was finally exhibited at the first ever exhibition of the Grosvenor Gallery in 1877.[17] There it caused a sensation. It was one of eight works by Burne-Jones exhibited in the show. Displayed together, beautifully spaced on crimson damask (the artist had doubts about the colour of the latter), the group was a significant statement in Aesthetic ideals.[18] Following its success at the Grosvenor Gallery, the painting was exhibited at the Exposition Universelle in Paris in 1878, marking the beginning of the artist's success on the international stage.

This painting illustrates the story of Nimue, Lady of the Lake. She enchants an infatuated Merlin and he, trapped in the tangles of a sprawling hawthorn bush, is helpless against her powers. The daring tall, thin format, the swirling drapery and tangled hawthorn create an atmosphere of almost suffocating intensity. This and the suggested pungent, overpowering smell of hawthorn blossom add to the picture's emotive qualities. The close tonal range of the colours also acts to emphasise the sense of coherence. Burne-Jones used Maria Zambaco (1843–1914) as the model for Nimue. She was a member of the wealthy Ionides family, significant patrons of the arts in Victorian London. The two were involved in a scandalous love affair from the mid 1860s, remaining close until the early 1870s. The picture's overriding themes of love, infatuation, power, entrapment and betrayal mirrored the artist's personal history.[19]

In *The Tree of Forgiveness* (Fig.20), Burne-Jones again explores the theme of infatuation. As with *The Beguiling of Merlin*, the artist employs a close colour palette and a carefully balanced composition. The expressive power of the picture is accentuated by the countenances of the subjects. However, the androgynous figures of the earlier picture are replaced by a mannerist anatomy inspired by Michelangelo. The painting illustrates a classical legend, Phyllis and Demaphoön (c.f. Louise Jopling *Phyllis* see p.123). After the conquest of Troy,

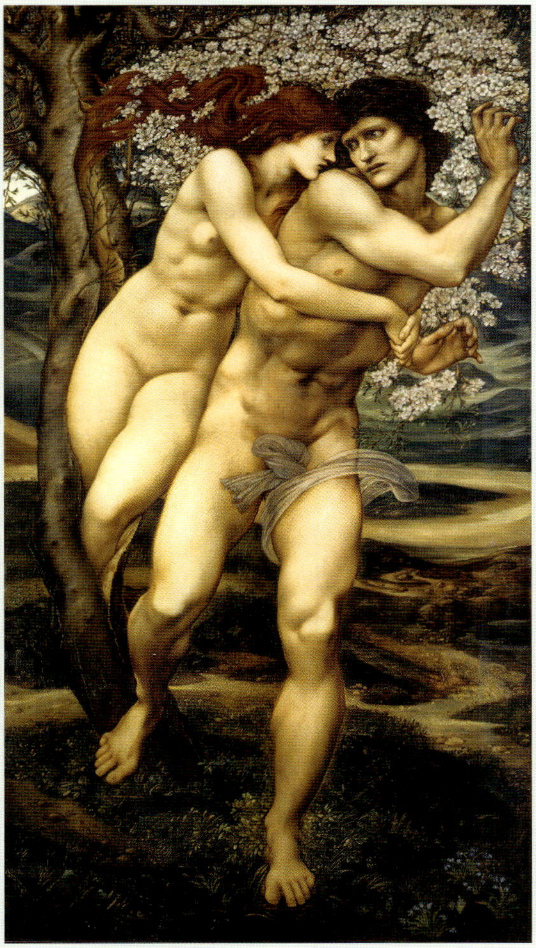

Fig. 20
EDWARD BURNE-JONES
The Tree of Forgiveness
1882
Oil on canvas
196 x 107
Purchased by William Hesketh Lever in 1918
LL 3635

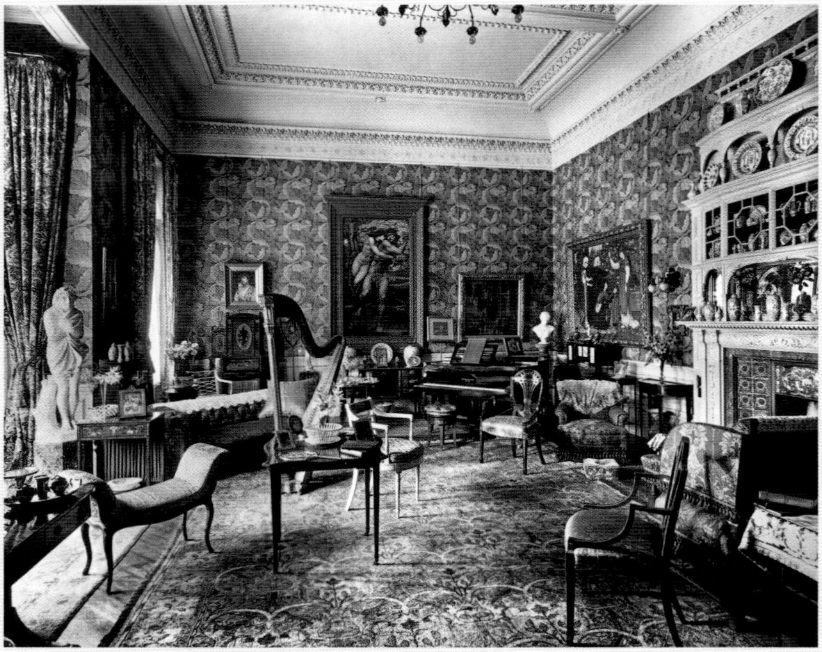

Fig. 21
HARRY BEDFORD LEMERE
The Music Room at Holmestead, Mossley Hill
1901
Bedford Lemere photographic archive
BL 16685

Demaphoön, the son of Theseus, stayed at the court of the King of Thrace. Phyllis, the king's daughter, fell in love with the visitor and he agreed to marry her but first had to return to Attica to sort out his personal affairs. Demaphoön was away so long that Phyllis lost hope of his return and in a fit of anguish killed herself. The gods took pity on her and turned her into an almond tree. When Demaphoön eventually did return he was filled with remorse and embraced the almond tree. Immediately the tree blossomed and Phyllis emerged to forgive her lover.[20] Again, the artist used Maria Zambaco, his infatuation, as facial model for the leading female character. The picture was a re-working of a watercolour produced by Burne-Jones in 1870 that was exhibited at the Old Water-Colour Society. Its display met with controversy due to Demaphoön's completely naked appearance. Following the narrow-minded reaction of the Society and critics to his work, Burne-Jones refused to exhibit again publicly until the launch of the Grosvenor Gallery.

The Tree of Forgiveness was exhibited at the Grosvenor Gallery in 1882 to mixed reviews. As usual, critics admired the artist's approach to colour and line but were dissatisfied with his unusual treatment of the figures. In the same year the painting was acquired by the Liverpool collector William Imrie (1836–1906) who ran the White Star shipping line. He, like his business partner, Thomas Ismay (1837–1899), was a keen collector of art. His collection was wide-ranging but put a particular emphasis on Arts and Crafts and Pre-Raphaelite art. A photograph of the Music Room in his Liverpool home, Holmestead, by Bedford Lemere and dated 1901 shows the Burne-Jones picture centre stage and displayed in an empathetic context of beautiful design (Fig.21).[21] The walls are covered with William Morris 'Acanthus' wallpaper, an extravagant mantelpiece is occupied by Chinese porcelain and 18th century furniture is tastefully positioned in the room. This carefully considered and complementary amalgamation of design styles was typical of interiors associated with Aestheticism. Collectors sought to reflect their Aesthetic interests not just in the acquisition and display of appropriate objects but also through their attitude to interior design. This fashion undoubtedly echoed artists' own insistence on the integration of art and design in their studio homes, such as Frederic Leighton's house in Holland Park.[22]

Burne-Jones's use of decorative compositional design continued until the end of his career. In a startlingly accomplished watercolour called *Sponsa de Libano* (see p.119), first exhibited at the modernist New Gallery in 1891 and purchased by the Walker Art Gallery in 1896, Burne-Jones shows off his absolute confidence as a designer.[23] The subject is based on the *Song of Solomon*, but even with no knowledge of the reference, the viewer is mesmerized by the beauty and emotive power of the work. The rhythm of movement in the swirling drapery, the way each section of the picture connects to another through colour and shape and the sheer awe-inspiring scale of the drawing are rightly impressive. This work is not just a tour-de-force of watercolour painting, it also speaks volumes about the concerns of Aestheticism. Of all the works referenced in this essay, it is the one with the most obvious visual relationship to the work of Mucha.

Aesthetic ideals were also employed by the Victorian classical painters Frederick Leighton and Albert Moore. Leighton, very much considered an artist of the establishment, was concerned with the illustration of classical literature and the classical world. Running through his artistic output is a keen interest in human anatomy. But Leighton, particularly in his later work, was also concerned with the use of colour and design to convey beauty and emotion. In *The Garden of the Hesperides* of 1892 (Fig.22), Leighton draws together perfectly his classical interests with an exploration of design and colour. The Hesperides were the daughters of Hesperus, the god of evening. They were guardians of the golden apples given to them by Juno (Jupiter) on the occasion of their marriage. The dragon Ladon assisted them. The apples were eventually stolen by Hercules. In his painting, Leighton replaced the dragon of the myth with a snake.[24] Leighton' s picture is daring: executed in the round, it no doubt presented challenging compositional problems, but the format is perfect for suggesting a claustrophobic atmosphere. Trapped in their duty of guarding the golden apples and made sleepy by the heat and their own music, they seemingly melt into a dream-like state, entwined with each other and the snake. The viewer's eye is drawn around the picture in a circular pattern, never escaping the languid, sensuous environment. In Moore's *A Summer Night* (Fig.23), there is also concern with design, colour and anatomy, but whereas Leighton's work is saturated with atmosphere and movement, Moore's picture is one of understatement and elegance. The figures seem captured in stillness like a photograph or classical frieze. In fact Moore's inspiration may have been the famous Portland Vase (c.AD 5–25: British Museum, London).[25] The carefully chosen poses suggest a series of consecutive movements, which, matched with the harmonising use of colour, create a beautiful rhythmic image. Oriental objects decorate the classical space. Moore's work, like that of all the artists discussed, shows an assimilation of many disparate elements. He used his knowledge of classical architecture and art as a source for his work. His study of the Elgin marbles and other Greek artefacts encouraged his use of drapery to reveal the form of the human figure. In addition Moore was very aware of architectural principles of composition, so that his preparatory drawings reveal an expert use of geometry and mathematics to guide his designs.[26] Undoubtedly, Moore's extensive knowledge of the principles of landscape painting also had an impact on his approach to composition. Moore was essentially interested in the formal, abstract properties of beauty. In a calm and assured way, he draws on our senses and emotions. Knowing this, it is perhaps easy to understand his relationship with Whistler.

In modern art history there has been a tendency to compartmentalise artists into like and chronologically ordered groups. Their styles are described in straightforward terms (e.g. Pre-Raphaelite, Classical etc.) but an examination of this group of works from our collection emphasises the real complexity of artists' methodologies and

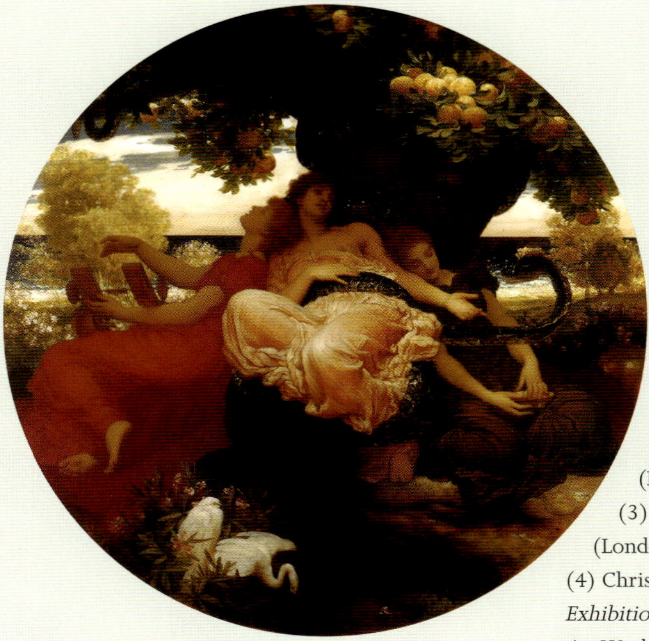

Fig. 22
FREDERIC LORD LEIGHTON
Garden of the Hesperides
1892
Oil on canvas
169 x 169
Purchased by William Hesketh Lever in 1913
LL 3139

intellectual interests. For Rossetti and Burne-Jones their artistic notions were very much rooted in Pre-Raphaelitism but their concerns extended to more abstract messages around women, emotion and colour. Similarly, Leighton and Moore might well be artists interested in the classical world but they were also interested in beauty, colour and emotion. This mixing of ideas was all perfectly natural. None of the artists worked in a vacuum, they were influenced by whom they met, what they saw, what they read, fashions, the interests of their patrons. Moore the Victorian classical painter was great friends with Whistler the advocate of colour and virtual abstraction. Leighton, Burne-Jones, and Rossetti were connected through mutual friends such as Val Prinsep (1838–1904) of Little Holland House. Together they produced paintings that exemplify perfectly Aestheticism. Most simply put, each is beautiful.

NOTES

(1) Sidney Colvin, 'English Painters and Painting in 1867', *Fortnightly Review,* 1 October 1867

(2) E. Prettejohn (ed), *After the Pre-Raphaelites: Art and Aestheticism in Victorian England,* (Manchester University Press, 1999), pp.1–12.

(3) Lionel Lambourne, *The Aesthetic Movement* (London, Phaidon, 1996), pp.112–133.

(4) Christopher Newall, *The Grosvenor Gallery Exhibitions: Change and Continuity in the Victorian Art World* (Cambridge University Press, 1995).

(5) Georgiana Burne-Jones, *Memorials of Edward Burne-Jones*, 2 volumes (London, Macmillan & Co. 1904), vol. II, p.69.

(6) Julian Treuherz, Elizabeth Prettejohn, Edwin Becker, *Dante Gabriel Rossetti* (Zwolle, Waanders Publishers, 2003), pp.11–49.

(7) Ibid., pp.51–109

(8) See Alistair Grieve, 'Rossetti and the scandal of art for art's sake in the early 1860', in E. Prettejohn (ed), *After the Pre-Raphaelites: Art and Aestheticism in Victorian England,* (Manchester University Press, 1999), pp.23–26

(9) As quoted in Mary Bennett, *Artists of the Pre-Raphaelite Circle: The First Generation* (London, Lund Humphries, 1988), p.170.

(10) As discussed in Julian Treuherz, Elizabeth Prettejohn, Edwin Becker, *Dante Gabriel Rossetti* (Zwolle, Waanders Publishers, 2003), p.192.

(11) The important work of Bedford Lemere in recording buildings and interiors is described in Nicholas Cooper, *The Photography of Bedford Lemere & Co: An Age of Confidence* (London, English Heritage, 2011).

(12) http://archive.historicengland.org.uk/SingleResult/Default.aspx?id=989591&t=Quick&cr=frederick+leyland&io=False&l=all. Reference BL 11528.

(13) Mary Bennett, *Artists of the Pre-Raphaelite Circle: The First Generation* (London, Lund Humphries, 1988), p.179.

Fig. 23
ALBERT MOORE
A Summer Night
First exhibited 1890
Oil on canvas
132 x 228
Purchased from the artist in 1890
WAG 2125

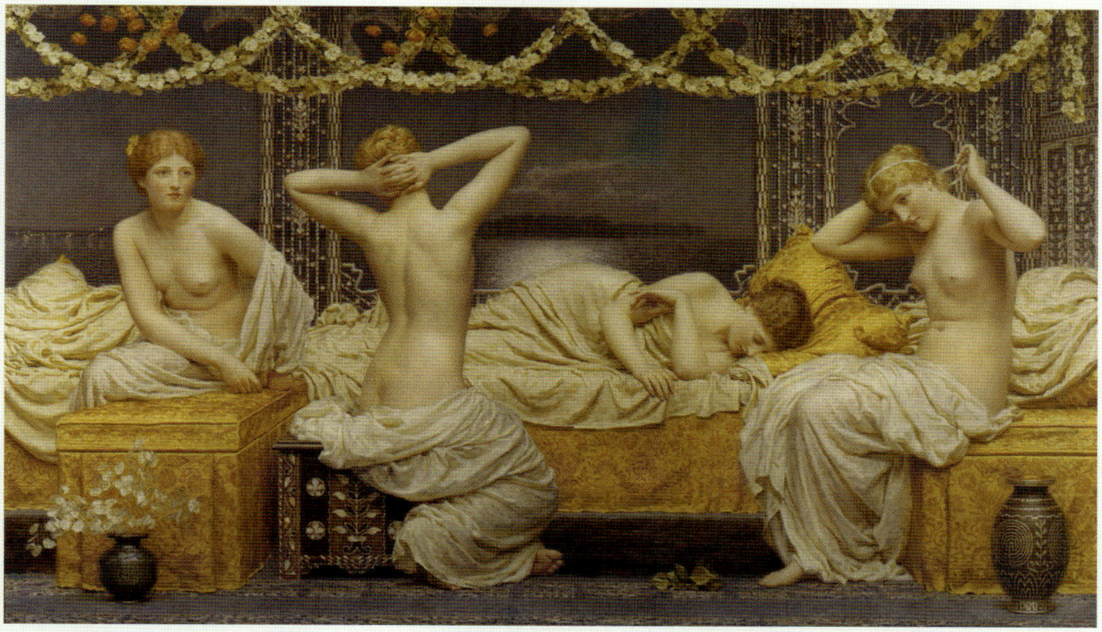

(14) Ibid. p.179.
(15) The first verse demonstrates this perfectly:

The blessed damozel leaned out
From the gold bar of Heaven;
Her eyes were deeper than the depth
Of waters stilled at even;
She had three lilies in her hand,
And the stars in her hair were seven.

Dante Gabriel Rossetti
The Works of Dante Gabriel Rossetti
ed. William Michael Rossetti (London 1911), p.3.

(16) As the critic Lionel Robinson noted in his description of Leyland's collection in the *Art Journal* of 1892, *'It is evident that the merely decorative use of pictures was in his [Leyland's] mind subordinate to the ideas they conveyed and the poetic feeling they stimulated. The explanation of his strongly-marked preference for the mystic, super-sensuous art of D.G. Rossetti does not concern us. It is enough to know that he and Mr Graham of Glasgow were the instruments by which this interesting phase of nineteenth-century Art was stimulated. Without these patrons Rossetti would have been forced to adapt his powers to pleasing the popular taste, but by their help he was able to work out his own theories of Art.'.* Quoted in Mary Bennett, *Artists of the Pre-Raphaelite Circle: The First Generation* (London, Lund Humphries, 1988), p.179.
(17) See Edward Morris, *Victorian and Edwardian Paintings in the Lady Lever Art Gallery* (London, HMSO), pp.7–11.
(18) Georgiana Burne-Jones, *Memorials of Edward Burne-Jones,* 2 volumes (London, Macmillan & Co. 1904), vol. II, p.77.
(19) See Edward Morris, *Victorian and Edwardian Paintings in the Lady Lever Art Gallery* (London, HMSO), p.7.
(20) Ibid., pp.15–19.
(21) Joseph Sharples, *Merchant Palaces: Liverpool and Wirral Mansions photographed by Bedford Lemere & Co* (Liverpool, The Bluecoat Press, 2007), pp.74–75.
(22) For a detailed exploration of the phenomenon of the artist's studio home at this time see Charlotte Gere, Artistic Circles: Design and decoration in the Aesthetic Movement (London, V&A Publishing, 2010).
(23) For discussion of the subject and comparison to preparatory studies see Jessica Feather et al., *British Watercolours and Drawings: Lord Leverhulme's Collection in the Lady Lever Art Gallery* (Liverpool University Press and National Museums Liverpool, 2010), pp.36–37.
(24) See Edward Morris, *Victorian and Edwardian Paintings in the Lady Lever Art Gallery* (London, HMSO), pp.71–75.
(25) Robyn Asleson, *Albert Moore* (London, Phaidon, 2000), pp.184–189.
(26) Robyn Asleson, 'Nature and abstraction in the aesthetic development of Albert Moore', in E. Prettejohn (ed), *After the Pre-Raphaelites: Art and Aestheticism in Victorian England,* (Manchester University Press, 1999), pp.115–134

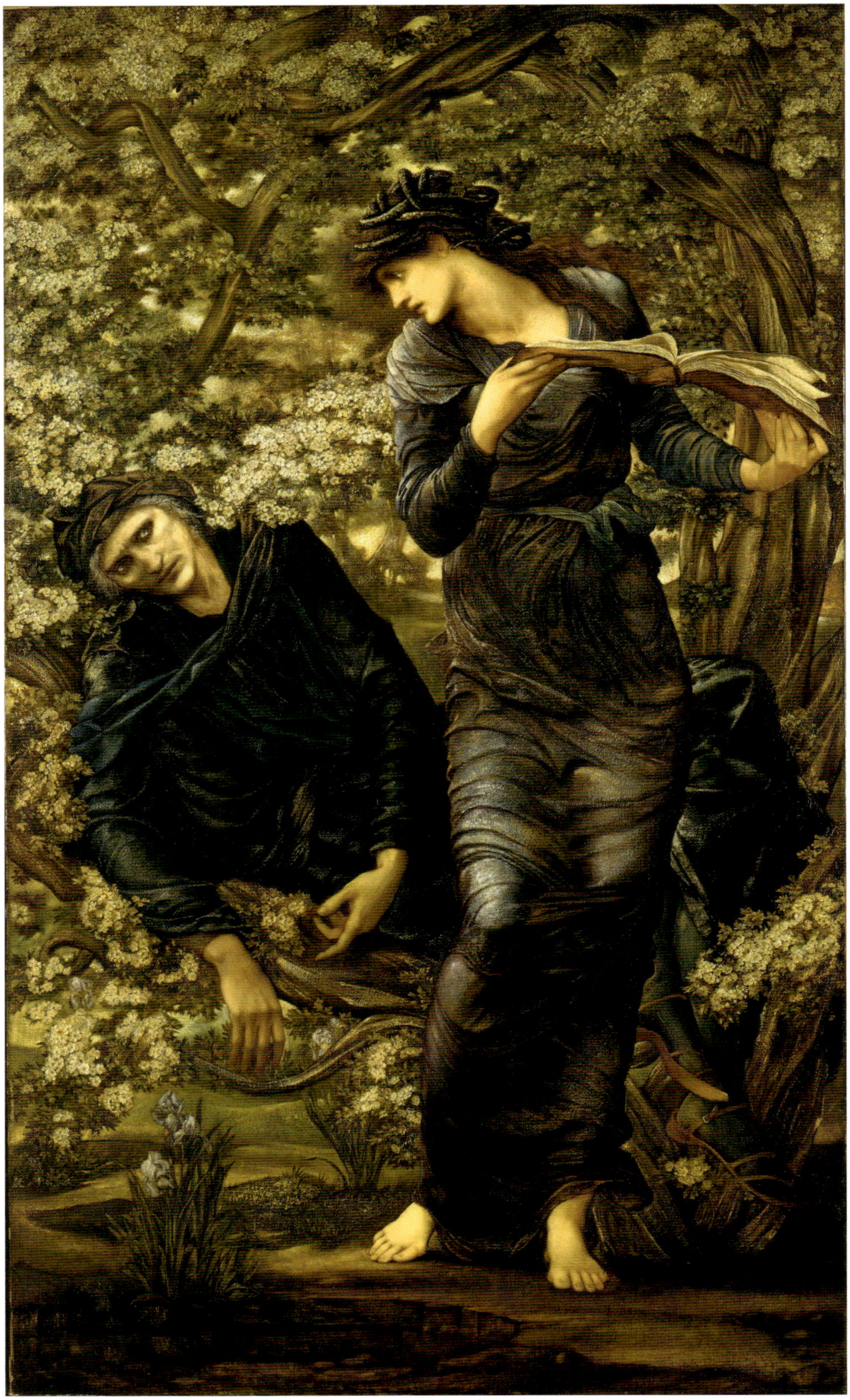

EDWARD BURNE-JONES
(1833–1898)
THE BEGUILING OF MERLIN
1872–1877
Oil on canvas
186 x 111
Purchased by William Hesketh Lever in 1918.
LL3121

Merlin, besotted by the Lady of the Lake, Nimue, is enchanted into deep sleep by her. Whilst under her power she gains his book of magic spells. Burne-Jones was fascinated by the medieval legends of King Arthur, and by the model for Nimue, who was his mistress Maria Zambaco, a sculptor herself. Burne-Jones' pattern-making, with Nimue's curving body mirroring the frieze of hawthorn branches, influenced the development of the Aesthetic and Art Nouveau styles.

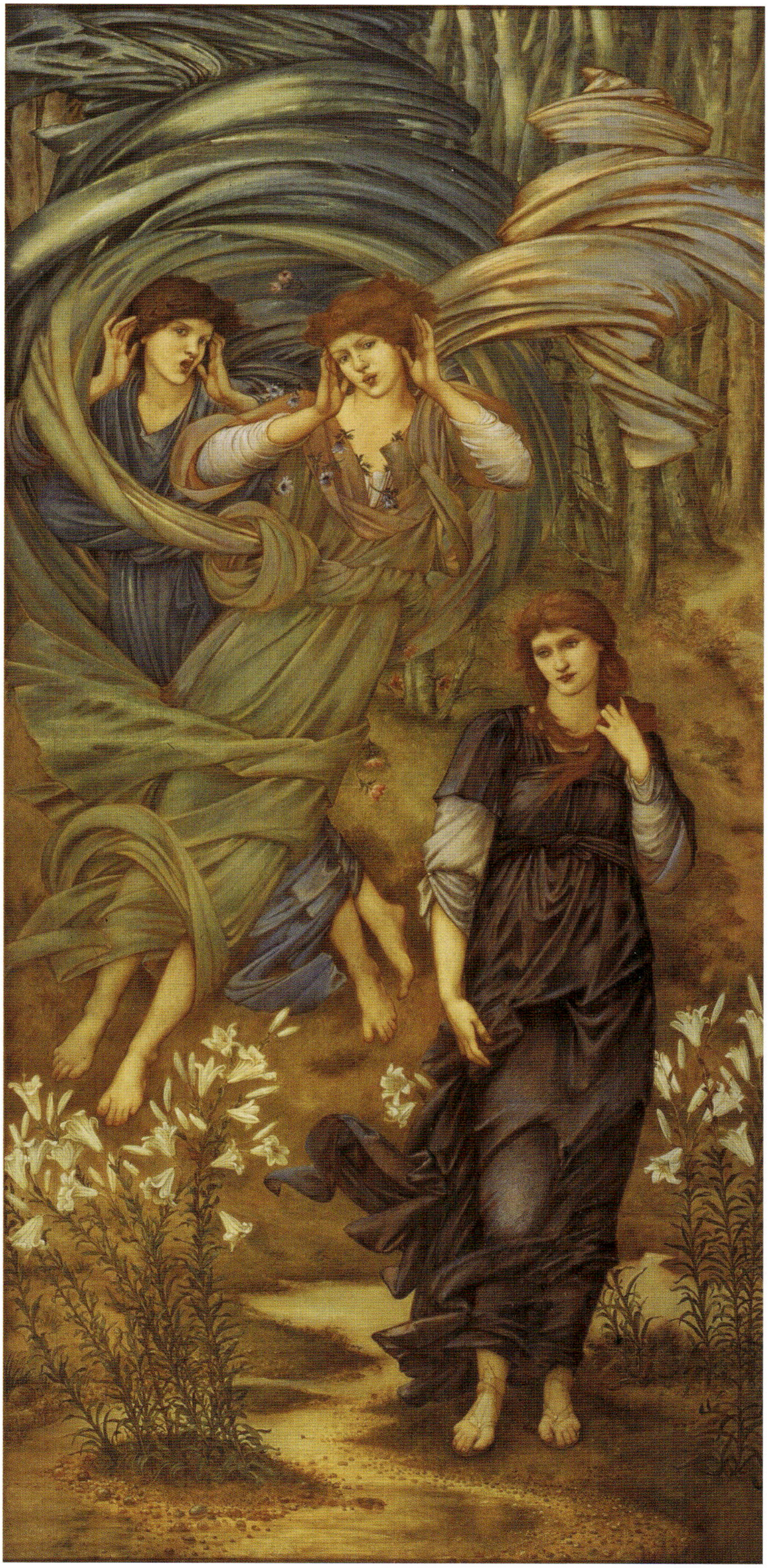

EDWARD BURNE-JONES
(1833–1898)
SPONSA DI LIBANO
(THE BRIDE OF LEBANON)
1891
Watercolour and tempera on
paper backed by panel
332.5 x 158
Purchased from the Liverpool
Autumn Exhibition 1896.
WAG113

This tall watercolour was inspired by the lines from the biblical mystical poem *The Song of Solomon*: 'Awake O North Wind, and come thou South, blow upon my garden that the spices thereof may flow out.' It shows a typically dreamy Burne-Jones' Bride wafted through a flowering field by the North and South Winds swirling above. Before being shown at the Walker in Liverpool it was exhibited in Liège, Belgium, in 1896.

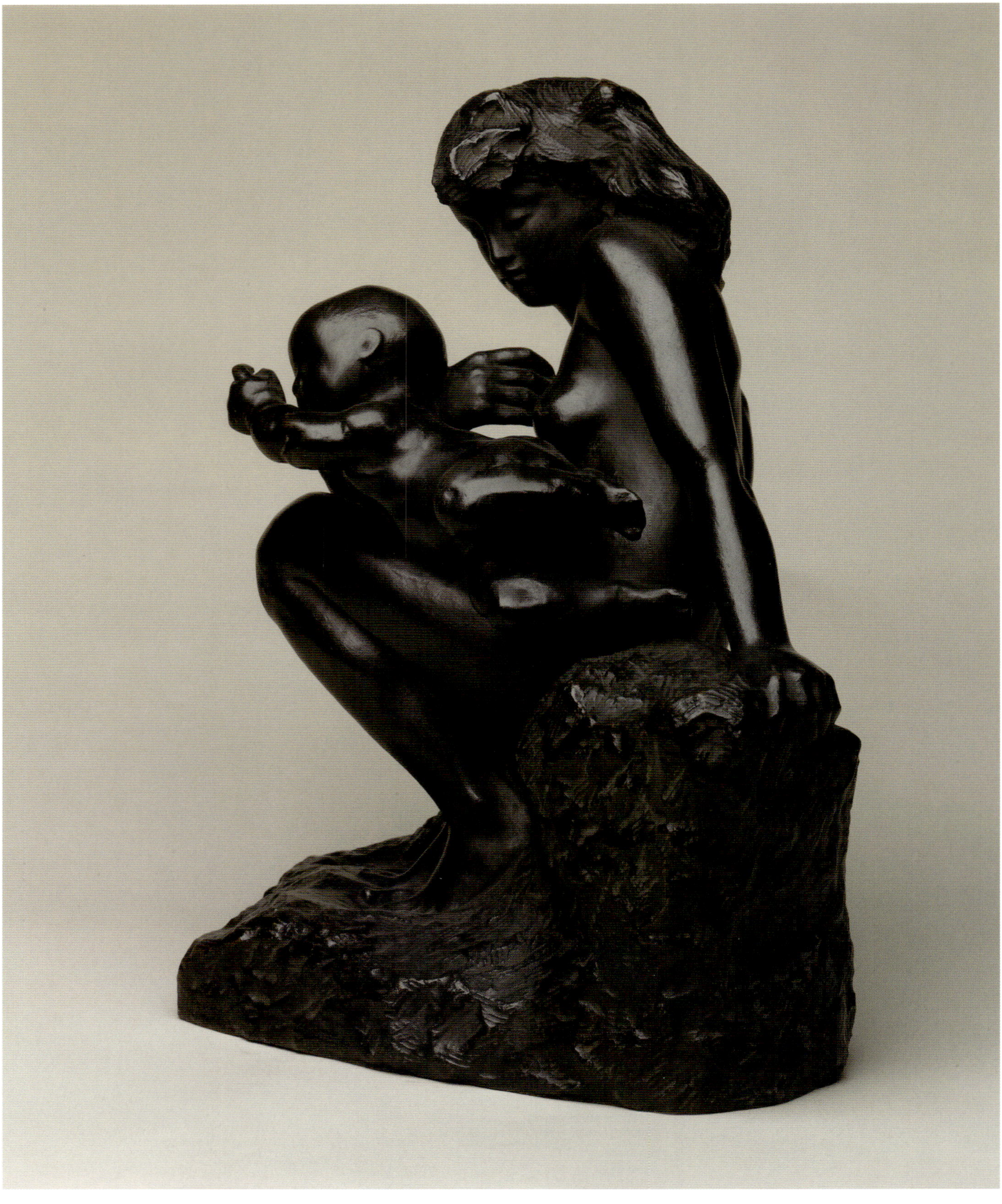

AUGUSTE RODIN (1840–1917)
FLEETING LOVE (ALSO KNOWN AS 'NYMPH AND CHILD')
Before 1899
Cast in bronze
40 x 25.5 x 33
Bequeathed by James Smith in 1927
WAG3176

Rodin encouraged the ambiguity of both symbolism and form in his sculptures. Small Rodin bronzes, often of female nudes, were popular with British collectors. This one was bought in 1899 by the Liverpool French wine importer James Smith (1831–1923) who met Rodin on his trips to Paris. By 1905 Smith owned seven Rodin works, six of which were given to the Walker.

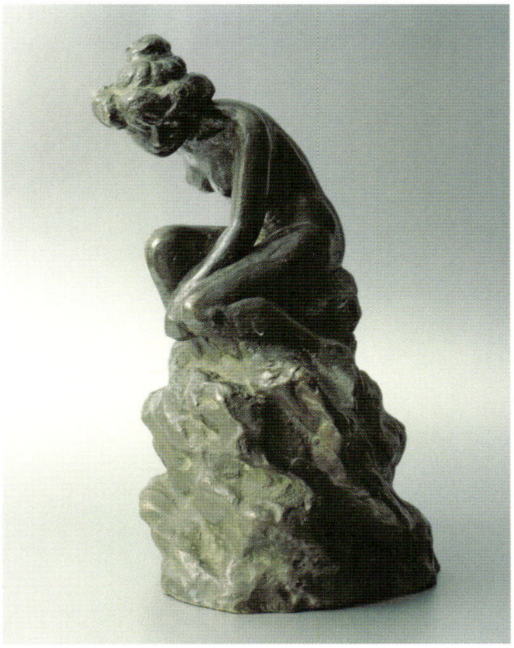

Fig. 24
NUDE ON A ROCK BY MUCHA
1899
Bronze
(height) 27
Mucha Trust

Inspired by Rodin, Mucha produced this rare sculpture, which captures the slender figure of a girl gazing down at her reflection in the water below the rock on which she is seated. Cast from a hand-build mass of clay, the expressive rendering of the forms show an influence from Rodin's work such as Fleeting Love shown here. (TS)

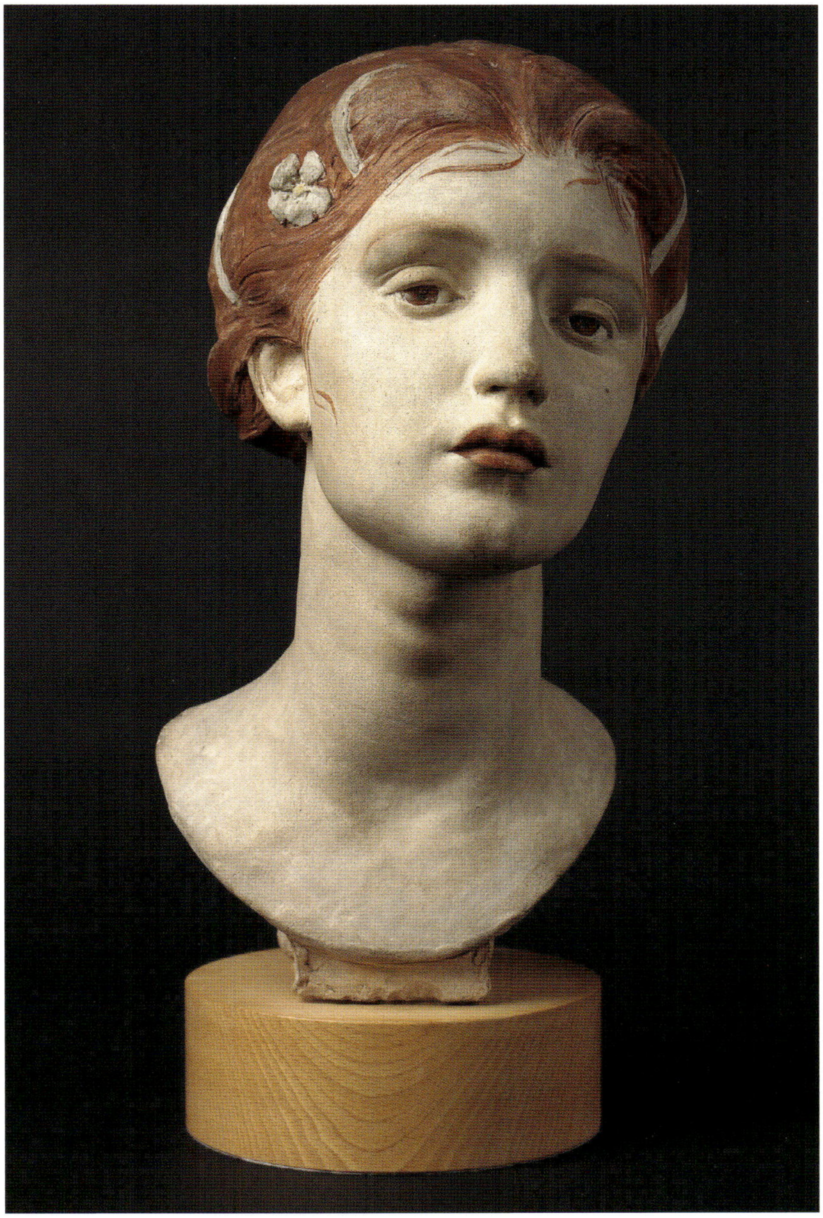

CONRAD DRESSLER (1856–1940)
NITA, MRS CONRAD DRESSLER
1893
Painted terracotta
37.5 x 20 x 26; (base height) 6
Presented by Mrs. V. E. Cotton in 1974
WAG8622

Conrad Dressler, the London-born sculptor of German descent, worked at the Birkenhead Della Robbia Pottery between 1894 and 1897 where he sculpted glazed earthenware architectural reliefs. This painted bust is thought to portray his Austrian wife Nita (1864–1928) a year after their marriage. Dressler admired the colour and purity of line of Italian Renaissance sculpture and ceramic reliefs.

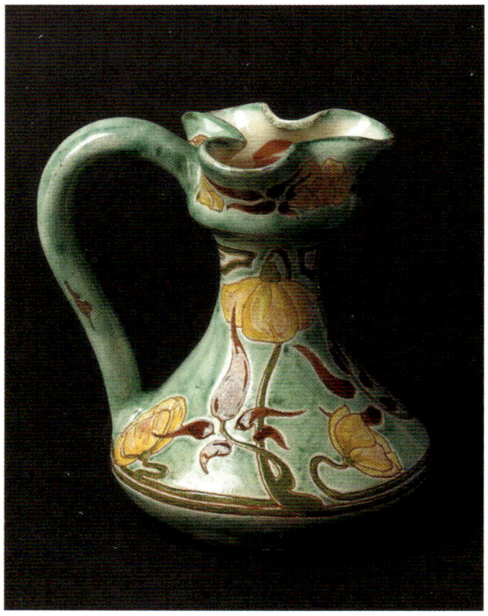

THE DELLA ROBBIA POTTERY, BIRKENHEAD (1894–1906)
DESIGNED BY CASSANDRA ANNIE WALKER, PAINTED BY LIZ WILKINS
JUG
1901
Earthenware
17 x 16.2 x 13.3
Presented by Miss May Rathbone, 1938
No.38.111

Cassandra Annie Walker is regarded as one of the most skilled designers and painters ever employed by the Della Robbia Pottery. She worked there throughout the Pottery's existence and produced some of its finest pieces. Her training at art schools in Liverpool and London meant that she was well aware of the emergence of the Art Nouveau style, which she applied to many of her works including this jug.

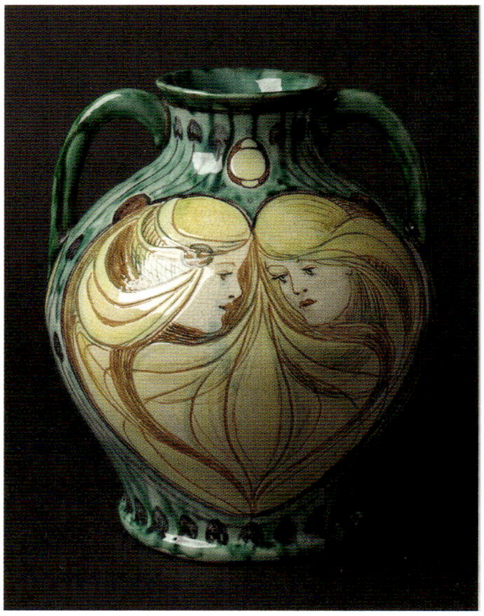

THE DELLA ROBBIA POTTERY, BIRKENHEAD (1894–1906)
DESIGNED BY RUTH BARE
VASE
1903
Earthenware
29.5 x 24.5 x 24.5
Presented by Arthur and Helen Grogan through The Art Fund, 2009
WAG2009.9

Ruth Bare was one of the most accomplished designers at the Della Robbia Pottery. She trained at Liverpool School of Applied Art, known as the 'Art Sheds', where she was taught by Herbert McNair, one of the 'Glasgow School' of artists who developed a particularly British form of Art Nouveau. McNair's influence can be clearly seen in the design of this vase.

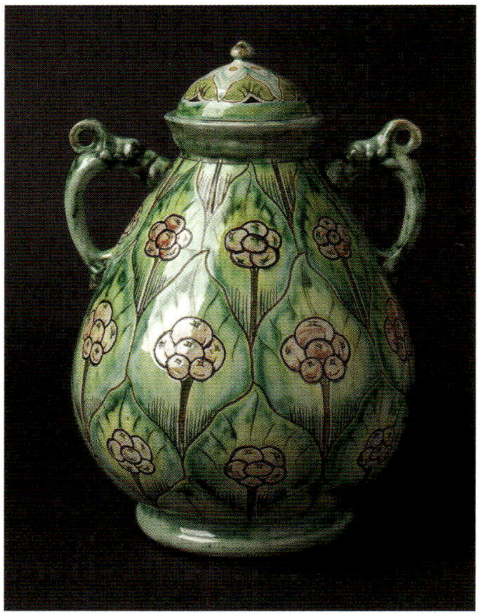

THE DELLA ROBBIA POTTERY, BIRKENHEAD (1894–1906)
DESIGNED BY CHARLES COLLIS, PAINTED BY PERCY JACQUES
JAR AND COVER
c. 1905
Earthenware
38 x 25.8 x 25.8
Presented by Miss L. Day, 1953
No. 53.52.11

Charles Collis joined the Della Robbia Pottery in 1895, aged 15. He worked at the Pottery for three distinct periods during its existence and in between was employed by the Doulton Pottery in Burslem and William Ault's Art Pottery in Swadlincote, Burton-on-Trent. It was at these other potteries that he first became aware of the Art Nouveau style, applying it to his designs for Della Robbia upon his return there.

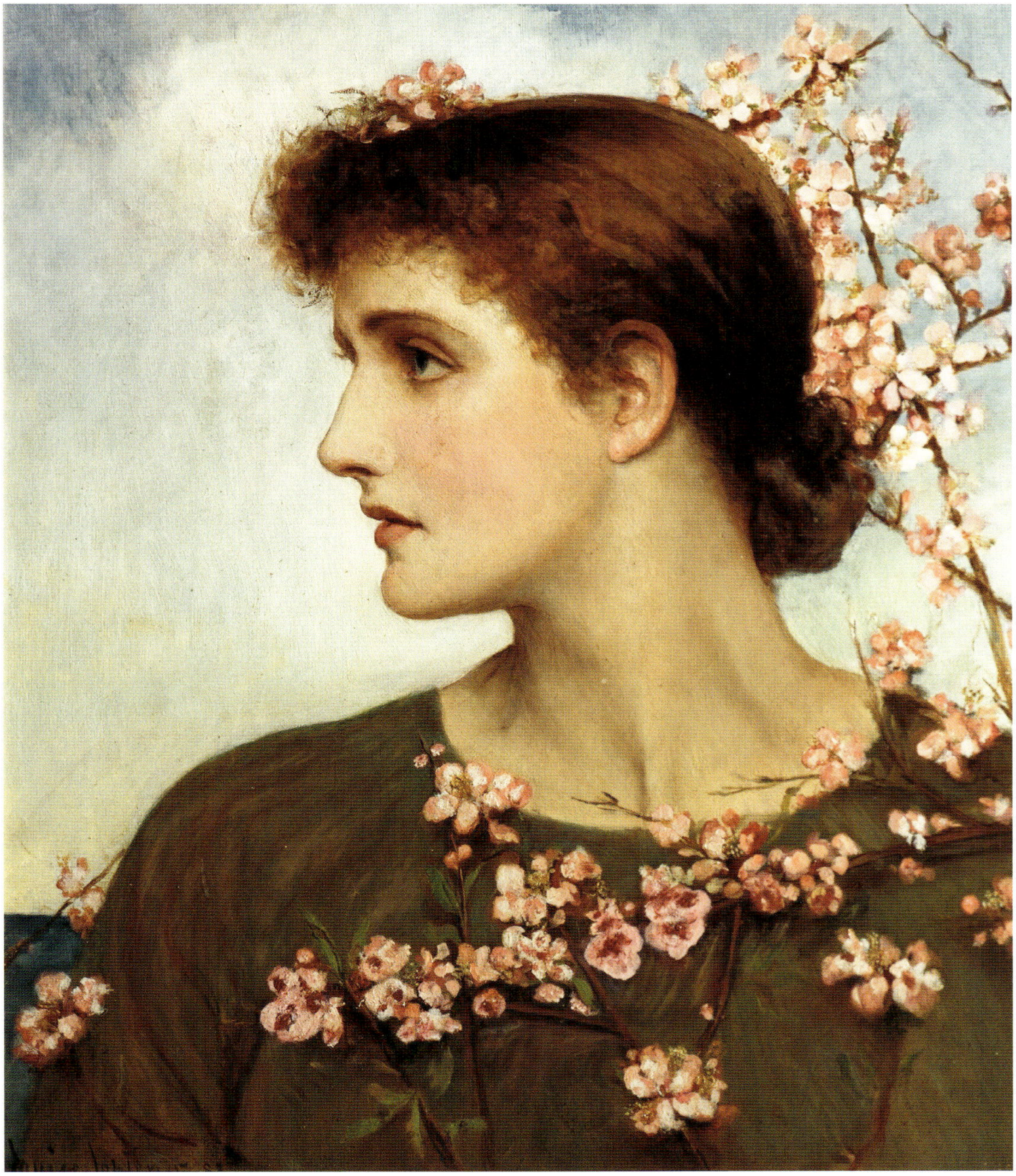

LOUISE JOPLING (1843–1933)
PHYLLIS
1883
Oil on canvas
52 x 44
Russell-Cotes Art Gallery & Museum
BORGM 01167

Jopling was a successful portrait painter who mixed with the fashionable society of London, which included famous writers and artists such as Oscar Wilde and John Singer Sargent (1856–1925). In this painting, Jopling drew the subject from the tragedy of Phyllis, a princess in Greek mythology who marries Demaphoön, King of Athens, but commits suicide when she gives up all hope of her husband returning to her after his long absence. When Demaphoön eventually returns home, he finds an almond tree over her grave, which instantly blossoms. The episode is captured here symbolically in a simple composition, featuring the bust of a beautiful woman entwined with the branches of an almond tree.

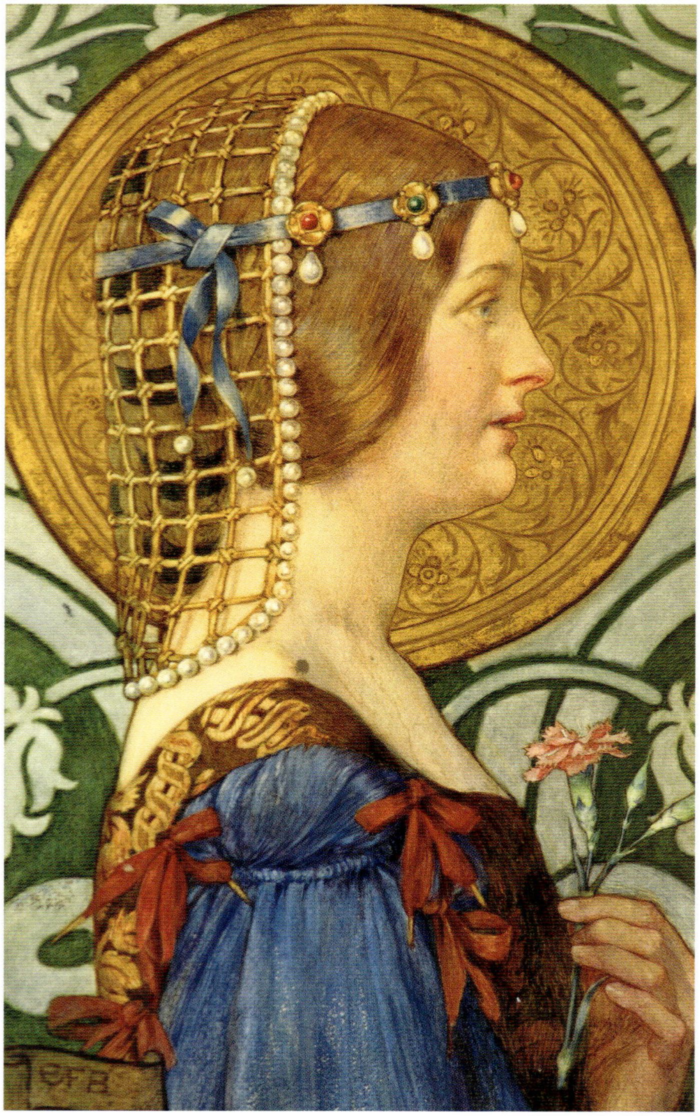

ELEANOR FORTESCUE-BRICKDALE (1871–1945)
IF ONE COULD HAVE THAT LITTLE HEAD OF HERS
c.1909
Oil on canvas
31.8 X 19
Russell-Cotes Art Gallery & Museum
BORGM 00360

This painting is a response to Robert Browning's (1812–1889) poem 'A Face', which was inspired by the Renaissance paintings that Browning saw in Florence. The first lines of the poem read:

'If one could have that little head of hers!
Painted upon a background of pale gold,
Such as the Tuscan's early art prefers!'

Fortescue-Brickdale was a close friend of John Byam Shaw (1872–1919), her contemporary at the Royal Academy and the Pre-Raphaelite follower. She became one of the early members of the teaching staff at Byam Shaw's art school founded in 1910, which was absorbed by Central Saint Martin's College of Art and Design in 2003.

DANTE GABRIEL ROSSETTI (1828–1882)
VENUS VERTOCORDIA
1864–68
Oil on canvas
81.3 x 68
Russell-Cotes Art Gallery & Museum
Purchased with the assistance of the Art Fund
BORGM 01897

A founder of the Pre-Raphaelite Brotherhood, Rossetti was also renowned as a poet, and this is one of his 'double works' where a poem provides context and extra meaning to the picture. The original frame of this painting is accompanied by this poem.

She hath the apple in her hand for thee,
Yet almost in her heart would hold it back;
She muses, with her eyes upon the track
Of that which in thy spirit they can see.
Haply, 'Behold, he is at peace,' saith she;
'Alas! The apple for his lips, – the dart
That follows its brief sweetness to his heart, –
The wandering of his feet perpetually!'

A little space her glance is still and coy;
But if she give the fruit that works her spell,
Those eyes shall flame as for her Phrygian boy.
Then shall her bird's strained throat the woe
foretell,
And her far seas moan as a single shell,
And through her dark grove strike the light of Troy.

In the painting, Venus, goddess of love and 'turner of men's hearts', is shown with one of her son Cupid's arrows and the Apple of Discord awarded to her by Paris of Troy. The butterfly, honeysuckle flowers and bird represent the fleeting nature of love.

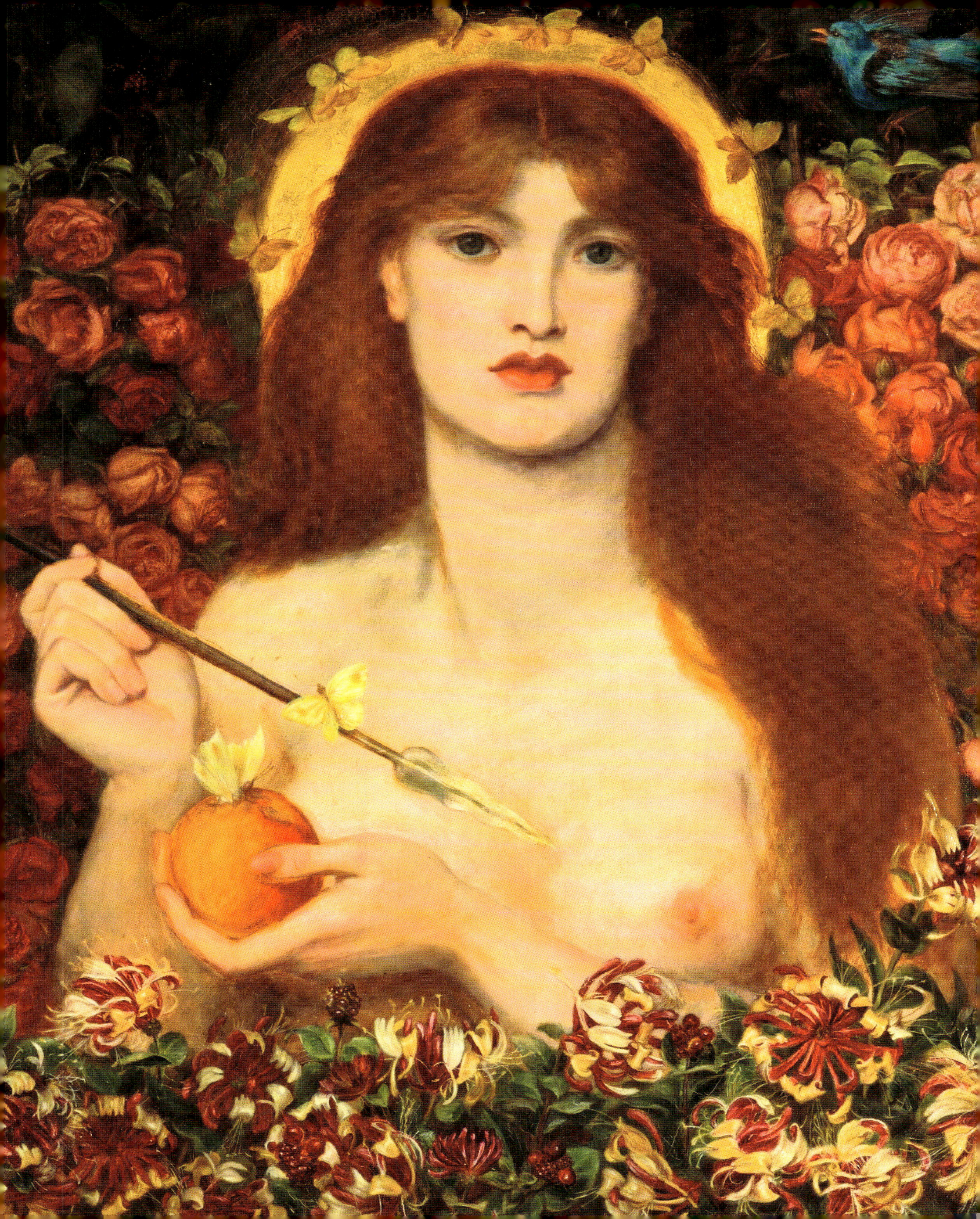

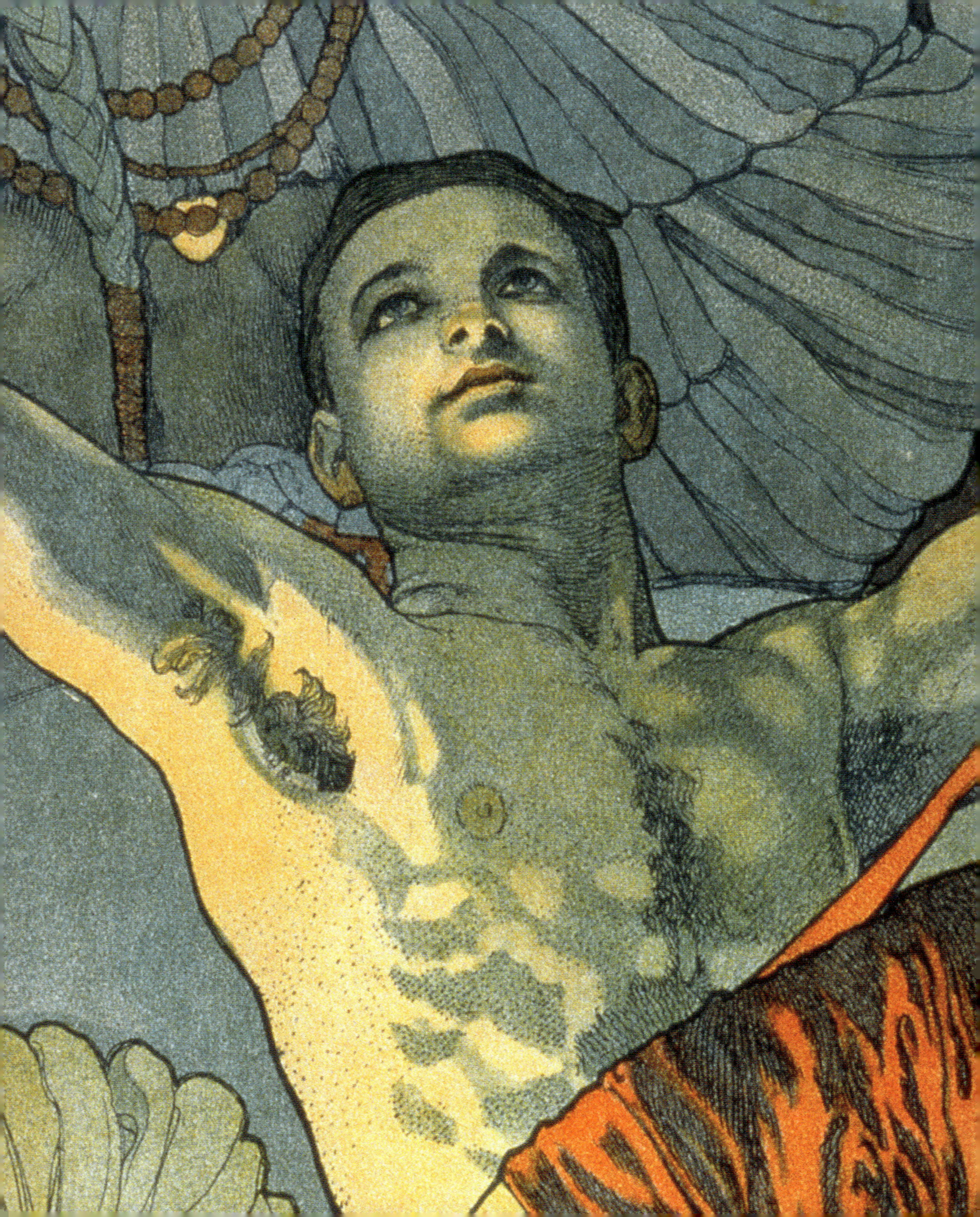

III

BEAUTY – POWER OF INSPIRATION

In 1910 Mucha returned to his homeland after an almost continuous absence of twenty-five years. His intention was to fulfil his long-term ambition to work for his country's political freedom using his art. He pursued this goal single-mindedly, working on his private project, *The Slav Epic* (see p.138), for the next seventeen years while taking commissions for causes that were close to his heart.

Prior to his homecoming Mucha had visited the United States five times between 1904 and 1909 in order to fundraise for this project, and he had met Charles Richard Crane (1858-1939), a philanthropist and wealthy businessman from Chicago who was to become the sponsor of Mucha's *Slav Epic.* A keen Slavophil and a friend of Tomáš Masaryk (1850–1937), the future president of Czechoslovakia, Crane contributed to the foundation of Slavonic Studies at the University of Chicago and he became interested in Mucha's 'messianic' visions for a new Europe with independent Slavic states. Mucha secured Crane's agreement for financial backing to *The Slav Epic* towards the end of 1909.

On his return to his native Czech lands, Mucha dedicated his life to the creation of *The Slav Epic.* He also worked for public projects for the nation, including the decoration of the Municipal House in Prague (see p.131), the design of a stained-glass window for St.Vitus Cathedral in Prague (1931), and the official poster for the 10th anniversary of the formation of Czechoslovakia (see p.137 right). In Mucha's Czech-themed posters and paintings, women remained central to the composition but they now became spiritual symbols clad in ceremonial folk costumes – 'the soul of the nation' according to Mucha – to inspire and unite the Slavic peoples under common political goals (see pp.129, 134–135).

Throughout this period, Mucha continued to develop *le style Mucha* as a universal visual language for the expression of timeless beauty, and applied this to his new works, both posters and large-scale paintings such as *The Slav Epic.* One of the best examples of the latter is the final painting of the cycle, *The Apotheosis of the Slavs: Slavs for Humanity* (see p.139). In this complex composition Mucha expressed his view of Slavic history as an organic movement – a spiral of continuous historical events, which surround the present state of the Slavic peoples after the victory of 1918, presented in the centre. From the celebrations at the centre of the painting, the curving lines of ribbons and rainbow lead the viewer's eyes to the future Slavic apotheosis where the Slavs would contribute towards the progress and peace of humanity, symbolised by the figure of a blossoming young man and the illuminating light of hope protected by a girl in white, both emerging from the celebratory group.

> *'The artist must remain faithful to himself and to his national roots.'*
>
> *Alphonse Mucha*

THE 8th SOKOL FESTIVAL, PRAGUE 1926: PAGEANT ON THE VLTAVA RIVER
(detail)
see p. 137 left

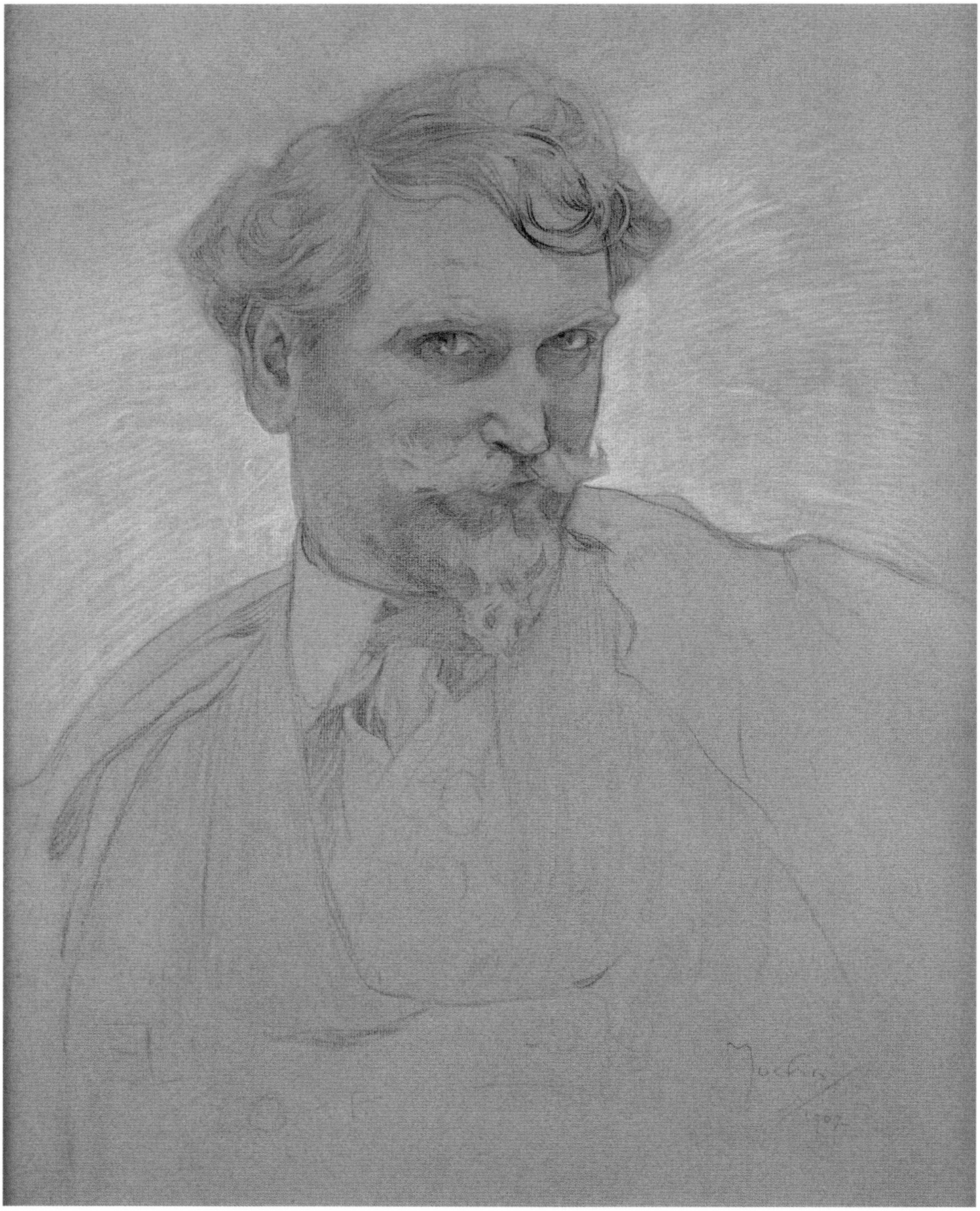

SELF-PORTRAIT
1907
Blue and white crayon on paper
55 x 42

The self-portrait was a recurring theme in Mucha's paintings, drawings and photographs. In this drawing, which was made in 1907 in America, the artist's penetrating eyes seem to stare into his own soul, reaffirming his artistic goal – the realisation of the *Slav Epic* project. Between 1906 and 1909 Mucha was engaged in regular teaching at the Art Institute of Chicago, where he was a popular teacher with a clear vision concerning the roles of art and the artist and well-devised theories that had evolved from his experience in Paris. His surviving lecture notes from this period, which were to be published posthumously in 1975 as *Alphonse Mucha: Lectures on Art*, give a glimpse of his theoretical basis for the creation of *le style Mucha*. (see p. 8)

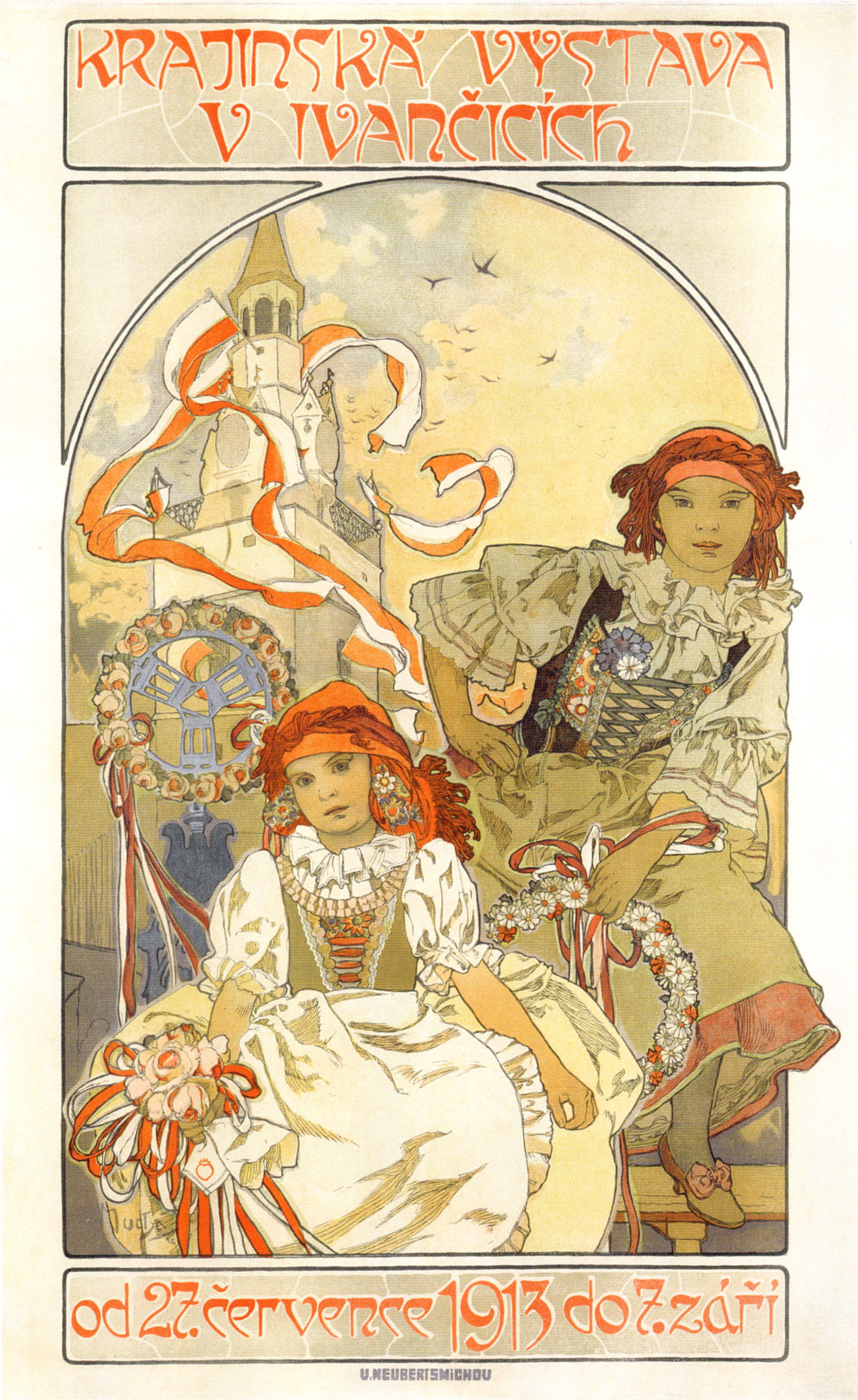

REGIONAL FAIR
AT IVANČICE
1912
Colour lithograph
93 x 59

This poster was prepared for a regional fair planned for Mucha's birthplace of Ivančice. The fair was supposed to open on 27 July 1913 but, in the event, it never happened. Nevertheless the poster remains as Mucha's tribute to his hometown, with which he stayed in close touch while he was working abroad. The poster shows two Moravian girls wearing the festive costume of the region and, in the background, the tower of the local church where the young Mucha used to sing as a choirboy. The image of the Ivančice church tower with the swallows flying round is a recurring motif in Mucha's work and alludes to homecoming.

ALLEGORY OF PRAGUE: PRAGUE SUBJUGATED
1911
Study for a panel of the Small Reception Room at the Lord Mayor's Hall in the Municipal House, Prague
Pen and ink and watercolour on paper
30 x 93.5

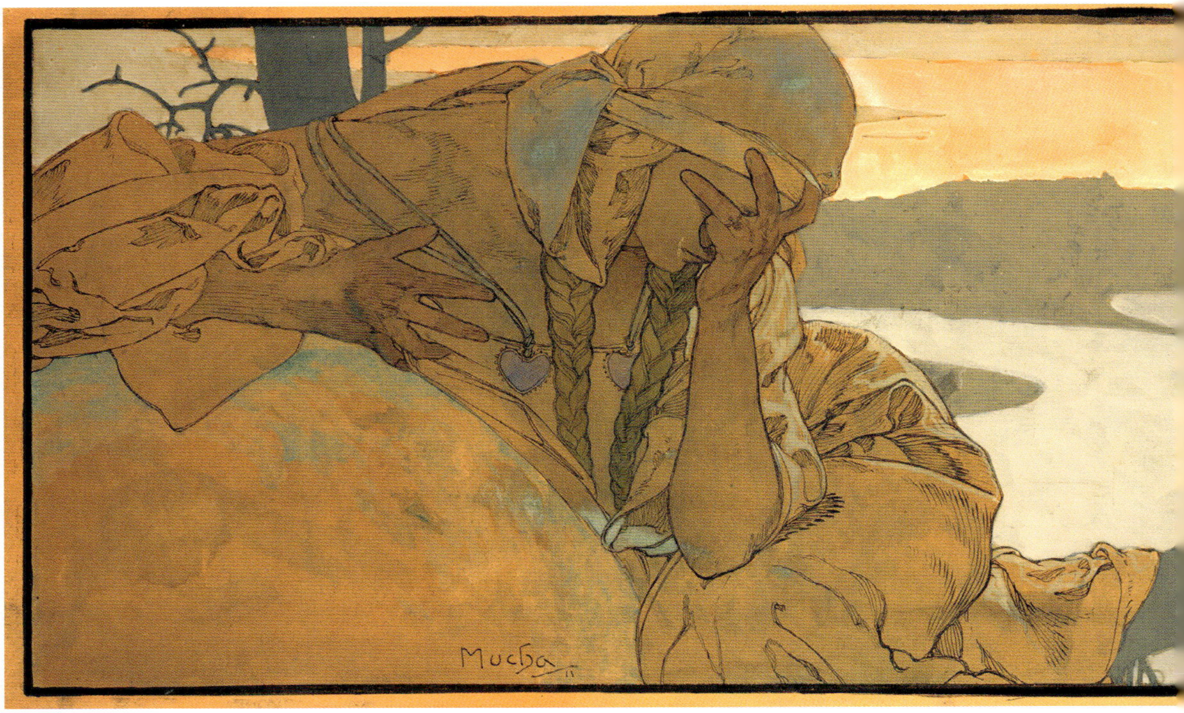

ALLEGORY OF PRAGUE: DREAMING OF FREEDOM
1911
Study for a panel of the Small Reception Room at the Lord Mayor's Hall in the Municipal House, Prague
Pen and ink and watercolour on paper
30 x 93.5

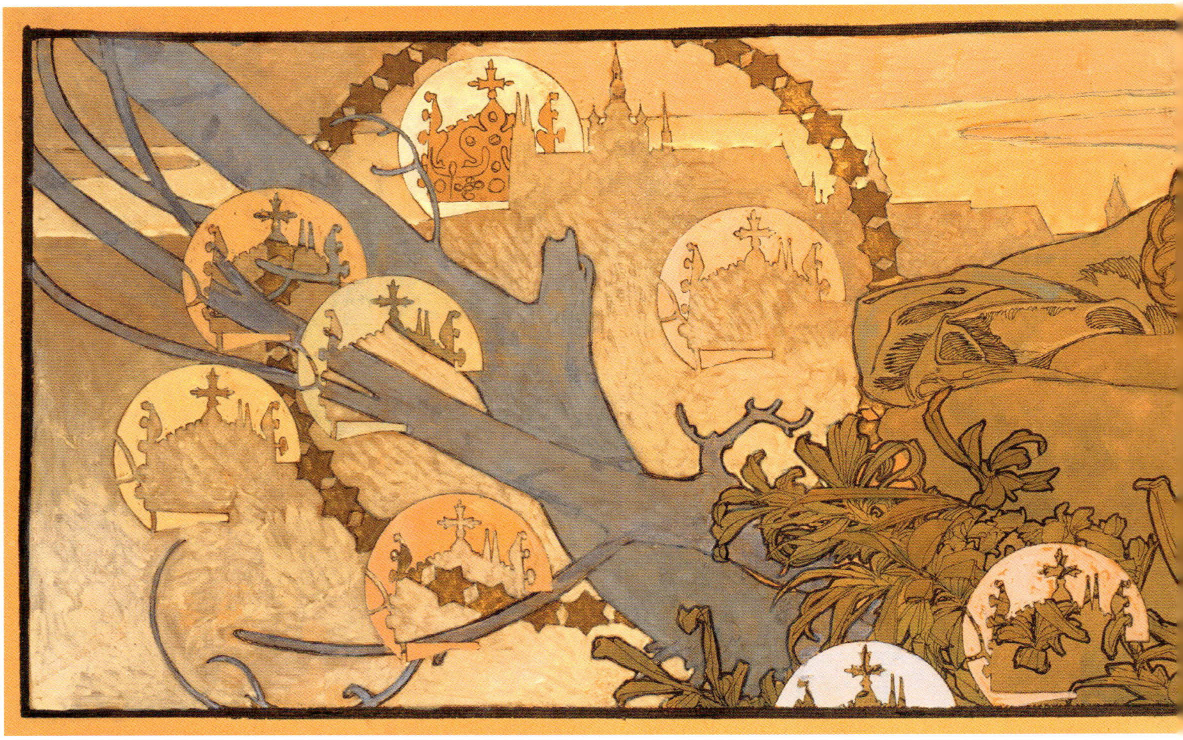

The two watercolours shown here are final studies for the pair of panel paintings, *Allegory of Prague*, in the Small Reception Room in the Lord Mayor's Hall. They allude respectively to the current state of the city under Habsburg rule and the glorious future of a liberated Prague.

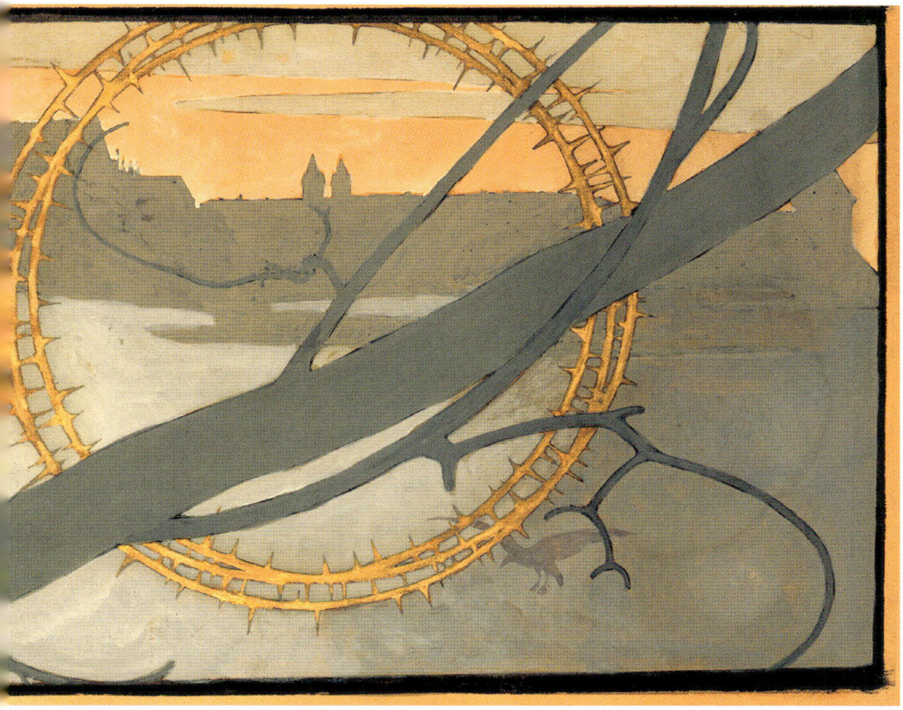

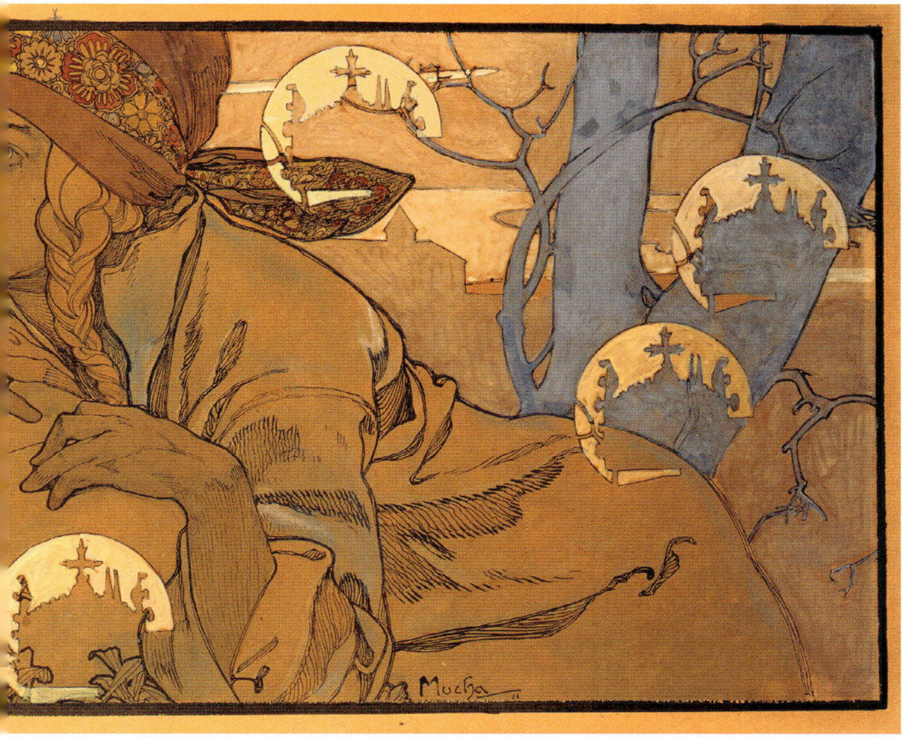

THE MUNICIPAL HOUSE, PRAGUE

Mucha's first work for his homeland was the decoration of the Municipal House (Obecní dům) in Prague, which was built between 1905 and 1912. Designed as an expression of civic pride and of the Czech National Revival – a movement to restore Czech culture and national identity – by Antonín Balšánek (1865–1921) and Osvald Polívka (1859–1931), the decoration of the building was carried out by many leading Czech artists at the time. Mucha was responsible for the decoration of the Lord Mayor's Hall, contributing both murals and furnishings.

Overleaf
Fig. 25
THE MUNICIPAL HOUSE, PRAGUE
Lord Mayor's Hall with murals and furnishings by Mucha
1910–1911

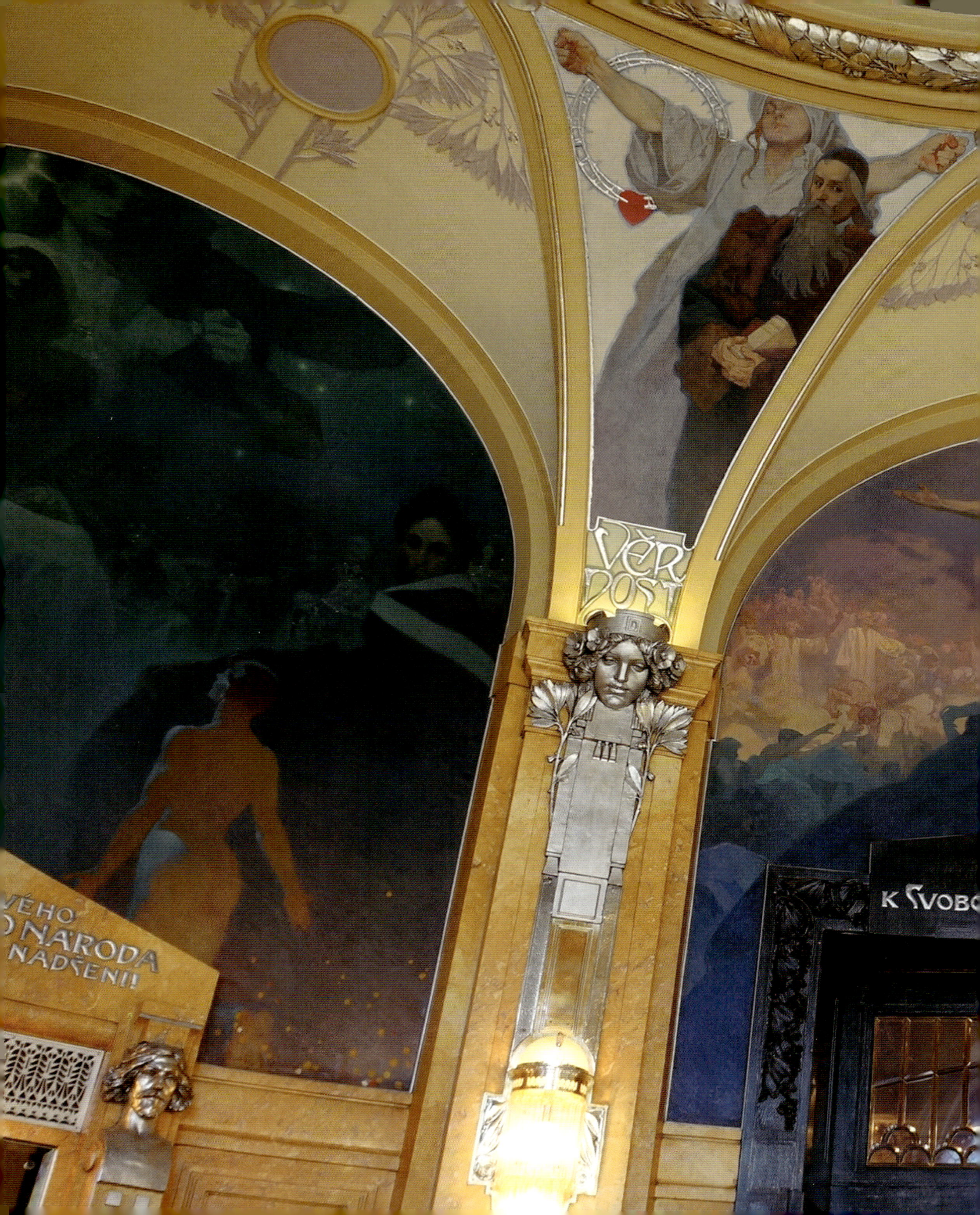
VĚR
NOST
VÉHO
NÁRODA
NADŠENÍ!
K SVOBO

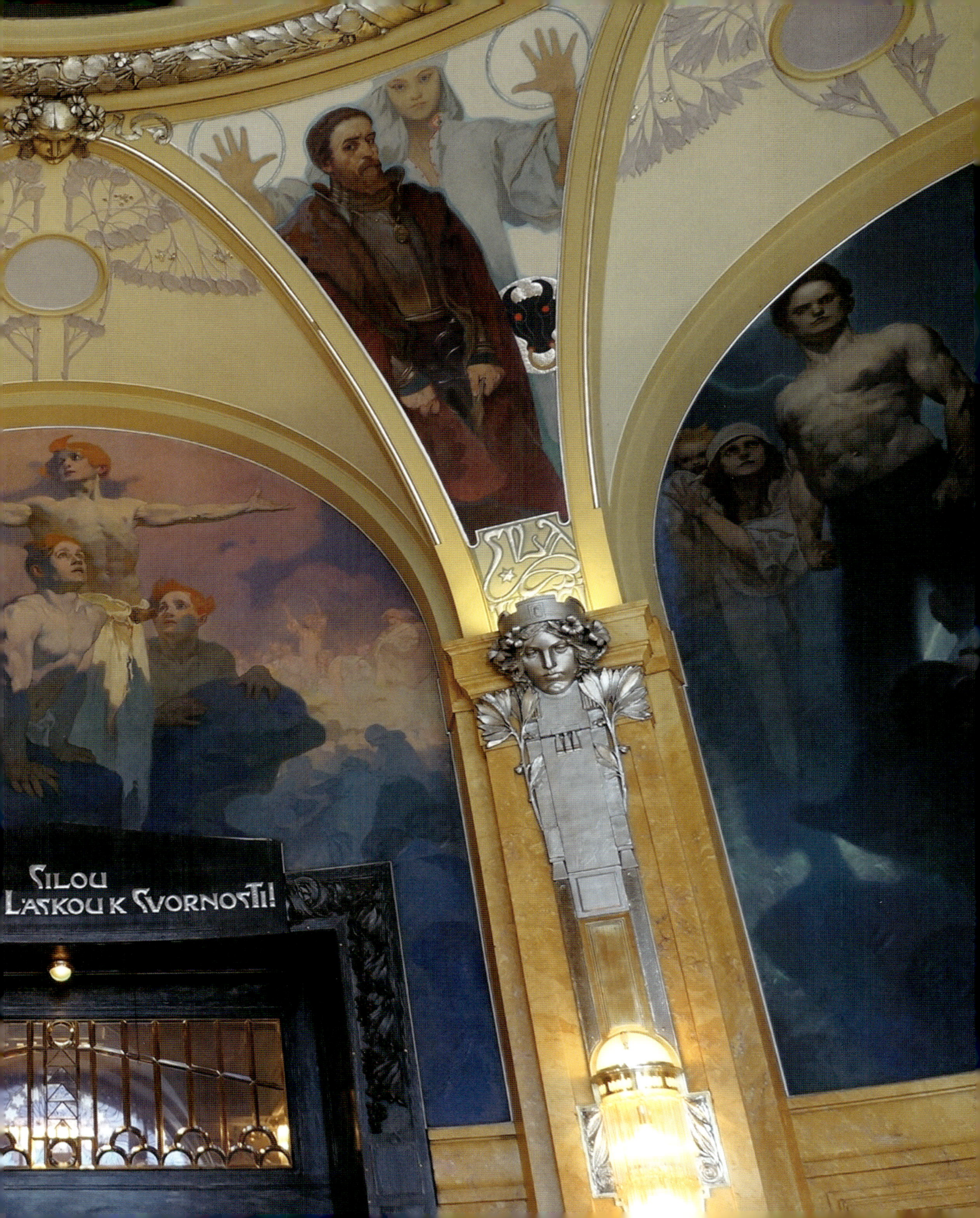
SILOU
LÁSKOU K SVORNOSTI!

SONG OF BOHEMIA
1918
Oil on canvas
100 x 138

At the time when Mucha produced this painting he could perhaps sense his dream coming true since in June 1918 the Allied governments officially recognised the Czechoslovak people's national aspirations. The painting was reproduced in the July 10 1918 issue of *Zlatá Praha* magazine under the title 'Our Song'. Reflecting the optimistic mood in the air, the picture shows three girls in national costume resting on a hilltop overlooking a great expanse of the Bohemian countryside. With a sense of rapture, the girl in the centre listens to the song uniting the Czech people.

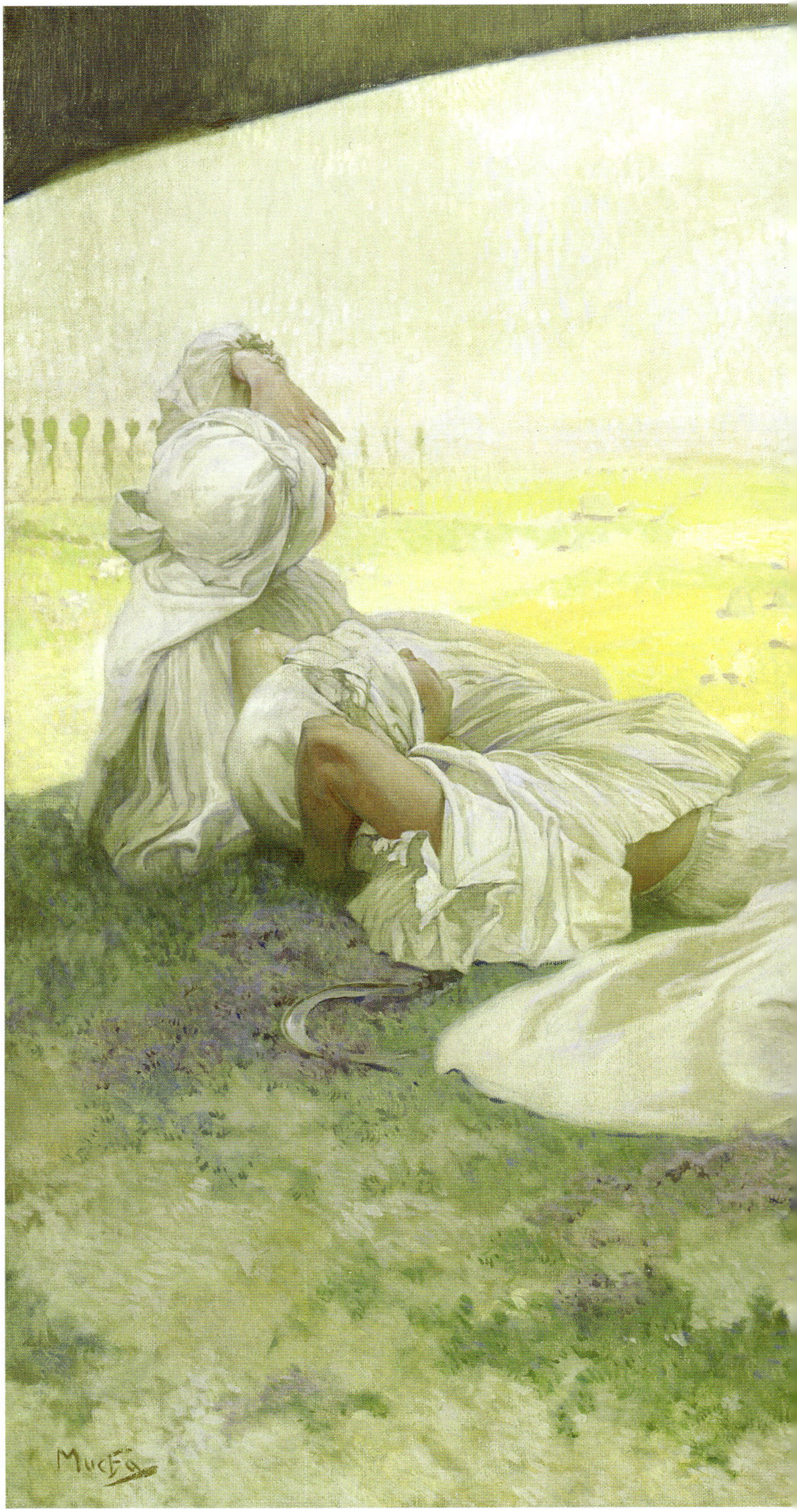

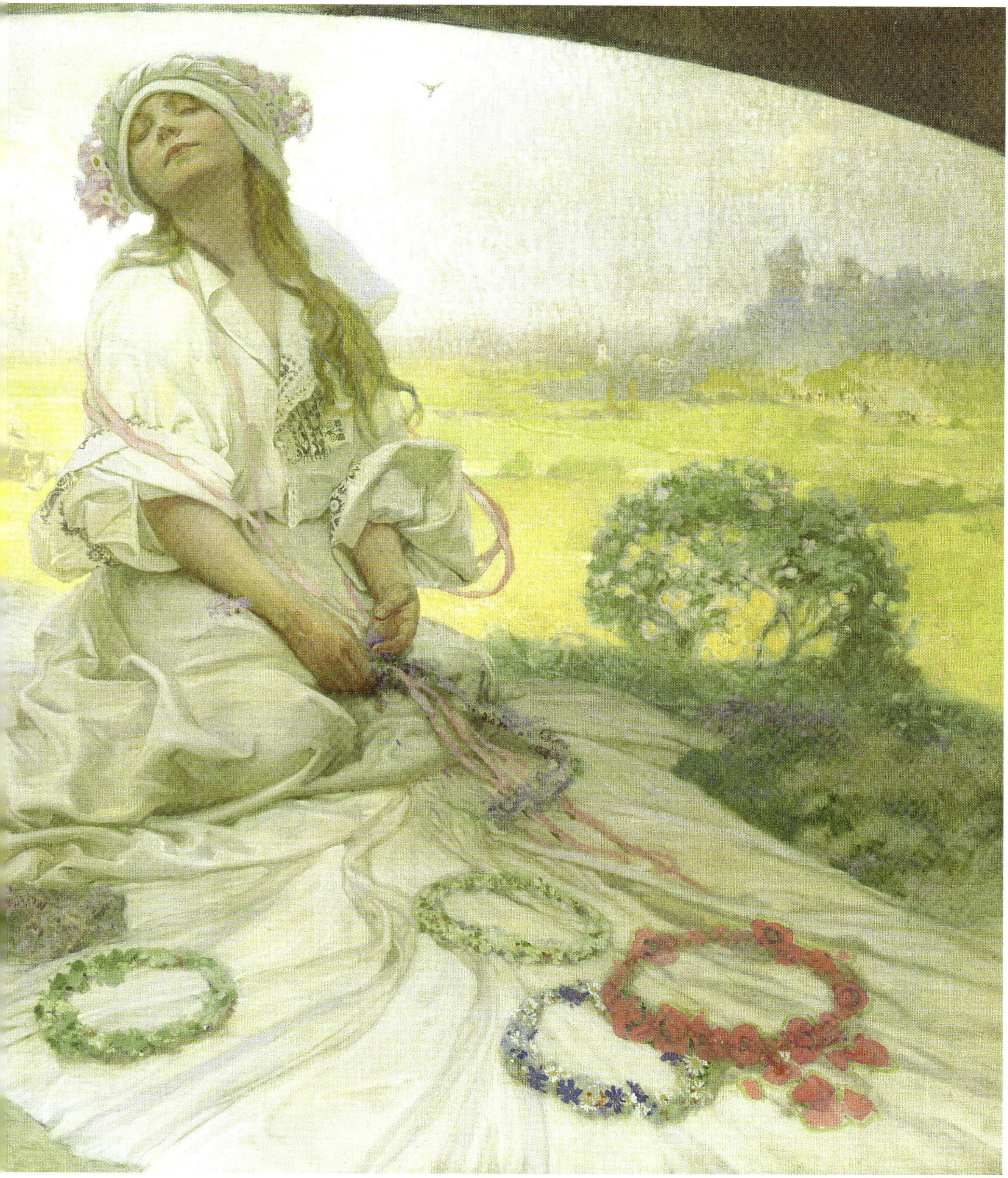

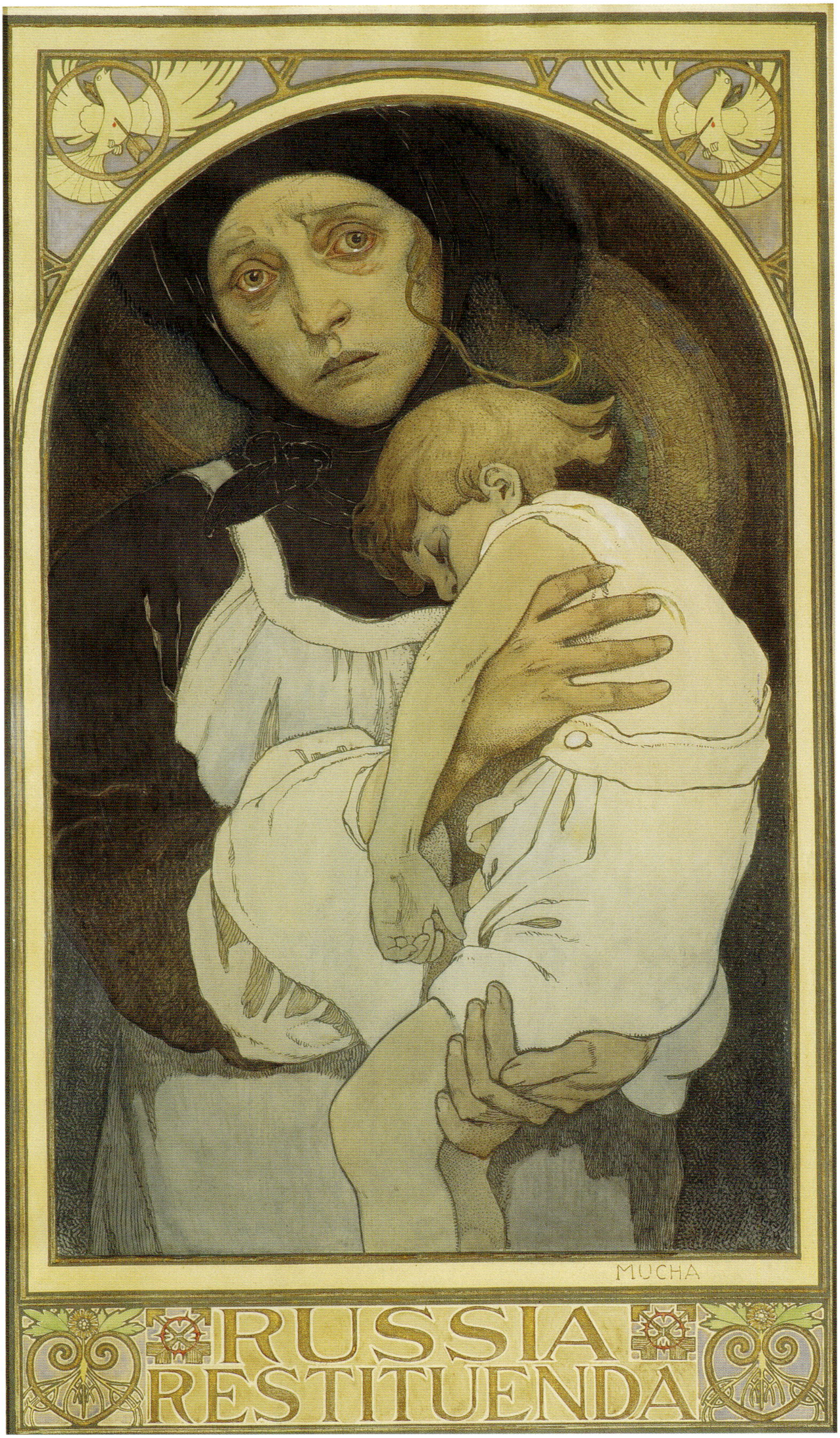

RUSSIA RESTITUENDA
1922
Study for the poster
Outline lithograph hand-coloured with ink, watercolour and gouache with gold
50 x 30.2

This poster served as a plea for help for starving children in the aftermath of the Russian Civil War (1917–1922), which paralyzed the country and killed millions through widespread disease and starvation. The situation was further worsened by a catastrophic famine, which broke out in the Volga-Ural region in 1921, prompting international relief efforts. Mucha's poster conveys a compassionate message through the image of a distressed peasant woman holding a dying child – an image adapted from the Christian iconography of Mother and Child. For the message at the bottom 'Russia Must Recover' Mucha chose to use Latin, a universal language, to indicate the impartiality and internationalism of this humanitarian effort.

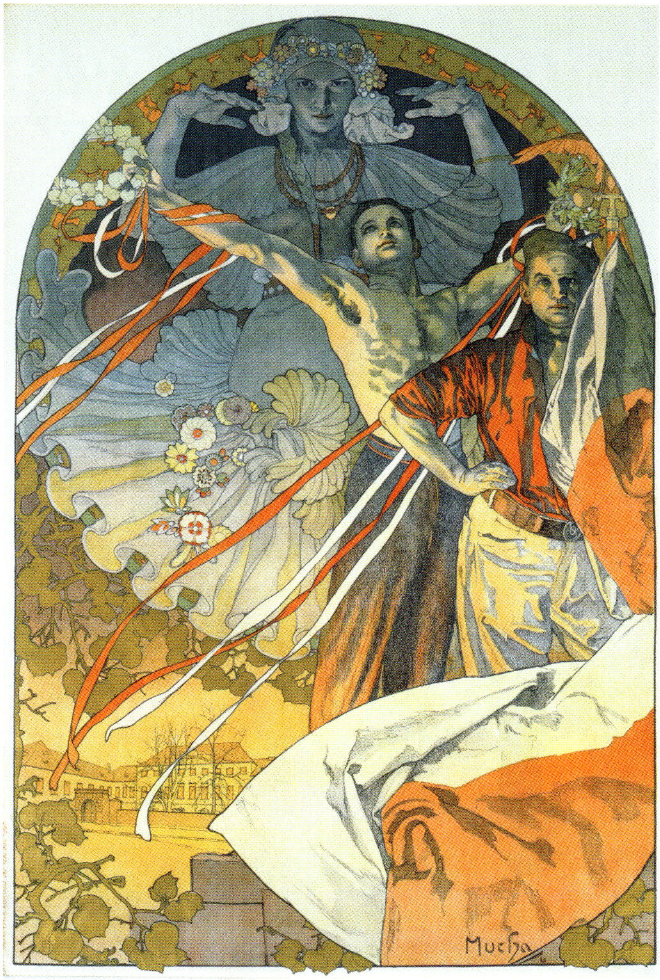

THE 8th SOKOL FESTIVAL, PRAGUE 1926: PAGEANT ON THE VLTAVA RIVER
1925
Colour lithograph
123 × 82.7

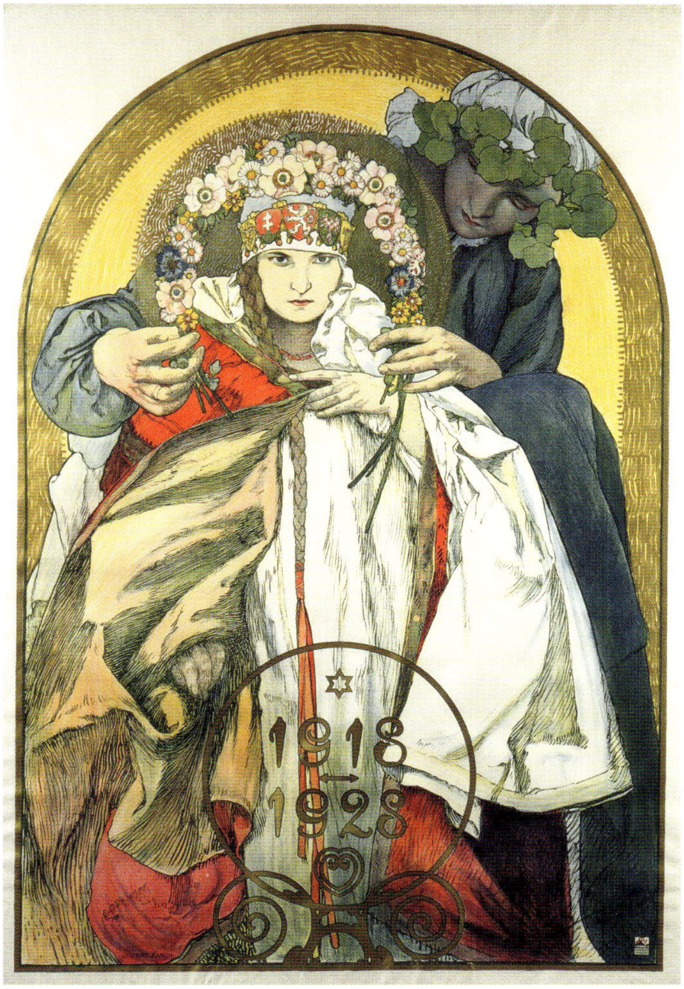

1918 –1928
1928
Official poster celebrating the 10th anniversary of the founding of Czechoslovakia
Colour lithograph
121 × 83.8

Promoting Czech nationalism (see pp.10–11) the Sokol festival was held every four years as a major national sporting event, combined with patriotic activities. This poster was made for a celebration planned to coincide with the Sokol Festival of 1926. Here Mucha synthesises the real world in the foreground – the two Sokol youths behind the Bohemian flag – with the spiritual world in the background, where the mythical Slavia, the personification of Slavic unity, gives them her blessing.

In this poster Mucha depicted the nation as a young woman in a ceremonial robe with a headdress decorated with the emblems of the ethnic regions constituting Czechoslovakia: Bohemia (the lion), Moravia (the chequered eagle), Slovakia (the cross), Silesia (the eagle with the clover stalk) and Ruthenia (the bear). Here she is being crowned with a garland of flowers by a spiritual being behind her representing the Allies in the World War I who supported the nation's independence.

THE SLAV EPIC

The Slav Epic is a series of twenty murals painted on enormous canvases (the largest measuring over 6 by 8 meters). Depicting the history of all the Slavic peoples – their sufferings and accomplishments over the past one thousand years – Mucha wished not only to inspire them to work together for their immediate objective, political independence, but also to suggest their goal for the future, the maintenance of peace among the Slavs as well as of all mankind. In 1918, when he was halfway through the project, his country was reborn as Czechoslovakia and in 1928, on the occasion of the 10th anniversary of the nation's independence, Mucha and Crane officially presented the complete series of the *Slav Epic* canvases to the City of Prague.

During World War II the canvases were rolled up and hidden in secret storage for fear of their destruction by the occupying Germans. The canvases reappeared in the 1960s in the small Moravian town of Moravský Krumlov. After extensive restoration work on the canvases, Mucha's *Slav Epic* was placed on public display in the castle of Moravský Krumlov from 1968 until 2011, when the City of Prague transferred all 20 canvases to Prague; they are at present on temporary exhibition at the Trade Fair Palace (National Gallery of Prague).

Fig.27
THE SLAV EPIC (CYCLE No.20): THE APOTHEOSIS OF THE SLAVS – SLAVS FOR HUMANITY
1926
Egg tempera and oil on canvas
480 x 405
City Gallery, Prague

For this composition Mucha introduced a colour scheme to represent four distinct periods: blue for the early years of Slavic civilisation in the bottom right; red for the flourishing Middle Ages in the upper left; black for the time of oppression, and luminous yellow for the liberation of 1918 celebrated in the centre. The upper part of the composition is dominated by the monumental figure of a youth embodying the new nation; he holds the wreaths of freedom and unity and is blessed by Christ behind him.

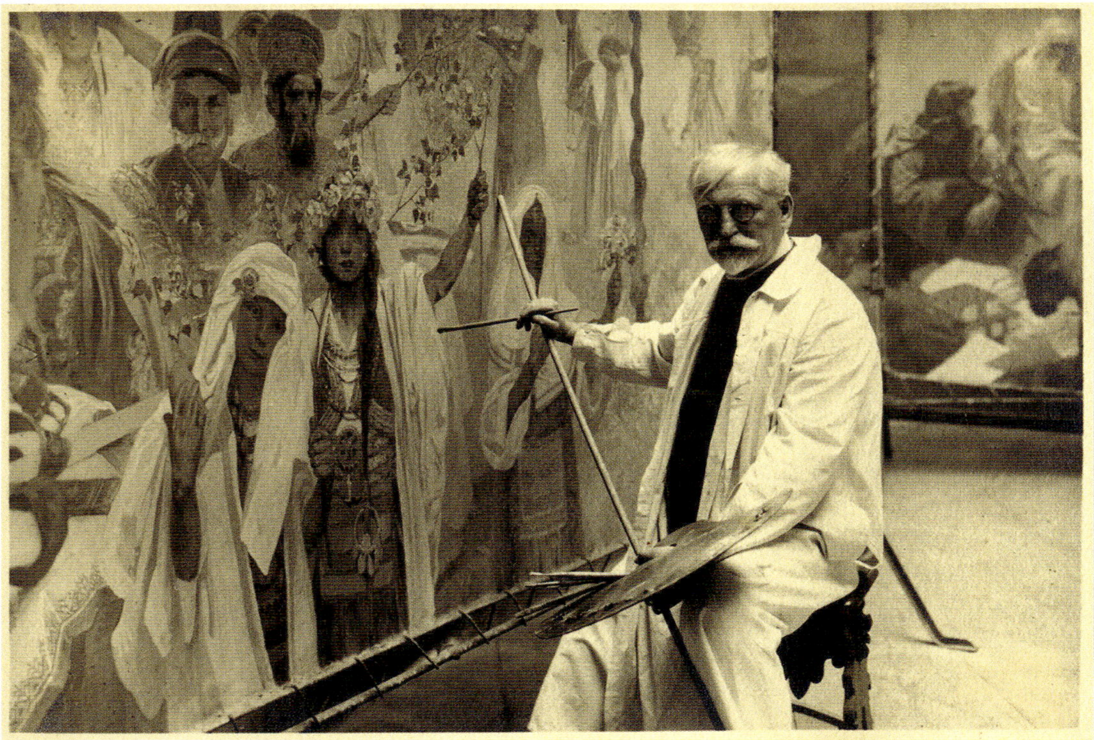

Fig.26
MUCHA IN HIS STUDIO AT ZBIROH CASTLE WORKING ON *THE SLAV EPIC: THE CORONATION OF THE SERBIAN TSAR ŠTĚPÁN DUŠAN AS EAST ROMAN EMPEROR* (1924)
c. 1923–1924
Vintage print

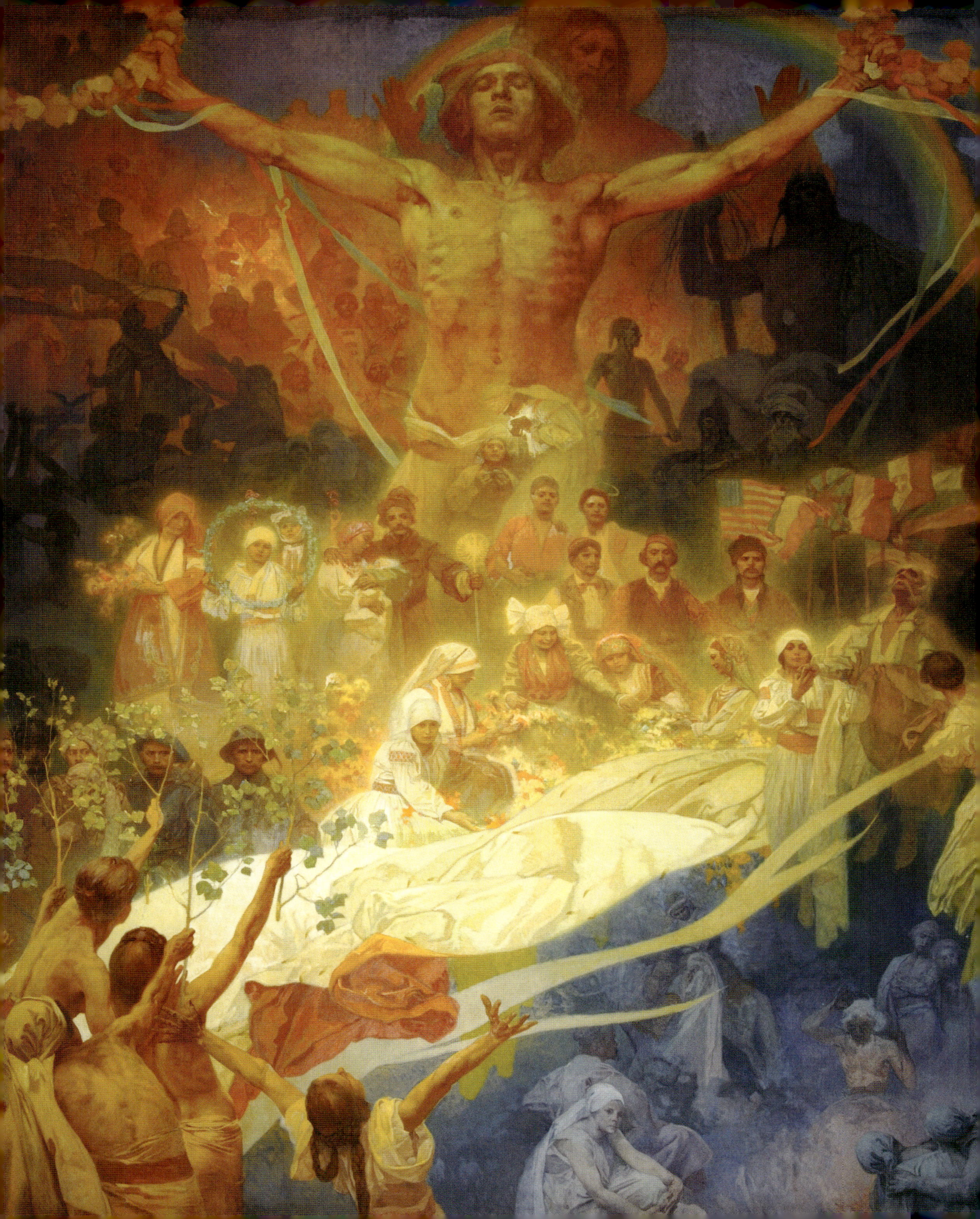

THE CELTIC REVIVAL IN SCOTLAND: THE GLASGOW BOYS AND THE EDINBURGH CELTIC RENASCENCE

JO MEACOCK

The Celtic Revival in Scotland, one of many historic revivals in the mid-late nineteenth century, was part of a Europe-wide renewal of interest in ancient history, philology, folklore and indigenous tradition. Richard Wagner's (1813–1883) operas, based on Germanic legend and old German poetry, were a product, as were Mucha's celebration of Slav history and mythology in his monumental *Slav Epic* (see p.138). In Scotland the movement was linked to a growing appreciation of Scottish national identity and culture, fuelled by archaeological discoveries and antiquarian interest in ancient monuments, manuscripts and relics, as well as a desire to record Gaelic oral tradition, folk tale and song. The roots of the revival lay in the eighteenth century. In 1778 the Highland Society had been founded in London and in 1780 the Society of Antiquaries of Scotland was established in Edinburgh. Despite being a literary hoax, James Macpherson's (1736–1796) 'translations' of the epic poems of third-century Gaelic bard Ossian (1760–1763) proved immensely influential and were acclaimed and translated throughout Europe.

A key figure in the Celtic Revival in Scotland in the nineteenth century was the biologist, town-planner, sociologist and reformer Patrick Geddes (1854–1932). Geddes promoted Highland culture, folklore and design as the richest and most important of surviving ancient traditions, uncorrupted by classical Greece or Rome, mediaeval or Renaissance thinking, or the materialism of contemporary society. Despite this, his outlook was not parochial but international, desiring to restore Scotland's former illustrious position in Europe, with Edinburgh as a centre for education, national art and literature.[1] Closely allied with Geddes in rekindling interest in Celtic myth and folklore was the Scottish journalist, writer and poet William Sharp (1855–1905), who from 1894 published under the persona of Fiona Macleod, a visionary and mystic Gaelic poet who was credited by Geddes as the originator, and central to the success, of the Edinburgh Celtic Renascence.[2] However, the stirrings of an artistic response to Scotland's ancient past were felt several years earlier in Glasgow among a group of painters who became known as the Glasgow Boys. Reviewing their work at the 1888 International Exhibition in Glasgow, Geddes described them as: 'the most important contemporary movement in Scottish, perhaps even British, art.' [3]

The Glasgow Boys' early preoccupation with rustic cottages and rural labour was inspired to a large extent by the French Naturalist painter Jules Bastien-Lepage (1848–1884), whose work the Boys held in high esteem. However, their interest in vernacular Scotland can also be seen to be part of a celebration of the indigenous, analogous to the poems of Robert Burns (1759–1796), often referred to as the Ploughman Poet, and the rural genre paintings of David Wilkie (1785–1841), albeit without their sentimentality or narrative impulse. The Boys' crofts and cottages were in many ways anti-Romantic, anti-heroic, reacting against the Scotland of Walter Scott (1771–1832) and Ossian and purposefully not referencing literature or history. Geddes was to argue that Celtic art was an art of the people, inherently connected with nature and a simple rural existence, not an historical fact but a living presence. Geddes saw this Celtic spirit in Burns, whereas Scott, he contended, displayed mere ignorance and prejudice in his depiction of the Celt. Arguably this Celtic spirit is a feature of the Glasgow Boys' work. In a letter of 1903, Robert Macaulay Stevenson (1854–1952), whom John Lavery (1856–1941) styled 'the prophet of our Glasgow School', compared the Boys' landscape art to the music of Wagner: 'how my heart swells and squirms within me when I see my ain countree [...] landscape art will yet write the Bible of this revelation for the common people [of Scotland] and they will hear the Gospel gladly.' In a Geddesian vein he declared it not the 'survival in me of the old notions' but 'the very breath of life for me.' [4]

Although the Boys were not a homogenous group with a set artistic credo, examples of their work from the mid-late1880s do attempt to capture something of the mystery and spirituality of the Scottish countryside in a way that relates to Geddes' and Sharp's Celtic evocations. George Henry (1858–1943) wrote admiringly to Edward Atkinson Hornel (1864–1933) in 1885 of Thomas Millie Dow's (1848–1919) atmospheric landscapes: 'I don't know of any other Fellow who has managed to make one feel on seeing those pictures so much of the spirituality of nature. They are intense in this way. One especially seems to make you weep with the strong quietness and mystery of nature.'[5] In the work of Henry, Hornel, James Guthrie (1859–1930), William Kennedy (1859–1918) and Dow, this Celtic spirit becomes increasingly apparent in decorative and symbolic representations of nature, paintings of the seasons and figures that merge with their woodland backgrounds, like wood spirits, as in Hornel's *The Goatherd* (1889: Glasgow Museums) or Henry's *Autumn* (1889: Glasgow Museums). The *Glasgow Herald* attributed the decorative and poetical impetus behind Hornel's *Summer* (1891: National Museums Liverpool), which 'lifts these children of the leafy glade above the common level of rusticity', to 'the faults of archaeology rather than of art'. [6]

Fig. 28
GEORGE HENRY
Gloamin'
1888–89
oil on canvas
24.4 x 30.8
Purchased with assistance of the National Fund for Acquisitions, 1980
Glasgow Museums 3361

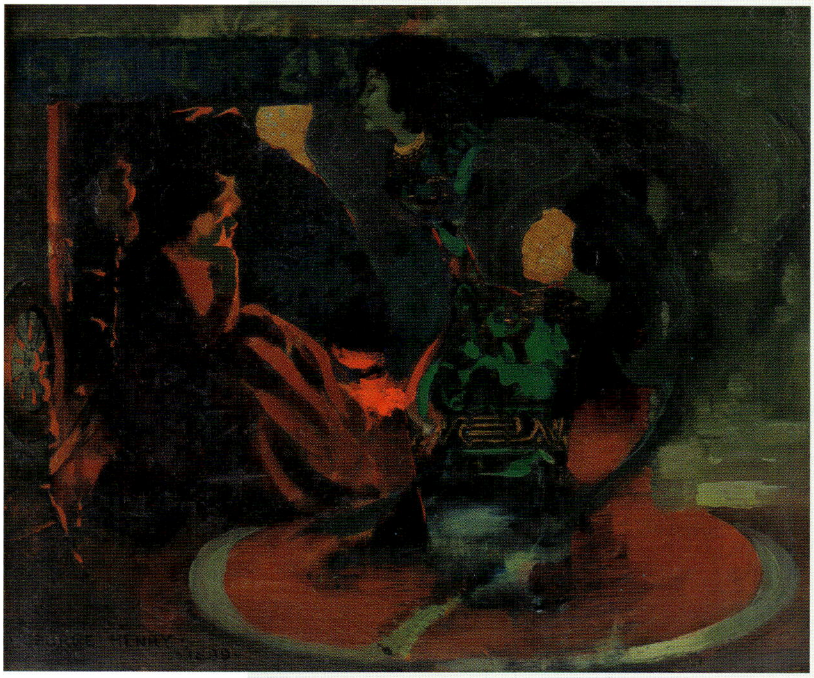

Celtic archaeology informed Henry's visionary *A Galloway Landscape* (1889: Glasgow Museums), which often excites comparison with the primitive symbolism of Gauguin and the Pont-Aven School. The sinuous curves of Henry's painting have been likened to ancient Pictish carvings and the emphasis on colour and form to the abstract nature of Celtic pattern and design. These rhythmic swirls are also compositional features of Henry's stylised *Gloamin'* (1888–89: Fig.28), with its Pictish-looking script above the fireplace and its eerie and evocative 'Celtic gloom', possibly based on local superstition or legend, and *The Witch-Ladye*, Henry's August 1889 frontispiece to the *Scottish Art Review,* a short-lived journal founded by the Glasgow Boys in 1888. Fascinatingly these forays into the Scottish supernatural were concurrent with an influential production of *Macbeth*, which opened at the London Lyceum on 27 December 1888 with Ellen Terry (1847–1928) as Lady Macbeth. It was reviewed and illustrated in the *Scottish Art Review* in January 1889; Terry's Celtic costume and her mystical, commanding presence were admired, as was the dramatic back lighting, which gave the production an air of wizardry.[7] The swirl of the witches' clothes and hair in the *Scottish Art Review*

illustration is tantalisingly close to Henry's painting and illustration. John Singer Sargent, who painted *Ellen Terry as Lady Macbeth* (1889: Tate Britain, London), designed a richly decorated Celtic knotwork frame to complement his composition, which was exhibited at the New Gallery in London in the spring of 1889. *The Times* had 'no doubt that this will be the most discussed painting of the year'.[8] In the same year Hornel decorated the frame of his *The Brownie of Blednoch* (1889: Fig.29) with carved Celtic symbols. These were the first instances of Celtic-inspired frame design. Sargent's more elaborate pattern, with interlacing, knotting and square-sectioned mouldings – those at the corners taken directly from Plate LXIII of Owen Jones' influential *Grammar of Ornament* (1856) showing Celtic ornament from a cross in Meigle, Strathmore – may have inspired the frame of Henry and Hornel's *The Druids – Bringing in the Mistletoe* (see p.149) of the following year. The square-sectioned Celtic designs in its corners are markedly similar to those on sculptured stones found in the graveyard of the Old Kirk in Govan, Glasgow; Henry was working in Govan in the late 1880s, having been commissioned by the Kyrle Society, along with several other of the Boys, to paint murals for Broomloan Hall.[9]

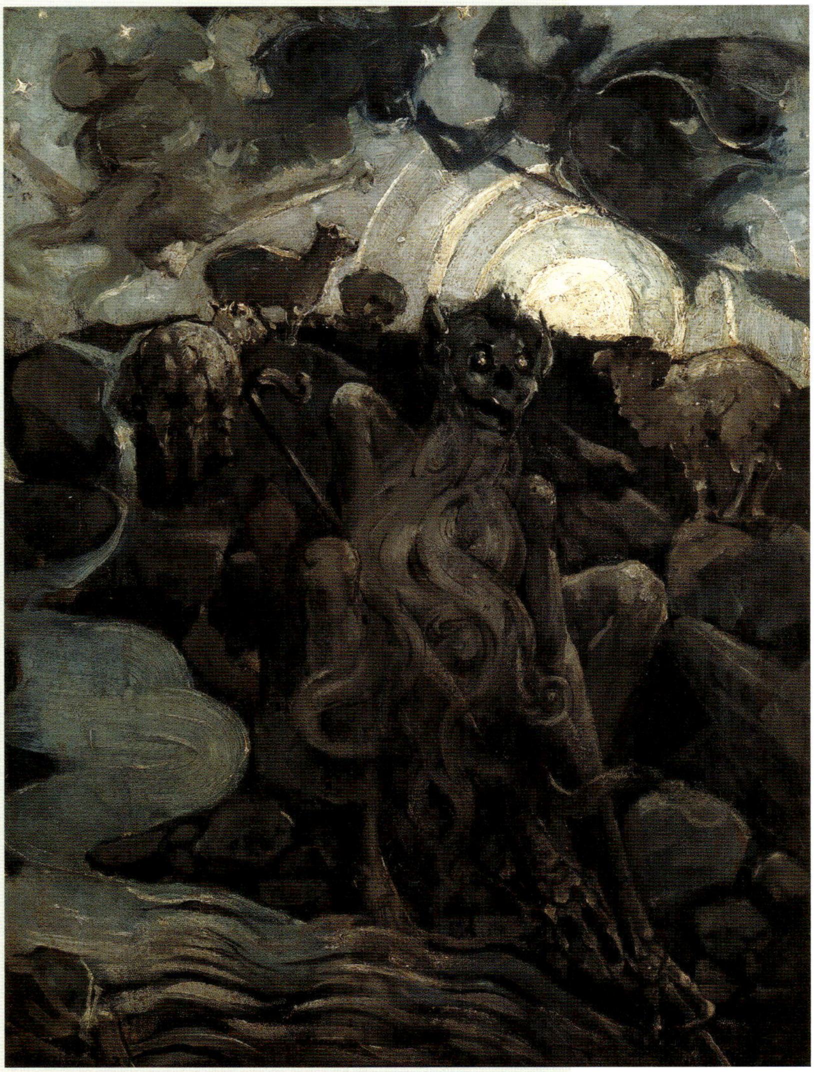

Fig. 29
E.A.HORNEL
The Brownie of Blednoch
1889
oil on canvas
61 x 45.7
Purchased 1945
Glasgow Museums 2479

Of the Boys, Hornel was the most drawn to the Celtic past. His library included a large number of books, articles, newspaper cuttings and pamphlets on Scottish history, archaeology and antiquities. His fascination with Celtic legend, myth and folk tales, particularly as associated with the Galloway landscape where he lived, became increasingly apparent in his paintings of 1889 and 1890. *The Brownie of Blednoch* was painted to illustrate a poem by William Nicholson (1782–1849), first published in *The Dumfries Monthly Magazine* in 1825, which was to appear in Malcolm Harper's poetry collection *The Bards of Galloway* (1889).[10] Going beyond the poem, Hornel painted witches on broomsticks flying overhead and a skull leering behind, alluding to the many local legends about brownies, witches, fairies and ghosts. In addition, Hornel painted the 'lang blue beard' of Aiken-drum curling and crossing like Celtic interlacing, further alluding to his archaeological interests. The sculptor, painter, poet, musician and outspoken nationalist James Pittendrigh Macgillivray (1856–1938), who was closely associated with the Glasgow Boys and nicknamed 'Macdevilry' by them, composed a bawdy, much recited poem in Scots, 'Hornel Exultant to his Goat on the Galloway Hills' (1888), in which he playfully poked fun at Hornel's obsession with ancient cup-and-ring markings, which the fictitious goat's markings resemble:

'My Gode, what's that on yer hide, ye B!
Thae markins in broon and white,
They're Hellish like Celtic designs, ye B!
In the study o' which I delight.' [11]

Hornel visually references these cup-and-ring marks in the stylised moon in *The Brownie of Blednoch*. According to the artist A.S. Hartrick (1864–1950), Hornel would go to any lengths to find these Bronze Age carvings. On one occasion Hartrick related that Hornel took him to see some examples near the cottage of a local character named Sinclair. During this visit the old man went into a kind of trance and began to describe 'a vision of a procession of priests with sacred instruments and cattle which somehow were connected with the cup-and-ring markings.'[12] This vision was inspirational for Henry and Hornel's *The Druids*. The painting was also the result of Hornel's researches; the patterning on the ceremonial robes, such as the snake on first Druid's robe, is analogous to designs on early carved stones at Aberlemno and Glamis in Angus, illustrated in Joseph Anderson's (1832–1916) *Early Christian Times*.[13] As well as containing this book, Hornel's library also notably held John Toland's (1670–1722) *History of the Druids* (new edn, 1814) and Herbert Eustace Maxwell's (1845–1937) *Primitive Implements, Weapons, Ornaments and Utensils from Wigtownshire* (1889) and George Hamilton's *Notices of Rock-Sculpturings of Cups and Circles in Kirkcudbrightshire* (1887), both from the *Proceedings of the Society of Antiquaries of Scotland*. On 11 September 1887, Hornel, along with a Mr Thompson and John McKie, the first honorary curator of Stewartry Museum, Kirkcudbright, made casts of the cup-and-ring marks recently found on the glaciated rock on the farm of High Banks, near the ancient village of Galtway.[14] Some of these casts were displayed as part of an impressive collection of Scottish archaeological and historical relics at the Bishop's Castle at the Glasgow International Exhibition in 1888.[15] This exhibition engendered fresh interest in Scottish Celtic history and may have encouraged Henry and Hornel that the time was right for a more overt Celticism in their paintings.

Geddes kept a close eye on happenings in Glasgow, and in Edinburgh in the early 1890s embarked on a series of mural decorations that were intended to embody Celtic spirit and culture, historic and contemporary, creating 'the vastest and most elaborate Celtic illumination in the modern world'.[16] In 1891 he bought Short's Observatory, renaming it the Outlook Tower, which became an ideological hub and museum for his Summer Meetings of artists, musicians, writers, teachers and students. He also bought Ramsay Lodge, the former home of the poet Allan Ramsay (1686–1758), as well as adjoining land in Ramsay Garden on which he created student and artist accommodation. He commissioned Dundee artist John Duncan (1866–1945) to paint *The Evolution of Pipe Music* on the walls of his music room in his flat at Ramsay Garden; Duncan joked that he was painting a history of the bagpipes.[17] Geddes also commissioned from Duncan seven large panels for the Common Room at Ramsay Garden, illustrating Scottish history and progress, stressing Celtic history, Scottish scientific tradition and the role of Scots in Europe: *The Awakening of Cuchullin, Fionn Wrestling with the King of Norway, The Taking of Excalibur, The Journey of St Mungo* (Fig.30), *The Vision of Johannes Scotus Erigena, Michael Scot* and *The Admirable Crichton*.[18] Celtic tracery borders were provided by Duncan's pupils Helen Hay, Nellie Baxter, Miss Mackie and Marion Mason, inspired by the intricate Celtic patternings of the Book of Kells (AD c.800). Geddes declared that: 'no more sustained and magnificent scheme of design and colour, no more vital symbolism has been produced by modern art in Scotland'.[19] In 1927–28 he commissioned Duncan to add Lord Napier of Merchiston, James

Watt, Walter Scott, Charles Darwin and Lord Lister to emphasise the continuity of the Celtic spirit in Scottish creativity and invention.[20]

In 1894 Geddes also set up a publishing firm, Patrick Geddes & Colleagues, specialising in Celtic and scientific literature. William Sharp was its manager and later literary advisor and the firm published both Macleod's powerful and melancholic Celtic tales and the editions of Celtic poetry that Sharp produced along with his wife Elizabeth, including *Lyra Celtica* (1896) and an edition of *Ossian* (1896). Additionally the firm produced a journal *The Evergreen: A Northern Seasonal*, which was intended to herald the spring of the Celtic Renascence in Edinburgh. In the first volume Geddes linked the publication to Allan Ramsay's collection of Scots poems *The Ever Green* (1724), which aimed to 'stimulate the return to local and national tradition and living nature'.[21] This essay was adapted to become a prefatory note to subsequent editions. The journal was illustrated by Duncan, Hay, Baxter, Charles Mackie, artist Robert Burns (1869–1941, James Cadenhead (1858–1927) and W. G. Burn Murdoch (1862–1932) among others, including Glasgow Boys Macgillivray and Hornel, and was decorated with Celtic initial letters and header and footer ornamentation. Duncan wrote to Geddes: 'I am sure that the harmony between the different ornaments throughout the book will go a good long way towards making it a thing of beauty.'[22] Duncan's vibrant and visionary *Anima Celtica* (Fig.31) in volume one demonstrates his awareness of European Symbolism and his research into Celtic archaeology. The bracelet that the dreaming woman wears is very similar to bronze armlets found in Banffshire, Aberdeenshire and Peebleshire, several examples of which were in the new National Museum of Antiquities in Edinburgh, which opened in 1858, and were illustrated in *Scotland in Pagan Times* (1883) by Joseph Anderson, the museum's Keeper (Fig.32). The brooch is comparable to the silver Cadboll brooches found in Rogart in Sutherland in 1868, illustrated in Anderson's *Scotland in Early Christian Times* (1879). Duncan recommended that his students should consult both books in addition to contacting local antiquaries.[23] Although initially criticising Duncan's design, Sharp proposed to Geddes in 1895 that it become the frontispiece for a new Anglo-Celtic quarterly to be called *The Celtic World,* to which Duncan was also to contribute an article on 'Celtic Ornament'; however the project never got off the ground.[24] *The Evergreen* itself foundered after four volumes due to adverse criticism, particularly from London, and the departure of Sharp, who had found international

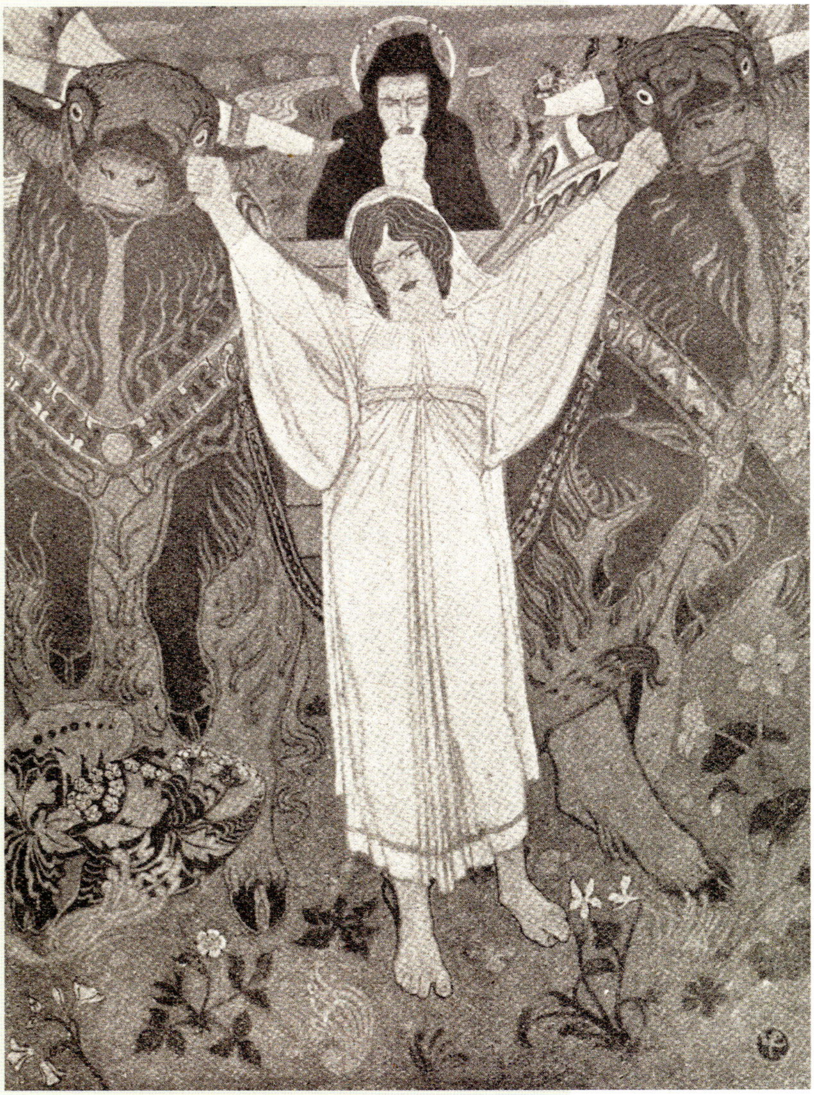

Fig. 30
JOHN DUNCAN
The Journey of St Mungo, mural, Common Room, Ramsay Garden, illustrated in Margaret Armour, 'Mural Decoration in Scotland. Part 1', *Studio,* vol. 10, no. 47, February 1897, p. 103

acclaim as Celtic bard Macleod. Geddes was disappointed, having hoped to find a market on the Continent.

In 1893 Geddes had set up Old Edinburgh School of Art, 'a *living* School of Art' [his emphasis], not just a place of teaching but of active production for public and domestic purposes that was to bring 'the Art student and the Art worker together', along with 'the student of History, the Antiquary and the scholar'.[25] Through the revival of Celtic art, Geddes hoped to introduce beauty cheaply and simply into objects of everyday utility. Classes were offered in architectural work, building construction, woodcarving, painting and decoration. Duncan, who became its Director, offered classes in modelling and decorative figure painting as well as day classes in Celtic ornament. The intention was to influence the output of the design industries in Edinburgh and the Highlands. Duncan encouraged Geddes to purchase examples of students' work to create a collection of

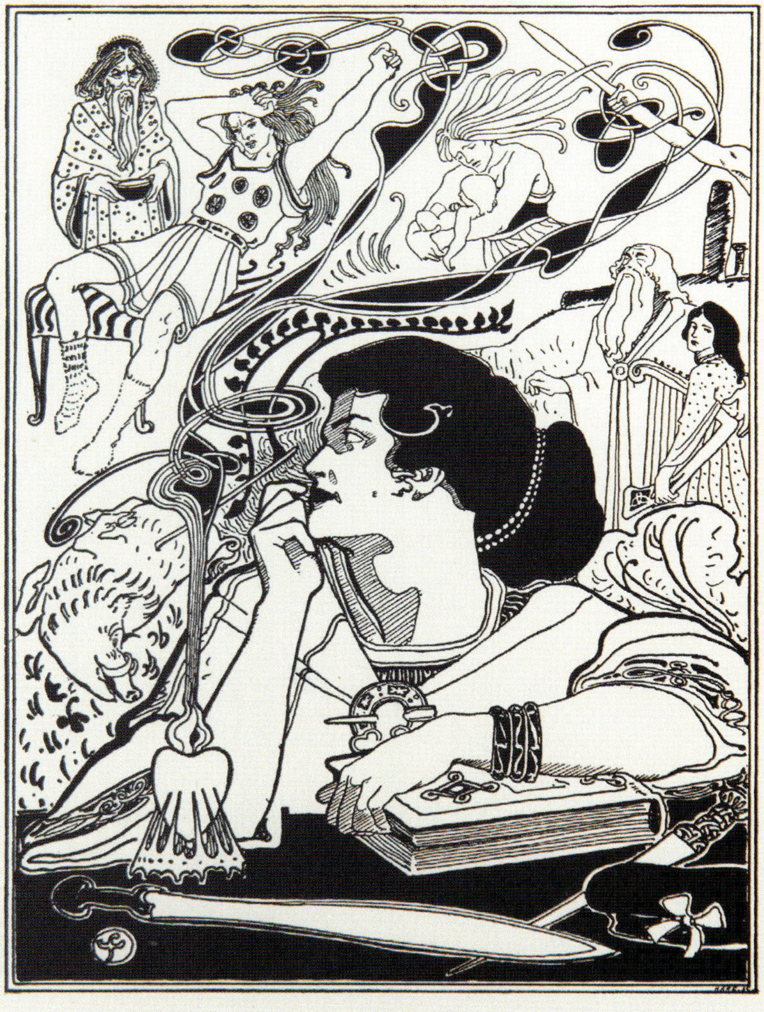

Fig. 31
JOHN DUNCAN
Anima Celtica, in *The Evergreen: A Northern Seasonal,*
spring 1895, Patrick Geddes & Colleagues, Edinburgh, 1895, p. 107 (Special Collections, Glasgow University Library, Sp Coll Ap-b. 49–52) with verse by Duncan:

'The visioned stories read,
the book is closed –
The Past has been and
shall not be again.
She dreams!... Yet comes
to her, disarmed, deposed
A wide new kingdom in
the minds of men.'

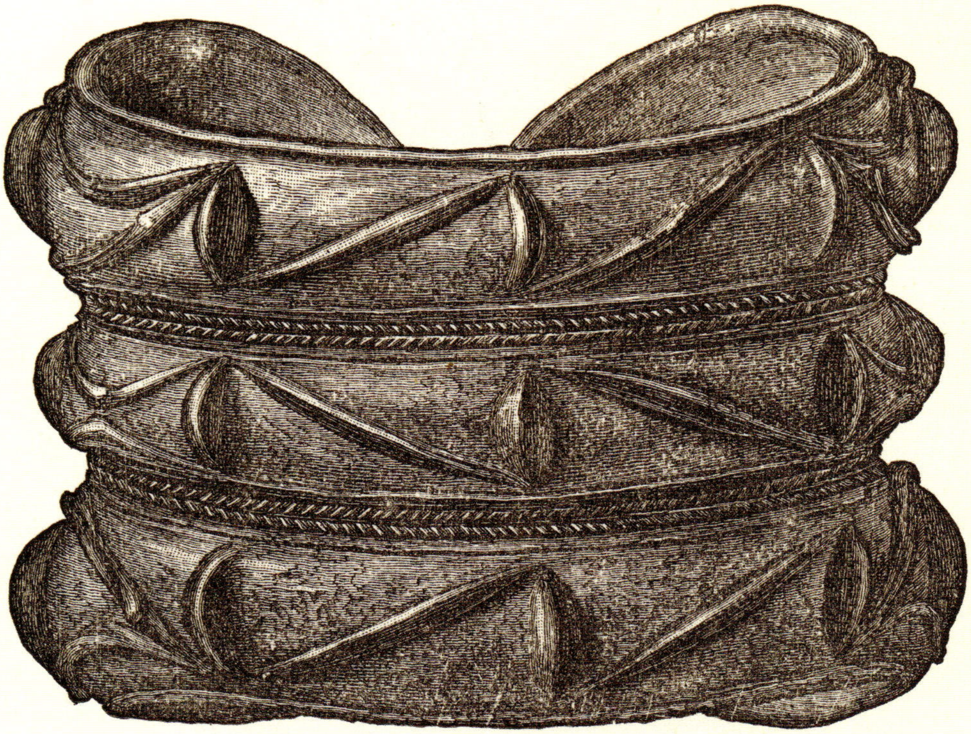

Fig. 32
Bronze armlet found at Drumside, Belhelvie, Aberdeenshire, illustrated in Joseph Anderson, *Scotland in Pagan Times: The Iron Age*, Edinburgh, 1883, p. 146, fig. 122

Celtic work in different media. Due to straitened financial circumstances the school closed in 1896/97 but Duncan tried to stay loyal to Geddes' vision. In the autumn/winter of 1898 he taught a class on Celtic ornament to architects, carpet designers, bookbinders and lithographers at the Young Men's Christian Association in Dundee and in 1904 at Eriskay he related to Geddes his plans to 'organise a little art community somewhere in the west Highlands for the cultivation of Celtic art'; in Eriskay he developed a close friendship with Marjory Kennedy-Fraser (1857–1930) who recorded and published traditional songs of the Hebrides.[26] In 1912 he contributed to the Celtic section of Geddes' magnificent *Masque of Ancient Learning*, a pageant illustrating the progress of culture and education from prehistoric, through ancient, to mediaeval and Renaissance times. A Celtic epilogue based on Duncan's Ramsay Lodge murals ended the *Ancient Masque*, demonstrating how key Geddes regarded this mural series, now almost 20 years old.

The Glasgow Boys' Celtic Revivalism at a time when attention was being drawn by historians and scholars to Celtic sources and archaeology, notably recent Bronze Age discoveries in Galloway, is fascinating. However, the Celtic Renascence that the dynamic polymath Geddes birthed in Edinburgh was part of a more systematic philosophy and educational and social strategy in which Duncan, an idealist and visionary artist who was sympathetic to many of Geddes' principles, found himself playing a key part. Hornel and MacGillivray's concurrent involvement in *The Evergreen* in 1895, when Duncan was living in Kirkcudbright and Charles Mackie nearby in Gatehouse of Fleet, is intriguing and suggests something of a Scottish east-west dialogue. In 1898 Duncan was invited to become one of twenty founder members of an Arts and Crafts Society in Glasgow, along with Burns, Phoebe Traquair (1852–1936), Rowand Anderson (1834–1921) and Glasgow Boys Macgillivray, Alexander

Roche (1861–1921) and David Gauld (1865–1936).[27] Duncan recognised that art workers needed to familiarise themselves not only with local crafts and materials, but also with folk art from other countries, such as Russia, Sweden, Lapland and America, in order to revitalise design in the Highlands. Geddes continually emphasised not only the local but also the international connections and ambitions of the Celtic Revival in Scotland. Fittingly it was *The Druids* that resulted in the Boys being invited to exhibit at the Munich Art Society exhibition in the Glaspalast, Munich, in 1890, bringing the Glasgow school international recognition and acclaim. Geddes' pronouncements on the decorative and imaginative as key aspects of Celtic design corresponded closely with European avant-garde thinking about the pre-eminence of line, colour and form in art, theories intimately connected with the artistic evolution of the Glasgow Boys, not to mention Duncan and indeed Mucha.

NOTES

(1) Patrick Geddes, 'Keltic Art', dictated 26 July 1899, p.6; University of Strathclyde Library, Department of Archives and Special Collections (SUA), T-GED 5/2/7.8.
(2) Geddes, 'Literature. The Celtic Revival', *Academy*, 11 July 1896, typescript; SUA, T-GED 5/2/1.
(3) Geddes, *Every Man His Own Art Critic (Glasgow Exhibition, 1888)*, Edinburgh & Glasgow, 1888, p.37.
(4) John Lavery, *The Life of a Painter*, London, 1940, pp.85–86.
(5) Henry to Hornel, Glasgow Art Club, 62 Bothwell Circus, [Oct–Dec 1885?]; Hornel Library, Broughton House.
(6) 'Fine-Art Institute', *Glasgow Herald*, 20 February 1892, p.4.
(7) William Archer, 'Scenic Aspects of the Lyceum Macbeth', *Scottish Art Review*, vol. 1, no. 8, January 1889, pp.249–55.
(8) 'The New Gallery. First Notice', *Times*, 3 May 1889, p.9.
(9) John Stuart, *Sculptured Stones of Scotland*, London, 1856, pp.43, 362, Plate CXXXVI, no.3. Roger Billcliffe, *The Glasgow Boys*, London, 2008, p.189.
(10) William Nicholson, 'The Brownie of Blednoch', *Dumfries Monthly Magazine*, October 1825, pp.327–30.
(11) A. S. Hartrick, *A Painter's Pilgrimage Through Fifty Years*, Cambridge, 1939, p.59.
(12) Hartrick, p.61.
(13) Joseph Anderson, *Scotland in Early Christian Times*, Edinburgh, 2nd series, 1881, pp.59, 64; figs.37, 41. It should be noted that an unspecified number of books were acquired by Hornel in the 1920s from the collection of the publisher and printer Thomas Fraser of Dalbeaty.
(14) Accession register, Stewartry Museum, Kirkcudbright, #2012.
(15) James Paton (ed.), *Scottish National Memorials. A Record of the Historical and Archaeological Collection in the Bishop's Castle, Glasgow*, 1888, Glasgow, 1890, pp.12–13.
(16) Geddes, *The Interpreter of Seven Pictures of Black and White*, Edinburgh, 1895, p.14.
(17) Margaret Armour, 'Mural Decoration in Scotland. Part 1', *Studio*, vol. 10, no.47, February 1897, pp.99–106.
(18) Geddes, 1895, p.15.
(19) Geddes, *The Masque of Ancient Learning and its Many Meanings*, Edinburgh, 1912, p.48.
(20) Geddes to Duncan, Collège des Ecossais, Plan des 4 Seigneurs, Montpellier, France, 2 February 1926; National Library of Scotland (NLS), MS 105517/67–68.
(21) Geddes, 'The Scots Renascence', *The Evergreen: A Northern Seasonal*, spring 1895, p.136.
(22) Duncan to Geddes, 13 Union Street, Kirkcudbright, 23 July 1895; SUA, T-GED 9/138.
(23) Duncan, notebook, pp.72–73; NLS, Ac.6866/4.
(24) Sharp to Geddes, Rutland House, Greencroft Gardens, South Hampstead, London, 3 March 1895; *The Celtic World prospectus*, 1895; NLS, MS.10563.
(25) Geddes, 'A Plea for Celtic Art', pp.1, 3, typescript; SUA, T-GED 5/2/3.
(26) Duncan to Geddes, 31 Albert Square, Dundee, 12 September 1898; NLS, MS.10531/152; Duncan to Geddes, Rudha Ban, Eriskay, 5 October 1904; SUA, T-GED 12/3/24. Kennedy-Fraser, *Songs of the Hebrides* (3 vols, 1909, 1917, 1921).
(27) Duncan to Geddes, 31 Albert Square, Dundee, 5 May 1898; NLS, MS 10530/122.
(28) John Duncan, notebook, n.d.; NLS, Acc. 6866/4, pp.72–73.

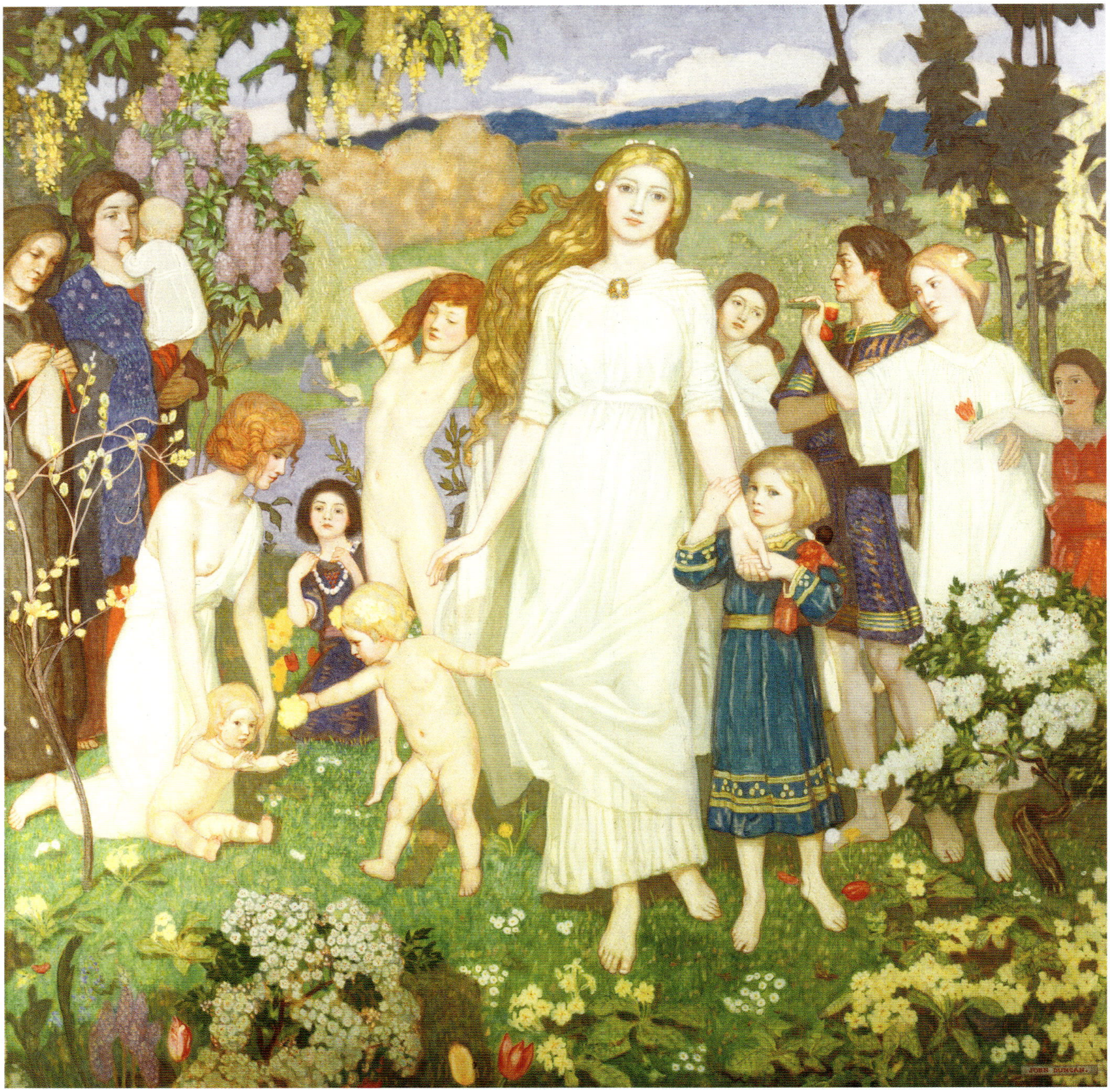

JOHN DUNCAN (1866–1945)
THE COMING OF BRIDE
1916–1917
Tempera on canvas
151.1 x 151.1
Purchased 1918
1457

This celebratory painting is based on the Celtic legend of Bride, who was held captive by Beira, Queen of Winter but was rescued by Angus on the first day of spring. The artist Cecile Walton described the painting as Duncan's 'happy picture'.

Duncan was profoundly influenced by two visits to Italy in 1890 and 1911. He particularly admired the flat, decorative beauty and spiritual purity of Fra Angelico (1395–1455) and Botticelli (1445–1510). He was delighted with the results of this painting, produced after much experimentation with the medium of tempera.

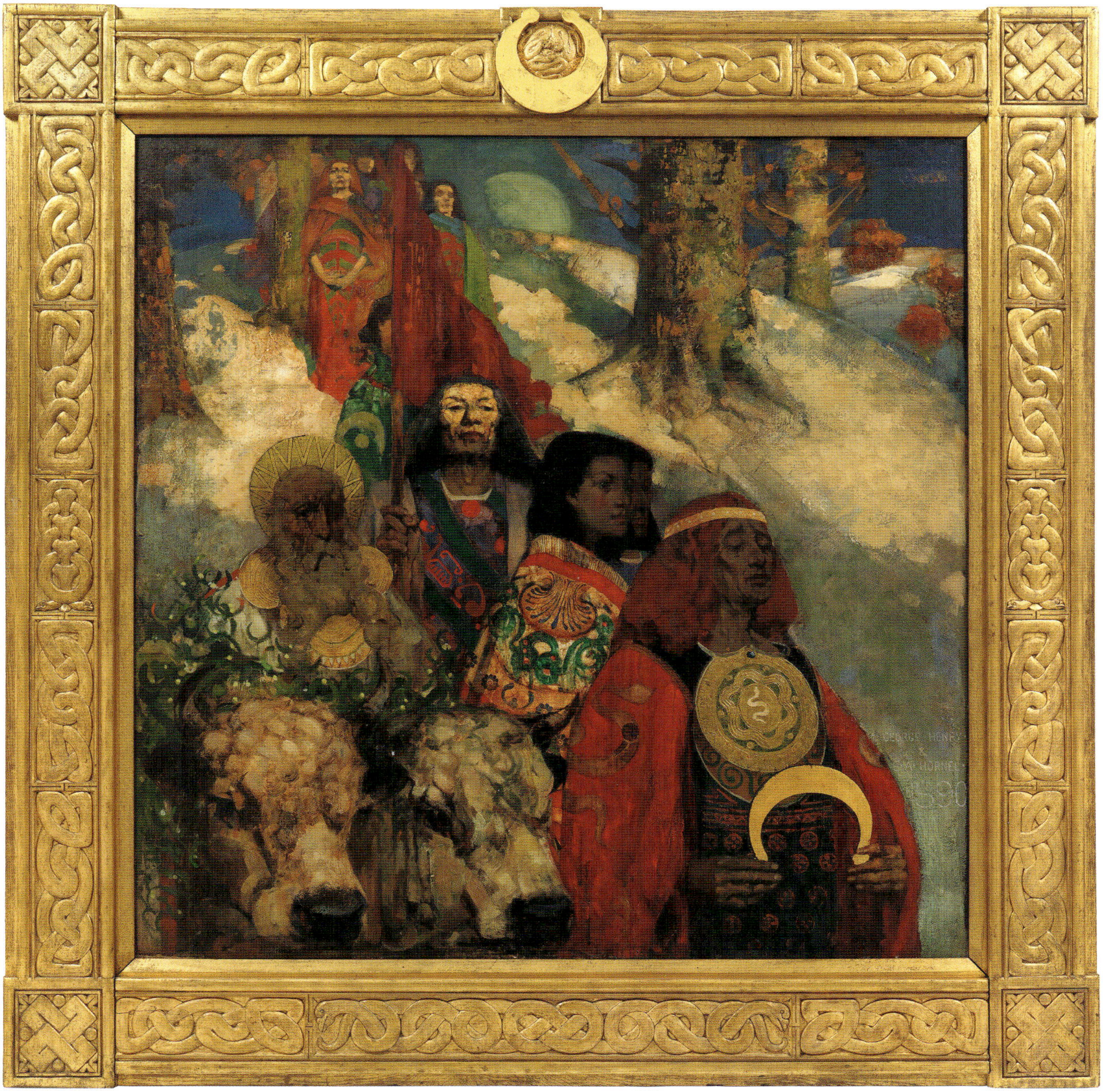

GEORGE HENRY (1858–1943) &
E.A. HORNEL (1864–1933)
THE DRUIDS – BRINGING IN THE MISTLETOE
1890
Oil on canvas
152.4 x 152.4
Purchased 1922
1534

Hornel, who was deeply interested in Scottish archaeology and folklore, probably suggested the subject matter of this visionary painting depicting Celtic priests or Druids processing in richly decorated ceremonial robes. In preparation the artists examined local cup-and-ring markings, druidical skulls and the Duke of Hamilton's herd of ancient white cattle. The journalist Neil Munro described the painting as 'Fiona MacLeodish in its Celticism.' The artists even designed its Celtic knotwork frame. Exhibited in the Grosvenor Gallery in 1890, it attracted much attention and resulted in the Glasgow Boys' invitation to exhibit in Munich.

ARTISTS' BIOGRAPHIES

KATIE DURAND

This list covers artists and manufacturers of exhibits selected by the four participating museums: Russell-Cotes Art Gallery and Museum, Bournemouth; Sainsbury Centre for Visual Art, Norwich; Kelvingrove Art Gallery and Museum, Glasgow; Walker Art Gallery, Liverpool.

BURNE-JONES, EDWARD (1833–1898)

Burne-Jones was born in Birmingham. In 1853 he took a place at Exeter College Oxford where he became close friends with fellow student William Morris (see p.10–11). Deeply influenced by the writings of John Ruskin, he and Morris believed that art provided a powerful means to revive lost traditions and values. The romantic symbolism of older painter Dante Gabriel Rossetti (see below), a fascination with mediaeval art and folklore and a close study of 15th Century Italian art led Burne-Jones to develop an idealised and sensual painting style, which appealed to wealthy patrons. In 1861 he helped Morris to found Morris & Co. and his stained glass designs were among the many items to be produced by the firm. Burne-Jones also designed bookplates, ceramic tiles, jewellery, tapestries and mosaics. Illustrated pp.113, 118, 119

THE DELLA ROBBIA POTTERY

Taking its name from Luca Della Robbia (c.1400–1482), a Florentine sculptor renowned for transforming the glazed terracotta technique, the Della Robbia Art Pottery was established in 1894 in Birkenhead, Merseyside. The firm was co-founded by the painter Harold Rathbone (1858–1929) and the two sculptors, Conrad Dressler (see below) and Carlo Manzoni (1855–1910); all were inspired by William Morris and his circle. Working with a group of local young potters and designers, they developed a highly distinctive style of pottery characterised by Art Nouveau style decorative motifs and vibrant turquoise glaze. The Della Robbia's artistically crafted pots were popular and widely sold by Liberty & Co., London, and through Morris & Co. The pottery closed in 1906.
Illustrated pp. 121, 122

DRESSLER, CONRAD (1856–1940)

Dressler studied sculpture under Joseph Edgar Boehm (1834–1890) and Edouard Lantéri (1848–1917) at the Royal College of Art. He joined the Art Workers' Guild in 1881 where members from all branches of visual arts and crafts met to discuss, demonstrate and share their working methods. In 1894 Dressler co-founded the Della Robbia Pottery in Birkenhead (see above) followed by Medmenham Pottery in Buckinghamshire, which specialised in architectural tiles and large wall panels. He worked in a variety of materials and techniques but is above all remembered for his sculpture, particularly busts of Arts and Crafts theorists John Ruskin and William Morris. After periods in Paris and the United States, Dressler settled in France in 1929.
Illustrated p.121

DUNCAN, JOHN MCKIRDY (1866–1945)

Duncan attended Dundee School of Art before working as an illustrator in London. He completed his studies in Antwerp and Dusseldorf and spent some time in Italy before settling in Edinburgh in 1892. Through association with the philosopher, sociologist, town planner and writer Patrick Geddes, Duncan became one of the leading Scottish proponents of the Celtic revival (see p.140). His symbolist murals, paintings, stained glass and book illustrations of mythical, legendary and religious subjects borrow decorative elements from early Celtic art and recall the work of the Pre-Raphaelites. Duncan was the first Director of Geddes' Old Edinburgh School of Art and taught in Chicago and at the Royal Scottish Academy School of Painting.
Illustrated pp. 144, 145, 148

FORTESCUE-BRICKDALE, ELEANOR (1871–1945)

Fortescue-Brickdale studied at Crystal Palace School of Art in Sydenham, London, and entered the Royal Academy in 1896. She had a successful career as a book illustrator, notably illustrating works by the poet Alfred Tennyson (1809–1892). She exhibited oils at the Royal Academy and was the first female artist admitted to the Institute of Painters in Oils in 1902. Fortescue-Brickdale also produced stained glass windows and biblical subjects in plaster. In 1920 she published the *Golden Book of Famous Women*, a compilation of stories about some of the most famous women in history and legend (Hodder & Stoughton). Her works emulate the sharp draughtsmanship, vibrant colours and allegorical subject matter of the Pre-Raphaelites.
Illustrated p.124

FOUQUET, GEORGES (1862–1957)

Son of the prominent Parisian jeweller, Alphonse Fouquet (1828–1911), Fouquet took the reins of the family firm in 1895 and commissioned artists and designers to create new and inventive designs that would appeal to a fashionable clientèle. His collaboration with Mucha between c.1898–1901 resulted in ornate and audacious pieces characterised by clusters of asymmetrical gem pendants (see p.50). From the 1920s Fouquet continued to work in gold, enamel and gemstones but moved away from Art Nouveau towards geometric Art Deco designs, often incorporating Egyptian motifs.
Illustrated pp. 50, 60

GALLÉ, EMILE (1846–1904)

Gallé was born in Nancy and became France's most celebrated *fin-de-siècle* glass maker and furniture designer. Following apprenticeships in Weimar and Meisenthal, Gallé took over his father's decoration business in 1877 and rose to fame with two successive participations in the Paris Exposition Universelle (1878 and 1889). His ornate glassware and detailed marquetry designs, dominated by naturalistic plant and flower motifs, put Nancy firmly on the map as a centre of Art Nouveau. By 1900 Gallé employed some 300 artisans. In 1901 he founded the École de Nancy, which proved instrumental in elevating decorative arts to the status of fine arts in France and around the world.

Illustrated p.61

HENRY, GEORGE (1858–1943)

Henry studied at Glasgow School of Art and in the studio of William York Macgregor (1855–1923). He was active in the circle of painters known as the Glasgow Boys (see p.140). In 1885 Henry met Edward Atkinson Hornel (see below) who introduced him to Galloway and his hometown of Kirkcudbright where the two produced striking landscapes and rural scenes characterised by rich colours and a flattened, decorative and highly textured picture plane. In 1893–94 Henry and Hornel spent 18 months in Japan during which Henry produced a great many watercolours. Henry gradually moved away from his experimental work and established a successful portrait studio in London.

Illustrated pp.141, 149

HORNEL, EDWARD ATKINSON (1864–1933)

Hornel was born in Australia but returned to his parents' native Kirkcudbright in Scotland as a small child. He studied at the Trustee's Academy in Edinburgh and the Academie des Beaux Arts in Antwerp. He settled in Kirkcudbright but travelled widely, notably to Japan in 1893–94 with his close friend George Henry (see above). Through Henry he became involved in the group of painters known as the Glasgow Boys who painted naturalistic rural scenes inspired by the French artist Jules Bastien-Lepage. Hornel and Henry's collaboration resulted in an increasingly decorative, textured and colourful painting style. Hornel's visionary scenes of local children in nature were acclaimed by artists and critics alike but did not sell well and in later years his work became increasingly formulaic as he submitted to public taste.

Illustrated pp.142, 149

JOPLING, LOUISE (1843–1933)

Jopling was born in Manchester and studied art in Paris under the romantic painter Charles Chaplin (1825–1891). With the support of patrons such as the de Rothschild family she became a successful portraitist, landscapist, and painter of genre scenes and one of the best-known female painters of the Victorian age. She exhibited at the Royal Academy and the Paris Salon and was the first woman to be admitted to the Royal Society of British Artists (1901). Jopling was a prominent figure in the artistic circles of the time and was close friends with fellow painters James Abbott McNeill Whistler and John Everett Millais. She established her own school of painting for women in 1887.

Illustrated p.123

KING, JESSIE MARION (1875–1949)

King was born in Bearsden, a suburb of Glasgow. She studied at Glasgow School of Art and on completing her studies began teaching book design while embarking on a successful career as an illustrator. Her distinctive designs, depicting slender girls adorned by floral arrangements in strong outlines and delicate colours, filled posters, bookplates, jewellery, ceramics, fabrics, wallpapers and murals. In 1908 she married fellow artist Ernest Archibald Taylor (1874–1951). After spending several years in Paris they settled in the fishing village of Kirkcudbright where the existing community of artists increased as women artists in particular gravitated to the couple's home in Greengate Close.

Illustrated pp.76, 77

LALIQUE, RENÉ (1860–1945)

Lalique was born in the Marne region of France. He attended evening classes at the Ecole des Arts Décoratifs in Paris while apprenticed to the Parisian jeweller Louis Aucoc (1850–1932) and completed h s studies at Crystal Palace School of Art in Sydenham, London. In 1885 he established his own workshop in Paris and his fanciful and organic pieces of jewellery, characterised by an inventive use of semi-precious stones, enamel, irregular pearls, horn, ivory and coral, rapidly found favour with a burgeoning clientèle thirsty for the latest in Art Nouveau designs. In the early 1900s he branched into glassware, and his stylistically and technologically innovative pieces earned him an international reputation.

Illustrated pp. 62, 63

LOETZ (OR LÖTZ) WITWE GLASSWORKS

Loetz Glassworks was founded in 1836 in the Southern Bohemian town of Klostermühle (today Klášterský Mlýn in the Czech Republic). In 1897, inspired by the work of the American Louis Comfort Tiffany (1848–1933), the firm began experimenting with iridescent glass, metallic sheens and rippled finishes. The Phänomen series, designed for the most part by Franz Hofstötter (1871–1959), was a resounding success at the 1900 Exposition Universelle in Paris (see p.49) and signalled the zenith of Loetz glass. The firm continued to produce pieces until its closure in 1947 but never replicated the success of its Art Nouveau period.

Illustrated p.64

LOGAN, GEORGE (1866–1939)

Logan was born in Beith, Ayrshire, and started his career as an upholsterer's apprentice in his hometown. In 1882 he joined the prestigious

Glasgow firm of Wylie & Lochhead (see below). At the Glasgow International Exhibition of 1901, Logan's designs for a library and bedroom suite were extolled by followers of the European avant-garde. His designs were also used by a number of Staffordshire potteries, including E. Brain & Co (under the trade name Foley Art China Peacock Pottery), Keeling & Co and Wedgwood & Co. Logan was also an accomplished painter, and while he continued to work for Wylie & Lochhead until 1937 he focused primarily on painting in his later years.
Illustrated p.77

MACKINTOSH, CHARLES RENNIE (1868–1928)

Mackintosh became an apprentice architect at the age of 16 while taking evening classes at Glasgow School of Art. Together with his friends Herbert McNair and sisters Margaret and Frances MacDonald, collectively known as 'The Four', he created posters and furniture in a new graphic style characterised by delicate colours, sinuous forms and symbolic subject matter. In 1896, Mackintosh won a commission to design the new Glasgow School of Art building. Thereafter followed a succession of commissions for buildings and domestic schemes, which all demonstrate his distinctive interplay of lines, geometric forms and stylised floral motifs. After some years in England where he struggled to find work he spent the last five years of his life in the South of France.
Illustrated pp. 71, 72, 74, 75

MORRIS, TALWIN (1865–1911)

Morris was born in Winchester and was apprenticed to his uncle, the Reading-based architect Joseph Morris (1836–1913), before joining a London firm. In 1893, he was appointed Art Manager of the Glasgow publisher, Blackie & Son. He became friends with Charles Rennie Mackintosh (see above) and his circle and was responsible for introducing the curved lines, stylised flowers and architectural forms of the 'Glasgow Style' into book design. Morris's work was exhibited at the 1902 Prima Esposizione Internazionale d'Arte Decorativa Moderna in Turin and had a significant impact on turn of the century book design. He also designed textiles, furniture and metalwork.
Illustrated p.76

RIESSNER, STELLMACHER UND KESSEL

Based in Turn-Teplitz, Bohemia (today Trnovany in the Czech Republic), the Riessner, Stellmacher und Kessel firm was founded in 1892 by partners Eduard Stellmacher, his brothers-in-law Hans and Karl Riessner, and Rudolf Kessel. The firm employed Stellmacher's son-in-law, the designer Paul Dachsel, and together Stellmacher and Dachsel experimented with organic motifs incorporating plants and animals, mythological creatures and applied flowers, fruits and precious stones. The firm's intricately shaped ceramics, marked with the name 'Amphora', won prizes at the World's Columbian Exposition in Chicago in 1893, at the Exposition Universelle in Paris in 1900 (see p.49) and at the World Fair in St Louis in 1904.
Illustrated p.65

RODIN, AUGUSTE (1840–1917)

Rodin was refused entry at the École des Beaux-Arts in Paris and instead served a long apprenticeship under Albert-Ernest Carrier-Belleuse (1824–1887). In 1876, he travelled to Italy where the work of Michelangelo made a great impression on him. His first full-scale figure, *The Age of Bronze* (1875–1877), was purchased by the French Ministry of Fine Arts for the Luxembourg Gardens in Paris in 1877. In 1880 he received the first of many commissions from the French Government, *The Gates of Hell* (1880–1917). The monumental portal, incorporating a vast repertoire of figures in sculptural relief, was only assembled and cast in its entirety following the artist's death. Widely recognised as the father of modern sculpture, Rodin was invited to exhibit his work throughout Europe and North America.
Illustrated p.120

ROSSETTI, DANTE GABRIEL (1828–1882)

Rossetti was born in London to Italian parents. After leaving school he followed a brief apprenticeship with painter Ford Madox Brown (1821–1893) and in 1848 he founded the Pre-Raphaelite Brotherhood with six other painters and poets including William Holman Hunt and John Everett Millais. The group contested the accepted academic style of painting, calling instead for a return to the serious subject matter, rich colour palette and attention to detail of the late medieval and early Renaissance period. Rossetti began exhibiting in the late 1840s and had a marked effect on a second generation of artists and writers including William Morris and Edward Burne-Jones (see above).
Illustrated pp. 109, 112, 125

WYLIE & LOCHHEAD

Wylie & Lochhead began business as undertakers during a major epidemic of Asiatic cholera in early 19th century Glasgow. By 1862 the firm had branched into a number of activities including cabinetmaking, paper staining, upholstering, carving and gilding. By 1900 they were the leading cabinetmakers and upholsterers in Glasgow and also had branches in London and Manchester. The 1901 Glasgow International Exhibition provided an opportunity to showcase lines developed in the distinctive Glasgow Style by designers John Ednie (1876–1934), George Logan (see above) and E.A. Taylor (1874–1951). Wylie & Lochhead was acquired by the department store chain House of Fraser in 1957. The undertakers side of the business continues to this day.
Illustrated p.77

SELECT BIBLIOGRAPHY

This short bibliography covers the topics explored in this book, selected for general readership and featuring English-language publications only.

Victor Arwas, Jana Brabcová-Orlíková and Anna Dvořák (eds.), *Alphonse Mucha: The Spirit of Art Nouveau* (US travelling exh. cat., 1998–2000). Alexandria, Virginia: Art Services International, 1998.

Robyn Asleson, *Albert Moore*. London: Phaidon Press, 2000.

Mary Bennet, *Artists of the Pre-Raphaelite Circle: The First Generation*. London: Lund Humphries, 1988.

Roger Billcliffe, *The Glasgow Boys*. London: Francis Lincoln Publishers (revised edition), 2008.

Ann Bridges (ed.), *Alphonse Mucha: The Complete Graphic Works*. London: Academy Editions, 1980.

Jude Burkhauser (ed.), *Glasgow Girls: Women in Art and Design 1880–1920* (exh. cat.. Glasgow Art Galleries & Museums and The Glasgow School of Art, 1990). Edinburgh: Canongate Publishing Limited, 1990.

Stephen Calloway and Lynn Federle Orr (eds.), *The Cult of Beauty: The Aesthetic Movement 1860–1900* (exh. cat., London, Paris and San Francisco, 2011–2012). London: V&A Publishing, 2011.

Anna Dvořák, Helen Bieri Thomson and Bernadette de Boysson, *Alphonse Mucha – Paris 1900: Le Pater/The Lord Prayer* (exh. cat., Gingins, Prague, Bordeaux and Mariemont, Belgium, 2001–2004). Prague: Obecní dům, 2002.

Frances Fowle and Belinda Thomson, *Patrick Geddes: The French Connection*. Wendlebury, Bicester: White Cockade Publishing, 2004.

Isabelle Frank (ed.), *The Theory of Decorative Art: An Anthology of European and American Writings, 1750–1940*. New Haven and London: Yale University Press, 2000.

Jean Louis Gaillemin, Christiane Lange, Michel Hilaire and Agnes Husslein-Arco (eds.), *Alphonse Mucha* (exh. cat., Vienna, Montpellier and Munich 2009–2010). Munich, Berlin, London and New York: Prestel, 2009.

Amanda Geitner and Emma Hazell (eds.), *The Anderson Collection of Art Nouveau*. Norwich: Sainsbury Centre for Visual Arts, University of East Anglia, 2003.

Hardy S. George (ed.), *Paris 1900* (exh. cat., Oklahoma City Museum of Art, 2007).

Charlotte Gere, *Artistic Circles: Design and Decoration in the Aesthetic Movement*. London: V&A Publishing, 2010.

Paul Greenhalgh, *Art Nouveau: 1890–1914* (exh.cat., London, Washington D.C. and Tokyo, 2000–2001). London: V&A Publishing, 2000.

John Hoole and Tomoko Sato (eds.), *Alphonse Mucha* (exh. cat., Barbican Art Gallery, London, 1993). London: Lund Humphries, 1993.

Jeremy Howard, *Art Nouveau: International and National Styles in Europe*. Manchester & New York: Manchester University Press, 1996.

Thomas Howarth, *Charles Rennie Mackintosh and the Modern Movement*. London: Routledge and Kegan Paul Ltd., 1952.

Perilla Kinchin and Juliet Kinchin with Neil Baxter, *Glasgow's Great Exhibitions 1888 · 1901 · 1911 · 1938 · 1988*. Wendlebury, Bicester: White Cockade Publishing, 1988.

Lionel Lambourne, *The Aesthetic Movement*. London: Phaidon Press, 1996.

John Lavery, *The Life of a Painter*. Boston: Little Brown and Company, 1940.

Henry F. Lenning, *The Art Nouveau*. The Hague: Martinus Nijhoff, 1951.

Hermann Muthesius, *The English House* (first English edition edited by Dennis Sharp). London: Lockwood Staples, 1979.

Edward Morris, *Victorian and Edwardian Paintings in the Lady Lever Art Gallery*. London: HMSO, 1994.

Alphonse Mucha, *Alphonse Mucha: Lectures on Art*. London: Academy Editions and New York: St. Martin's Press, 1975.

Jiří Mucha. *Alphonse Mucha: The Master of Art Nouveau*. Prague: Knihtisk Artia, 1966.

Jiří Mucha. *Alphonse Maria Mucha: His Life and Art*. London: Academy Editions, 1989.

Sarah Mucha (ed.) with Ronald F. Lipp, Victor Arwas, Anna Dvořák, Jan Mlčoch and Petr Wittlich, *Alphonse Mucha*. Prague: Mucha Limited, 2000.

Gillian Naylor, *The Arts and Crafts Movement: A Study of Its Sources, Ideals, and Influences on Design Theory*. London: Studio Vista and Cambridge, Mass.: The MIT Press, 1980.

Christopher Newall, *The Grosvenor Gallery Exhibitions: Change and Continuity in the Victorian Art World*. Cambridge University Press, 1995.

Elizabeth Prettejohn (ed.), *After the Pre-Raphaelites: Art and Aestheticism in Victorian England*. Manchester University Press, 1999.

Brian Reade, *Art Nouveau and Alphonse Mucha* (exh. cat., Victoria & Albert Museum, London, 1963). London: HMSO, 1963.

Jack Rennert and Alain Weill, *Alphonse Mucha: The Complete Posters and Panels*. Uppsala, Sweden: Hjert & Hjert, 1984.

James Maude Richards and Nikolaus Pevsner (eds.), *The Anti-rationalists*. London: Architectural Press, 1973.

Tomoko Sato, *Alphonse Mucha 1860–1939: The Artist as Visionary*. Cologne: Taschen, 2015.

Derek Sayer, *The Coasts of Bohemia: A Czech History*. Princeton and New Jersey: Princeton University Press, 1998.

Peter Selz and Mildred Constantine (eds.), *Art Nouveau: Art and Design at the Turn of the Century* (exh. cat., Museum of Modern Art, New York, 1960).

Marta Sylvestrová and Petr Štembera, *Alfons Mucha: Czech Master of the Belle Époque* (exh. cat., Budapest and Brno, 2009–2010). Budapest: Museum of Fine Arts and Brno: Moravian Gallery, 2009.

Julian Treuherz, Elizabeth Prettejohn and Edwin Becker, *Dante Gabriel Rossetti* (exh. cat., Liverpool and Amsterdam, 2003). Zwolle: Waanders Publishers and London: Thames & Hudson, 2003.

Petr Wittlich. *Prague: Fin de Siècle*. Paris: Flammarion, 1992.

Gabriel P. Weisberg, Edwin Becker and Évelyne Possémé (eds.), *The Origins of L'Art Nouveau: The Bing Empire* (exh. cat., Amsterdam, Munich, Barcelona and Paris, 2005–2006). Amsterdam: Van Gogh Museum, Paris: Les Arts décoratifs and Antwerp: Mercantorfonds, 2004.

CHRONOLOGY
ALPHONSE MUCHA AND HIS TIMES

ALPHONSE MUCHA: BIOGRAPHY

1860
24 July: Alphonse Maria Mucha born in Ivančice, a South Moravian town under Austrian administration, to the family of Ondřej Mucha, a court usher.

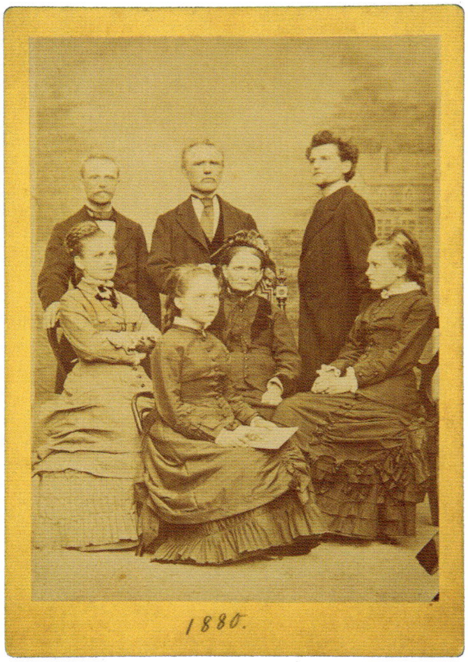

The Mucha family 1880: (standing from left to right) Mucha's step-brother August, father Ondřej and Mucha himself; (seated, same order) sister Anna, youngest sister Anděla, mother Amálie and step-sister Antonia

1867
Austrian Empire transformed into the dual monarchy Austro-Hungarian Empire following the disastrous defeat in the Austro-Prussian War of 1866; the Prussian occupation of Ivančice for a few months had an enduring influence on Mucha.

1868
By this year Mucha has been regularly singing as a choirboy for a local church in Ivančice. Makes his earliest surviving drawing, *Crucifixion*.

1872
Autumn: moves to Brno, the Moravian capital, where he becomes a boarding scholar and chorister at the Cathedral of St. Peter and Paul while studying at the Slovanské Gymnasium. Meets the future composer Leoš Janáček.

CONTEMPORARY ARTISTIC AND CULTURAL EVENTS

1860
First foreign editions of seminal *On the Origin of Species* by Charles Darwin (originally published in London in 1859) appear in the US, Germany and the Netherlands; the book brings public attention to the significance of the organic world.

1861
Morris, Marshall and Faulkner founded by William Morris with friends from the Pre-Raphaelites promoting honesty of craftsmanship.

1862
International Exhibition in London, which shows the largest ever display of Japanese art seen in the West at the time, mainly drawn from the collection of Sir Rutherford Alcock, the first British Consul-General in a newly opened Japan.

1863
Charles Baudelaire's essay, 'Le Peintre de la vie moderne', published in *Le Figaro*. Salon des Refusés founded by Napoleon III: the first exhibition includes *Le déjeuner sur l'herbe* (1862–1863) by Édouard Manet and *Symphony in White No. 1: The White Girl* (1861–1862) by James McNeill Whistler.

1867
Exposition Universelle in Paris presents official Japanese exhibits for the first time in a national pavilion: this triggers a long-lasting Japanese-art craze in Europe.

1875

Summer: on his visit to a church in the East Bohemian town, Ústí nad Orlicí, Mucha is deeply impressed by murals by Jan Umlauf, a painter in the Czech Baroque tradition. This experience leads him to the decision to be a professional painter.

1877

Expelled from school due to his poor academic performance; his father finds Mucha work as a court clerk in Ivančice. Devotes his free time to drawing, taking lessons from Josef Zelený, Moravian painter and his former art teacher.

1878

September: Mucha's application to the Prague Academy of Fine Arts is turned down. Involved in amateur theatre performances as an actor-director and decorator while contributing illustrations to local satirical magazines.

1879

Joins the Sokol organisation. Autumn: goes to Vienna to work as an apprentice scene painter for the firm of Kautsky-Brioschi-Burghardt.

1880–1881

In his spare time, attends evening art classes and visits art galleries to study Old Masters and contemporary artists, in particular, Hans Makart. December 1881: dismissed from work after a major fire burns down the Ringtheater, his employer's best customer.

1882

Goes to Mikulov, South Moravia where he earns a living by painting portraits for local notables.

1883–1884

By 1883 has met the local landowner Count Eduard Khuen-Belasi; he employs Mucha to decorate his residence Emmahof Castle and later Gandegg Castle in the Tyrol for his brother Count Egon.

1875

Morris's decorative art company is renamed Morris & Co.; his social art doctrine and mediaeval aesthetics inspire the Arts and Crafts Movement in the 1880s. Arthur Lasenby Liberty opens luxury retail brand Liberty in London selling imported goods from Japan anc the East. Siegfried Bing expands his Japanese import business at the firm of Leullier et Bing in Paris following his fist visit to Japan this year.

1877

Grosvenor Gallery founded in London; the opening exhibition includes Whistler's *Nocturne in Black and Gold – The Falling Rocket* (c.1872–1877), which leads to the Whistler-Ruskin Trial (1878).

1878

Emile Gallé receives the Grand Prix at the Paris Exposition Universelle of this year for his glassware, which includes a vase with a carp motif inspired by a Hokusai woodcut.

1880

Commissioned by the Directorate of Fine Arts (the French state) in 1880, Auguste Rodin begins to work on the monumental sculpture group *The Gates of Hell,* which he continues to develop until his death in 1917.

1882

The Century Guild of Artists formed by Arthur Mackmurdo, Herbert Horne and Selwyn Image, forerunners of the Arts and Crafts Movement: their work is considered to herald the Art Nouveau style. The Society for Psychic Research founded in London as well as in Vienna.

1884

The first exhibition of Les XX held in Brussels; this is seminal for the development of Art Nouveau. Georges Seurat exhibits his first major painting *The Bathers at Asnières* (1884) at the Salon des Indépendants. Inspired by Morris, a group of British architects found the Art Workers' Guild to promote the 'unity of all the arts'.

1885

Travels in Northern Italy (Venice, Florence, Bologna and Milan) with Count Egon. Autumn: begins studies at the Munich Academy of Fine Arts with the sponsorship of Count Eduard. Through family contacts commissioned to paint an altarpiece *Saints Cyril and Methodius* (1886) for the Church of St. John of Nepomuk for a Czech community in Pisek, North Dakota, USA.

1885

Symbolist periodical *Revue wagnérienne* appears in Paris.

1886

Elected chairman of the Škréta Club, a society of Czech art students, and becomes editor of its journal *The Palette*. While in Munich Mucha makes a series of photographs on 7 × 7 cm glass-plate negatives.

1886

Paul Gauguin works with Émile Bernard in Pont-Aven. Whistler's retrospective held at the Petit Palais, Paris. Jean Moréas's manifesto for Symbolism appears in *Le Figaro*. Neo-Impressionist group formed around Seurat.

1887

Autumn: moves to Paris to study at the Académie Julian sponsored by Count Eduard Khuen-Belasi; he is taught by Jean-Paul Laurens, Gustave Boulanger and Jules-Joseph Lefebvre. Becomes chairman of the Lada Club, a society of Czech, Polish and Russian students.

1887

Construction of the Eiffel Tower begins (completed in 1889). Gauguin visits Martinique. Van Gogh organises an exhibition of Japanese prints at the café Le Tambourin, Paris. The Arts and Crafts Exhibition Society formed in London with the goal of breaking down the distinction between fine and decorative art.

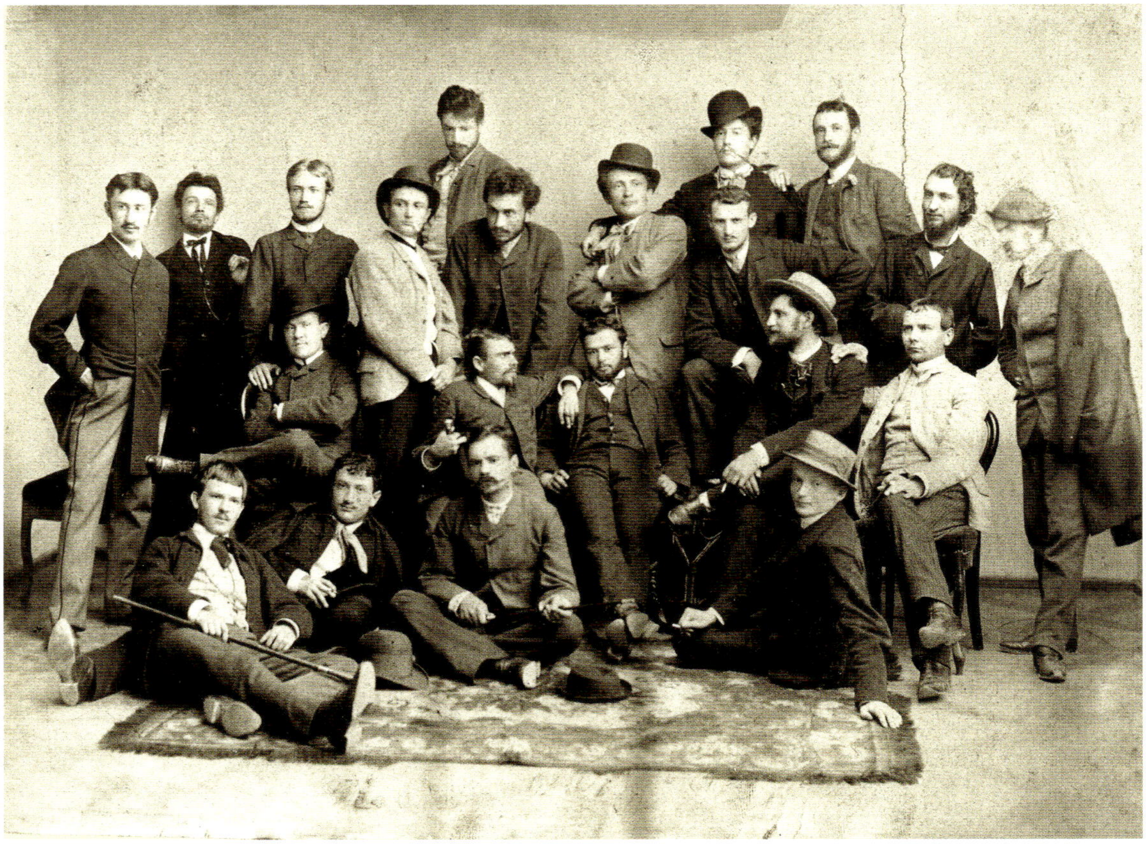

Members of the Škŕeta Club, Munich c.1886: Mucha (seated, second from right in profile) between David Widhopff (third from right) and Karel Václav Mašek (far right)

Mucha and friends at his studio in rue de la Grande Chaumière, Paris c.1893–1894. Left to right: Paul Gauguin, Mucha, Luděk Marold and Gauguin's mistress Anna 'La Javanaise'

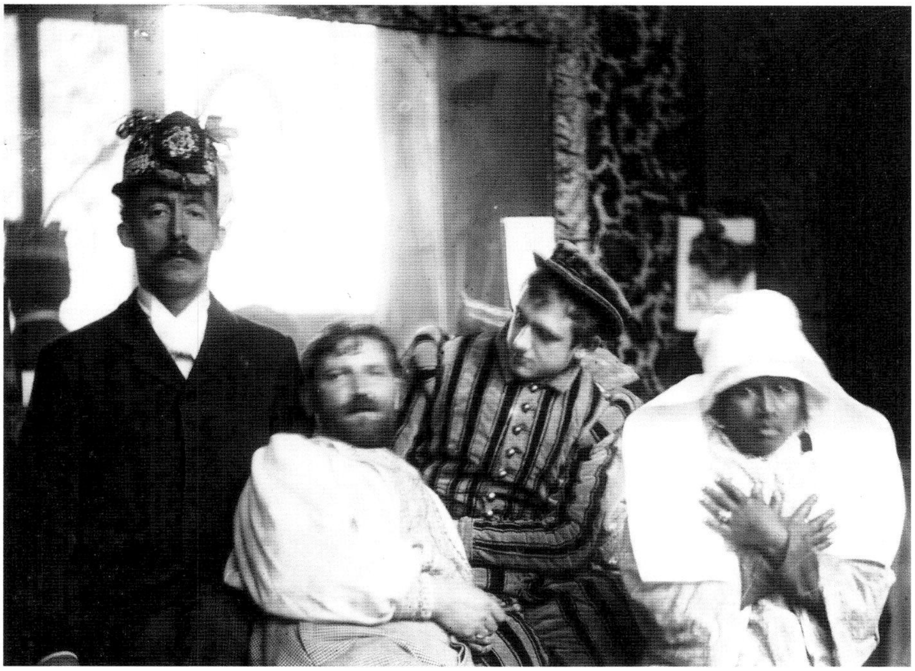

1888

November: enters the Académie Colarossi; the teaching staff includes Raphaël Collin, an influential figure in the artistic exchange between France and Japan at the time.

1888

Siegfried Bing launches an influential monthly journal, *Le Japon Artistique,* published in French, German and English. A group of art students from the Académie Julian form the Nabis, inspired by Gauguin's Synthetism. Van Gogh stays with Gauguin in Arles.

1889

Financial support from Count Eduard ends; begins to work as an illustrator for publishers in Paris and Prague.

1889

Morris attends the International Workers Congress in Paris as a delegate of England's Socialist League. The Paris Exposition Universelle is held: Burne-Jones's *King Cophetua and the Beggar Maid* (1884) receives wide acclaim and is awarded the Legion of Honour. Symbolist periodicals, *La Revue blanche* and *La Plume* founded.

1890

Through the introduction of the Polish painter Władysław Ślewiński, joins a circle of artists including Stanisław Wyspiański, Paul Sérusier and the Nabis who gather at Madame Charlotte Caron's Crèmerie at 13 rue de la Grande-Chaumière; moves to lodgings above the Crèmerie.

1890

Oscar Wilde's 'decadent' novel *The Picture of Dorian Grey* and his essay 'The True Function and Value of Criticism' (revised as 'The Critic as Artist' in 1891) appear in *Lippincott's Magazine* and in *The Nineteenth Century* respectively. Whistler's *The Gentle Art of Making Enemies* published.

1891

Spring: meets Paul Gauguin, then a temporary lodger at Madame Charlotte's before his first trip to Tahiti. Begins working for Parisian publisher Armand Colin, who commissions Mucha to illustrate *Scènes et Épisodes de l'Histoire d'Allemagne* by Charles Seignobos.

1891

First exhibition of the Nabis; Gauguin sails for Tahiti. Toulouse-Lautrec produces the poster *Moulin Rouge: La Goulue,* his first attempt at lithography. Whistler's *Arrangement in Grey and Black No.1* (1871) is bought by the French state.

1892
Begins to give drawing lessons at his studio; these later develop into Cours Mucha at the Académie Colarossi.

1893
By this year, Mucha has purchased his own camera, which takes 10 x 13 cm glass-plate negatives. Summer: Mucha's friendship with Gauguin resumed on the latter's return from Tahiti.

1894
Awarded a 'mention honorable' at the Paris Salon for oil studies for *Scènes et Épisodes de l'Histoire d'Allemagne*. Late in December: designs his first poster for Sarah Bernhardt, *Gismonda* (see p.22).

1895
1 January: the poster *Gismonda* appears in Paris causing a sensation. Signs a six-year contract with Bernhardt to design sets, costumes and posters for her productions. Mucha's circle of friends at Madame Charlotte's includes Swedish dramatist August Strindberg and English composer Frederick Delius. Later this year, meets the Lumière brothers, pioneers of filmmaking.

1896
Joins the Salon des Cent, the group of artists promoted by *La Plume* magazine (see p.39). Signs an exclusive contract with Parisian printer F. Champenois. Designs his first series of decorative panels, *The Seasons* (see pp.82–83). Summer: moves to a larger studio and apartment at 6 rue du Val-de-Grâce.

1897
By this year Mucha has met the socialist poet Henri Cazalis and participated in the theosophical circle led by Albert de Rochas and Camille Flammarion. February–March: Mucha's first solo exhibition held

1892
The Munich Secession is formed. First exhibition of the Salon de la Rose+Croix held at the Durand-Ruel Gallery promoting 'esoteric' Symbolist works. Sarah Bernhardt prepares to stage Wilde's play *Salomé*, written in French with her in mind, but the production is banned from public performance in England.

1893
Gauguin briefly shares Mucha's studio at 8, rue de la Grande-Chaumière, Paris, while preparing for the exhibition of his Tahitian works at the Durand-Ruel Gallery held in November. First exhibition of The Four – Herbert MacNair, Charles Rennie Mackintosh (see p.152) and the MacDonald sisters; their works are inspired by William Blake and Beardsley. Victor Horta's first town house, La Maison Autrique, Brussels, built in the Art Nouveau style.

1894
Wilde's play *Salomé* published in English with illustrations by Aubrey Beardsley. Henry van de Velde publishes *Déblaiement d'Art*, which calls for a unified environment for the arts and challenges the notion of a hierarchy between 'fine' and 'decorative' art. Beardsley's art magazine *The Yellow Book* is founded in London.

1895
The construction of Hector Guimard's first building in Paris, Castel Béranger, begins (completed in 1898). Later this year, Bing opens his new shop in Paris, *Maison de l'Art Nouveau*, with the interior designed by Van de Velde; the name of the shop contributes towards the wider circulation of the term referring to the newly emerging decorative style as 'Art Nouveau'.

1896
Art Nouveau magazine *Jugent* founded in Munich; this introduces Mucha's poster for *The 20th Exhibition of the Salon des Cent* (see p.7). Morris's Kelmscott Press publishes *The Works of Geoffrey Chaucer* with illustrations by Burne-Jones. The state visit of Tsar Nicholas II of Russia to France generates Slavophilism in Paris.

1897
The Vienna Secession formed by a group of Austrian artists including Gustav Klimt as its first president. Bram Stoker's Gothic horror novel *Dracula* published; its popularity is indicative of a fascination with the

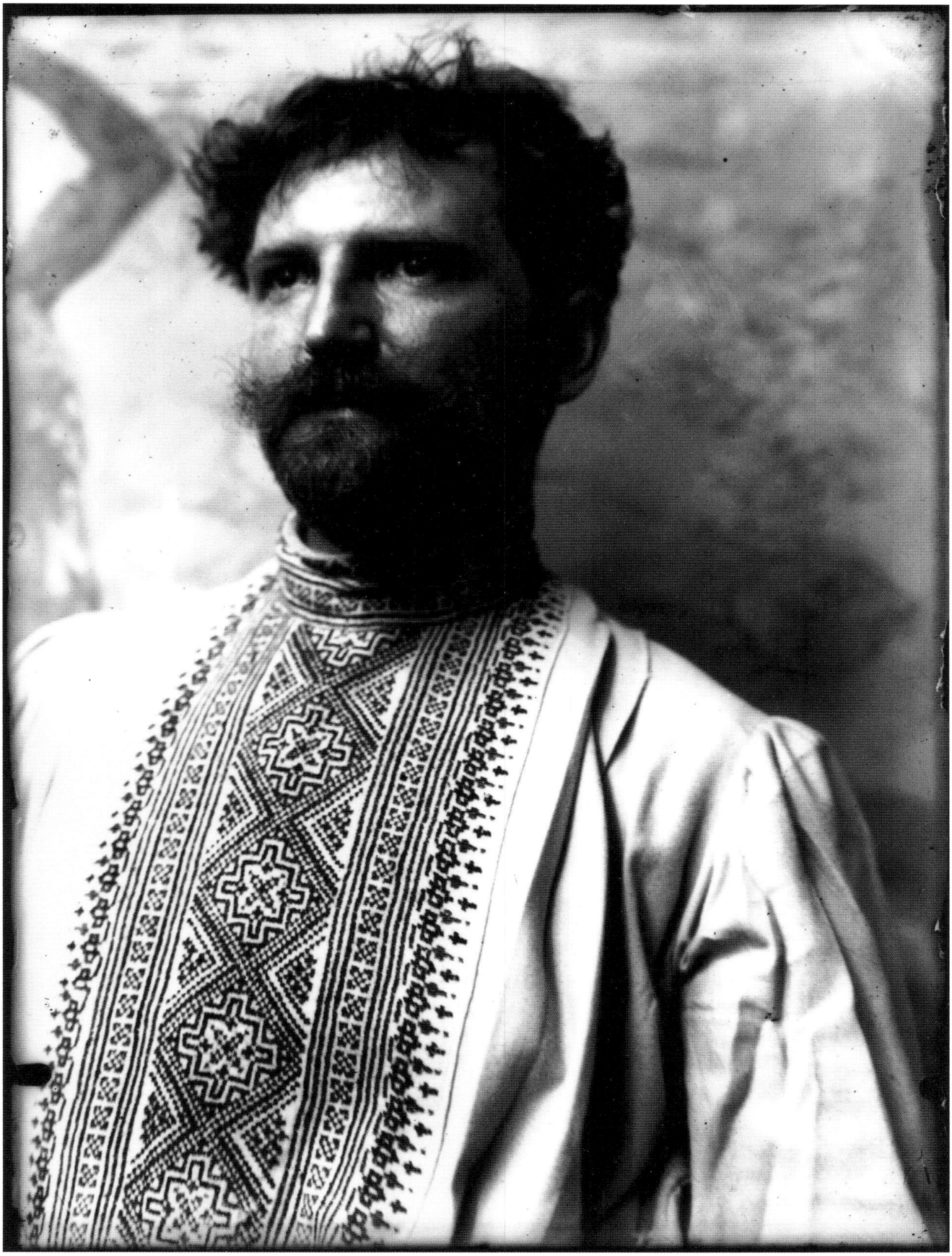

Mucha in a Russian shirt 'rubashka', at his studio in rue de la Grande Chaumière, Paris. Early 1890s

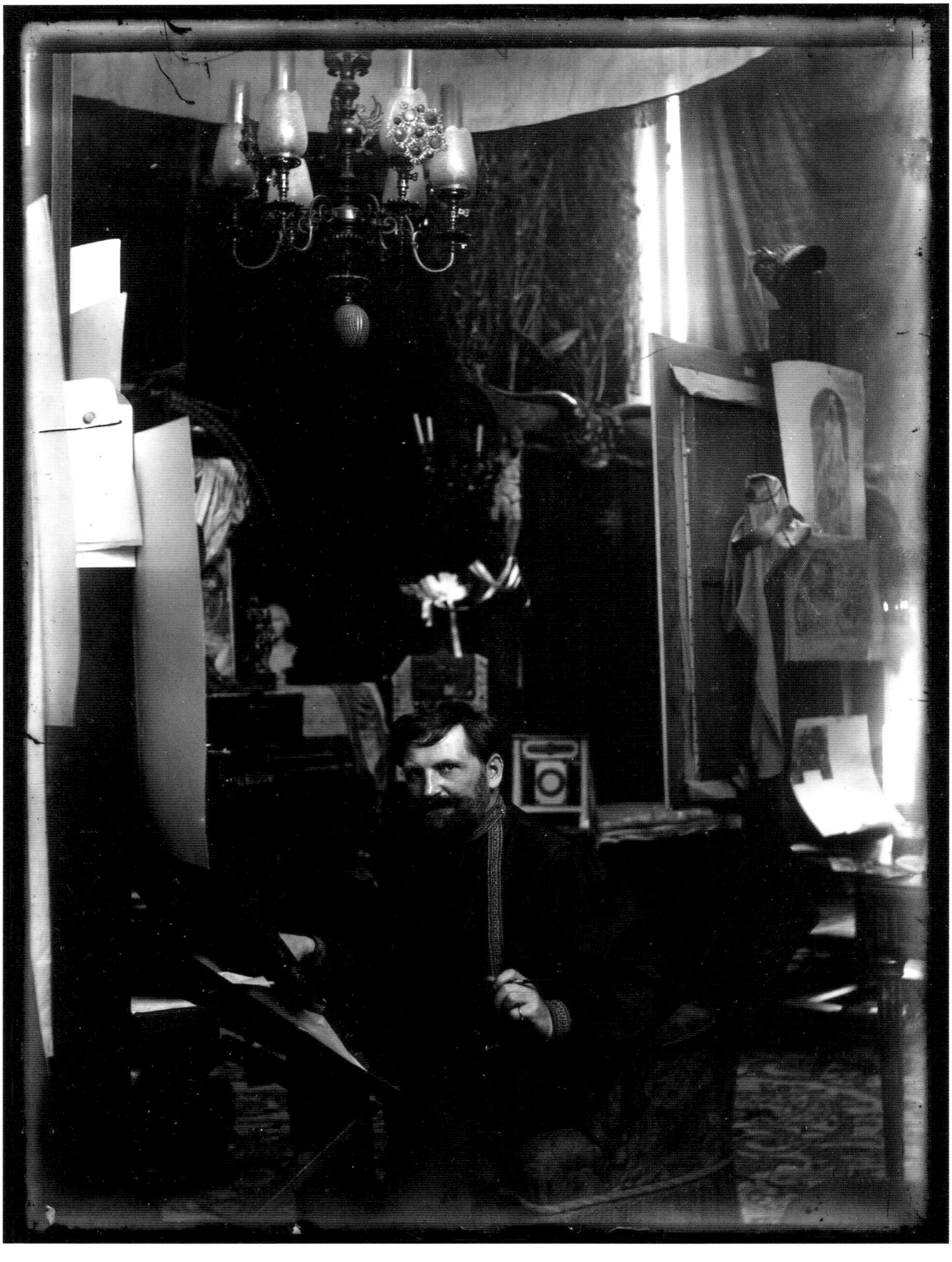

Mucha working at his studio in rue du Val-de Grâce, Paris c. 1898

at the Bodinière Gallery, showing 107 works. May–July: second solo exhibition at the Salon des Cent, featuring 448 works; *La Plume* issues a special number devoted to Mucha (see p.39).

1898
25 January: initiated into the Paris lodge of the Grand Orient de France, the oldest Masonic organisation in France. February: joins James McNeill Whistler's Académie Carmen to give drawing lessons. Participates in the first exhibition of the Vienna Secession. Around this year, begins a collaboration with Georges Fouquet. Also begins working in sculpture under influences from Auguste Seysses and Auguste Rodin (see p.121).

1899
Receives commissions from the Austrian government for the Paris Exposition Universelle of 1900, including the decoration of the Bosnia-Herzegovina Pavilion, one of three national pavilions to be exhibited by the Austro-Hungarian Empire. During his research trip to the Balkans for this project, his first ideas for *The Slav Epic* are formed. December: publishes his personal interpretation of the Lord's Prayer, *Le Pater*.

1900
Awarded a silver medal for the decoration of the Bosnia and Herzegovina Pavilion at the Paris Exposition Universelle and appointed a Knight of Order of the Emperor Franz Josef I for his contribution towards the Austro-Hungarian Empire. Commissioned by Georges Fouquet to design the interior and furnishings of the new Boutique Fouquet.

1901
Receives a Légion d'Honneur for his contribution towards the Paris Exposition Universelle. Elected a member of the Czech Academy of Sciences and Arts.

1902
Accompanies Rodin to Prague and Moravia on the occasion of the Rodin exhibition organised by the Manès Union of Artists, Prague. Publishes *Documents décoratifs* (see p.95).

gothic, an attribution to the darker side of the arts. The Buchanan Street Tearooms designed by Mackintosh and George Walton open in Glasgow.

1898
First exhibition of the Vienna Secession; the poster designed by Klimt. The New Gallery, London, promoter of the Aesthetic and the Arts and Crafts Movements, organises an exhibition of the work of French enamellers including René Lalique (see p.151) and Georges Fouquet (see p.150).

1899
The South Kensington Museum, established in 1852 following the Great Exhibition of 1851, becomes the Victoria and Albert Museum. Inspired by the ideal of the English Arts and Crafts Movement, Grand Duke Ernst Ludwig founds the Artists' Colony Mathildenhöhe in Darmstadt (completed in 1914).

1900
Paris Exposition Universelle (15 April – 12 November); the Grand Palais (the fair's main exhibition hall) is inaugurated along with the adjacent Petit Palais and Pont Alexandre III. At the Exposition Bing's Art Nouveau Pavilion receives international acclaim, consolidating the term 'Art Nouveau' as the name of the style defining the era. First line of the Paris Métro inaugurated between Porte de Vincennes and Porte Maillot with entrances designed by Guimard.

1901
Fouquet's new boutique opens at the rue Royale, Paris. Gallé founds the École de Nancy, together with Antonin Daum, Louis Majorelle and Eugène Vallin.

1902
First International Exhibition of Modern Decorative Arts held in Turin where works by Charles Rennie Mackintosh and the other Scottish contributors receive international attention. Max Klinger's polychrome Beethoven monument (1902) and Klimt's *Beethoven Frieze* (1901) displayed at the fourteenth exhibition of the Vienna Secession.

1903
October: meets Marie (Maruška) Chytilová, a Czech art student and his future wife.

1904
March–May: first visit to the US; paints society portraits following introductions by Baroness Adèle von Rothschild; meets Charles Richard Crane, his future sponsor for the *Slav Epic* project; becomes a founder member of the American Slav Society.

1905
Makes two more trips to the US, working on commissions and teaching at the New York School of Applied Design for Women. Publishes *Figures décoratives* (see p.101).

1906
10 June: marries Maruška in Prague. October: fourth trip to the US accompanied by Maruška. Mucha begins teaching at the Art Institute of Chicago (until 1909).

1907
Earns regular income from teaching at art schools in New York, Chicago and Philadelphia.

1908
Commissioned to decorate the new building of the German Theatre in New York. Summer: meets Woodrow Wilson, then President of Princeton University and future US President (1913–1921).

1909
15 March: birth of daughter Jaroslava in New York. Spends summer with his family in Bohemia and Moravia. October: makes his fifth trip to the US; Crane agrees to finance Mucha's *Slav Epic* project towards the end of this year.

1910
Spring: returns to Bohemia to work on the murals for the Municipal House, Prague (see p.131).

1903
The Grafton Gallery, London, holds an exhibition of Lalique. Salon d'Automne founded in Paris.

1905
Construction of the Municipal House (Obecní dům) in Prague begins, designed by Osvald Polívka and Antonín Balšánek. At the Salon d'Automne a group of artists led by Henri Matisse and André Derain gains the name 'fauves' (wild beasts) because of their boldly coloured paintings ignoring realism. German expressionist artists form the Die Brücke group in Dresden.

1907
Retrospective Cézanne exhibition held at the Salon d'Automne. Pablo Picasso paints the ground-breaking Cubist work *Les Demoiselles d'Avignon* and meets Georges Braque.

1908
The Franco-British Exhibition is held in London celebrating the Entente Cordiale signed in 1904 between Britain and France: it shows the largest display of French Art Nouveau objects ever seen in the country.

1909
The new building of the Glasgow School of Art is completed, designed by Mackintosh. *The Manifesto of Futurism* (1908), written by the Italian poet Filippo Tommaso Marinetti, appears in *Le Figaro*. Sergei Diaghilev brings the Ballet Russe to Paris.

1910
Wassily Kandinsky makes one of the earliest abstract works *Composition No.2*. The Functionalist Czech architect, Adolf Loos, gives a lecture *Ornament and Crime* (written in 1908) in Vienna attacking ornament in art. Roger Fry organises the Manet and Post-Impressionist Exhibition at the Grafton Gallery, London.

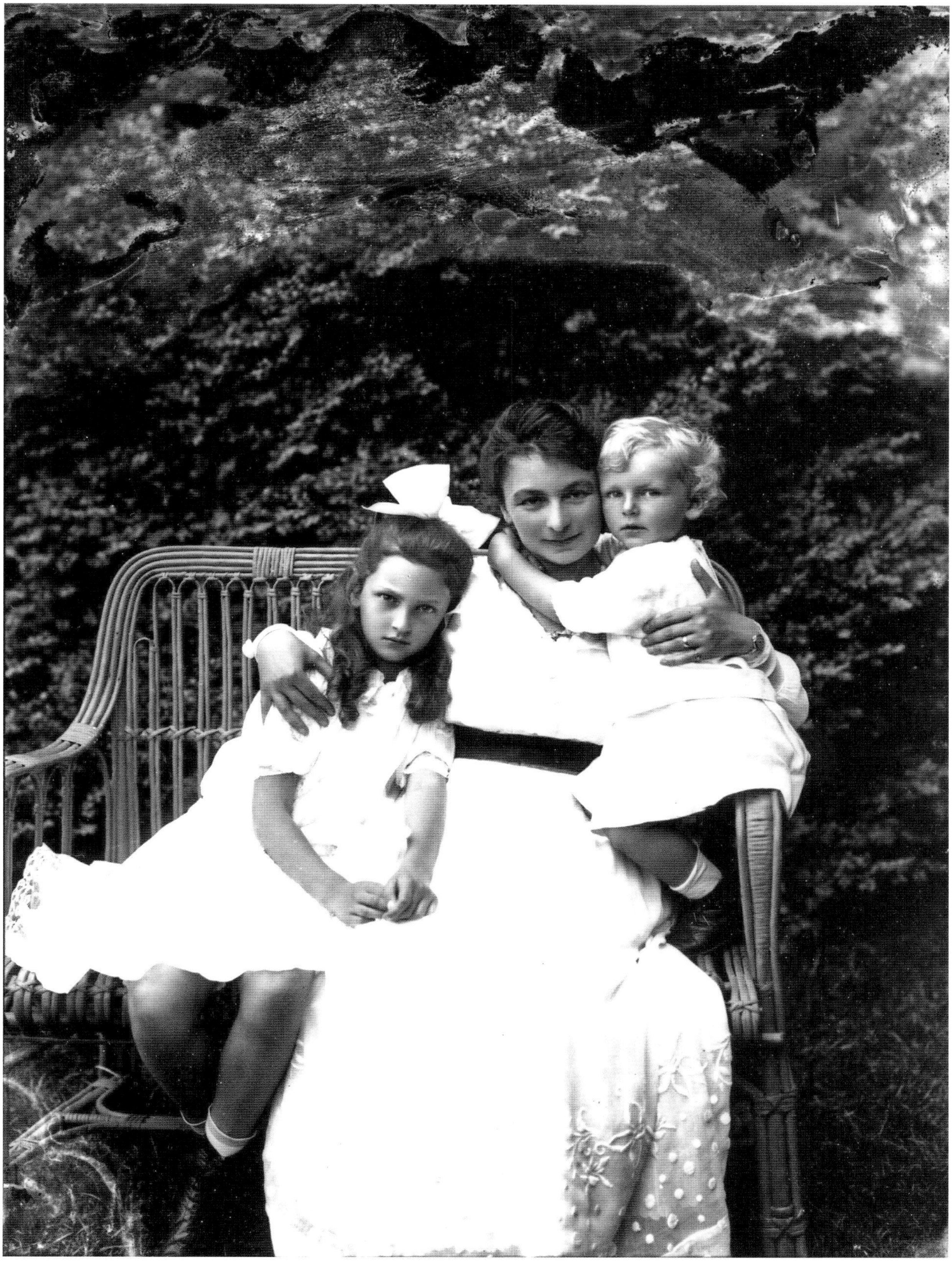

Maruška with daughter Jaroslava (left) and son Jiří (right) at Zbiroh Castle, western Bohemia. c.1917

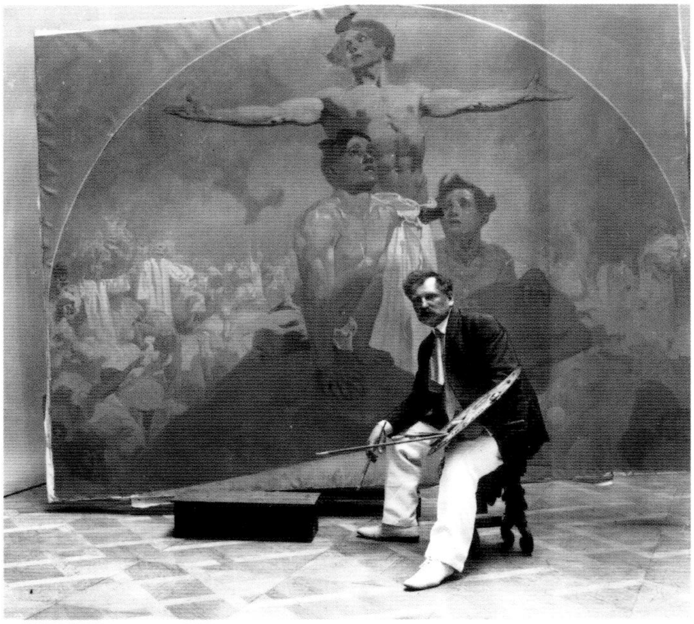

Mucha working on a mural for the Lord Mayor's Hall at the Municipal House in Prague
c.1910–1911

1911

On completion of the murals for the Municipal House, moves with his family to Zbiroh Castle, West Bohemia; starts working on first *Slav Epic* canvases.

1911

First group exhibition of Cubists shown at the Salon des Indépendants in Paris. Followers of Picasso and Braque form the Group of Creative Artists in Prague.

1913

February–March: sixth visit to the US; attends the opening of the Armory Show in New York. April–June: makes an extensive research trip to Poland and Russia for *The Slav Epic*.

1914

Outbreak of World War I; the Art Nouveau movement is in decline by this time

1915

12 March: son Jiří is born in Prague.

1916–1917

Produces three visionary drawings on the theme of war.

1916-1917

The anti-war and anti-art Dada movement begins in Zurich in 1916; this is followed by the publication of the art and literature review *Dada* in 1917. De Stijl founded by Piet Mondrian and Theo van Doesburg in Amsterdam in 1917.

1918

28 October: the independent state of Czechoslovakia is created as a result of the dissolution of the Austro-Hungarian Empire. Designs first postage stamps and bank-notes for the new state. By the end of this year Mucha has completed eleven canvases of *The Slav Epic*, including *Petr Chelčicky* (see pp.18–19).

1918

By the end of the war Art Nouveau has been widely criticised by writers and administrators in Europe as being decadent; the style is effectively finished as a progressive force.

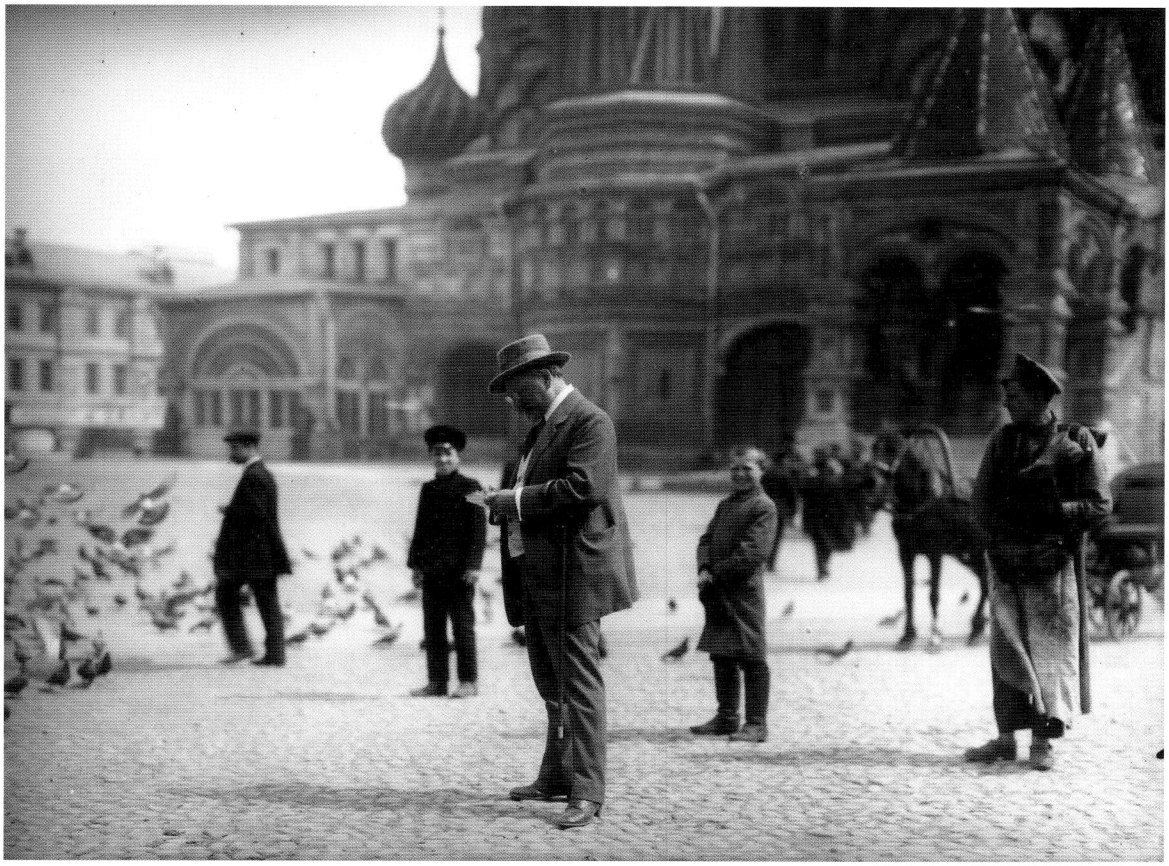

Mucha in Red Square, Moscow 1913, making sketches for *The Slav Epic: The Abolition of Serfdom in Russia*

1919

Becomes a founder member of the first Czech-speaking Masonic lodge, Jan Amos Komenský, Prague. 27 April: the opening of the first *Slav Epic* exhibition at the Klementinum, Prague, showing five canvases. With his family makes his seventh and last visit to the US later this year.

1919

Walter Gropius founds the Staatliches Bauhaus in Weimar.

1920

June–September: five canvases of *The Slav Epic* are presented at the Art Institute of Chicago.

1921

January–February: retrospective including the *Slav Epic* pieces from Chicago presented at the Brooklyn Museum, New York. Spring: returns to Czechoslovakia.

1921

Paul Klee starts teaching at the Bauhaus followed by Kandinsky in 1922.

1923

February: elected Sovereign Grand Commander of the Czech Supreme Council of Freemasons.

1923

Le Corbusier publishes a collection of his essays *Vers une architecture* exploring the concept of modern architecture. František Kupka publishes *Creation in the Plastic Arts* in Paris and Prague.

1924
Makes research trips to the Balkans for the remaining *Slav Epic* paintings; visits Mount Athos.

1924
André Breton publishes his first *Surrealist Manifesto*; the second follows in 1929.

1925
Lalique's crystal tower fountain becomes a prominent feature of the Exposition Internationale des Art Décoratifs et Industriels Modernes in Paris; The term 'Art Deco' is coined, derived by shortening the words 'Arts Décoratifs'. The Bauhaus moves to Dessau.

1928
Autumn: the complete cycle of *The Slav Epic* is officially presented to the City of Prague by Mucha and Crane and is shown at the Trade Fair Palace. The Mucha family moves back to Prague.

1931
Commissioned to design a stained-glass window for St. Vitus Cathedral, Prague.

1931
The Abstraction-Création group formed in Paris.

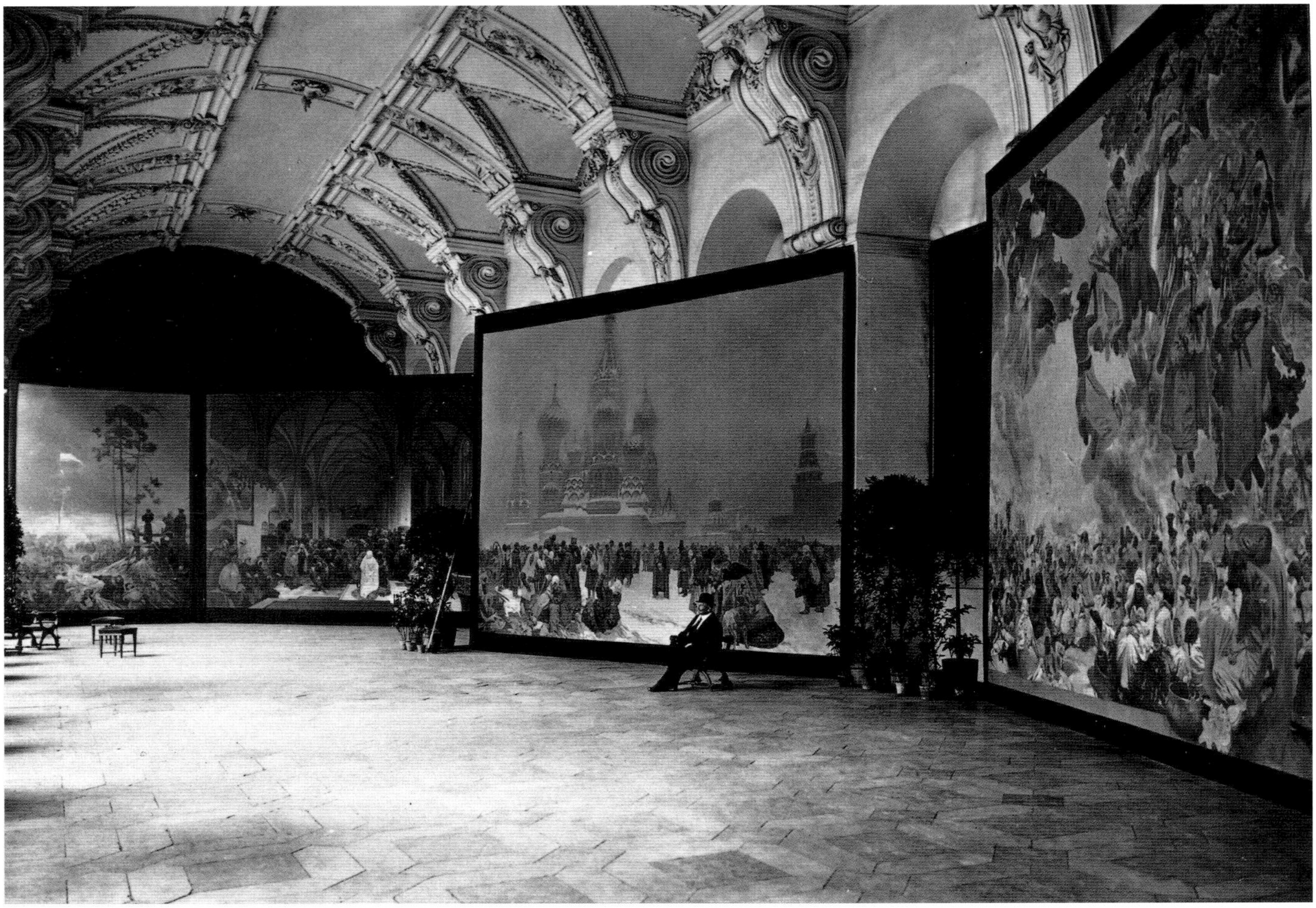

Mucha at the first *Slav Epic* exhibition at the Klementinum, Prague, 1919

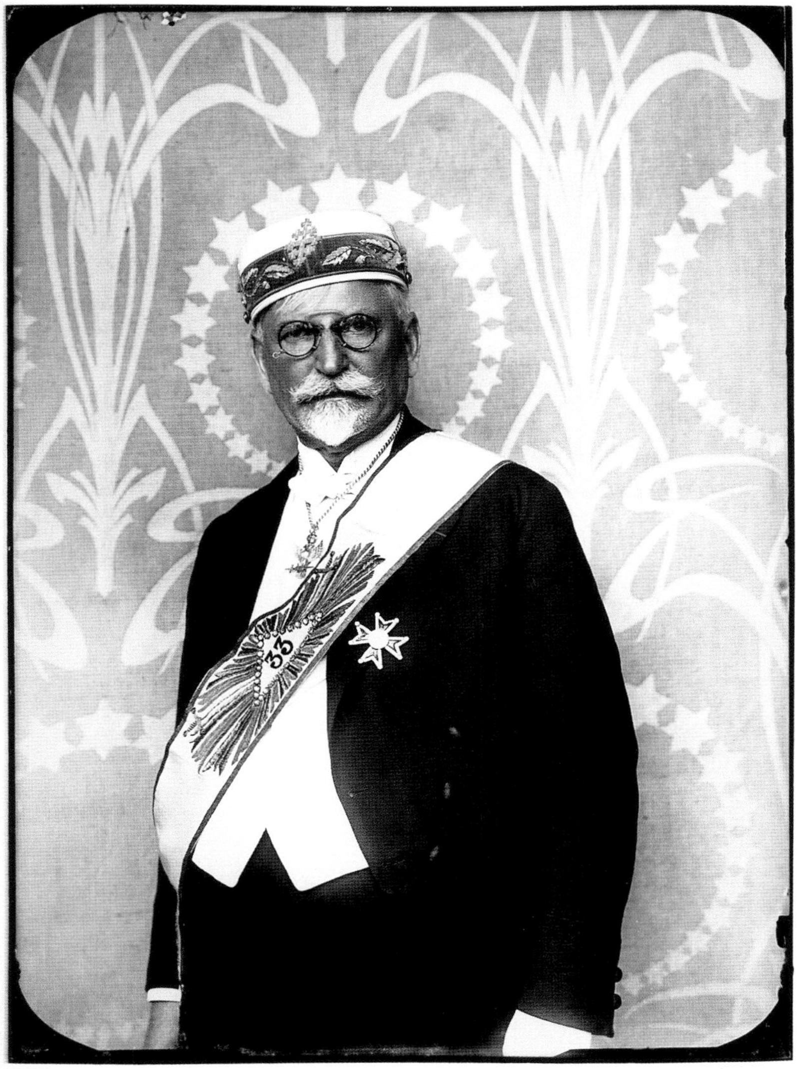

Mucha in formal maisonic regalia as Sovereign Grand Commander of the Czech Supreme Council of Freemasons
1923

1932
The Mucha family moves to Nice, living there for two years.

1936
Retrospectives at the Musée du Jeu de Paume, Paris, and the Moravian Museum of Decorative Arts, Brno. Begins to work on the triptych (unrealised) *The Age of Reason*, *The Age of Wisdom* and *The Age of Love*.

1939
March: German invasion of Czechoslovakia; Mucha is among the first to be arrested and interrogated by the Gestapo on account of his Masonic activities. Although released after several days, his health deteriorates. 14 July: dies in Prague; interred at Slavín (the Czech pantheon), Vyšehrad Cemetery.

1932
The Bauhaus moves to Berlin but is closed by the Nazis in 1933.

1939
Around 5000 works of graphic art considered to be 'degenerate art' by the Nazi Party are burned in Germany. Outbreak of World War II.

CREDITS AND ACKNOWLEDGMENTS

COPYRIGHT CREDITS

pp. 60–65 Works in the Anderson Collection of Art Nouveau © Sainsbury Centre for Visual Arts, University of East Anglia 2015

pp. 74–77 & 141–149 Works in the collection of Glasgow Museums © CSG CIC Glasgow Museums Collection 2015

pp. 109–122 Works in the collection of the National Museums Liverpool courtesy of National Museums Liverpool © National Museums Liverpool 2015

pp. 123–125 Works in the collection of Russell-Cotes Art Gallery & Museum reproduced with the kind permission of Russell-Cotes Art Gallery & Museum, Bournemouth © Russell-Cotes Art Gallery & Museum 2015

FURTHER PHOTOGRAPHIC CREDITS

Fig.7 Hermann Obrist, *Whiplash (Peitchenhieb)*, c.1895 © Münchner Stadtmuseum, Sammlung Mode/Textilien/Kostümbibliothek

Fig.8 Aubrey Beardsley, *J'ai baisé ta bouche Iokanaan*, Illustration for 'The Climax' from Oscar Wilde's *Salome*, 1894 © Victoria and Albert Museum, London

Fig.9 Henri de Toulouse-Lautrec, *Divan Japonais*, 1892 © Victoria and Albert Museum, London

Fig.10 Hector Guimard: Bench for a smoking parlour, 1897 Photo © RMN-Grand Palais (Musée d'Orsay) / Stéphane Maréchalle

Fig.11 "Edicule Guimard – Station de métro Boissière" by MOSSOT is licenced under Creative Commons Attribution 1.0 [URL: https://commons.wikimedia.org/wiki/File:Paris_16_- Edicule_Guimard_Station_Boissi%C3%A8re_-1.JPG]

Fig.12 "Hector Guimard Castel Béranger" by Geolina163 is licenced under Creative Commons Attribution-ShareAlike 3.0. [URL : https://commons.wikimedia.org/wiki/File:Hector_Guimard_Castel_B%C3%A9ranger.JPG]

Fig.13 Postcard showing the Glasgow School of Art, phase 1 (1897–1899), pasted into page 29, Volume 15, of William Young's Glasgow Scrapbooks. © CSG CIC Glasgow Museums and Libraries Collection: The Mitchell Library, Special Collections

Fig.14 The Immortals at Dunure, Ayrshire, about 1893 © The Glasgow School of Art

Fig.15 Photograph of a 'Drooko' poster, designed by Margaret and Frances Macdonald, printed by Carter and Pratt, Glasgow, about 1894–5 © The Hunterian, University of Glasgow 2015

Fig.16 Photograph of the Luncheon Room at Miss Cranston's Buchanan Street Tearooms © T & R Annan and Sons Ltd, Glasgow

Fig.17 The Ladies Luncheon Room, 1900–1 from the Ingram Street Tearooms © CSG CIC Glasgow Museums Collection

Fig.21 The Music Room Holmestead, Bedford Lemere photographic archive BL16685. Reproduced by permission of Historic England

Fig.30 John Duncan: *The Journey of St Mungo* mural, Common Room, Ramsay Garden. Courtesy of Special Collections, Glasgow University Library

Fig.31 John Duncan: *Anima Celtica*, in *The Evergreen: A Northern Seasonal*. Courtesy of Special Collections, Glasgow University Library

Fig.32 Bronze armlet found at Drumside, Belhelvie, Aberdeenshire, illustrated in Joseph Anderson, *Scotland in Pagan Times: The Iron Age*. Courtesy of Special Collections, Glasgow University Library

p.148 John Duncan: *The Coming of Bride* © Estate of John Duncan. All rights reserved, DACS 2014

Every effort has been made to acknowledge correct copyright of images where applicable. Any errors or omissions are unintentional and should be notified to the publisher who will arrange for corrections to appear in any reprints.

AUTHORS' CREDITS

Alphonse Mucha: In Quest of Beauty
© Tomoko Sato 2015

Verve and Logic: The Lineage of Art Nouveau
© Paul Greenhalgh and Claire Allerton 2015

The Glasgow Style, The Four, and the Controversial Poster Ghouls © Culture and Sport Glasgow (Museums), 2015

Beguiling Beauty: Aestheticism in Britain and Works from the Collection of the National Museums Liverpool © Sandra Penketh 2015

The Celtic Revival in Scotland: The Glasgow Boys and the Edinburgh Celtic Renascence
© Culture and Sport Glasgow (Museums), 2015

Anderson Collection of Art Nouveau: Descriptions of works © Sainsbury Centre for Visual Arts, University of East Anglia 2015

Glasgow Museums: Descriptions of works © Culture and Sport Glasgow (Museums), 2015

National Museums Liverpool: Descriptions of works © National Museums Liverpool 2015

Russell-Cotes Art Gallery & Museum: Descriptions of works © Russell-Cotes Art Gallery & Museum 2015

All other text © Mucha Foundation Publishing 2015